The Gift of the Middle Tanana

The Gift of the Middle Tanana

Dene Pre-Colonial History in the Alaskan Interior

Gerad M. Smith

Foreword by Charles E. Holmes

Afterword by Evelynn Combs

LEXINGTON BOOKS

Lanham • Boulder • New York • London

Published by Lexington Books
An imprint of The Rowman & Littlefield Publishing Group, Inc.
4501 Forbes Boulevard, Suite 200, Lanham, Maryland 20706
www.rowman.com

86-90 Paul Street, London EC2A 4NE

British Library Cataloguing in Publication Information Available

Library of Congress Cataloging-in-Publication Data

Names: Smith, Gerad M., 1981- author. | Holmes, Charles E., writer of foreword. |
  Combs, Evelynn, writer of afterword.
Title: The gift of the Middle Tanana : Dene pre-colonial history in the Alaskan interior /
  Gerad M. Smith ; foreword by Charles E. Holmes ; afterword by Evelynn Combs.
Description: Lanham : Lexington Books, 2022. | Includes bibliographical references and
  index. | Summary: "In this book, Gerad Smith explores the history, ethnography, and
  archaeological record of the Native people living in the Middle Tanana Valley in
  Alaska during the late Holocene. Smith illustrates how the role of deep-play rituals
  of   reciprocity shaped a traditional society that has lasted over a thousand years"
  — Provided by publisher.
Identifiers: LCCN 2021046602 (print) | LCCN 2021046603 (ebook) | ISBN
  9781793654762 (cloth) | ISBN 9781793654786 (paper) | ISBN 9781793654779
  (ebook)
Subjects: LCSH: Athapascan Indians—Alaska—Tanana River Valley—Antiquities. |
  Antiquities, Prehistoric—Alaska—Tanana River Valley. | Tanana River Valley
  (Alaska)—Antiquities.
Classification: LCC E99.A86 S65 2022 (print) | LCC E99.A86 (ebook) | DDC
  979.8/01—dc23/eng/20211102
LC record available at https://lccn.loc.gov/2021046602
LC ebook record available at https://lccn.loc.gov/2021046603

For all the descendants of the Middle Tanana people

Contents

Foreword

Charles E. Holmes

The Northern Boreal Forest is challenging to archaeologists. Many anthropologists and archaeologists have found the coastal regions of Alaska more inviting and rewarding, where villages full of semisubterranean houses, large middens full of well-preserved fauna and abundant artifacts are just waiting to be studied. Archaeological research in the interior forests of Alaska, home of the Northern Dene Native groups, has lagged behind investigations into the world of coastal maritime adapted cultures, for example, Aleut, Yupik, and Inuit. Evidence that documents the lifeways of Late Prehistoric Dene peoples is difficult to find and even more so for the prehistoric Holocene and Pleistocene inhabitants.

Pioneering work in the 1920s and 1930s was focused along rivers, for example, Frederica de Laguna, and roadways, for example, Froelich Rainey, because of easy access through the forests, but the results were underwhelming. It was not until the 1960s that the potential for a long, rich, and diverse archaeological record emerged through the work of Robert McKennan and John Cook at Healy Lake and Frederik Hadleigh West at sites in Denali National Park, the Campus Site at the University of Alaska Fairbanks, and Donnelly Ridge on Fort Greely. We archaeologists in the present are indebted to past scholars and strive to build upon their contributions. My career has benefited from Dr. Cook's mentoring and association with Drs. McKennan and Hadleigh West, as well as many other scholars. The sites, Pickupsticks and Swan Point, that I discovered, and that are analyzed in this book, are examples of how advances in archaeology can be achieved.

How do the recovered broken and discarded stone tools inform us about the people who produced them? The stones only testify to the fact that individuals were here. But the archaeologist has the duty to tell the most complete story possible. To do that, one might begin with recognizing and understanding who occupies the land in the present and how their ancestors lived. It helps, as Dr. Smith has done, to form a partnership with local Native people to tell the story. Consultation with linguists is extremely useful in deriving place names that inform about resources and the seasonal subsistence travel. As we depart on the journey to the past it is imperative to have as exact a footing as possible in the aboriginal culture before venturing into interpretations and experiments that become more abstract the farther back in time one goes. Dr. Smith endeavors to follow this path.

Charles E. Holmes, PhD
Affiliate Research Professor, University of Alaska Fairbanks

Acknowledgments

First, I want to acknowledge the Middle Tanana Alaska Native people, the Salchaket and Goodpaster Villages' descendants, and especially any Shaw Creek village descendants. This study took place and was written on their traditional lands. I am indebted to the current, historical, ethnographic, and archaeological record that they and their ancestors left, which is reconstructed here as best as I was able. Their ideology and cultural values have left an indelible mark on me. There are several Alaska Native cultural experts who I wish to personally thank for their insights: David John (Crooked Creek), MacArthur Tickett (Ambler), Dixie Dayo (Minto), and Wilson Justin (Nabesna). I am also profoundly grateful for the hospitality of Evelynn Combs and Melissa Erikson of Healy Lake. The multiple trips I made out there will remain some of the most valued memories of my life. During the time spent with them and other tribal members exploring the lake, rivers, and hill country surrounding the village, I informally discussed many of the themes and topics covered here.

Throughout the past 125 years, many Alaska Native traditional experts have provided or documented cultural information to other researchers, which is used here for this work. Most of their names are not known to me, but I am forever in their debt. This book is the product of over a decade of working with and thinking about the archaeology of the Alaskan interior. Due to all the interactions between myself and a spectrum of new students to senior researchers, I feel that this work is a product of everyone's ideas with whom I have shared topical discussions. I want to express my thanks to Ben Potter, who introduced and guided my initial research into the Northern Archaic and Athabascan traditions, to Josh Reuther, who encouraged my pursuits into geoarchaeology, social complexity, and household archaeology, to

Nancy Bigelow and Dan Mann for perspectives in paleoecology, Chris Hundertmark and John Burch for their insights into wildlife ecology, Ryan Harrod for bioanthropology guidance, Ted Parsons for learning photogrammetric methods, and especially to Charles Holmes, for the years of field research I conducted with him. I am incredibly grateful for the years I spent with James Kari documenting and mapping the traditional place names, analyzing Dene narratives, and learning the complexities of Dene grammatical structures. All indigenous place names in this work come from Kari's currently unpublished Middle Tanana dictionary unless otherwise noted. I am also especially thankful for the recent work by Chris Cannon, which has specifically investigated the Northern Dene spiritual and mythological culture as expressed through their sky lore and his interpretation of the stories of Traveler.

I am very thankful for all the hard work of my archaeological field school teaching assistants, students, and volunteers who excavated these sites between 2017 and 2019 put in: Thomas Allen, Jeffery Baird, John Bergner, Eleanor Bishop, Aidan Boeckmann, Nancy Boyer, Anna Burchfield, Christine Castro, Madison Chán, Cory Coulman, Alexandria Crowell, Alexandra Derrera, Eddie Edwards, Alyssa Flynn, Emma Frankevich, Lauren Gregory, Heather Greiner, Gabriel Hill, Dava Hollis, Joshua Huck, Miranda Jackovich, Jordyn Jones, Charlie Padget, Flora Peychère, Eddie Perez, Samantha Schaeffer, Steve Shoenhair, Nicholas Taylor, Tyler Teese Roberto Torres, Taylor Vollman, Richard Wilcock, Catherine Wolk, Xiaofei Zhang, and Roxanne Zorea. A special thanks goes out to the Summer Sessions staff of the University of Alaska Fairbanks, who worked hard to facilitate that course. I am also thankful to all the other former students and volunteers who worked at Swan Point and Pickupsticks since their discoveries, whose names are also not listed here.

I want to express further thanks to Barbara Crass for property access, the employees of Pogo Mine for providing road access to our sites, and to Richard VanderHoek and Judith Bittner at the Alaska State Office of History and Archaeology for providing excavation permits and access to the previous Swan Point collections. I am thankful to the University of Alaska Anchorage Anthropology Department, their Anthropology Laboratory for Cultural and Environmental Scanning, the University of Alaska Museum of the North, and the Alaska Consortium of Zooarchaeologists for lab access and their staff and volunteers' help. Special thanks also go to Tanana Chiefs Conference, the Otto William Geist Fund, and the David and Rachel Hopkins Fellowship for providing analytical funding. I am also thankful to Craig Mishler for allowing me to cite his taped interviews here.

Finally, I am deeply grateful to my partner, Nell Bishop, whose support through this process has been so helpful. I will always value her assistance with photographs, field efforts, her quality work creating the artifact photo plates, and general informal discussions on the topics here. I am grateful to my parents for their encouragement in pursuing scientific studies and a love for the outdoors throughout my childhood. I am also thankful for everyone in my current extensive, blended family. I discussed many of these themes over the years with all of them, and I am deeply appreciative of their insights.

To all the Middle Tanana people's descendants, I have tried my best to faithfully reconstruct the history, prehistory, and culture of this unique area. Any mistakes I may have introduced were unintentional, and I sincerely apologize for them. In recognition that this product was built upon information created by their ancestors and preserved by the ancestral lands that they help protect today, I have asked that all proceeds from this book be returned to the Healy Lake Tribal Council, many of whose members are descended from the Middle Tanana people.

Ten xwt'een nen' kaage dagha' k'aats'iide eł ts'edeedletth'ih
"We work and live on the land of the Tanana people"

Introduction

THE LEGACY OF AMERICAN ARCHAEOLOGY AND THE RESPONSIBILITY OF RESEARCH EQUITY

I stepped out of the old pickup into the Alaskan sun. It was the early summer of 2012. I walked to the back of the brown pickup, catching the word TAIGA on the license plate as Dr. Charles "Chuck" Holmes opened the tailgate. We grabbed our backpacks and checked for our bear protection (bear spray and a pistol). We crossed the dusty road and walked into the mixed spruce. For the first two-hundred yards, the trail was open, dry, and an easy walk. After walking through a stand of birch, it opened up into an open tussock field of mixed shrubs, grasses, and moss. Our XtraTuf boots came in handy there, as the trail became a mix of mud and standing water. Eventually, we skirted the edge of a stand of small diameter twisted black spruce and grass, where on a future project, we would often encounter a quietly grazing black bear sow and her two cubs. There were several more patches of tussock swamp and stands of spruce. Sometimes the trail was obvious; sometimes, it became a myriad of braided paths going several directions. Sometimes it disappeared into the moss. We walked on, and eventually our goal, a prominent ridgeline of white spruce, would become visible. Finally, we arrived at a pond with a lone swan resting on it. We crossed its outlet. It was a small trickle; in future summers, it would become worn into a treacherous thirty-meter-wide portage requiring a corduroy of sticks and small logs to cross safely.

Then we began to walk up the hill. The hike was about a mile in length, but the arduous nature often slowed the walk to about forty-five minutes. Bad weather could slow us even further. On top, it opened up into a dry clearing. Here we rested, and Dr. Holmes summarized to me the previous twenty years of excavations there at Swan Point. Eventually, we would wander off down the west side of the hill to a small lower terrace. There, a humble circular depression about four meters in diameter and half a meter deep awaited. This depression, Chuck said, was what he believed was the remains of an ancient house pit. His team had tested it six years previous with a trench and radiocarbon assays, which indicated the feature was about 1900 years old, much older than any other precolonial residences known in the Tanana Valley.

On a similar but much hotter day five years later, Chuck and I drove six miles further down the Pogo Mine Road. The road follows the western and northern margins of much of the Shaw Creek Valley. This time, we struck a bearing straight through the spruce forest, climbing up, then down a long hill. After crossing a small tussock bog and stream, an isolated hill covered in the stark, dead, burned trees came into view. We circled it, making our way through fallen trees and new growth. In 2012, a wildfire had torn through the area, roaring up the hill in a firestorm whose winds toppled the ancient trees, tossing them about like a game of pick-up sticks. The site was marked by another housepit feature, longer and deeper than the Swan Point feature. Chuck had also tested this site in previous years with another exploratory trench.

This book presents the results from investigations at these sites, Swan Point and Pickupsticks. Both are later Holocene precolonial household sites, located about five miles apart within the Shaw Creek Flats in the Middle Tanana Valley, Alaska. These residence features are temporally separated from each other by almost a millennium. The youngest of the two, Pickupsticks, is about 900 years old, and Swan Point about 1900. They both offer a comparative snapshot of family life, which is compared against the historic traditional households of the pre-contact nineteenth century. This unique perspective allowed me to compare the residential components of three periods, each separated by roughly a millennium, to investigate broad questions such as these: How does the material record inform us of the life histories of the artifacts of the people who lived there? How did family household construction develop over time? How similar or different were ancestral lives lived in each period of the past, concerning economics, technology, and cultural values? What was their technological, linguistic, and genetic contribution to the descendant communities of the Middle Tanana? How can this information be used to empower today's Alaska Native communities and advance the science of the collective human past?

This book discusses the Middle Tanana culture. Their people have experienced an extensive recent history of social, political, and individual abuse by the currently dominant Euro-American social group. Thus, any reconstruction of their past, especially if done by a member of the socially privileged group, becomes one that is inherently a narrative of empowerment of the author's values. Therefore, this introduction seeks to frame what archaeology is, how it is culturally defined and empowered, and who gets to control that narrative.

Interwoven within that is an ethical framework. That ethical foundation is discussed first in this book so that it does not become an afterthought.

Any generations' understanding of the past is heavily influenced by the zeitgeist of their coming-of-age years. Those who lived under the constant threat of nuclear annihilation found extensive inspiration to study theories of extraterrestrial impact-induced extinctions (i.e., Alvarez et al. 1980; Haynes 2008), while their parents and grandparents who were influenced by the rise of eugenic theories and the devastating impacts of the American Dust Bowl explained extinction through concepts of racial senility or climate change (i.e., Benton 1990).

Long-running research themes are often influenced by the overarching social questions unique to each generation. These investigation biases influence how each will interpret what defines valued cultural resources, how that heritage is perceived through education outlets, and where national resources will be directed toward protecting and interpreting them. Awareness of these factors allows us to understand that heritage does not exist as an entity in and of itself; instead, it is an emphasized subset of the past (i.e., historical sites, books, etc.) that reinforces idiosyncratic yet dominant cultural values. Therefore, self-awareness in this sphere becomes an exercise in introspection of the person's inner values concerning the past and its interaction with their society's values concerning the same resources. Each will be uniquely biased by its preferential focus. Archaeology as an American vocation is tasked with identifying these biases and studying the ignored, undeveloped, or not yet recognized aspects.

As an archaeologist trained as an anthropologist in the Americanist tradition, I cannot look at the archaeological record without reflections on past and present social and cultural systems. These have informed and produced the desire to study it in the way I present here. The exploration of these ancient cultural traces of economics, technology, and community interactions can help us to reflect upon the relative importance of social networks, economic behaviors, and cultural values that appear to have been successful to those unique periods of the past, and which ones were successful across vast periods of time and space. Ultimately, these questions and answers are absorbed internally and help navigate and reevaluate the social constructs we value today.

PERSONAL IDENTITY STATEMENT

In recognition that the most productive research follows current social problems and interests, I had several fruitful discussions over the years with my brother, Zach Smith. He was then studying at the American Film Institute in

Los Angeles. The arts are often the most sensitive to subtle emerging shifts in social values, being natural outlets deemed culturally appropriate for exploring otherwise dissenting norms. These embryonic themes often influence the sciences later on. We recognized that over the past decade (2010–2020), the overarching ideas in the arts and humanities have highlighted that those narratives which overemphasize the perspective of Euro-American, male-focused, heteronormativity are at best intellectually passé and creatively bankrupt. At worst, it continues to foster ignorance of the actual past and present experiences of other social groups and identities. If not addressed, this narrowed perspective by empowered identities simply passively enforces silencing the experiences and control of the narratives of the past, present, and future of other identity groups, which is why resources and effort must actively be directed toward changing this narrative.

Intellectual equity might be criticized as creating an environment that at best normalizes dissenting experiences and viewpoints, and at worst provides federal support for minority spiritual experiences at the expense of the majority's (e.g., Weiss and Springer 2020). In reality, equity in research highlights and equalizes our different perspectives, promoting an intellectual environment that is non-monolithic. This process has been ongoing for centuries on this continent, with each generation finding unique social tools for integration and empowerment. In my generation (the Millennials), the novel tremendous social balancing innovation was the construction of the free-access global Internet, which equalized all persons' voices and access to information unlike anything had before. On the positive side, this tool has fueled novel social justice movements throughout the world. On a negative note, most digital search platforms' predictive algorithms became designed to produce results increasingly tailored to fit the user's preconceived desires, resulting in reinforced fixed concepts rather than a balanced information product, heightening social polarization.

During the decade that this research work was undertaken (2010–2020), a unique and turbulent global social movement rose, Fourth-Wave Feminism, seeking to further the goals of cultural and individual equity. It focused on illuminating the persistent gendered and racial-based cultural norms that contribute to ongoing patterns of oppression and marginalization despite extensive legislation. This movement has emerged from the intersectionality studies of the 1990s, which studied how sociopolitical identities combine to create unique modes of discrimination and privilege. The new wave of feminist theory has focused on the realms of the population that remain oppressed, marginalized, and silenced in our current economic and political spheres: women of color, immigrants, transgender, and the economically impoverished, among others.

What do novel intellectual paradigms involving social empowerment have to do with archaeology? Investigating these paradigms and their reverberating effects through the sciences requires the researcher to recognize their own ascribed and chosen identities that have formed their experience with the world, and how that informs their research interest and ease of access to that process. As a Euro-American, heterosexual, cisgender male from a modest, lower-income but culturally middle-class, rural American background, my personal struggles for empowerment are essentially only reflective of a narrative of economic struggle. This narrative once blinded me to the far-more difficult road to personal freedom and empowerment that other chosen and ascribed identities face in my country. My struggles for success are not exacerbated by my gender, sexual identity, ethnic or racial background, or chosen spiritual enlightenment path, and thus, my experience is one of a privileged minority.

Producing this work became an internal process of learning, recognizing, and understanding the complex, ongoing experiences that marginalized communities continue to face in our society. The point of acknowledging systemic societal inequality and of one's own socially privileged position is not to produce a sense of gender, class, ethnic, or racial guilt; after all, we are all the accidental product of birth. Acknowledging these factors allows the more empowered sectors of society to identify unique and systemic problems (in the case of this work, to the Alaskan Native identity and experience) to work together to solve them equitably. Those of us that form the current privileged societal identities cannot take sole leadership against solving ongoing discrimination and inequality. We can only use our social privilege to raise our partners' voices and provide guidance and leadership opportunities when asked. Otherwise, we appropriate the struggle. This book is designed to frame the history of the Middle Tanana people in a way that provides empowerment to the descendant community, and uses their voice and experience as an interpretive perspective.

FINDING NATIVE ALASKAN THEORETICAL PERSPECTIVES ON THE PAST

In a sense, this work reflects my personal journey of discovery, working alongside one such marginalized group of indigenous American citizens, the families of the Healy Lake Tribe, many of whom are also descendants of the original Middle Tanana families. This book seeks to find the Native American voice in my research, not as an "other," or an abstract, long-gone culture, or an idealized Native culture, but as one that is actively promoting an identity that is at once equal to, contemporary with, and as dynamic as my own cultural experience. Therefore, this work seeks not to present archaeology as a dead historical account or as a purely intellectual exercise, but to explore the ongoing dynamic traditional culture of the Middle Tanana people and apply that to the archaeological record to understand how to recognize the local Dene people's antiquity, origins, and continuing cultural contributions to the world.

Presently, Euro-American culture continues to fetishize the crafted, twentieth-century image of a nineteenth century aboriginal people fighting against their inevitable doom in the face of American expansionism. At the same time, it denies the twentieth-century narrative of a people who rebounded from the brink of demographic and cultural genocide, fought for their rights of freedom to live and worship as they pleased, and regaining political power. The current Native American experience is that of a post-apocalyptic community, a concept that can only be understood in the abstract by most Euro-American persons. The road these communities face of cultural reconstruction and full empowerment in American society is long from over.

Anthropological research concerning Native Alaskans in the Alaskan interior began with the Great Depression Era, and archaeological research there largely does not predate the 1960s. Both have been the research and interest domain of the currently empowered middle-class Euro-American population. It reflects the perceptions of materialistic and ascetic values of those researchers and bureaucrats who predominantly ascribe to that community's identity. In recognition that the precolonial record in Alaska entirely represents the ancestry of Alaska Natives and that their values toward, and narratives of, the past can be at odds with Euro-American perspectives, since the 1990s, the Alaska state universities have made a concerted effort to teach and prepare Alaska Native students in order to enable them to take these research and bureaucratic roles if desired. Theoretically, this effort helps empower these groups to control how their cultural heritage is protected, promoted, curated, and interpreted. This model's problem is that it forces these individuals to bend their cultural values to the overarching Euro-American education, economic, and bureaucratic system.

While conducting archaeological fieldwork through private consulting contracts during the first years of this project's work, I began to form the core questions concerning how a non-Euro-American-informed archaeological theory might look. I discussed it often with the Alaska Native informants and elders who worked with us. In particular, I informally posed the following question to several Alaska Native coworkers: "Where do we begin in order to study and understand the archaeological record from a uniquely Alaska Native perspective?" Overwhelmingly, I was encouraged to begin learning the traditional place names; they contain the answers to many cultural-specific research questions we commonly investigated. Identity, history, values, and land use are inherently tied to place, and the names derive their meaning from them. Traditional ecological knowledge and traditional cultural knowledge form the backbone of this work. It is so integral that it is often woven in without overt reference, and I hope that the reader can recognize its influence.

With the rise of liberal democracy and republican ideals since the nineteenth century worldwide, nation-building has been closely tied with creating new ethnicity constructs. Today, as throughout the past, language continues to form an integral part of community identity at local, regional, and national levels. It has always carried a central place in the intellectual investigations of the Alaska Dene people and their past. This book will summarize my work with Dr. James Kari on recording and mapping Alaska's traditional Dene place names in their twelve languages. While this aspect only forms one chapter focusing mainly on the Middle Tanana, the place names analysis represents the most significant level of effort. The chapter provides an in-depth discussion of the reconstruction of the Dene Atlas and compares the dataset against the current English one. It relies on editorial work conducted mainly by Kari since the early 2000s. Kari's work has illuminated many lines of evidence that the ancestral linguistic reconstruction of Proto-Dene appears to reflect an ancient expansion throughout Alaska in a landscape devoid of any prior (or co-residing) non-Dene language. Since we do not see any periodic human population replacements in the Alaskan interior, it suggests great regional antiquity for the Dene language family. This hypothesis has been difficult to accept for many Quaternary Beringian researchers, likely due to a lack of training in lexicographic or historical linguistic methods, which would allow them to critique the merit of the theory adequately. To help frame Kari's arguments, I have included a discussion of the linguistic interactions between English and Dene.

For clarity, there are twelve languages spoken in Alaska that belong to the Dene language family. All Native words in this text should be assumed to be derived from Middle Tanana unless otherwise noted by a proceeding abbreviation (table 0.1). Included are obsolete English names for those languages as well, since use of them continues to occasionally arise, and can be confusing for researchers unfamiliar with the region or literature advances.

8   *Introduction*

Table 0.1.   **Alaska Dene Language Names and Abbreviations**

No.	Abbreviation	Language	Obsolete Name(s)
1	AT	Ahtna	Ahtena
2	DH	Deg Hit'an	Ingalik
3	DN	Dena'ina	Tanaina
4	GW	Gwich'in	Kutchin
5	HN	Hän	Han
6	HO	Holikachuk	Ingalik
7	KY	Koyukon	
8	LT	Lower Tanana	Tanana
9	MT	Middle Tanana	Lower Tanana, Tanana
10	TC	Tanacross	Tanana
11	UK	Upper Kuskokwim	Ingalik, Kolchan
12	UT	Upper Tanana	Nabesna, Tanana

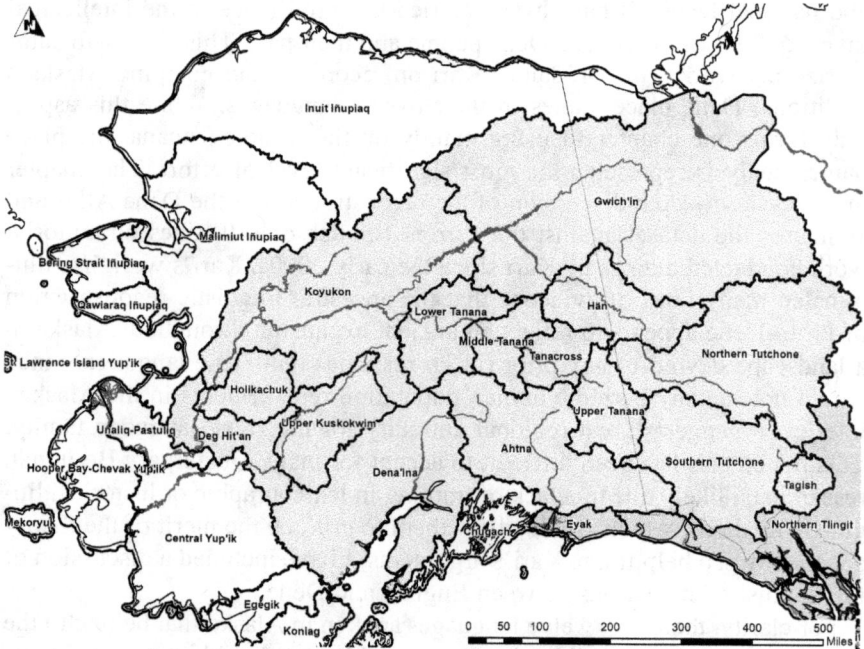

Figure 0.1.   Northern Dene languages of mainland Alaska, latter nineteenth century, with surrounding unrelated Native Alaskan languages labeled. Additional Canadian language boundaries not depicted.

GUIDE

Archaeological books are often structured according to a historical narrative, beginning with a summary of research methods and models, then embarking on a narrative that begins in the distant past and moves forward through time. Conversely, I have found that when one begins teaching archaeology and paleoanthropology first from a cultural anthropology standpoint, then systematically moving into the archaeological applications of those methods to progressively deeper periods of the past, the best comprehension results are achieved, and I have structured the book similarly. First, I will demonstrate how we form our hypotheses and research conclusions by studying living populations and then applying those ideas to the past, acknowledging problems arising for interpreting systems with no present analog. This approach requires less faith-like adherence to the producer's methods and findings. Instead, the consumer can more readily employ a logical response to personally evaluate why, how, and what we have concluded from the archaeological and fossil records.

This text is structured opposite that of a historical narrative, as if one was turning back time. The temporal flow begins with the present and moves steadily deeper into the past. It is constructed as such to help the reader understand how an archaeologist constructs a framework of the past when confronting a site whose components and history are yet unknown. Assuming the law of superposition holds true at a site, excavations usually begin by moving through the recent past, located in the uppermost layers of a site where more information can be correlated with the known culture's past and ending with the far distant past in the lowest levels of which far less proxy information is known (e.g., Holly 2002, 11 –12). Finally, while my career has taken me to many places in this beautiful state, one other culturally related region to the Middle Tanana is the Middle Susitna River basin, and I have used several of my personal experiences there to illustrate ideas throughout this work.

Chapter One

The Middle Tanana People
Modern and Historical Identities

It was a long drive down the Richardson Highway from Fairbanks to Delta Junction. From there, we drove up the ALCAN Highway and over the Gerstle River bridge. Then we turned north on a gravel road for several miles before turning off on a small, unmaintained two-track trail through the dense boreal forest that ended on the south bank of the Tanana River. After parking the truck, Evelynn and I stepped onto her mother Melissa Erikson's riverboat and rode off with several dogs and Evie's young nephew Odin in tow.

The boat ride took us several miles down the river, then up a small outlet of Healy Lake, slowly winding through the thick lake grass. We crossed the water to a prominent flat point and stopped there to walk around. On that point were the remains of the original Native village, built in the early twentieth century, then abandoned during the early 1940s, and subsequently reestablished several miles further east along the lakeshore. On the rocky beach, broken pieces of antique chinaware could be seen. "Those are from Chief John Healy's great potlatch of 1927," Melissa said. Large bones, likely moose remains, could also be seen eroding out of the bluff edge in places. I saw a small olive-colored stone scraper among the debris.

We climbed up the steep embankment. The corners of several notched-log cabins could still be seen standing upright just above the chest-high grass. We walked about, mostly silent. This place was the Village Site where John Cook and Robert McKennan conducted excavations in the 1960s, under the observation of Melissa's grandmother, Margaret Kirsteatter. This place was sacred on many levels. Many ancestors were interred there during the last great pandemic of the early 1940s, which had spelled the death-knell of that village location. Cook's work here and at other locations around the lake had become the first definitively demonstrated human occupation in the Middle Tanana region that extended into the final few millennia of the last ice age. During

those early excavations, a young Charles Holmes first volunteered, resulting in a prolific career. Many later interior archaeologists would credit their
research sites as being initially discovered by his prolific exploratory forays.
Later, Dr. Holmes recalled listening to news of the Apollo 11 moon landing
on a radio while excavating the remains of the terminal Pleistocene-age occupation in the lowest levels at the base of the site. In the deepest components
of those sites, the famous typological artifact, the teardrop-shaped Chindadn
point, was recovered. "Chindadn" is an anglicized loanword of *ch'endĕddh'*,
a local Tanacross word meaning elder (Holton 2009).

Healy Lake represents one of the important origin points of modern
archaeological research for the Alaskan interior. It provided the initial regional
cultural chronology of the early Chindadn complex, middle-Holocene Transitional period, and later Athapaskan tradition. The chronology initially spanned
the entirety of human occupation from the late Pleistocene to the Historic
period, demonstrating cultural connections between them. For the local residents, these initial studies brought a mix of reactions, but the legacy is one of
pride based on antiquity, melding their own traditions of having been there
since time immemorial with the Western traditions of measured chronology.

The Alaska Native community at Healy Lake today is comprised of members whose ancestries are drawn from many villages throughout the Middle
Tanana Valley, from Salcha to Dot Lake, many which have long since dissolved. That long-term consolidation of communities is the result of multiple
dynamic social processes of the past 150 years, and is explored here to provide a point of reference for non-Native readers.

This book is focused on the cultural history of the Native Middle Tanana
people, with specific emphasis on the last 8,000 years of their known
14,000-year-long archaeological record demonstrated throughout the nearby
valley of Shaw Creek. Shaw Creek is geographically located near the present-
day community of Quartz Lake, midway between the two principal villages of
the late nineteenth century of the Middle Tanana people, Goodpaster and Salcha. The book explores the intersection of ethnography, oral history, traditional
place names, paleoecology, and archaeology in order to understand constructs
of identity, ancestry, and our culturally informed reconstructions of the past.

As a discipline, Americanist archaeology is not to history what paleontol-
ogy is to biology, being a pale reflection of the latter. It is fundamentally
an anthropological investigation into the past. It robustly investigates questions of the past through the lens of our present social values and conflicts
(e.g., Yoffee 2007). Since this work is primarily archaeological and builds
upon ethnographic, linguistic, and ecological models to inform the material-
cultural record, it will begin first with the present and then move to the recent
past, moving progressively deeper into time. At each archaeological site,

excavators must first explore and understand the uppermost younger components before moving on to the deeper and older ones. This style of exploration of the past is called the direct historical approach, where comparisons can be made between materials and the documented historic culture of the local inhabitants, and project those cultural connections deep into the past by recognizing related artifact forms. In North America, the uppermost protohistoric components are often initially investigated as the direct ancestral remains of the Native groups on whose traditional lands they are found until demonstrated otherwise.

However, before exploring the archaeological past, it is necessary to understand who the Native Middle Tanana people are today, how community identity is currently maintained, how those processes have historically changed, and identify the factors contributing to concepts of identity, community, and home. That introduction will help frame the cultural context of the recent archaeological past from the ethnographic record and explore factors that led to modern Native identity.

COMMUNITY IDENTITY DURING THE STATEHOOD ERA (PRESENT TO 1959 AD)

Throughout the twentieth century, the Middle Tanana people were referred to by the Euro-American community as part of the greater ethnonym "Athabascans." The anthropologist Robert McKennan (1959, 15–17) provided a history of the use of that term (originally spelled "Athapaskan"), which originated as a place name describing net-like grass in northern Canada, and its adoption by Euro-Americans as a cultural signifier for all Native people across northwestern Canada and Alaska who spoke related languages. In 1997, the Tanana Chiefs Conference in Fairbanks formalized the Alaskan spelling as Athabascan (Resolution 97–35). More recently, the Canadian First Nations and anthropologists have begun to use Dene as an appropriate English identifier, and the term "Athapaskan" is now considered to be negatively tied to colonial impositions, and its use in Canada is currently heavily discouraged. The term Dene represents a loanword whose similar forms in the donor languages simply mean "people." Currently in Alaska, both Dene and Athabascan are still considered acceptable, but it is likely the latter term will eventually become a harmful ethnic descriptor in the United States as well. Recognizing this, "Dene" will be used here when referring to the people to appeal to groups on both sides of the border appropriately, and perhaps the future as well. "Athabascan" will only be used when referring to the archaeological expression of Dene culture. I use this term with apologies to any who might find offense; the topic of changing the term "Athabascan tradition," which for archaeologists means the recognizable material culture of the Dene people prior to the colonial period, to "Dene tradition" or something appropriately similar has not yet been widely discussed. Additionally, in this book," Salcha" refers to the Euro-American community, and *Salcheege* (anglicized as Salchaket) refers to the original Alaska Native community and people; they were geographically located in the same place. All Native words are given in the Middle Tanana language unless otherwise noted.

Today, in the early twenty-first century, over 100 years of access to wage labor, the railroad and highway hubs, and the presence of the University in Fairbanks has caused many Native Tanana people to relocate there on both a permanent and semi-permanent basis. These factors have helped facilitate Fairbanks in becoming the long-term sociopolitical center of the Tanana Valley. The Tanana Chiefs Conference (TCC) continues to meet there, and the headquarters of Doyon, Limited (one of the twelve regional Alaska Native corporations formed in 1971 (Arnold [1976] 1978) are also located there. The offices of several Tribal councils and smaller village corporations representing communities elsewhere in the valley are also in Fairbanks. The Alaska Native villages that remain populated today in the Tanana Valley have retained their presence as important traditional cultural centers. Federal and corporation funds are allocated to Tribal entities to maintain this valued system (Simeone 1995). Today, some members will actively maintain a multimodal career, moving between more traditional village life and the modes of wage labor in the service industry, trades, political, and academic spheres as they feel is personally necessitated. Many fulfill multiple administrative roles within Tribal corporations, and others hold active research positions at the university.

Despite the economic and political dominance that Fairbanks draws for the Native community, the smaller remote villages are still considered the focal point of maintaining traditional cultural identity in the face of the overwhelming omnipresent Euro-American Alaskan culture and its capitalist market-driven political economy. Maintaining many villages' isolation from the road system is often vital for cultural survival and traditional subsistence living (Simeone 1995). This process has helped create a modern, broadly unified interior Alaskan Native culture. The visible social differences are mainly due to capital income levels and personal participation in the traditional rural subsistence lifestyle. English has been the dominant first language for most people beginning with those born during the Cold War era. The traditional languages of the region are now imperfectly learned at varying levels as a second language. In recognition of the unfortunate historical processes of language erasure, this chapter covering the twentieth and twenty-first centuries will only refer to place names by their latest English form, reflecting how many younger people now know their ancestral landscape. When the book discusses earlier times, the traditional Native names will also be used when known.

The twentieth century saw several major socioeconomic factors that continue to heavily influence the residential movements of Alaska Natives in the Tanana Valley. The act of statehood in 1959 spurred the need to legally settle territorial land claims between Alaska Natives with the Federal Government, an effort that remains ongoing. Alaska Native land claims had to be settled before the United States government could grant legal title to the State of Alaska for lands the United States had purchased from the Russian Empire. The Alaska Native Claims Settlement Act (ANCSA) of 1971 (Arnold [1976] 1978) solidified and halted older socio-economic processes imposed by the Euro-Americans from the early twentieth century that resulted in the geographical splitting of the local Native community into Upper and Lower Tanana Valley groups. Those groups are now centered upriver at Tok and downriver in Fairbanks and Nenana. Smaller villages such as Healy Lake, Tanacross, Dot Lake, Tetlin, Northway, and Mentasta Lake have retained small but dynamic Alaska Native populations (<500 persons) more or less permanently the Upper Tanana area. The communities of Minto, Manley Hot Springs, and Tanana have maintained their small communities in the Lower Tanana Valley (figure 1.1). No Native communities in the Middle Tanana Valley remain substantially populated today. Extended familial ties, however, continue to transcend this current geographical divide.

ANCSA created a new interaction between the United States and tribal sovereign governments in Alaska. Instead of tribal membership being determined through blood quantum and reservations, tribal affiliation was determined by ancestral village, and community members were given both land allotments that could be demonstrated to have been traditionally used by Tribal members, and shares in for-profit community and regional corporations upon legal settlement (Peter 2009; Pratt 2009). TCC became the ANCSA Native association, tasked with handling most of the internal bureaucratic activities and government-to-government affairs between tribes and the US Federal administration.

All the Tanana communities additionally were also subsumed under a single Alaska Native regional for-profit corporation, Doyon, Limited. The corporation also includes most of the Dene villages of the middle Yukon, upper Kuskokwim, Koyukon, and Tanana watersheds. Unlike the similar Alaska Permanent Fund Dividend, where shareholders are determined by only state residency, corporate shareholding is determined by residency, blood quantum, and chosen inheritance. When the Alaska Native tribal groups accepted the ANCSA settlements, each enrolled member was given an equal number

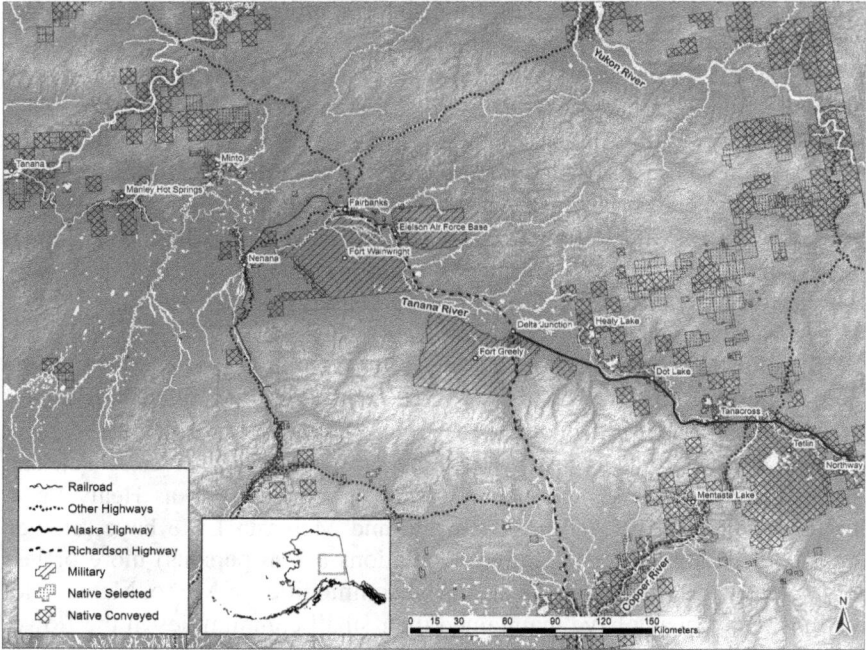

Figure 1.1. Modern Alaska Native villages of the Tanana Valley, Native selected or patented land status, and US military lands, post–World War II.

of shares in their regional and village corporations. Shareholders maintained full authority over determining the inheritance of those shares. Five decades of this ascribed inheritance practice has resulted in a dual split in the Alaska Native community; those who are shareholders and receive dividends and those who are not. Importantly, Alaska Native women were immediately granted equal access to shareholder and land claim enrollment regardless of marital status, an action that would have been unlikely at any earlier period of US jurisdiction.

All thirty-seven Tanana Valley Tribes actively engage with the US government through TCC. Due to historical processes outlined below, Alaska Native Tribes are defined differently than elsewhere in the nation. Today, each Alaska Federally recognized tribe is simply defined as being one of 229 recognized Alaska Native villages. Each is considered to be a separate sovereign nation protected in perpetual legal trust by the US government. Membership (or citizenship) enrollment is documented through proof of parental or ancestral residency in each village, and is independent of corporate shareholder status. Some villages/tribes allow dual enrollment, but most are exclusive.

Enrollment provides access to federal services promised (but not always honored) by the United States government in perpetuity in exchange for the permanent settlement of traditional land claims (Schneider 2018; TCC n.d.).

Current identities as a Native person of the Tanana Valley are multimodal. It heavily favors identity concepts that value the individual and natal family. It is externally determined through Euro-American ideas of personal, genetic, and linguistic ancestral residency based on legal land title and Euro-American traditional economic concepts of inheritance and corporate ownership. Notably, the ancestral languages of communities have become an academic ethnicity marker. This identity through ancestral language is also a western imposition. Despite these relatively new ideas, traditional Dene concepts of identity persist. They focusing instead on extended familial clan ties and those traditional familial forms remain actively maintained, and are considered critical to the potlatch ceremony. Traditional elders continue to be revered and are considered to be active maintainers and teachers of traditional culture (Simeone 1995).

The region that this book is concerned with, the Middle Tanana, and the traditional villages that once existed between the modern Euro-American communities of Big Delta and Salcha, was almost entirely depopulated of its Native population before the rise of Alaska Native political activity associated with statehood (1959) and ANCSA (1971) and is explored in the next section. This did not occur through social violence or government-enforced expulsion as in other parts of the continent, but rather through socioecological developments described in the next section.

It is important to realize that the continued maintenance of traditional kinship networks and the uninterrupted, free movement of Alaska Natives throughout the Historical and Modern periods has resulted in a minimized concept of a diaspora community compared with other US and Canadian regions. A sense of loss of traditional lands as might be experienced by Native people elsewhere is only somewhat present here, mainly restricted to loss of land and resource rights (Peter 2009, 181). Intercommunity residential movements are considered traditionally acceptable. Today, realms of political conflict tend to be focused on traditional resource acquisition claims and entitlements at the local, state, and federal levels.

THE TERRITORIAL ERA OF DIRECT CONTACT (1959–1897 AD)

An important external factor influencing the Euro-American population's dispersal throughout the Territory of Alaska was the construction of the ALCAN Highway (also known as the Alaska-Canadian, or Alaska Highway).

The highway was built in 1942, just before Alaska's statehood in 1959, from Dawson Creek, British Columbia, to Delta Junction, Alaska. The road partially fulfilled the need to transport military equipment to the territory in response to the invasion of the Aleutian Islands by the Empire of Japan. This road was the first such constructed through the Upper Tanana region. The Alaskan section was built by the African-American 97th Engineer Regiment (1,200 enlisted men and 50 officers), 18 private contractors from the American Midwest, and 1,300 further civilian employees (Duesenberg 1994). The road opened the Upper Tanana to more expansive commerce and direct settlement by outside populations (Lane 1942). The earlier construction of the Richardson Highway along older Native trails that passed from Valdez to Fairbanks through Big Delta, beginning in 1910, had a similar effect in opening the Middle Tanana region to Euro-American settlement (Woster 2016) (figure 1.1).

As the military pushed the ALCAN Highway through the Upper Tanana country, a wave of sickness and death was introduced through the area (Haynes and Simeone 2007). Prior to this, the central Tanana village at Healy Lake had maintained a dynamic Native population. The devastating respiratory illness hit their community and caused a dramatic population loss and subsequent dispersal of the survivors throughout the Upper Tanana region in 1943 (Andrews 1975; Ferguson 2002). Most of the survivors eventually settled at Dot Lake (figure 1.2). Margaret Kirsteatter was a resident whose life and residency spanned the 1940s epidemic. She was influential in maintaining a presence and rebuilding the community at Healy Lake after the 1950s and preserving the traditional lifeways. She conducted the first private collection of artifacts from around the lake, a practice her son Fred continued. Margaret became one of archaeologist John Cook's primary informants when he was conducting excavations there for his dissertation during the 1960s (Cook 1969) under the supervision of Robert McKennan, who had learned of the collection (Younie 2015, 3). She had been born upriver in Mansfield village in 1916, tracing her lineage through her mother, Agnes Sam from Healy Lake, and maternal grandmother Belle Hatchet Sam, who was born in the village of Joseph located on the Middle Fork Fortymile River. Belle Hatchet's mother was married to *Kataba* who was the brother of Belle's husband Old Chief Sam, a lifelong member of the Healy Lake band. Old Chief Sam and Kataba's father was a powerful shaman, counterpart to elder Chief John Healy, who played an important role in the community's movement from the Fortymile country to Healy Lake. Margaret's family and descendants (children Fred and Linda Kirsteatter, Linda's daughter Melissa Erikson, and Melissa's daughter Evelynn Combs) have worked closely with many anthropologists and archaeologists working in the Upper Tanana since the 1960s,

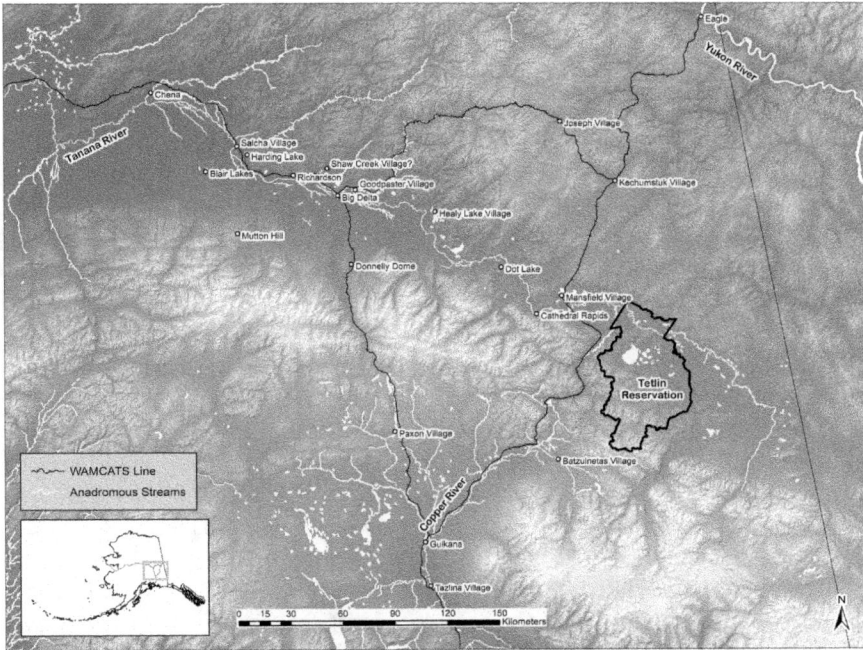

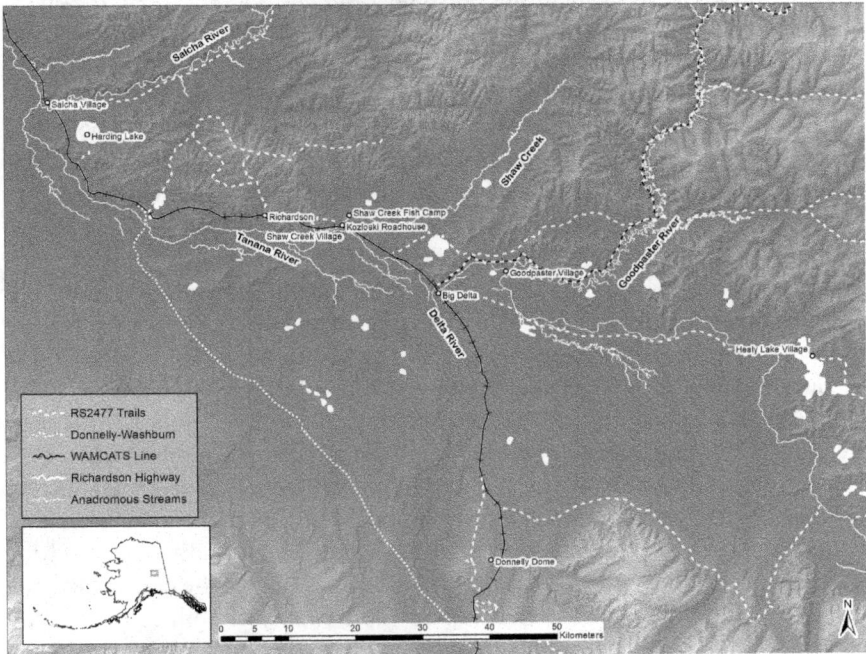

Figure 1.2. Geographic references for the early historic period, around 1890 AD to World War I.

and their family's influence on the development of both regional and North American anthropological and archaeological theory is incalculable (genealogies from Callaway and Miller-Friend 2001, iv; Mishler 1986, 23).

World War II and the subsequent Cold War eras also saw the construction and development of military reservations in the Middle Tanana Valley and the bases of Fort Greely, Eielson Airforce Base, Ladd Army Airfield, and Fort Wainwright that restricted large swaths of land from public access south of the Tanana River from the Delta to Nenana Rivers, and between the Chena and Salcha River drainages north of the Tanana (figure 1.1). Before World War II, these areas comprised much of the traditional land used by the Chena, Wood River, and Delta-Goodpaster Dene bands. Today the US military remains a widely respected social institution for the Tanana Valley Natives. Still, as a land-management agency, negativity is expressed toward them regarding access restrictions to traditional lands, historic resource depletion, and environmental degradation (e.g., Easton 2005, 221–224, 242; Hollinger 2003, 9–10, 55–56, 58; see also petroleum spills and toxic contamination associated with the military's Haines-Fairbanks Pipeline and accompanying twenty-five-foot corridor, built following the ALCAN and Richardson highways (operating between 1954 and 1973) (USACE 2004).

During the prewar years, two non-Native men had an especially impactful effect on the local Native community. They were the early twentieth century immigrant brothers John and Milo Hajdukovich, who played an essential lasting role in developing the fur trade on the Upper Tanana country above Big Delta. They facilitated and promoted the continued traditional landscape use in the region by local Natives, discouraging settlement pressure from other Euro-Americans. Other places in the interior areas of Alaska, such as Eagle and Fairbanks, experienced opposite trends (Ferguson 2002).

Partly due to the Hajdukovich brothers and the other early merchants, Ted Lowell and Herman Kessler's influence, and partly from the desire for market independence from the Euro-American-owned trading posts by the Upper Tanana people, one Native reservation was formed in the Tetlin area in 1930, later dissolved under ANCSA in 1971 (Heaton 2012) (figure 1.2). Homesteading in the Tanana had been open to Alaska Natives after the Indian Citizenship Act in 1924. However, the idea of residential permanency and career farming under the Euro-American traditional land tenure system on either homesteads or reservations was rejected by both many individuals and the initial Tanana Chiefs Conference in Fairbanks in 1915. At the conference, the leaders opted to maintain the status quo, where people of both cultures could continue using the land simultaneously as they saw fit (Schneider 2018). None of the Upper Tanana chiefs attended the meeting, with the exception of Chief Joe, who represented the *Salcheege* people, having moved there from the village of Joseph, his namesake. Chief Joe, brother of Belle Hatchet Sam, was the maternal uncle of the younger Chief John Healy (d. 1947), he initially led Joseph Village but became the chief at *Salcheege* after a controversial marriage to his second wife Agnes, the recent widow of Chief Jarvis. Chief Joe (or Joseph) had initially made his fortune guiding Lt. Mitchel through the Goodpaster (Callaway and Miller-Friend 2001, iv; Mishler 1986, 23).

Social factors that influenced shifts in the traditional seasonal nomadic lifestyle before World War II was primarily driven by the fur trade. Many Natives (usually men) ran legal traplines or supported the riverboats to obtain a cash income. Seasonal jobs and traplines dictated men's winter movements and residences during this period. At the same time, their families often stayed at permanent homes near what had been previously seasonal fish camps or winter villages located near new trading posts, schools, and missions (Cook 1989; Hilmer 2019; John 1996; Luke 1998; Thomas 2005).

Anthropologist Robert McKennan noted during his fieldwork in the Upper Tanana in 1929 that much social prestige was gained for chiefs who could obtain a mission or government school for their village (Mishler and Simeone 2006, 150–151). When the Episcopalian missionary teachers arrived in the Tanana villages, they actively sought to isolate the traditional shamans, called *deyinenh*, or sleep doctors, through economic disenfranchisement (today, some consider the term "shaman" to carry stigma following early missionary teachings and prefer "medicine man" or "spiritual person" (Cannon et al. 2020, 21). This practice helped create a new power opportunity for young adults seeking leadership positions by employing Christianity as a mechanism for social organization, marginalizing older individuals who preferred the old spiritual authority paths.

During this period, school attendance became mandatory. Many children were removed from their villages through a mix of force and personal choice (dependent on age) to religious boarding schools. It was unknown to the traditional leaders at the time the traumatic effect that this experience would ultimately have on first-generation students. When the fieldwork for this project was undertaken (2013–2020), this initial boarding school generation formed the elder generation for the Tanana people. Their experience was mixed; many endured physical, mental, and sexual abuse by a subset of predatory school leaders who were never disciplined or prosecuted. Many younger members did not understand where they were or why they had been removed from their communities and families and forgot their villages and kin. There was no communication with families and little control for documentation of where children came from or who their relatives were, and many were ultimately adopted out to Euro-American families elsewhere in the United

States. In the absence of detailed census records, it remains unknown how many children were lost to adoption or death.

Learning English and adapting to the American secular-religious schooling curriculum was a traumatizing process. Some teaching methods, considered brutal by today's standards, were standard practice then across most American public schools but were especially intensified in the Native boarding schools. These experiences are recorded in Legacy of Our Elders (TCC 2017, 2018). Though the overarching narrative of the boarding school period was disastrous and negative, some experiences were positive, especially for primary schools and orphanages located in rural villages. One particular positive result from this experience was that the cross-cultural relationships formed between older students facilitated intercommunity political organization during the early statehood era. The adverse effects resulted in the end of many cultural practices including the indigenous languages being taught as a vital first language to the subsequent generations. The individuals who survived and returned brought the legacy of the mental, physical, and sexual abuse back to their communities with devastating effects. In many villages, this generation presently forms the only remaining speakers of their original dialects.

Returning to community economics during the latter territorial era, in addition to obtaining furs for trade, Natives also supported the briefly occupied mining and military highway construction communities by providing fresh meat (typically large game and salmon). Paul Kirsteatter of Healy Lake reported that during the 1913 Chisana Gold Stampede (see also Powell 1909), the Native communities actively saved the incoming Euro-Americans, who were at that time primarily prospectors, from starvation on numerous occasions by gifting them an abundance of food when needed and refusing any sort of repayment (Kirsteatter 2000). "Gifting" or "potlatching" is used here in their colloquial verb forms, specifically referring to the context of giving something to another person with ceremonial intent; that is, both the giver and the gifted understand the cultural ramifications of the event and the implied expectations of ritual reciprocity. The diction is specifically chosen for use here for lack of a better English term and due to its regionally accepted use in this context. Cash as a medium of exchange only slowly became necessary for use later during the 1920s and 1930s, primarily to circumvent trading post monopolies who often operated trade through in-store credit (e.g., Halpin 1987, 9–11).

As contact became more long-term between the Native and Euro-American cultures, it became understood to the Natives that the immigrant Euro-Americans often had radically different ideas concerning the purpose of wealth accumulation and the role of reciprocity. The Tanana people never hesitated to gift food and clothing to the immigrants. It was a social action shrewdly engineered to peacefully incorporate them into the traditional gift-economy of the potlatch based on reciprocal gift exchanges determined by familial relationship (the word "potlatch" comes from Chinook meaning "to give" (Hibben [1889] 2011). By doing so, they indebted the new population to the old through the conventional rules of nonviolent reciprocal gift exchange between rival factions (Mauss [1925] 2016, 62–63; see Simeone 1995 for detailed information about this practice). As this book will show, this had been a successful tool of social integration and governance used by the Tanana Dene for millennia. The Native communities would have expected the mining community to eventually return the favor when their fortunes had changed for the better and to be showered with gifts and wealth in gratitude. The early prospectors appear to have, in some cases, considered the food as a selfless gift that required no reciprocity, but in many other cases, they were well aware of the implications and dully reciprocated. The potlatch ceremony was then well known and understood throughout the Euro-American community of the North American West Coast (Mauss 2016, 62; Powell 1909). Upon leaving the country, the miners would often "potlatch" their leftover supplies to the nearest Native group. However, several influential non-Native missionaries and patrons did not perceive the potlatch formality positively. They worked actively to suppress the ceremony as they alleged it to be detrimental to concepts of individual ownership and accumulation of personal wealth for old age (Simeone 1998). This negative attitude did not carry over to local Native Christians, who continued to positively view the practice. This cultural divide concerning the sociopolitical ramifications of gift exchange continues to color the Alaska Native perceptions of Euro-American Alaskans and their legal obligations toward them (Simeone 1995).

An earlier wave of deadly epidemics in the Middle Tanana occurred during the 1920s (including the 1918 Spanish Influenza), accompanying the Richardson Highway's initial construction along the Delta and middle Tanana Rivers. The Influenza epidemic was particularly devastating: almost 82 percent of the 1,113 deaths attributed to the outbreak in Alaska occurred among the Native population, which hit all age, health, and gender groups more or less equally (~75 percent of attributed deaths happened during the month of November 1918) (Crosby 1989; Mamelund et al. 2013). The loss of about 8 percent of the Native population, who comprised about 48 percent of the overall territorial population, was a traumatic shock to the villages. Former journalist and author Jack de Yonge (2010, 207–208) recalled visiting *Salcheege* village with his father during the Depression years following the epidemic. He remarked that the village had become entirely depopulated except for elderly members. Many of the younger generations who had survived had permanently left the community for wage labor opportunities elsewhere. Since the World War II era, Salcha has been considered a Euro-American community and is officially known by its shortened anglicized loanword form.

Pandemics were rampant from the early-nineteenth through mid-twentieth centuries and were responsible for reducing the original Native population by up to 30–70 percent during this period from previous estimates (Boyd 1990; Easton 2005, 61–65). Tuberculosis, in particular, became endemic during the nineteenth century, with rates of infection estimated to be from 25 to 50 percent of village populations. It was the leading cause of death for all age groups, with 35 percent of mortality attributed to the disease before the 1950s (Chandler 2017).

While tuberculosis was then a leading cause of death for all social and ethnic classifications worldwide, the widespread pattern of highly visible mortality rates in response to novel diseases among the Native Americans across the continent resulted in a concept perpetuated by the empowered Euro-American community of ascribing inferior racial fitness as evidenced by community health as being inherent within the Native nations. The false idea that a genetic basis as defined by racial boundaries is the primary cause of health disparities in minority populations unfortunately still permeates Euro-American popular culture. In actuality, the high mortality numbers have long been demonstrated to not be due to any genetic deficit. Instead, for past populations, they are understood to be the result of the combination of social factors such as the lack of preventative practices influenced by germ theory-in traditional medicine, family-based health practices, lack of exposure to disease during early childhood, increased exposure throughout life to higher daily health risks, and repetitive seasonal nutritional deficits.

Today, the US economic and political spheres continue to largely ignore the minority and low-income working-class experience regarding access to adequate healthcare and its devastating effects on those communities. It has resulted in a long-term skewed understanding of community health toward these marginalized groups by wealthier Euro-Americans (Riley 2012). These historical trends continue to have a marked effect, especially on the Native American and Alaska Native populations today and continue to have a negative influence (Sarche and Spicer 2008).

Before the presence of the highways in the Tanana, population movement and commerce were constrained mainly by river travel and overland seasonal pack trails. The Richardson Highway was an expansion of the earlier Valdez-Fairbanks Trail, a winter-use trail that was cleared and built in 1902–1903 along an older Native trail (Reckord 1983). The construction was associated with the Washington-Alaska Military Cable and Telegraph System (WAM-CATS) line built from Valdez to Eagle. Both became the first of many large infrastructure projects to disrupt the traditional lifeways throughout the valley. The telegraph line was constructed between 1901 and 1904, bisecting the valley. One leg ran from the village of Kechumstuk south to Gakona Junction, crossing the Tanana River at Tanacross. Another leg ran north from the Gulkana River in the Copper River Valley, following the Delta River to Big Delta, where it crossed the Tanana River and then traveled northeast along the Goodpaster River to Ketchumstuk, then to Eagle. As a result, the Goodpaster to Kechumstuk section became abandoned between 1907 and 1910 (Solka 1994; Tweiten 1990). Lieutenant William Mitchell directed the telegraph line construction, surveying from Eagle to Chena in 1903 while making detailed notes of the Native village at Goodpaster (Mitchell 1982). The line was maintained by the US Army Signal Corps, who manned service cabins located along the line approximately every ten to twenty miles apart (Andrews 1980; Tweiten 1990). The section from Goodpaster to Kechumstuk was built along an older Native trail (Andrews 1980, 40–43). The Valdez-Fairbanks Trail split at Donnelly Roadhouse, with one spur traveling north to Big Delta and a second spur going northwest to cross the Tanana at Washburn (Peterson 1982) (figure 1.2).

While at Goodpaster Village in 1903, Lt. Mitchell noted that while English was beginning to be spoken by a few individuals, Chinook Jargon was a much better-known *lingua franca* (Mitchell 1982, 73; see also Powell 1909, 57). Chinook was a creole/pigeon trade language considered to have originated in the Columbia River mouth, eventually spreading extensively northwards along the Pacific drainages during the nineteenth century. In the eastern Yukon-Tanana Uplands, the historic village name of Kechumstuk may be derived from this language (Hibben [1889] 2011). The name means "catching-stick" or "catching-fence," in Chinook, likely referring to the extensive, twenty-mile long, plus eighty-mile network of caribou fences and corrals that were used there (e.g., Brooks [1953] 1973, 78–79). Another possible origin was provided by Andrew Isaac who reported that the name referred to harvesting hay for horses in the early twentieth century (Andrews 1980, 3). The previous name of the village was *Saages Cheeg*: meaning "sun fork mouth/gap" (Kari 2011a). Diction used by authors such as Fredrick Currier (2018) and Robert McKennan (Mishler and Simeone 2006) suggests a heavily-Chinook-influenced pidgin English may have been used between the prospector and Native communities of interior Alaska.

The US Signal Corps initially maintained a permanent presence along the line at the service cabins. Each was operated by two men, who rotated out every few months (Mishler 1986). One such cabin was built near the Native village at the mouth of the Goodpaster River. Soon after construction, the village was permanently abandoned. The population dispersed up and down the valley after one of the corps personnel became drunk, raping and killing a very young girl during the winter of 1904–1905. The girl was the sister of Abraham Luke, who became anthropologist Craig Mishler's primary informant (Mishler 1986). The Signal Corps cabin burned under suspicious circumstances soon after, either as a retaliatory act by the girl's family or as an act of arson by the Signal Corps officers themselves who were looking to relieve their daily monotony and isolation. The station was relocated to Big Delta near Rika's Roadhouse in 1907. The Roadhouse, highway, and the Tanana ferry there became a central hub for the local Euro-American community and was called Big Delta, built where the older Native community, the Tth'ihtl'aa iin, had once lived. During the 1940s and 1950s, the community shifted south to the ALCAN Highway terminus, as the construction of Fort Greely drew people ten miles away to Buffalo Center, the present-day location of the city of Delta Junction (Ferguson 2002). The earlier name referred to the introduction of a small herd of twenty-three plains bison from Montana in 1928.

In this region, many English place names incorporate the term "Delta" as part of their descriptor, recorded by the earliest Euro-American explorers. Both Lt. Allen (1985) and the geographer Donald Orth (1971) provide descriptive landscape reasons for these toponyms, but it should be pointed out that the phrase "ddhel' tah" in the Middle Tanana language means "among the mountains" (Kari n.d.). This phrase would have likely been often overheard by the early American explorers as their Native guides discussed the region in their own languages and may have influenced the English names.

THE SHAW CREEK PEOPLE (1860–1915 AD)

A neighboring Native community to the Big Delta and Goodpaster villages was located just downriver in the next major south-flowing drainage at Shaw Creek (figure 1.2). This community is much more poorly documented. Several locations for the Shaw Creek Native village have been elicited, one nineteenth-century site near the Shaw Creek Bridge on the Richardson Highway (visited by Abraham Luke and excavated by Froelich Rainey (XDB-00190) (Rainey 1939b), and another unknown location farther up the valley (ANLC0881b 1983; Solka 1994). Rainey described his site as just above Kozloski's Roadhouse, being a large midden (2.5 ft. deep x 10 ft. wide) and the site of an earlier large trade camp.

A brief influx of as many as eighty Euro-American prospectors spent 1901–1904 scouring the Salcha River, Shaw Creek, and Goodpaster River areas. The mining community of Richardson, located about ten miles downriver from Shaw Creek at Banner Creek, was established as a result. In about 1908, a homestead was filed on the mouth of Shaw Creek by Polish immigrant Anthony Kozloski, who maintained a roadhouse there until 1918 (Solka 1994). Kozloski built an active fishwheel at the mouth. The creek supported a salmon spawning habitat then and a potato plot on top of the nearby rocky bluff, which supplied local produce for the Richardson community just downstream on the Tanana. In response, the Shaw Creek Native village relocated from the mouth to about a mile up Shaw Creek between the mouths of Rosa and Caribou Creeks, which may have also been one of the traditional locations of the summer fish camps (figure 1.2).

Kozloski soon suffered a head injury from a horse kick, resulting in extreme behavioral changes that included severe paranoia. For the next ten years, when he was not tending his fishwheel or potato crop, he actively patrolled the Shaw Creek basin, claiming exclusive use and threatening violence on anyone he encountered. Local historian Paul Solka (1994), who grew up in Richardson, wrote that the Shaw Creek Native families permanently abandoned the area due to his erratic behavior. Most travelers on the Richardson Trail at that time also apparently avoided staying at Kozloski's Roadhouse during his tenure after the accident. In a taped recording by Jim Kari curated at the Alaska Native Language Center Archives, informant Eva Moffit of *Salcheege* (d. 1993) recalled her family, father A. Mumus (or Mumfus John) Barnabas, mother Bessie Barnabas (1884–1986), and herself needing to sneak by his homestead in a boat during early morning hours while he slept to avoid his armed threats in order to engage in subsistence activities on the creek. She did not mention meeting any other Natives during that trip (ANLC0959 1991).

Once they had abandoned Shaw Creek, the families would have had the option to join their close relatives, who were likely associated with the neighboring community to the west, *Salcheege*. This opaque name can literally be translated as "sun mouth," though many other puns can be elicited (Kari 2015). This form of purposely using an ambiguous name is termed *deliberate opacity*, and Kari argues it indicates great antiquity of the name.

About the time of the Native depopulation of Shaw Creek, most of the people of the Big Delta and Goodpaster villages likely had already abandoned their villages in favor of living at *Salcheege*. However, a few Goodpaster families chose to relocate instead of the village of Joseph to the northeast, named after its headman. Joseph had been settled there before 1901 under the direction of his elder brother Chief John Healy (d. 1929) of Healy Lake. Joseph village was located to the east of the upper Goodpaster River headwaters on the Middle Fork Fortymile River (Andrews 1980). Joseph village was in the traditional winter-use area of the Healy Lake band (Kirsteatter

2000) (figure 1.2). Local prospectors named them after a family the Healy Lake people never met—trader John J. Healy, his wife Belle, and his brother Joseph of Fort Cudahy and Dawson (Tolton 2014).

Another story potentially concerning the fate of the Shaw Creek band was given by Cecelia Balch, Bessie Barnabas's last living daughter. When her grandfather Chief John was a younger man, perhaps in the 1880s, he was bringing his new wife from the Tazlina area on the Copper River to his home at *Salcheege*. Along the way, they were ambushed by a band of men bearing muzzle-loading rifles near a stream called Clearwater River. The attacking men were wiped out in the skirmish, and Chief John and the *Salcheege* families adopted the surviving women and children (Ferguson 2016).

The only official English-named "Clearwater Creek" is to the east of the Delta River, flowing north into the Tanana just upstream from the Goodpaster. This stream seems to be well out of the way for a person traveling by foot from Copper River to *Salcheege* village. Other alternatives are found in the traditional Middle and Lower Tanana Place Names databases, which were well known to Celia (Kari and Smith 2017). Two other north-flowing streams, one with no English name, carry the translated name "clearwater stream." They are located between the Delta and Salcha Rivers. The traditional name "clear water stream" often denotes an optimal location for a summer fish camp and salmon weir, where the clear water of the smaller north-flowing streams meets the silty opaque water of the Tanana. One of these, Clear Creek, is just upstream from Delta Creek, flowing parallel to the Tanana River on its southern bank, just opposite of Shaw Creek. This creek also had a village near its mouth which was closely associated with the Shaw Creek village. Those families' territory is included in the reconstructed Shaw Creek people's catchment area. The other is a small creek with no English name that enters the Tanana just downstream from the Salcha River. This story may be more associated with the fate of Clearwater village than Shaw Creek village.

Abraham Luke told one final traditional story concerning the demise of the Shaw Creek people. He maintained that one of his great-grandfathers had been a powerful shaman from Shaw Creek village who was murdered by his nephew after an ominous dream. He was killed and cremated several times as his spirit would not pass over. Eventually, his ghost returned to the village and killing everyone it found there. One of the surviving families left permanently, joining the Wood River band (ANLC0882a). The story, given in mixed English and Middle Tanana, suggests that these events may be more strongly associated with a third village at Tenderfoot Creek, which was also closely tied to the Shaw Creek and Clear Creek families. These three differing accounts suggest that the region's abandonment and its Native settlements were a complicated, multi-causal, and unrelated series of events between the 1880s and 1910s.

Another factor influencing community dissolution throughout the Middle Tanana was shifting concepts of personal wealth during this time. Participation in the international fur trade steadily became a dominant part of the Tanana Native economy during the latter nineteenth and early twentieth centuries. At Goodpaster village, all trade furs taken by individuals for market sale were considered the chief's communal property, who personally took them to the Tanana or Eagle trading posts. However, at *Salcheege*, individuals retained personal ownership of their furs, including husbands and wives, who kept separate accounts of their wealth. Andrews (1975) considers this difference to have been a driving factor influencing individuals to abandon Goodpaster and moving to *Salcheege* and Joseph permanently. Log cabins and canvas wall tents became a popular Native residence choice in the early twentieth century as soon as axes and canvas became readily available at the trading posts.

Under the leadership and missionizing activities of a charismatic man, Jarvis John, born at Paxson Lake but who became a resident of Goodpaster village as a young adult (figure 1.2), remaining members of the Native population between the Goodpaster and Salcha Rivers became centered at *Salcheege* village by 1907. An Episcopalian mission was built there at the same time the Richardson Highway was completed. The Middle and Upper Tanana Episcopal Missions were operated by unmarried Euro-American laywomen and ministered to by a circuit minister who traveled seasonally by dogsled or boat.

Many families continued moving seasonally between *Salcheege* and various traplines throughout the territorial years, while some family members permanently stayed tending gardens and small children in the village. Chief Jarvis eventually died in a suspicious drowning incident in 1914 at forty years old on Blue Creek, a slough near Big Delta. By the 1930s, almost all of the *Salcheege* Native inhabitants had left the community. Many moved upriver, joining the Healy Lake village. Others, including Bessie Barnabas and her daughter, Eva Moffit, moved to Fairbanks or the later community of North Pole. Helen Charlie, originally of Goodpaster village, also moved to Fairbanks, where her daughter Laura Anderson (1957) wrote and published her memoirs in *According to Mama*.

The Territorial period in the Middle Tanana was marked by a gradual, decades-long dissolution of the Native population there. The depopulation appears to have primarily been an internal process of community responses to pandemics, wage labor, trapping economics, and a few critical instances of interpersonal violence. The Middle Tanana's original people did not remain a unified presence there long enough to have become recognized by the US Government as a separate tribe in the legal sense that the Native communities are today. Today, their descendants are active members of many other vibrant, officially recognized villages throughout the Tanana Valley.

THE NINETEENTH CENTURY AND THE
END OF CULTURAL AUTONOMY

Before 1897 AD, the nineteenth century primarily saw the Tanana Valley untouched by direct contact with the colonial powers. The Tanana River was the last major river valley to be explored by any non-Native group in North America. Before the influx of early twentieth-century Euro-American prospectors, only a limited number of outside US visitors were documented visiting the valley. The last was led by US Army Lieutenant Joseph C. Castner, who traversed overland from Cook Inlet to the Delta River and down the Tanana in 1898 (Woodman 1984). Lt. Castner described portions of the Goodpaster, Salcha, and Chena Rivers and mentioned meeting several groups of prospectors along his journey. During the same season, geologist Alfred Brooks (whose namesake is the Brooks Range in northern Alaska) also traversed the river (Woodman 1984). The first recorded Americans to visit were led by US Army Lieutenant Henry T. Allen. He led a party mapping the Tanana River from Mentasta Lake in its headwater's country to its confluence with the Yukon River in 1885. Lt. Allen's excursion included the Copper River and lower Yukon Rivers. Allen's (1985) narrative of the Tanana is brief, as he met very few Natives along the river after leaving the headwaters country. All explorers reported that villages and residences were constructed in traditional manners, as western-style log cabins had not yet diffused there before the 1890s. Another early traverse was by the merchant Charlie Hamilton (1892), who traveled up the Tanana to the Goodpaster area, then on to the Fortymile River region (Mishler 1986, 76).

Before the American's traverses, three incursions on the river by British-Canadian explorers have been historically recorded: the Anglican minister Jules Prevost completed an ascent of the Tanana into the Fortymile country in 1893 (Cook 1989). Earlier (1885), an ascent of the river was done by the Anglican missionary Vincent Sim from the mouth almost as far upstream to *Salcheege* (Mishler 1986, 74). The earliest documented reconnaissance was by the independent Canadian fur traders Arthur Harper and Mr. Bates during the 1870s (McKennan 1969, 24). Harper's son Walter would be the first to stand on the highest peak of Denali. They were independent fur trappers associated with the Hudson Bay Company who came overland from the Yukon and traversed the river from approximately Cathedral Rapids to its mouth (Schwatka 1893, 3). Harper's namesake is currently on a peak at the headwaters of the Healy River. These three events remain the only documented incursions on the Tanana by the British-Canadians. The Canadian presence, mainly via the Hudson Bay Company's sphere of influence, in interior Alaska was confined mainly on the central Yukon River, between the mouth of the Porcupine River to the mouth of the Tozitna River, principally at their trading outpost of Fort Yukon (1847–1869: Brooks [1953] 1973, 219; Mercier 1986, ix) and nominally at Noukelakayet Station, about fifteen miles downstream from the mouth of the Tanana (1868–1869) (Turck and Turck 1992). Fort Yukon was officially handed over to the Americans by formal request in 1869 following US Captain C. W. Raymond's arrival via steamboat, confirming that the fort was within the United States' territorial claims via the Russian Empire's prior claims.

The Russian American Company's assets were sold to the American firm Hutchinson, Kohl, and Co. after the territorial purchase in 1867, the culmination of political processes beginning in the 1840s (Brooks [1953] 1973; Loyens 1966, 100–110). The Russian explorers are only known to have penetrated up the Yukon River beyond their sub-post at Nulato into the Koyukuk River once in 1863, and as far as the mouth of the Tanana just before 1861, attempting to ascertain the location of Fort Yukon and confirm the British territorial incursion (Brooks [1953] 1973, 218–219, 233; Dall 1870, 276). Most researchers presently agree that there is no evidence that the many Copper River explorations by the Russians ever made it farther north than Batzulnetas in the south-facing foothills of the Alaska Range (Simeone 2009) near present-day Slana. The headwaters of the Susitna may have also been reached once by the Russian explorers, as well as the Kuskokwim (Brooks [1953] 1973, 235). No Russian explorers are definitively known to have ever entered the Tanana Valley, but Brooks infers that a Russian party was once reported on the Fortymile River ([1953] 1973, 236). A story of Aleut raiders is also maintained by the Healy Lake people, referenced here since the Russian exploration parties were primarily made up by Aleut and Creole members (Ferguson 2002).

Abraham Luke of Goodpaster and Big Delta retained some knowledge of the Russian vocabulary (ANLC0881b 1983), suggesting that this trade language once used by the Dena'ina and Ahtna may have also diffused during the nineteenth century into the central Tanana region (also attested to by Brooks [1953] 1973, 96). Luke had learned bits of the language from his father, whose mother was a "Russian" (i.e., Creole, probably the recent descendant of a Russian or Cossack explorer) from Paxson Lake. Luke mentioned that his father had also visited the Russian trading post at Nuchek in Prince

William Sound at least once but never provided more information. Several Creole villages are documented through oral history along the lower Susitna River (Kari and Fall 2016). At least thirteen Russian-sponsored expeditions entered the Copper River Basin between 1796 and 1848 (Grinev 1993). Three of the Copper River expeditions ended in the mixed Russian/Aleut parties being massacred in response to various provocations. The demise of those three groups often overshadows the legacy of the Empire there. Interactions between the Copper River people and the Russian Empire's agents were complicated. The Ahtna chiefs sought to both facilitate trade while maintaining a monopoly on their production of furs and copper, thwarting the Russian efforts (primarily through peaceful means) to gain access to these economic spheres in the valley (Grinev 1993).

During the nineteenth and early twentieth century, some of the Middle Tanana people were also noted to have traveled to the American trading posts at Cordova and Valdez, via the Copper River, and the British and later American trading posts on the Yukon River, indicating the long-range trading forays some members were willing to take. However, both Lt.'s Castner and Allen's Native guides expressed severe aversions to traveling through other groups' hunting territories. Sometimes they would abandon the expeditions altogether when the lieutenants refused to pay them and terminate their agreements early as they passed farther and farther from their home territories. Their aversion to passing through neighboring areas without prior invitation suggests that these long-distance trading travels were likely more an exception for specific individuals rather than an annual occurrence for the average person. For many of the guides that continued with either military expedition, it remains unknown if they were able to return safely to their natal villages.

Native trade networks facilitated the diffusion of western trade goods throughout the Tanana Valley, along with the English language, before actual contact with agents of those new cultures. Knowledge of relations between Native groups and the Russian Empire, British Empire, and the United States elsewhere on the continent was also widespread in the Tanana Valley before contact. The first contact with Europeans in the Copper River basin to the south was at the Copper River mouth in 1796 by Demitri Tarkhanov (Grinev 1987, 99, in Grinev 1993). The Upper Tanana chiefs expressed knowledge about the US government's negative interactions with Native nations elsewhere on the continent on several occasions (Allen 1985; Schwatka 1893; Woodman 1984). While Lt. Allen had almost no knowledge of the Tanana Valley when he arrived, the Upper Tanana delegates who met with him had already incorporated Western period suit clothing into their traditional formal attire. Children were brought to the lieutenant who could recite some basic English education lessons.

Little direct historical knowledge about the people of the Tanana Valley during the nineteenth century is available. A vague picture has emerged from oral history and extra-regional historical documents that during the latter half of the nineteenth century, the Middle Tanana population may have fluctuated between 100 and 700 individuals (Andrews 1975, 25–28). Demographic numbers were affected by epidemics, little of which is known for this regional period, and very high natural infant mortality. The visits by Lt.'s Allen and Schwatka both mention that adult males in the Tanana Valley outnumbered adult females considerably. However, it is unknown if this reflected typical demographic structure, social health unique to the late nineteenth century, a preference for the survival of male children, or women not being present or visible during the visits (Simeone et al. 2019, 106).

When Western trade goods were incorporated into the Native economy (Haynes and Simeone 2007, 56; Strong 1976, 160–161), they were valued at three relative levels:

1. Items of Western manufacture that replaced Native aboriginal means of production, such as firearms, gunpowder, and iron or steel tools.
2. Trade goods that were consumed and considered "minor luxuries," including tea, sugar, tobacco, blankets, cloth, and clothing.
3. Products that became part of the Native "prestige economy" and were used as potlatch gifts, such as the role that dentalium shells and glass beads had filled traditionally. Later, this category would expand to include firearms and blankets.

During the mid-nineteenth century, a period of dramatic internal Alaska Native wars was induced partly by the disruption of the ancient trade flow. This series of battles profoundly disrupted the lifeways of the Lower Tanana and Lower Yukon Natives. However, they may have only had negligible effects for the Upper Tanana. Informant Abraham Luke maintained that except for a few instances, those wars did not extend upriver beyond the Lower Tanana region (ANLC0883a 1983); however, Simeone et al. (2019) and McKennan's (1959) informants indicate otherwise describing an important series of raids originating from the Kluane Lake region and extending into the Dot Lake area (figure 1.2). McKennan (1959, 97, 170–174) documented several oral histories of and the behaviors reserved for warfare, but these appear to have been a rare final solution to any interclan conflict. Overall, it would appear that the Middle and Upper Tanana areas' populations survived the nineteenth century Warring Period relatively unscathed, aside for some inter-village raiding, compared to elsewhere in the state (see also Patrick Saylor's interview in Callaway and Miller-Friend 2001).

During this period, the Anglican branch of Christianity first diffused into eastern Alaska with missionaries following the Hudson Bay Company's trading routes down the Porcupine and Yukon Rivers and up the Tanana. Beginning with Reverend Robert McDonald's efforts in 1862 (Johnson 1985), this early influence resulted in the Tanana Valley being assigned to the Episcopalian Church for missionizing focus under Rev. Sheldon Jackson's overarching plan for the Christian education of the Alaska Native population in the late nineteenth century. The Salcha mission school was built in 1909 and closed in 1920, run by Ms. Margaret Wightman (Andrews 1975). The Anglican/Episcopalian Church remains influential among the Native population of the region.

Before this, a heavily Native-influenced version of Russian Orthodoxy diffused a generation or two earlier via the Cook Inlet area into the Copper River Valley where the chief of Taral, living at the confluence of the Copper and Chitina Rivers, decided to accept baptism. Chief Nicolai's influential conversion and charisma spread the beliefs north from there into the Middle Tanana (Grinev 1993; see also Znamenski 2003). For cultural practices, this belief system seems to have mainly only affected burials, promoting inhumation over cremation, the practice of burying the dead beneath the small canvas and timber-framed grave houses, the use of Russian Orthodox-style crosses as grave markers (McKennan 1959), and some shamanic beliefs and practices. Many Natives of those contact generations saw little difference between the Euro-Americans' teachings of Christ or their own traditional morality concepts as laid forth by Traveler, whose *Salcheege* name was *Saatedlech'eeghe*, discussed in more depth in the following chapter. Often, they considered the two belief systems to either be complementary or simply compartmentalized differences between them (Easton 2005, 15; see also Mishler and Simeone 2006, 116), an understanding that continues for many today. These earliest forms of Christianity seem to have passed into the Middle Tanana not through missionary activity but initially through kinship and shamanic knowledge networks.

Robert McKennan's experiences also illustrate the early viewpoint of compartmentalizing the differences between Christianity and traditional beliefs. He refers in his diaries to several instances of private conversations with village leaders where talks became directed toward sharing cultural information about distant past stories. In these conversations, McKennan was asked to recount both biblical and scientific perspectives on that ancient period. They were framed not as teaching moments but as two knowledgeable experts comparing and contrasting cultural perspectives on similar events (Mishler and Simeone 2006).

Later, the children and grandchildren of those first generations mission-ized by Euro-American Christians often either felt the desire or were pres-sured to experience a "purer" Christianity (i.e., more Euro-American cultural conforming) devoid of older traditional beliefs. The enculturation process may be partially influenced by the final form of Christianity to arrive (in this region mainly post 1930s), American Evangelical Protestantism, and the heavy indoctrination received in the boarding schools. Evangelicalism was unique from the Anglican Communion and Russian Orthodoxy. The form that arrived in Alaska during this time was heavily influenced by the American Social Gospel movement of the early twentieth century. This influence prescribed secular cultural conformity within the boarding schools and stressed individualized spirituality and emphasized denial of community agency, especially in traditional forms.

The Evangelical attitude toward negatively perceiving traditional non-Christian indigenous cultural and spiritual expressions among indigenous groups worldwide remains high today, but began to soften after the 1970s, significantly impacted by the populist work of Don Richardson (1974). Some Alaskan mission efforts since then, like that of Raymond and Sally Jo Collins in McGrath, Nikolai, and Telida, Alaska, have worked hard to reverse the effects of the deep cultural and personal trauma. However, the permanent negative aspects of the American Evangelical diffusion resulted in a long-term de-emphasis of older traditional cultural group expressions of devoutness (Simeone 2018, 114). Today, the informal, everyday spirituality practiced by the Tanana Natives often incorporates aspects of all these histor-ically present forms of Christianity, including the older Native beliefs. It also includes influences from Roman Catholicism, which had established a later presence at the village of Tanana, located at the confluence of the Tanana and Yukon Rivers (Cannon et al. 2020, 20; Loyens 1966, 116; Thomas 1967).

It is helpful to understand that attitudes toward Christianity remain inter-preted through the traditional perceptions concerning spiritual experience of the Tanana people. Individual experience, personal interpretation, freedom to seek or reject guidance from self-styled leaders, and the value of self-education over formal education remain core to the Dene's identity. Rather than seeing Dene Christianity as a passive, haphazard result of cultural bor-rowings from Euro-American religious traditions, Dene Christian expressions are instead better understood as the result of active internal scrutiny and breakdown of Euro-American spiritual teachings in contrast to the traditional core morality system of *'engii*, and the mythological experience of Traveler and other important similar core morality teachers.

Individualized spiritual experience is also traditionally valued and posi-tively accepted by modern non-Native Euro-American culture (Cannon et al.

2020, 5; Mishler and Simeone 2006, 116). This tradition has been embedded deeply within American religious ethos since the first emigrations to North America in the seventeenth century, such as was popularized by the early American religious and political philosopher Roger Williams. His fundamentalist philosophy of personal salvation, soul liberty, individual freedom, human rights, direct democracy, minimalist government, and separation of church and state, influenced by his Narragansett and Wampanoag teachers, became central to Euro-American and historic Evangelical identity. While born in Europe's Humanist awakenings, these early ideas found proof-of-concept in the ancient values of the Native American societies of New England and elsewhere. Later European thinkers Locke, Montesquieu, Voltaire, Hume, Rousseau, and American philosophers Franklin, Jefferson, and Adams further popularized them (Stubben 2000). Thus, those Euro-American values, being the result of early cultural sharing between Europeans and Native Americans, were found to be at once both foreign and deeply familiar to the Dene.

During the latter part of the nineteenth century, western trade goods, religion, and language diffused through various agencies and preceded direct Euro-American contact. These all had their unique impacts on the lived cultural patterns of the Tanana Dene and how those changed throughout the Territorial and Statehood periods. Continued religious attitudes have primarily reflected the predominant colonial power of the time. These are reflected in the archaeological record through burial practices and the incorporation of western trade goods, particularly glass beads manufactured and traded from China, Russia, and Italy, into otherwise traditional uninterrupted behaviors (Grover 2016; Kunz and Mills 2021). A growing emphasis on acquiring fur-bearing animals for western trade posts was likely the most significant aspect influencing settlement strategies. Therefore, settlement patterns, family identity, trade economics, and new religious burial practices can be considered to be innovative cultural influences during this time, affecting the archaeological record.

CONCLUSION

The first half of the twentieth century was the period of the highest socio-cultural stress for the Tanana people. In the early Historic Period, the Middle Tanana people ceased to exist as a separate community in the sense that others have become under ANCSA and federal legal recognition of the modern Statehood era. This appears recorded at the Swan Point archaeological site by the incorporation of western clothing items and food goods into otherwise traditional subsistence lifestyle, and its abrupt cessation of use around World War I. While the Middle Tanana language and villages no longer exist as separate viable entities, their people continue to maintain their presence and identity through traditional family ties. They are active members, teachers, and leaders within the local sociocultural and political spheres.

Historic and modern factors that have affected the current concepts of cultural identity, dissolution, and continuity of the Middle Tanana Native community are as follows: availability of wage labor, federal and tribal village residency and parental ancestry requirements, permanent legal land titles that restrict persons from moving back to pre-titled traditional lands, the long-term effects of past pandemics, mining and extra subsistence pressure on wildlife resources, and the mission schools. These six factors have primarily driven the creation of the modern Native identity in this region. During the preceding nineteenth century, three earlier novel factors affected the traditional socioeconomic sphere and represented new influences in the archaeological record. These were the growing importance of the international fur trade on local resources, widespread depopulation due to pandemics.

Chapter Two

The Ethnographic Reconstruction of the Past

The Middle Tanana People and a Theory of Deep Reciprocity

We pulled our snowmachines to a stop and killed the engines. It was Christmas week, 2014, and I had spent it at the Healy Lake village with Melissa Erikson, her daughters Evelynn and Lorinda, and Lorinda's newborn son, Odin. Melissa, Evie, and I had decided to ride up a tributary to visit the old village site, which had been inhabited before the historic lakeshore site. The snow was several feet thick, and we had stopped twenty or thirty feet from a single standing cabin. Despite being over a century old, the cabin was in excellent condition, well built, with sheets of metal roofing added at a later time, preserving the structural integrity.

"It was originally built by Chief Healy," Melissa said.

Cables of wolf skulls adorned the walls, strung later by other men of the community, recalling the period of bounties placed on the predators by a government unfamiliar with critical roles they played in the ecological web. Neither Melissa nor Evie approached the cabin, and I sensed it would be the 'engii for myself to do so or to photograph it.

"When the snows are gone, you can see the depressions of other houses," she continued.

We contemplated the cabin from afar, and I imperfectly considered how past events between the rival factions within the protohistoric community continued to strongly affect the present behaviors of Melissa and Evie. My professional work over the next few years in the academic and private spheres of archaeology would give me a deeper understanding of how our present behaviors affect our constructs of the past. Despite the singular march of time, the entanglement of the past, present, and future continue to change our perceptions of the events of each, patterning our physical traces in the biosphere, irrespective of temporal distance.

Before contact with Euro-Americans, the Tanana' people's primary concept of time was cyclical rather than linear. Recent work by Chris Cannon has focused on reconstructing the cosmology of the Northern Dene, as reflected through the mythology depicted in their unique, shared whole-sky constellation (Cannon et al. 2020). The shared mythology is summarized as such: the world passes through four great cycles of time, each ending in chaos and beginning with a newly established order, a common motif shared across many North American Native cosmologies (Mayor 2005). Each age was associated with a smaller constellation and a prophecy, which summarized the distant past, present, and future of the world. The tales of Raven and Traveler often include background elements equivalent to events and things recognizable to the late Pleistocene and early Holocene world. At the same time, they also have elements of later pre-colonial history, reflecting efforts to keep the tales contemporary and relevant. Framing the past in nonlinear models like this is similar to human memory formation and preservation; any event of the past can be sought and examined and reframed regardless of chronological order.

During the first, the Distant Time cycle, animals and humans could share language, and their physical forms were interchangeable. This was the creation that Raven manipulated, shaping into the world we recognize today. Raven is not the original creator, but through his chaotic actions, he gave the world much of its present form (Chapman 1921, 309). Raven is a trickster and through his tricks, he magically changed reality around him, shifting the world to his own immediate narcissistic desires. Magic, tricks, subterfuge, puns, and riddles all need the creative energetic urge to either change the nature of reality or change the way reality is perceived by the observer. Because stasis states, or maintenance of the eco-cultural system was desirable for all members of the community, individuals who were adept at puns, riddles, singing, dancing, illusion, and true magic, were restricted to practicing these at appropriate ceremonies and seasons. Especially powerful shamans were considered "outside" their community due to their dangerous ability to upset the balance and cause change, setting in motion the novel forces of destruction and creation. They were feared, extolled, and regarded with care, as is evinced by the first shaman, Traveler, an otherwise benevolent person who always put his vision quest ahead of his family and love interests.

The Raven story cycle represents an earlier time than the Traveler cycle, and some stories seem to recall memories of the changing Pleistocene ecosystem. One example is reflected in a tale where Raven eschews the rules of *'engii*, wearing false finery and bringing taboo food to a feast and causes the world to permanently, partially flood, evoking imagery of the coastal inundation of central Beringia (de Laguna and DeArmond 1995, 262–265).

While the Raven stories are widely shared across multiple cultures and linguistic groups, the Traveler stories are specific to northern Dene (de Laguna and DeArmond 1995). While cognates to Traveler are recognized in surrounding non-Dene groups, the subtle aspects of the Dene Traveler stories are entirely analyzable within Dene culture. The Traveler stories are set toward the end of the first age. During this time *Saatedlech'eeghe* (Traveler; lit.: One who goes in anger at the sun), furious that people had lost respect for righteous living, left his home to begin his spirit quest. Initially he was followed by his younger wife, and according to some stories he traveled with the giant *Yaachox* (Big Sky). He walked and paddled about the earth, always beginning from upstream on major rivers ending toward the sea, changing animals into their smaller forms, bringing general order, and establishing the sacred reciprocal relationships of *'engii* between people and nature. *'Engii* is the encoded right and wrong ways of doing all things in Dene culture, which, when practiced correctly, brings balance between all things in the universe.

The First Age of time ended when the rules of *'engii* were forgotten, and the world of the archaic Dene descended into violence and conflict. The Second Age began when Traveler, who after he reached the sea at the end of his life had ascended into the sky to hold back an ancient evil force, sent the Little People to remind the Dene of the ancient traditions (Cannon et al. 2020). During this time, the Little People taught the ancestral Dene sacred language, but their teachings were only imperfectly applied. Thus, it is each person's duty to discover, understand, and apply these teachings to themselves as they see fit. The Little People's appearances require ceremonial gifts and can be interpreted as reminders to practice proper traditional ways to avert disaster. Increasingly common sightings are thus considered an ominous foretelling, and their appearances today, during this time of unprecedented destruction of the natural world, is especially valued. It is a reminder that the traditions of the ancestors still have power, and that the overwhelming march of industry empowered by an ideology of consumerism is alien to this land and is not necessary the overwhelming conclusion of human civilization. This age is considered to encompass all of the pre-colonial history specific to Dene culture.

The Historic Period and the appearance of people traveling by sailing ships and bearing books are associated with the Third Age. The third cycle has been an increasingly chaotic period. Once again, the ancient teachings have either taken secondary precedence to materialistic pursuits or have become altogether forgotten during the ensuing cultural struggles. Because of this, the world's eco-cultural system has slowly, dangerously, shifted out of balance into increasing disharmony.

The Fourth Age will begin when the Earth's climate has degraded and heated to the point that the perennial snows disappear from the mountains and grasslands of the ancient habitats reappear once again in Alaska. Humanity will be faced with a choice; if they do not take the necessary steps to correct the eco-cultural disharmony, the world system will collapse and the great ancient evil force embodied as a giant prehistoric cat-like monster that Traveler has held back in the sky returns (Cannon et al. 2020, 6–7, 12). Like the seasons, the great cycles are believed to repeat themselves, and *Saatedlech'eeghe* will return once again to set the following world back in order (see Boraas and Peter 2008, 191).

The belief of Traveler's ancient journey and establishment of the cultural covenant between the Dene and creation is found within all northern Dene, suggesting an oral history as old as their cultural-linguistic origins. Within the Pacific Northwest and Northwestern interior region of North America, their territory has been recognized since the early twentieth century by anthropologists as unique, representing societies with social and resource networks far more complex than those generally maintained by non-agrarian societies. These include both the Dene and other traditional communities of the Pacific Northwest Coast (Clark 1984; Suttles 1990), Cook Inlet (Osgood [1937] 1966), the Aleutian Islands (Lantis 1984), Bristol Bay (Van Stone 1984), and the Bering Strait and Chukchi Sea regions (Burch 2006). These societies have presented anthropologists and archaeologists with a wealth of socially complex situations where agriculture did not play a definitive role in providing the necessary energy surplus typically needed to maintain the increasingly complex social networks. For these northern coastal societies, the excess energy was primarily supplied by marine resources (Betts 2013). This excess allowed for the development of sophisticated technology, complex warfare strategies and responses, working relationships, craft specialists, a slave class, and maintenance of prominent families. Arising from this concept was wealth retention and redistribution, resource and land ownership, large-scale food and craft item storage, population growth, and extensive social inequality (Adams 2001; Barton 2013; Burch 1974; Carballo et al. 2013; Cowgill 2004; Feinman 1998, 2011; Maschner 1997; Mason 2012; Smith 2009).

In Alaska, socially complex coastal societies were the immediate neighbors to the inland Dene people, who exhibited decreasing sociocultural complexity as one traveled further north. As a coexisting sociocultural sphere that was in close contact with the coastal people, the cultural concepts of the interior people reflected the complex social systems observed in the coastal communities. These likely drifted inland as cultural borrowings via trade, marriage, and shared knowledge networks rather than arising independently. Relatively increased social complexity was documented among the inland Dena'ina

(Townsend 1981), Ahtna (de Laguna and McClellan 1981), and Tanana people (McKennan 1981) and is reflected in extended familial networks. For the Upper Tanana people, the ritualized potlatch ceremony was all at once a reflection, maintenance, and intensification symbol of this complexity (Guédon 1981). As an intensification ceremonial ritual and an act of deep play, the potlatch (*titl*), when practiced, reaffirmed family ties, social status, personal prestige, nonviolent competition between non-relatives, and emphasized the fact that the Dene society's dual nature of two-non-related competing sides as necessary and fundamental.

The people of the Middle Tanana were deeply invested in the regional potlatch. The ritualized kinship system organized all local clans into one of two moieties, seeking to bring together non-related individuals into the same domestic space through lifelong economic partnerships between unrelated family leaders, which symbolically reflected the inhabited environment. The potlatch formed an extra-regional web that knitted communities together across a vast region beyond band or tribal identities. Euro-Americans have often focused on simplifying the system to its grand periodic feasts where powerful clans and families, under the direction of a centralized personality, gifted all their annual wealth to those considered sociopolitical competitors. However, this was simply one part, an intensification ritual, symbolizing an ancient, complex, systemic whole designed to ensure regional, cultural, and ecological stability and continuity.

Western narratives of this event often focus on the largescale physical and social nature of these events, which were often given to honor an individual's life events. For the Middle Tanana, potlatches could be given for any event, large or small. They could be delivered, for example, on the death of a favorite dog, or even for minor burn victims, and dictated acts of sharing and gifting food and other material and immaterial items (Andrews TNS 973 A1973; Mauss [1925] 2016, 123), illustrating the depth of reverence that all aspects of life, culture, and events were held in and that the concept of reciprocity permeated all things. Through this, a balance was symbolically maintained between persons, between humans and animals, and between humankind and the universe.

In order to observe the development and antiquity of social complexity in the Tanana Valley in the archaeological record, standard material proxies are needed to be recognized. These can only be demonstrated through a comprehensive summary of the aspects of the ethnographic record that will leave a marked trace in the archaeological record. Since this study is focused on the cultural and ecological interactions of Middle Tanana Alaska Natives from the perspective of two precolonial sites in the Shaw Creek basin, the following summary of the regional ethnographic history will highlight patterns of cultural connections between these assemblages and the Alaska Native people who traditionally used the Middle Tanana River. It will explore what anthropologists and historians have documented during the recent past as interpretive frameworks for understanding progressively deeper time depths of the region. This type of cultural chronological framework will emphasize shifts in technology and resource use to highlight potentially adaptive behaviors that might have both driven cultural changes and maintained cultural practices in the past.

The utility of using the ethnohistoric record as a reconstructive proxy for investigating precolonial human behaviors will naturally have decreasing efficacy as time increases from the historic period. Given enough remoteness into the past, ecological and geological proxies' relative efficacy increases as explanatory mechanisms necessary for cultural interpretations. These extra-cultural proxies provide a contextual dataset within which cultural histories and behavioral strategies are constructed. They can provide exploratory devices informing how past cultural systems were maintained or changed by extraneous environmental factors and provide contexts for designing hypotheses pertaining to cultural change and resilience.

North American ethnographic work and archaeological applications referencing them have been criticized for being constructed on Euro-American and androcentric-biased perspectives, which continue to color their narratives. Thus, they often represent imbalanced culturally informed value interpretations toward roles of gender and age-graded information (e.g., Kehoe 2013). Anthropological publications primarily represent a legacy of heteronormative authors and western identity constructs influenced during the nineteenth and twentieth centuries; therefore, the following discussions of gender identity and roles are framed by understanding the traditional rules of *'engii,* rather than Euro-American values (see interpretive discussions in Fulkerson 2017). Despite acknowledging the reality of erroneous or improperly applied cultural perspectives, it should be understood that the history of ethnographic work among the Dene people of the Tanana Valley has left a largely positive legacy. Most anthropologists and archaeologists who have worked with the Native groups here since the 1930s continue to be remembered and discussed with respect by descendant communities. However, criticisms regarding specific instances by those same researchers are not concealed.

The following history and ethnography sections are reconstructed from Elizabeth Andrews's (1975) and Craig Mishler's (1986) first-hand ethnographic studies and their curated raw data pertaining to the Middle Tanana people unless otherwise cited. Andrews's work concerning the *Salcheege* people was designed to complete the earlier unpublished ethnographic work (1964–1967) of anthropologist Mertie Baggen, who passed away before its completion. Her papers remain curated at the Rasmuson Library at the University of Alaska Fairbanks. Mishler's work on the Goodpaster people was completed as part of a state-funded study early in his career. Both Mishler and Andrews continued to work prolifically throughout the region during their careers. Their initial work resulted in many taped recordings with informants that have been digitally curated and made available by the Alaska Native Language Center archives and are used here with permission. Many of those recordings were reviewed and partially transcribed by the author to illuminate the cultural record here, as they contain a wealth of data not summarized in the final ethnographies.

Oral history is referenced here as a respected resource illuminating the past. Oral traditions represent rich datasets meant to guide a person through life in a culturally acceptable manner. They are constructed and passed on so that their interpretations can be flexible to the culture-bearers experience. Some traditions are meant to be taken literally, and others in an abstract sense. As such, their utility and construal may be different for each person and between generations, without changing the core of the given story. Thus, the user is expected to cull from their ancestral traditions for anecdotes on both successful day-to-day and life-altering situations. Thus, the traditions become ancient knowledge, retaining their core message (Levi-Strauss 1963, 207–208).

For anthropologists trained as cultural outsiders, oral traditions represent a subjective and culturally bounded information dataset that can be unintentionally biased by the interviewers' original methods and goals (Kirby 2008). Thus, their use can potentially improperly support anthropological conclusions, creating "just-so stories." Oral history can often focus on the important and unique, while archaeology draws its conclusions from demonstrating what was once normal and mundane. It can appear then that oral history and scientific conclusions are incompatible with each other. Indeed, they are if the user is unaware of the goals and limitations of each. But if understood in their proper context, each can be considered a different tool of understanding the past. Their comparisons can generate a novel understanding of our shared ancient history.

My friendships with Evelynn Combs, Melissa Erikson, and their extended family of Healy Lake have greatly enhanced my understanding of this ethnohistoric data and guided its interpretation. My several extended trips and subsequent interactions with residents between there and Fairbanks proved invaluable, helping me learn and understand the local contemporary perspective of the region's cultural history. Often, discussing archaeological or place name findings with them spurred informal analogies or comparisons with their own oral histories; therefore, their use here is considered culturally appropriate. Having said that, it is understood that each reader will have a different and unique experience and interpretation of that methodological use and the meaning of those stories, and may reach different conclusions or entirely reject my application of them. Since the role of oral history is traditionally focused on the personal experience, those reactions are considered appropriate.

The Middle Tanana people (the *Salcheege* and Goodpaster bands) form the cultural core of this study. Thus, given the historical processes outlined earlier, the Upper Tanana people are considered part of the greater cultural periphery but more relevant to the core than those of the Lower Tanana. The Middle Tanana people were also tied much closer through kinship to the Upper Tanana people rather than the Lower, despite sharing a salmon industry, language ties, and cultural aspects with the downriver people (Vitt 1971). Therefore, the ethnographic works of Robert McKennan (1959), Roger Pitts (1972), William Simeone (1995; Haynes and Simeone 2007), and Ramon Vitt (1971) are included. The Lower Tanana was also once within the greater cultural periphery, and ethnohistoric work completed for Lower Tanana people (Olson 1968; Raboff 2001) is also reviewed here.

Evidence concerning ethnic identification within the archaeological record is often ambiguous at best. Currently, Alaskan anthropologists prefer referring to the Alaska Natives by their language family or specific language following Krauss et al.'s (2011) designations, since tribal boundaries were nonexistent. However, this ethnolinguistic designation is a western intellectual imposition, a legacy of nineteenth-century nation-building concepts rooted in ancient European traditional agrarian land-tenure systems, where a people's identity became closely tied with their village or locale of origin (Willems 1970). As shown in detail later, for the people of the Tanana Valley, identity was drawn first through relative extra-regional kinship networks (a permanent fixture) and second through the village and river of current residence (a flexible fixture). Understanding the traditional form of identity, which emphasized extraterritorial unity and multi-group unity, is essential to understanding the transmission of cultural knowledge among individuals and from one generation to the next (Clark 2001, 9).

This chapter provides a cultural frame of reference for interpreting the archaeological record of the Middle Tanana Valley. The subsequent sections outline how the lives of the Tanana Valley people from its headwaters to its mouth were determined by the highly predictable seasonal availability of resources and extensive kinship networks. The particular seasonal availability of salmonid species below the Volkmar River resulted in a divided subsistence strategy that has strongly affected settlement strategies for at least the past one-thousand years on the lower half of the Tanana River (Boraas 2007). The result was a salmon-oriented strategy on the Middle and Lower

Tanana areas and a non-anadromous lake fish (whitefish) oriented strategy on the Upper Tanana above the Volkmar River (Shinkwin et al. 1980). Salmon harvested above the Goodpaster River were considered only edible by dogs (Mishler 1986, 13). Other ecological-based economic factors seem to have been similar in practice between the regions.

This chapter will explore how traditional extended familial networks were, and continue to be, maintained between the Upper, Middle, and Lower Tanana groups, and others to the north and south, which resulted in a highly stable, ancient bifurcated sociopolitical system that promoted extra-regional and extra-familial cooperation. I explore here the idea that an archaeological proxy for this system may be the spread and development of seasonal semi-permanent house forms, villages, and fish camps as a settlement strategy. Together, these places, especially the villages, were cyclically returned to on an annual basis and inhabited for months on end, resulting in the construction of permanent housing, resource-acquisition, and food storage features that required a significant dedication of initial work to construct and maintenance to curate among non-related groups (Anderson 1988, 2008). The seasonal residential features appear in the regional archaeological record throughout the past 1,500 years (e.g., Hays et al. 2014) but are especially visible during the past five-hundred years (e.g., Coffman et al. 2018). Before the adoption of seasonal sedentism and salmon intensification, other factors point to ancient connections in the region through genetics, language, technology, and subsistence use during the middle Holocene Northern Archaic tradition and into the earlier Holocene American Paleoarctic tradition (Dumond 2010; Kari and Potter 2010; Moreno-Mayar et al. 2018; Potter 2008a, 2008b). The ethnographic and archaeological information here summarizes the types of cultural data that are more likely to have influenced the archaeological remains.

This chapter also details the rules of *'engii*, a term that roughly means prohibited actions, which if occurred, could result in bringing bad luck to the person and community (Mishler 1986, 28–29). The rules of *'engii* framed one's cultural norms. They represented an ancient system of agreement between humans and nature, traditionally considered to have been created by the first shaman/sleep doctor, *Saatedlech'eeghe*. The cultural hero traveled about the earth in ancient times, transforming the creatures of the ancient world into their smaller, recognizable forms of today, separating their languages and bodily forms from that of earlier giant animals and humans, establishing the rules of everyday life and interactions with the natural and spiritual realms (Attla 1990; Cannon et al. 2020; Friend 2010; Wright 1977). As Mishler hypothesized, the system of *'engii* appears to have had such an effect on the daily life of the Dene that the artifact record reflects its rules.

TRADITIONAL IDENTITY AND SOCIAL ORGANIZATION

The Tanana watershed encompasses roughly 120,000 km², and the early territorial censuses suggest an estimate of 400–1,200 Native persons living throughout the valley at the turn of the twentieth century (McKennan 1969). The estimate equates to a rough population density mean of one person per 100 km². If Robert Boyd's (1990) pandemic mortality estimates of 30–70 percent are correct, a peak estimate of 1,700–4,000 persons (or one person per 30–70 km²) may be considered an appropriate population peak at the beginning of the eighteenth century. Early informants supported this idea, stressing that their population had been decimated by diseases throughout the nineteenth century (Guédon 1974, 10; McKennan1959, 19).

At the time of direct regional Euro-American contact, the Tanana River exhibited five distinct Native languages, spoken by perhaps about 1,200 people existing as a dialectical continuum downriver to upriver: Upper Koyukon, Lower Tanana, Middle Tanana, Tanacross, and Upper Tanana (McKennan 1981) (figure 2.1). Koyukon is thought to have been a recent incursion into the Kantishna Drainage, a development of the early to mid-nineteenth century warring period and subsequent depopulation there (Raboff 2001). While previous social identity was derived through kinship via extended matrilineal descent clans, and to a lesser extent, the village and its associated primary drainage system, today, the American patrilineal kinship system, with its economic focus on the natal family and the individual, has subsequently been adopted for its greater social ease within US and Canadian law (Olson 1968). It confers to Natives equal legal privileges as Euro-Americans; however, the traditional matrilineal clans' extended familial system has also survived and is actively used in social gatherings, playing a definitive role in maintaining traditional networks (Simeone 1995).

THE MOIETY KINSHIP SYSTEM

The Tanana people traditionally used the following extended kinship network in part to enhance survival and social networks valley-wide and extra-regionally. The dynamic interaction of this extended kinship system ensured its widespread utility by strengthening social stability. This system allowed for the boreal forest-adapted individuals and communities to fix access to resources across a broader geographic region than they could effectively otherwise directly control as endogamous bands or tribes (Ives 1990). At its core, Dene concepts of relatedness follows the Dravidian system of cross-cousin marriage and the Iroquoian system of equating one's parallel cousins as their

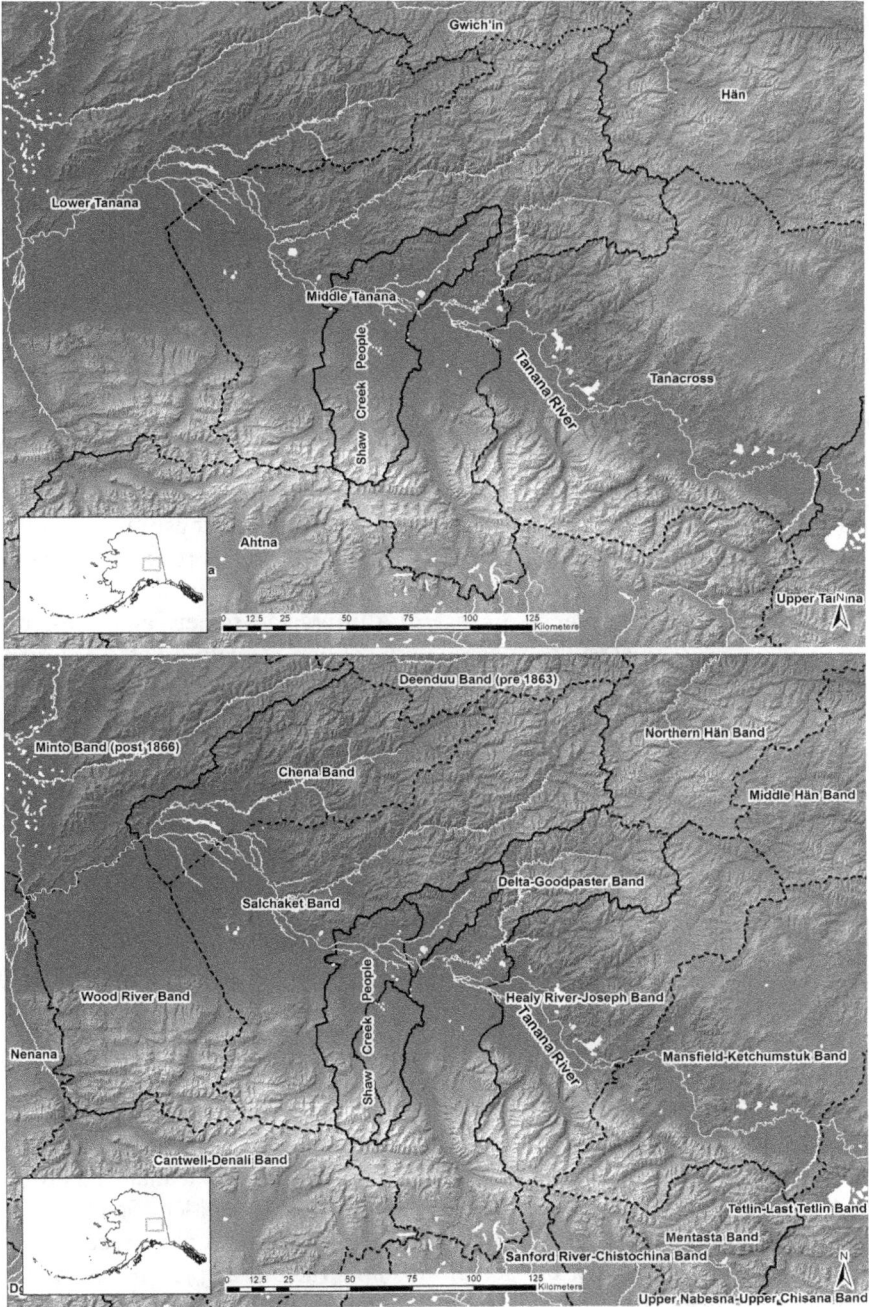

Figure 2.1. Recognized late nineteenth-century language groups of the Tanana Valley and surrounding area (top) and major band resource territories, with anadromous streams depicted. The reconstructed minor Shaw Creek Band territory is also depicted.

natal siblings within a matrilineal and matrilocal descent system (Ives et al. 2010). The kinship system resulted in and emphasized a dual split in society, where clans were matrilineally related to only one side or another. Marriage across the social divide was encouraged, and marriage between members of clans considered to be on the same side was incestuous. There were exceptions: the *Ałts'ę' Neeyi* clan was unique in allowing the practice of endogamy (Simeone 2018, 82). For the *Ałts'ę' Neeyi*, who, according to some origin stories, are indigenous to the Upper Tanana region, the differing marriage rules may have been a relict practice predating the widespread adoption of the moiety system.

The concept of a dual kinship split appears to be deeply embedded in Dene antiquity. It has linguistically been reconstructed for Proto-Dene, the theorized common ancestor of the Na-Dene language family. It tends to be absent or vague for Dene groups that have been historically less sedentary and less populous. The kinship terminology is not ubiquitously used across the Na-Dene language family, suggesting that shifting concepts of relatedness may not have occurred in tandem with the language's spread but developed later (Ives 1998). However, the sense of a bifurcated society and stress on exogamy appears to been shared with the linguistically-related Siberian Ket, further evidence of great antiquity (Ives et al. 2010).

All villages on the Tanana were designed to have a minimum of at least two exogamous cross-cousin clans (Andrews 1975; McKennan 1959), but some could have as many as three. More than three were rare in a single village due to overall low demographics throughout the region. Andrews (1975, 85–96) identified six clans among the *Salcheege* people, and Mishler identified a seventh at Goodpaster (1986, 24). Norm Easton has identified eight clans throughout the Upper Tanana (2005, 120). These names and sides generally follow the structure of the Ahtna to the south, who have seven clans documented for the Seagull moiety, and six for the Raven side; however, the totemic symbols of the clans can be quite different extra-regionally (Simeone 2018, 80) (see Osgood ([1937] 1966, 128–129) for the Dena'ina classification of this system).

James Kari's lexicographical work on Middle Tanana (n.d.) has reconstructed the following classification structure from primary work with informants Bessie Barnabas, Eva Moffit, and Abraham Luke. The clans recorded in the dictionary have been assigned to the moiety side, as identified by Bessie Barnabas and Eva Moffit in Andrews (1975). The following reconstruction should closely reflect the actual kinship structure as present or known about in *Salcheege* during the late nineteenth century:

- Side 1 Moiety: *Tikaan Dneey* (male), *Tikaan Ts'eeyi* (female) (Wolf People):

  - *Tsisyu* (Ochre)
  - *Ch'echeelyu* (Fish Tail)
  - *Ch'ek'aagiyu* (Flying Seeds)
  - *Udziyh toxt'een* (Caribou Clan)

- Side 2 Moiety: *Ch'ezhenn'* (Bald Eagle):

  - *Naltsin* (Made Descending; or, Sky Clan, also called Caribou Tail People)
  - *Ałts'ę' Neeyi* (Right-Way, or, One-Way Clan, also called Bear Clan)

- Middle Sub-Moiety: *Taniidze Gheltsiiłne* (Born in the Middle; reserved for people of unknown, mixed clan, and non-Dene ancestry):

  - *Dzenh Tohwt'eene* (Muskrat People, specifically reserved for people of intermixed clans)

- Clans of an unspecified moiety:

  - *Ch'ebaan' deneey* (Edge of Skin Clan)

The opposing moiety clans were consistently associated with either the moiety totemic figures of Raven, Eagle, or Wolf/Seagull. Marie-Françoise Guédon (1974) considers this side to be Seagull downriver from Nabesna and Wolf upriver (see also Pitts 1972, 29). It is important to note that the English clan and moiety names represent symbolic translations and are not necessarily literal meanings. Each was symbolically represented by multiple animals, objects, and colors.

It is important to note that the dual-moiety system with a third fringe group was consistent throughout the Tanana, but the clan affiliation to moiety side often shifts by region throughout the Tanana Valley. Thus, in the extant literature there is some discrepancy about which side a clan might be associated with. If one considers the clan list provided by Kenny Thomas (2005, 14) of Tanacross, the clans are grouped differently by moiety compared to Andrews' Middle Tanana list. The discrepancy concerning the shifting clans by moiety between villages in the Tanana has concerned some elders, but if true, is likely to be reflective of either the valley's low population density (requiring periodic negotiations of moiety affiliation if opposing clans were not present to fulfill opposing role expectations, perhaps an adaptation in response to the extensive depopulations of the nineteenth–twentieth centuries), or confusion due to distant memory and the boarding school's aggressive deculturization program. Thomas often emphasized the arduous nature of memorizing the kinship structure. Complex kinship systems like this rarely develop in regions of low demographic pressure, so the Tanana represents a unique case study (Guèdon 1974). For the Gwich'in to the north, society was split into only two exogamous clans with a middle clan again reserved for persons of unknown ancestry, which generally followed the rules of the Tanana moieties, perhaps reflecting a more ancient form.

There were vital social roles attached to the clans of each side. One was always expected to support their maternal clan and affinal relatives in all social situations. A widow was expected to marry into her deceased husband's family unless given explicit permission by them to marry outside this levirate system. Some groups also followed a sororate system expecting widowers to marry into their deceased wife's family (McFadyen Clark 1996). Each clan's socioeconomic and political rivals were formed from those of the opposite moiety. It also dictated who could form extra-familial partnerships, which both facilitated nonviolent competition and social cohesiveness. Male hunting partners were expected to come from opposing (unrelated) clans. They could often be intergenerational, and these roles and relationships generally dictated how a person or family was expected to act or support when interacting with the opposing clan, such as rules guiding trade, war, marriage, medicine, funerals, and potlatching (Andrews 1975; McKennan 1959; Mishler 1986).

To summarize, the traditional kinship and social roles resulted in a dualistic society where extensive social mechanisms ritually interlaced all actors (people who are actively trying to live up to a social role) into a single social system. It simultaneously emphasized intense competition and reciprocity across the clans and moieties. Social cohesiveness was built, and inter-clan violence was minimized through the reconciliation mechanisms and the symbolic conflict and competition roles during the potlatch (Mauss [1925] 2016, 115–117). These rules for the Tanana reflected those of the Dena'ina and Ahtna to the south and were shared in a more generalized form with the Gwich'in to the north (Ives et al. 2010). Multiple clans were usually known by various names (typically animal) up and down the Tanana River that were associated with one moiety side or another inconsistently. Clans might have been able to negotiate to switch their respective sides if there were not enough members of the opposing clan to carry out the social obligations in the village setting. The third moiety formed a sort of fringe group that could be reserved for members of unknown ancestry, mixed ancestry, or clans that were nearly extinct. Those persons could assume the required roles of either opposing clans as necessary during social events. Today, non-Natives attending traditional events fall under the rules of the third group and can take active gender-appropriate roles if requested (Simeone 1995). Finally, one's clan and moiety were permanently marked through facial tattoos for women and chest tattoos and face paint for men (Mishler 1986, 40–41).

THE PHRATRY SYSTEM

Social organization and descent in the Middle Tanana were fundamentally matrilocal. Communities were loosely organized through male and female traditional leaders who were often elders, who might be further organized through the leadership of a middle-aged charismatic individual, who was also often considered a powerful sleep doctor (Andrews 1975, 112). Traditional elders could be shamans, although every individual held varying degrees of spiritual power or spiritual connection with the entangled cosmos. Those individuals specifically called shamans/sleep doctors had demonstrated especially strong abilities. Each was sought for expert advice in gendered activities/economics/behaviors, and were not necessarily married to each other.

In the Upper Tanana, villages could organize under a group of male leaders who were often related. These male leadership groups, phratries, considered inheritance rights of residency to be passed from a male ego to his sister's son (McKennan 1959; Pitts 1972, 70). Documented phratry names are identical to moiety and clan names, making reconstructions confusing; the reason for this is that they are likely identical, with different gendered leadership and teaching roles. Sons received their clan's name through their mother and learned male-specific labor practices from their mother's brothers, who took on much of their later upbringing. It likely assisted in organizing lifelong economic partnerships between unrelated men. The role of natal fathers was limited to providing emotional support for children. For females, leadership and teaching roles were passed from generational grandmothers to generational mothers to daughters. In the Dene kinship sense, one's siblings, mothers, and grandmothers would, in Euro-American terms, be considered cousins, aunts, and great-aunts.

For the Upper Tanana, Roger Pitts reconstructed three phratries (in addition to the two moieties) with five, nine, and one clan associated with each (1972, 85–91). The system of village phratry inheritance may not have been as necessary or may even have been nonexistent in the Middle Tanana. Throughout the Tanana, residency was typically expected to be matrilocal; men moved in with their wife's family after a year or two of bride service. Village heads were typically male, and were often polygamous in reflection of their role as good providers and wealth builders. Women also assumed

leadership roles; in this, they might, on the rarer occasion, also marry multiple husbands in recognition of their prestigious role (Van Stone 1974, 53,
81) or to mitigate social stress (McFadyan Clark 1996, 30). These leadership
positions were held as long as the band could trust their leaders' success in
organizing game acquisition, trade, and war.

CLAN ORIGINS AND SOCIAL COMPLEXITY

Clan origin stories in the Dena'ina, Ahtna, and Tanana regions are associated
with real geographic places and appear singular in place. Clan names do not
appear to be associated with multiple location origins for disparate regions
(Kari and Fall 2016; Simeone et al. 2019). Place names associated with the
Caribou clan are given an origin story associated with Upper Tangle Lake
and nearby Dickey Lake at the headwaters of the Delta River (Reckord 1983),
and Sky clan descended from the perennial ice of Mt. Wrangell (figure 2.2).
The clan origin stories collected by Robert McKennan (1959) from the Upper
Tanana told that these had originated to the south of the Alaska Range in Ahtna
country, diffusing into the Tanana via the Copper River region, likely borrowed
there from the coastal people beyond the Chugach Range: the Eyak and Łingít.
Albert Heinrich provides an origin story for the clans of the Raven Moiety, also
agreeing that this side originated in Ahtna country to the south in the Copper
River Basin and had long ago migrated north into the Tanana Valley:

> After arrival on the Upper Tanana, the Naltsíín [Caribou] "made peace," "made
> villages," and "found" other clans; in other words, they conquered the country,
> settled it, and incorporated other groups, while the Tígaxíyu [Sky], further south
> did likewise . . . the Ałatdindei [Bear] were found on an island in Midway Lake.
> . . . [T]he Naltsíín discovered their plight, ferried them across to land, and took
> them in. As the Tígaxíyu moved northward, and the Naltsíín southward, they
> met in the neighborhood of Tonsina [on the Lower Copper River] and joined
> forces on equal terms. (in Pitts 1972, 79) (figure 2.2).

It is more challenging to organize the origin of the moiety names. The
moiety system's origin myth is told as a story of three sisters, each ancestral to a moiety, traveling and settling throughout southcentral Alaska and
the Tanana Valley. This myth is shared throughout the Ahtna, Upper Cook
Inlet Dena'ina, and Tanana peoples (Pitts 1972). One moiety is formally
termed Wolf east of Nabesna in the Upper Tanana and Tutchone, and Bald
Eagle in the Middle and Lower Tanana to the west. The Tanacross villages,
which traditionally associate it with Seagull, follow the Ahtna to the south
(de Laguna and McClellan 1981). Raven as the traditional symbolic animal

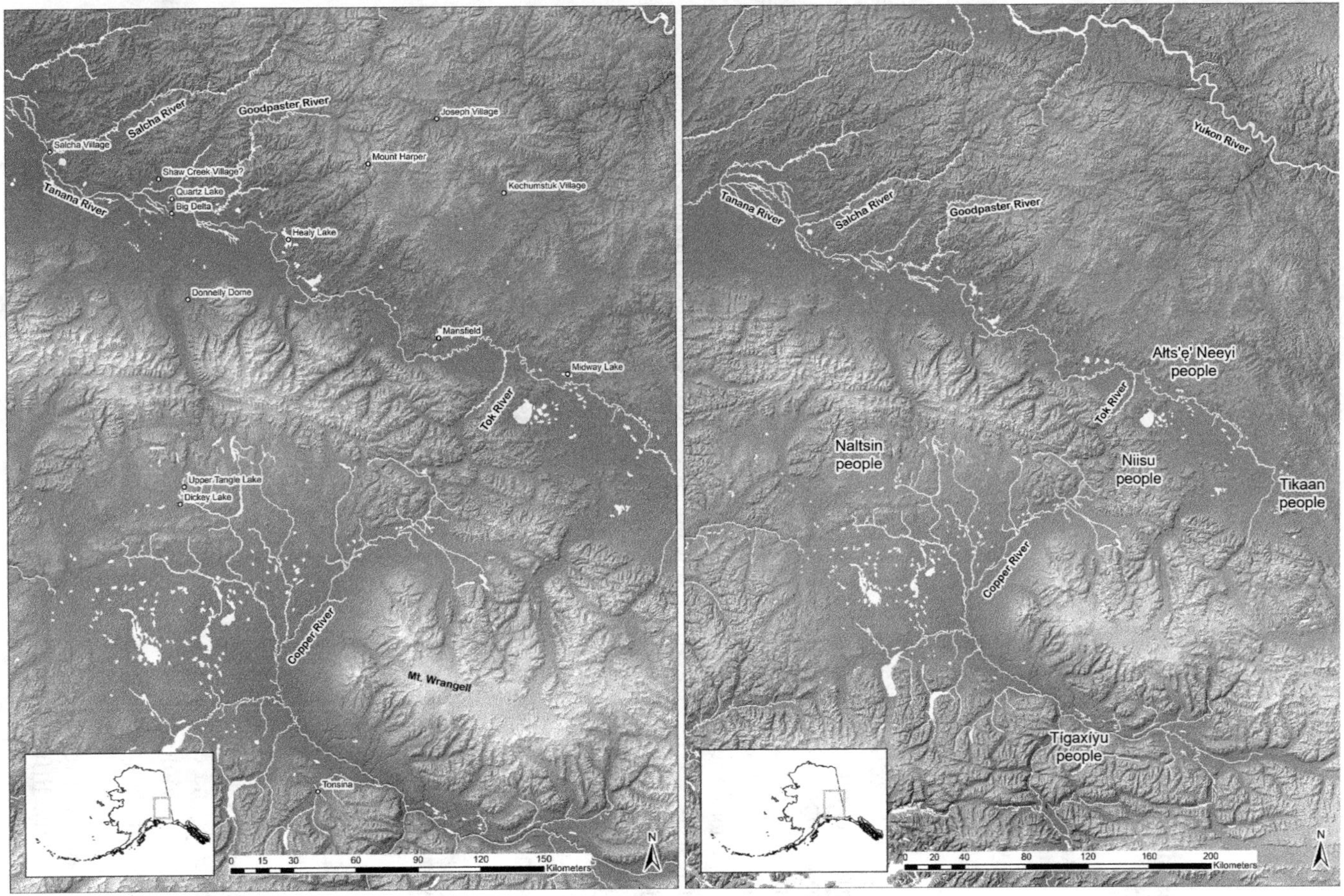

Figure 2.2. Geographic references pertaining to the ethnohistoric reconstruction (right) and reconstructed clan origin locations (left).

of one moiety group also often appears. When patterns of clan affiliations to moiety side are observed, it likely means relatively recent changes. Shifts in moiety names represent much more substantial cultural beliefs, and may be reflective of older larger-scale population movements either through migration or long-term marriage patterns. The moiety patterns can be indicative if Tanana families were closer tied to the Copper River Ahtna people or southern Yukon provincial areas.

The Upper and Middle Tanana ethnographic informants of McKennan and Andrews agree that initially, in the Tanana Valley, an endogamous clan system was the custom. It was only later that the exogamous, dual-sided moiety system concept was adopted, either directly borrowed or diffused through marriages into the Tanana from the south and east. McKennan and Pitts considered the phratry system to be a relict form of leadership associated with the older endogamous clan system (Pitts 1972, 79–81). These original phratries were *Tcion* (Wolf), *Neltcin* (Caribou), and *Niisu* (Marten or Rabbit Skin). *Tcion* was considered to represent a westward expansion of people into the upper Tanana from the White River and beyond; *Neltcin* had been a northward expansion from the upper Copper River. *Niisu* was endemic to the upper Tanana and later merged with the *Neltcin* phratry.

A general theme emerges of an ancient substantial population flow moving north from the Copper River into the Middle and Upper Tanana, a smaller population flow from the east into the Upper Tanana headwaters, and a merging of both migrations with preexisting populations and clans that were endemic to the Tanana Valley. The subsequent increased demographic pressure required the innovative integration of phratry clans into the older moiety system of the Ahtna. The moiety system and associated symbolic potlatch are considered here to have developed as a social mechanism to mitigate interband stress due to rising demographic pressure. It has been held in *Salcheege* oral traditions that Raven created the first potlatch, and organized the clans into opposing sides (Andrews 1975, 85–87). Perhaps this indicates that the initial emphasis for this new social order was offered through the clans associated with Bald Eagle moiety, who is associated with Raven elsewhere (the *Naltsin* and *Ałts'ę' Neeyi* families).

The moiety system, symbolized and organized through the potlatch, was a necessary innovation upon the older social order, adopting novel forms of residency and emphasizing non-kin partnerships in order to avoid long-term large-scale violence (Mauss [1925] 2016, 115–117; Pitts 1972, 80). Increasing social complexity arose in the Tanana Valley, similar to that seen with the Ahtna, Tutchone, and Dena'ina (Cooper 2012, 567–568), except that the social roles of inherited nobility and slaves in these southern people did not necessarily fully diffuse into the Tanana River Valley. Themes of wealth disparity arising between the village leader's immediate family and others and an idea of inherited leadership likely facilitated the adoption of the potlatch ceremony. It could be used to ease social tensions that arose from this new social order by regifting of wealth and aggrandizing prestige through that process (Cooper 2006, 2012; Simeone 1995). Andrews (1975, 85–86) did not tie clan origin stories for the *Salcheege* people to actual geographic places. However, she provides an origin story that confirms that the novel kinship system was symbolically linked with the potlatch and mass game hunts' origin.

It is important to note here that the migration reconstruction does not correlate with the Na-Dene language family's theorized spread, which diffused into Alaska from the northeast, spreading down the Tanana and entering the Copper River from the Middle Tanana region (Kari and Fall 2016, 145). Therefore, these two sociocultural diffusions—the development and dispersal of the moiety system and the spread of the Na-Dene language family—should not be equated with each other and likely represent separate unrelated events.

VILLAGE IDENTITY, SOCIAL ROLES, AND WATERSHED TENURE

The inter-band kinship networks were maintained across a vast territory. Most related individuals who found themselves more distant than three or four villages away might only rarely meet each other in person during their lifetime. Kinship determined the degree that individuals and families could safely move about the landscape. Relationships were actively memorized and orally recited both informally and formally during large group gatherings and were an especially vital part of the potlatch. The difficulty in orally maintaining these extended kinship networks is often reiterated, and their mastery commanded a high degree of social respect. Kinship ties dictated social obligations that were ritualized in the grand gifting ceremony of the potlatch, where the role of deep play (Geertz 1973) is entered by the potlatch giver and their hosting clan (Thomas 2005). At a superficial level, the gifting ceremony was expected to be positively reciprocal, meaning the guest/host roles would eventually be switched, and a future ceremony would likely exceed the value of the former potlatch. At a deeper level, the hosting head person was proving their worth as a clan and village provider. Significant also was the fact that until the giftees could ceremonially reciprocate, they were held under a sense of indebtedness to the gifters. On an even more important symbolic level of deep play, the gifter acted out and entered into the role of species' guardian spirits who would give or withhold individual animals as food to sustain the village. A slight misstep during the ceremony would result in the permanent loss of prestige, political position, and personal luck/power/magic for the potlatch giver (Mauss [1925] 2016, 115–117). In a sense, the roles of deep play and universal reciprocity merge to form the concept of deep reciprocity. When one enters into the culture of Dene gift exchange, they are interacting with the fundamental network of the universe.

While individuals primarily identified themselves through their mother's birth clan, they secondarily identified themselves through their village of current residence, which usually carried the name of the primary water feature that the settlement was located near. Regional exonyms appear to have been used as identifiers to refer to the people who utilized that region. Resource acquisition areas were denoted by stream catchment areas, a system known as Watershed Tenure (WT) (Kari 2019b). Villages could have a nearby twin community separated by only a few miles, such as the Goodpaster and Big Delta Native villages, or even three, such as the Shaw Creek (XBD-00190), Clear Creek (XBD-00192), and Tenderfoot Creek Native villages (no documented site). The Goodpaster-Big Delta Band traveled together south, up the Delta River, to hunt in the Donnelly Dome area during winter. Later in spring, they would move back north toward the headwaters of Goodpaster near Mount Harper to hunt caribou (a profoundly sacred place, e.g., Tweiten 1990) (figure 2.3). They maintained summer fish traps on Blue Creek and the Goodpaster River and also utilized Quartz Lake. Both Mishler and Andrews's informants and Ronald Skoog's (1968) reconstructed migratory caribou behavior suggest that during the end of the nineteenth century, when the Fortymile caribou herd was at a population maximum, a portion of this herd migrated north/south across the Tanana between Big Delta and Healy Lake, perhaps indicating why these village locations were chosen. Elsewhere in the valley, they migrated west-east north of the Tanana River. At least one caribou fence was maintained at Big Delta near Rika's Roadhouse.

The *Salcheege* Band moved from the mouth of the Salcha River to upper Dry Creek above Blair Lakes to the Little Delta River's headwaters for autumn and winter hunts and then back and partway up the Salcha River for the spring hunts, staying near the mouths of the clear water creeks and rivers for the summer salmon runs. The two accounts indicate that the *Salcheege* and Goodpaster bands had neighboring, non-overlapping hunting territories south of the Tanana. There may have been a regional gap between their land use territories to the north, between the Salcha and Goodpaster River watersheds.

When families from the same winter village seasonally dispersed, they confirmed their planned destinations with each other under the direction of the headman. If resources failed a family, they would attempt to find one of the other families, especially the headman's, before considering venturing into a neighboring band's territory (ANLC0922 1983). WT and clan membership rules dictated whether or not a group could hunt or borrow food in a

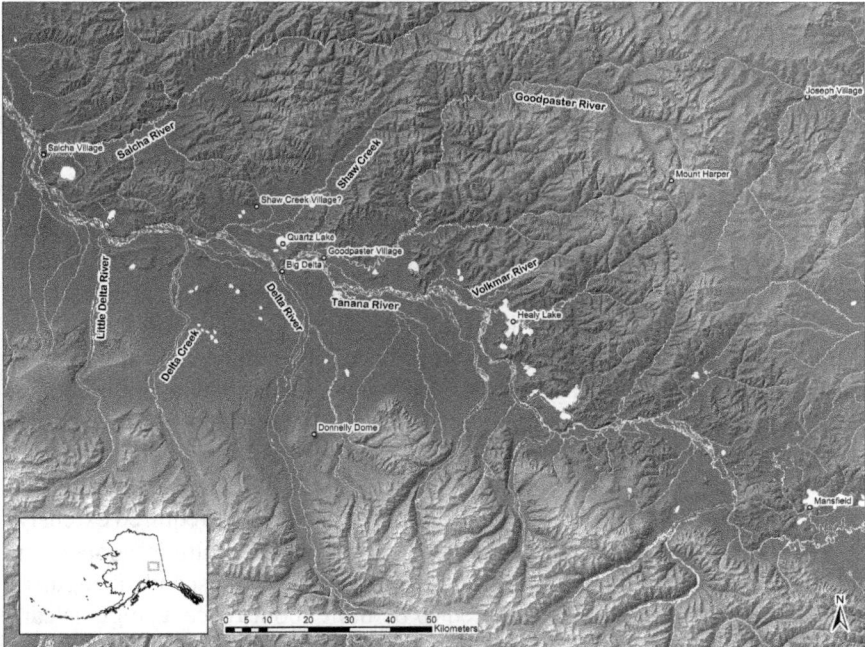

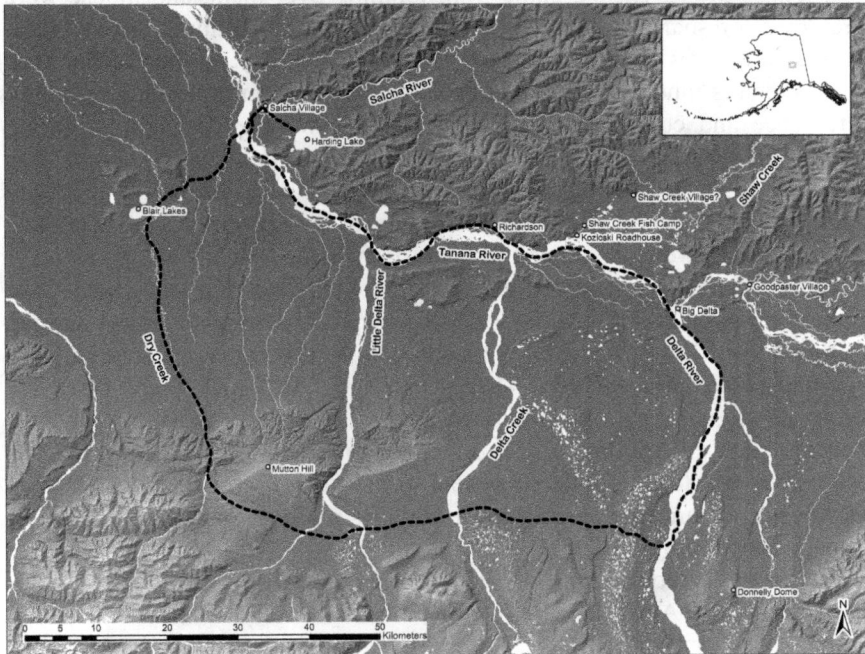

Figure 2.3. Top: geographic references pertaining to the ethnohistoric reconstruction. Bottom: a rough trail described by the Salcheege band's nineteenth century winter circuit (~250km) (ANLC0922 1983).

neighboring group's territory without explicit prior permission. It was considered theft unless the tenured group had specifically gifted an unrelated clan or village the resource rights to an area (Easton 2005, 122). If this were unavoidable, the hunting party would leave a sign of their identity as a promissory note.

At some point during the nineteenth century, the *Udzisyu* clan (AT; MT: *Udziyh toxt'een*) of *Tikaan* (Wolf Moiety) on the Gulkana River gifted through a potlatch the tenure of the north half of Paxson Lake to the *Naltsin* clan of *Ch'ezhenn'* (Bald Eagle Moiety) of the Tanana River, as a peaceful resolution to violent conflict between the clans (Reckord 1983; Simeone 2018, 25, 81–83). This event would have necessitated the need for a reciprocal occasion of equal or higher value. A potential candidate event may have been the great Healy Lake potlatch of 1927, a village where the *Naltsin* clan of the Tanana dominated by numbers. Many Gulkana village members were included among the guests of honor (Demit 2000; Endicott 1928).

The construction of caribou/moose fences and fish weirs required extensive social cooperation. The maintenance of both required multiple cooperating families, sometimes involving social interaction that transcended linguistic barriers. Moose fences were required to be built about twice as high as caribou fences to prevent the game from jumping over them, and moose were preferred for snares because they tended to not thrash about once caught, unlike caribou, where corrals were needed (Vitt 1971). In the Kechumstuk region, chiefs inherited sections of the extensive, about 80-mile-long ungulate fence and corral network. Their families were expected to maintain them (Andrews 1980). Fish weir sites also required centralized organization and were linked in places to family inheritance. During the early nineteenth century, fish weirs were abandoned in favor of the European fish wheel, and caribou fences were abandoned in favor of the rifle.

Both feature types allowed groups to capitalize on migratory behaviors, permitting large quantities of food to be taken in a relatively short amount of time at predictable spots on the landscape. It further necessitated the storage and preservation of these energy packages, for which cache pits were designed (figure 2.4). The ability to amass large stores of wealth as food helped create the opportunity for organized distribution of goods, providing an opportunity for the potlatch system to develop. The appearance of these features in the archaeological record provides a proxy for these social functions' antiquity (Boraas 2007).

Cache pit features were especially favored for large-scale food preservation throughout Alaska in the later Holocene (Arndt 1977; Mishler 1986; Rogers 2015; Smith 2012). They represent a practice stretching back at least into the middle Holocene at the nearby Mead Site (Ben Potter, personal communication), and potentially the early Holocene Hollembaek's Hill Site near the Gerstle River mouth (Lanoë et al. 2019b).

Figure 2.4. Top: intact Historic-Era cache pit, likely for fish storage used by the Healy Lake band, covered and filled with sawn logs to deter bear pilfering at the North Gerstle Point site (XMH-00163) downriver from the mouth of the Gerstle River. Bottom: intact protohistoric cache pit associated with caribou remains at the Cripple Creek site (CIR-00003) on the upper Chatanika River.

Above-ground caches, or "high caches," in the notched-log style likely do not predate direct contact with trading posts in the Tanana Valley (Fair 1997), as steel axes were an integral part of their construction. The traditional raised rack or platform preceded the notched-log cache construction form. During the Historic Period, below-ground cache pits traditionally used precolonially tended to be moved inside houses under wood-plank flooring as log cabins became the dominant form of architecture. The practice of bringing the cache into the home may also represent the shifting conceptualization of communal access to personal property during this time.

THE SHAW CREEK PEOPLE

Shaw Creek is located on the north side of the Tanana between the Good-paster and Salcha Rivers. There isn't a directly identified or ethnographically known band directly associated with the drainage; however, oral history provided by Abraham Luke and other historic documents describe that several closely related villages were present, near the mouths of Shaw, Tenderfoot, and Clear Creeks. This book is focused on reconstructing their culture and history. The reconstruction identifier for the Shaw Creek families would be *Debedee Na' Iin* (Sheep Creek People or Sheep Creek Family). They were a band of Middle Tanana–speaking families who maintained summer fish camps at various locations along the lower Shaw Creek. Several winter village locations have also been elicited along Shaw Creek, suggesting that the idea of a "village" should not be considered in the geographically static sense but could be moved as resources necessitated (figure 2.5).

While one village location was attested to near the mouth of Shaw Creek, which is today the site of a private boat landing, Abraham Luke recalled that a second location for the Shaw Creek village existed upstream "[a]bout 5, 6 mile(s). Right now, where the (pond?) . . . and you pass about another mile and a half on the hillside, that's a big village. A big village" (ANLC3676a 1980, 1:11). A series of undated edited US Geological Survey maps from the 1980s with notes made by Mishler and Andrews during his work with Luke marks this location as near the archaeological site XBD-00413's current location. This site, the Lower Caribou Ridge Site, was unknown to Mishler or Andrews at the time, not recorded for another thirty years, when three cache-pit-sized surface depressions were recorded (Meitl et al. 2015). The Gilles Creek site several miles further upstream (XBD-00235) also has one possible described residential feature that dates to the recent precolonial past (200±40 BP, Beta-160826: Yarborough 2003).

Luke maintained that Quartz Lake to the east of Shaw Creek was within the Goodpaster/Big Delta band's traditional round. Luke considered that the

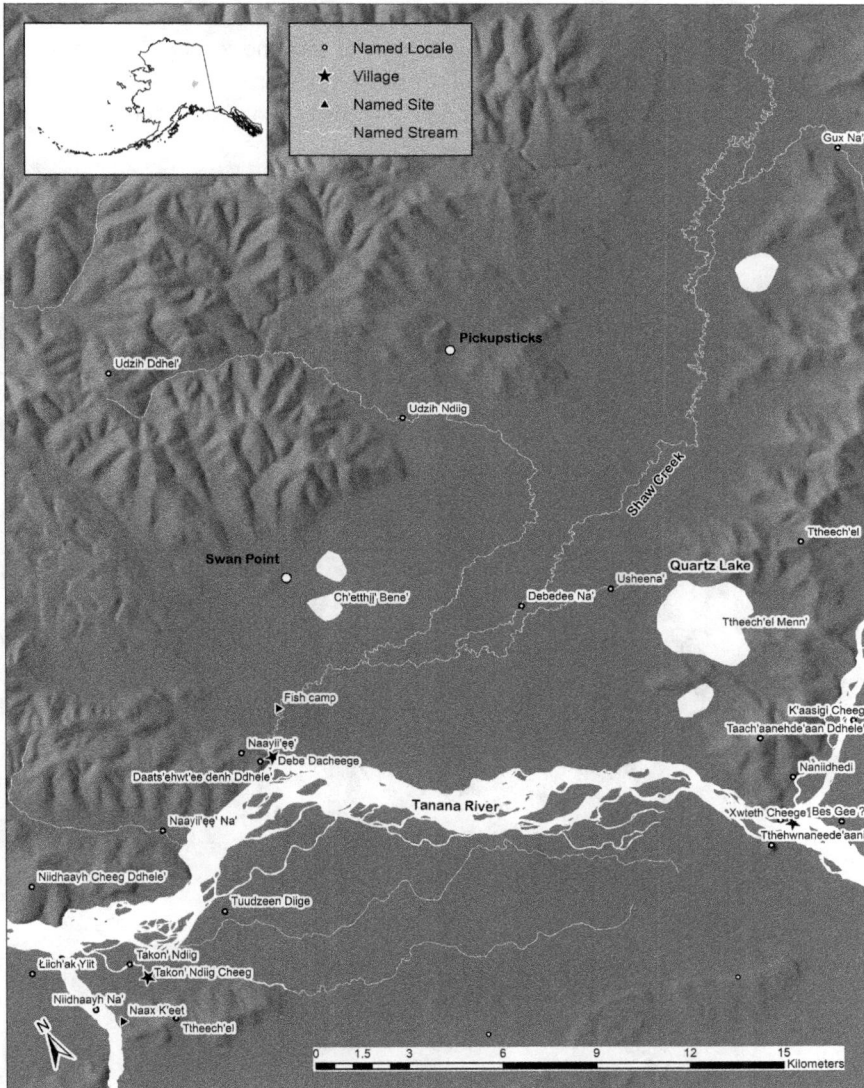

Figure 2.5. Traditional Middle Tanana place names of lower Shaw Creek and Quartz Lake and the investigation sites.

Indigenous name for Shaw Creek, *Debedee Na'* [Sheep Horn Creek], was named for the sheep actively hunted in Shaw Creek and Goodpaster River's headwater country. If so, it suggests that the area was not exclusively used but shared with the Goodpaster band. Lower Shaw Creek was also considered to be a late summer resource use area to harvest and cache moose and caribou by

Salcheege people (Andrews 1975, 49). These accounts either indicate expansion of the Goodpaster and *Salcheege* territories into the recently depopulated territory between them or that the families who were centrally located on Shaw Creek shared it jointly with related families from both the *Salcheege* and Goodpaster villages.

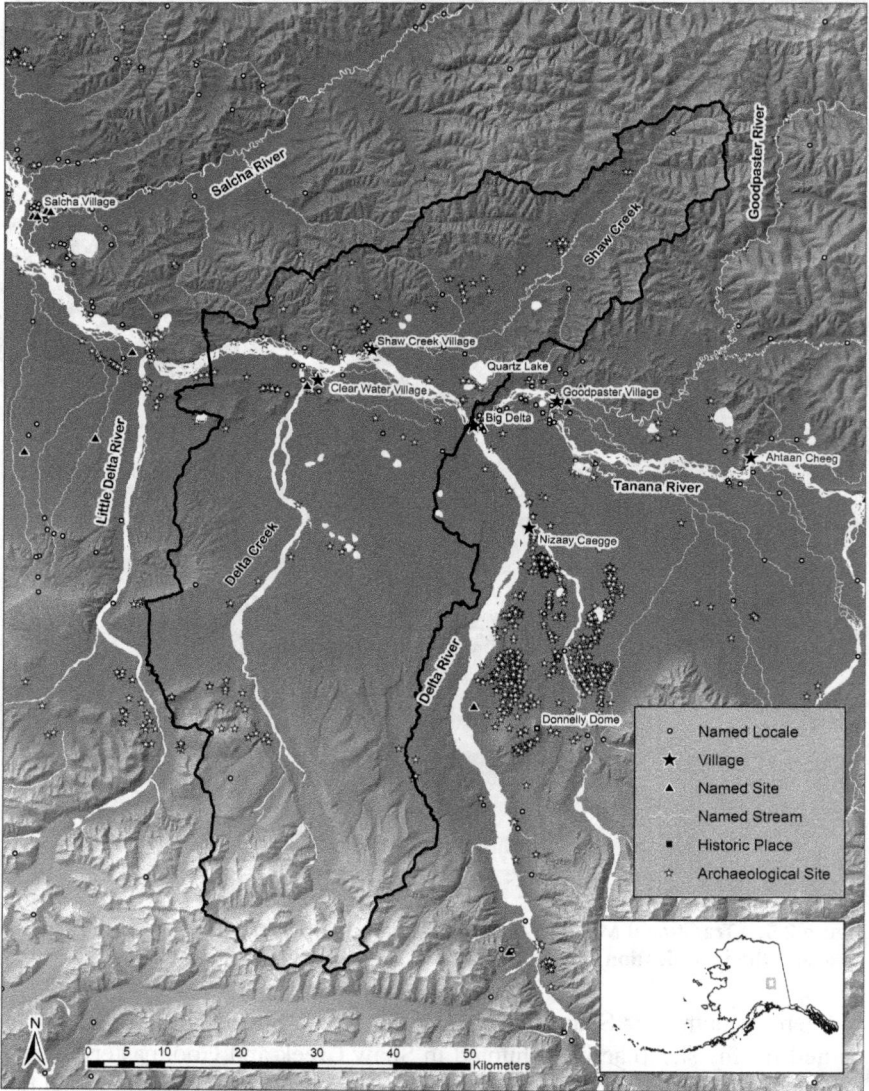

Figure 2.6. Reconstructed Territorial Catchment Basin for the Shaw Creek Band.

As discussed earlier, several sister villages to the Shaw Creek community were attested to by Abraham Luke. One was a village associated with a powerful shaman located on the nearby Tenderfoot Creek, where the Richardson Highway leaves the Tanana River, and their WT area was likely identical to Shaw Creek. A third sister village was located opposite Shaw Creek's mouth between Delta Creek and Clear Creek. The Delta Creek band's WT area to the south could have likely been shared with the families of Shaw and Tenderfoot Creek villages if these three were indeed occupied simultaneously. Ethnographic patterns throughout the Middle and Upper Tanana indicate that bands actively used both north and south-flowing secondary streams that entered the Tanana River near each other (figure 2.6).

COSMOLOGY

By the time McKennan (1959) published his ethnography of the Upper Tanana (written almost thirty years prior), most of the significant Alaskan Dene groups also had their own cultural descriptions published. The shared cultural similarities and cosmology were being actively drawn across Dene groups of northwestern North America.

The similarity of a shared belief system throughout the Alaskan Dene societies was not lost on McKennan. It conceived of all material things being imbued with life with the ego as a sort of central but smallest part of the universe, with higher peripheral dimensions extending beyond it (Jerry Isaac, TCC 2017). The first dimension consisted of the "body and breath" of the individual (Boraas and Peter 2008). The second dimension was comprised of the soul and shadow of the individual. One's shadow spirit could traverse the dream world and thus pass into other dimensions. If one could lucidly direct these travels, they could become a sleep doctor (de Laguna and McClellan 1981, 656; see also Cannon et al. 2020). The third dimension was a transitory place of deceased human souls that had not yet achieved their life's purpose. The souls' journey to this place could be interrupted, especially if cremation and the funeral potlatch were not correctly observed, burials were disturbed, or even if their names were elicited after death. It was desirable for the deceased to enter this place because spirits who lingered in the physical world could ultimately only have a negative effect on the living. Eventually, the spirits' journey would lead to reincarnation, usually in human form, but one could also be reborn as an animal or even something considered by Western materialist philosophy as inanimate forces, such as joining or becoming a wind or whirlwind (Powell 1909, 293–294).

Animal spirits inhabited the fourth dimension. Each species had a form of conscious guardian spirit. These could become a desirable spirit helper for strong individuals, and strict, proper behavior was necessary to maintain a positive relationship with them. The fifth dimension was one of high power, being the mountain spirits (sometimes translated as "giants," meaning "immense beings" (Fast 2008), guardian animal spirits, and the mother of the animals. Individuals avoided calling the attention of these powerful spirits to themselves. Circumlocution (avoidance speech) was a highly utilized practice by the Dene to prevent the individual from becoming overwhelmed by inadvertently focusing the intense power from that which was being described to the speaker. In the Tanana Valley, mountains and their inner spirits were believed to control and create the weather. The phenomenon of lenticular cloud formation above the high peaks of the Alaska Range was often described as the result of the resident spirits' hearths built deep inside (Paul 1957, 20–21). The final highest dimension was that of the supreme being, exemplified by pure love, who, for the Upper Tanana and Ahtna, was embodied by *K'eh'een*, Mt. Wrangell, a shield volcano to the east of Copper River and one of the most massive mountains on Earth (Boraas and Peter 2008; Kari 2019b).

The spiritual importance of landforms was not restricted to only the most massive mountains; smaller landforms that were visually prominent could also possess much power. Place names attached to landforms may often reflect avoidance language (Kari 2011b, 248). It is rare to find toponyms directly referencing supernatural beings, individuals, or commemorative events (Kari 2011b, 248). Both Abraham Luke and Eva Moffit identified Bluff Cabin Ridge near Big Delta as the place of Christianity's original appearance in the Middle Tanana Valley (Mishler 1986). They also identified it as the location of Christ's future return through a very unique and interesting cycle of stories that weave themes of traditional magic, myth, and historical elements (ANLC0921 1983, 26:20–39, 45; ANLC2874b 1984, 19: 18, 30–30). The close association of Christ and Traveler by the early pre- and post-contact generations may indicate that this landform was associated with Travelers' sacred travels and may have been considered the place of his future return.

Each individual needed to achieve a strong sense of balance or find the place of purity by practicing *'engii*, a system of rules that assisted one along this path. An individual began at a young age to seek a relationship with an animal spirit helper and of being able to lucidly dream. To do so, one would attempt to master the correct behavior of undertaking all things in life, including mundane tasks. McKennan (1959) describes this using the English terms of taboos and avoidance of bad luck. Alan Boraas described this for the Dena'ina in terms of *beggesh* (impurity) and *begesha* (absence of impurity).

One would try in all areas of life to maintain a constant sense of *begesha*. One could become polluted by *beggesh* through either intent or action, and the essence of it could be retained in an object affecting all who unknowingly came into contact with it in the future. To avoid obtaining any inadvertent *beggesh*, one should only hunt animals with pure intent and respect (avoiding attitudes such as pride during their harvest as each animal was considered to choose to give their body for the hunter's families sustenance—the ultimate gift as it could not be repaid in life), dispose of their bodies properly, thanking the spirits for the food (Boraas and Peter 2008). An animal's spirit could linger for several days, observing how their body's gift was utilized and treated, reporting these behaviors to their guardian spirit, which would affect future hunting success. Food was shared between hunting partners and their village, and the hunter was expected only to receive a small share of their own kill to help ensure humility (Simeone 2018).

All forms of singing were considered sacred and always framed as prayer (Haynes and Simeone 2007, 73). It was the language used to speak with the spiritual dimensions, and animals whose vocalizations were song-like could be considered to be communicating with the powerful spirit beings. It is important to understand the role of singing: it explains why hunters used songs to communicate with both animals and their spirit guides and why singing formed a central role in so many social interactions. Especially powerful singers and their songs could be used to control the weather and all forms of prestige luck beyond just hunting (McKennan 1959, 165–166). Songs were also considered an appropriate potlatching gift, and it was a high honor when one village gave another a song. Gifted songs and dances could be curated by a village and eventually given back to the original community if they had lost them.

HOUSING TYPES

Villages were small and could exhibit one to several large main houses depending on the population size; some smaller communities may have only had one large main house, with smaller, more temporary living shelters associated. In both villages and camps, residences were ideally organized around a semispherical axis reflecting the local familial clan and moiety connections (Pitts 1972, 74). The Birches site (MMK-00005) at Lake Minchumina displays this idea (West 1978, 34). Basic shelters included hide or bark tents (~4.5–12 m diameter) and brush shelters (~1.5 m diameter) covered in bark that could be stretched over logs or against a standing spruce tree. Also utilized were bark lean-tos (~1.8 m long) and double lean-tos (up to 6 m long). These were used during seasonal migration times, but single men

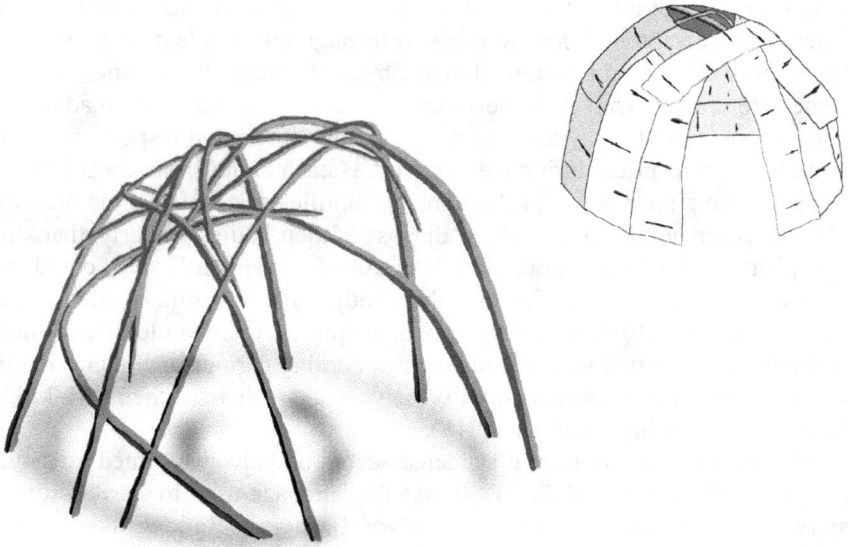

Figure 2.7. The traditional domed small house. In summer, the stick frame would be covered in bark, and in the winter, covered in caribou or moose hide. Hearths might be inside or outside the structure. Two domed tents might be joined together to form a larger oval-shaped structure with a central hearth shared by two unrelated partnered families (based on Pitts 1972: 110, 179–180).

and women might live in a hide tent or teepee/wikiup (~2.5–7 m diameter) in a village (Pitts 1972, 106). Sometimes several small families might share a dome/beehive-shaped hide tent or join tents together with a shared fire (Vitt 1971, 98) (figure 2.7). These usually were between families whose men were joined in a hunting partnership (Kirsteatter 2000) (dimensions from Cook 1977, 176).

Larger dome-shaped semi-subterranean hide-covered winter houses could be built to house two families in a hunting partnership. The house type that required the most labor investment, the double-walled rectangular bark/moss house, might be made (Pitts 1972). Other unique tents involved the menstruation hood: a giant moose-hide cowl that measured several meters long. It was worn and lived in by girls for up to several months upon first menstruation (Andrews 1975, 118–120). The hood was so large and heavy that it forced the wearer to stay in one place. For the Ahtna, the puberty hood was altered to be small enough that the wearer had freedom of movement but was worn so that it covered the eyes, forcing the wearer to look down, avoiding eye contact with all persons (Simeone 2018, 93). Another structure was a spruce-bow birthing hut built over a small dugout pit (Andrews 1975, 116). Houses involving below-ground pits are usually associated with winter, while summer houses were tall ovoid domes or wikiup-cones built on the surface. This other flooring form was likely a practical response to the summer rainstorms, which can quickly fill any surface depression with several inches of water and mud, as those involved in the field excavations required for this work experienced every year. Sweat houses were added as smaller extra rooms but were thought to be a recent innovation borrowed from coastal people (Pitts 1972, 112). Traditionally, they were separate dome-shaped buildings, restricted to men's use, considered essential to prevent laziness.

Other important widespread cultural pit features that need to be differentiated from housepits can include birthing pits (Ruth Ridley: TCC 2018), cooking pits (Potter et al. 2011; Rogers and Stone 2010), food storage (cache) pits (Mishler 1986), cremation pits (Potter et al. 2011), inhumation pits (Potter et al. 2014), pitfall traps (McKennan 1959), smokehouses (McKennan 1959, Pitts 1972), temporary shelters (McKennan 1959, Pitts 1972), drinking water wells (Rogers and Stone 2010).

Annette McFadyen Clark (1996, 165–166) provides a comparative guide for Alaska Native winter house constructions. However, no Tanana Valley residential features were included in her otherwise comprehensive analysis. Mishler's work with Abraham Luke (1986, 30–31) provides detailed notes and sketches of the double-walled moss house of the Middle Tanana, and Pitts provides them for the Upper Tanana (1972, 114–115) (figure 2.8). The houses could be large enough to house up to three to four families. Lt. Allen noted ten to twenty people per home in the villages he visited. Prestigious men and women who maintained extended families generally built houses big enough to be shared by two natal families with additional unattached structures for others. Pitts's Upper Tanana informants differentiated between the headman's semi-subterranean spruce bark house and the average family's semi-subterranean moss and hide house (figure 2.9). Spruce bark could only be harvested in sheets during the spring, indicating construction time. The hide house was built over a centralized pit with a berm packed around the tent's edge. Small-diameter logs were bent across the pit, and hides sewn together were drawn across it, leaving an opening for the door and overhead smoke-hole (McKennan 1959; Osgood 1971; Pitts 1972). The Upper Tanana people considered the ovoid, dome-shaped winter skin house to represent an older house form than the later semi-subterranean moss houses.

Secondary rooms housing a sauna were rare for the Tanana, unlike the Ahtna to the south. Sweat baths seem to have been a separate construction (McKennan 1959, 76). A bench was constructed around the inner periphery where members could sit, and activities could occur around a central excavated pit and fire. Smoke exited through a hole in the roof, and the door was

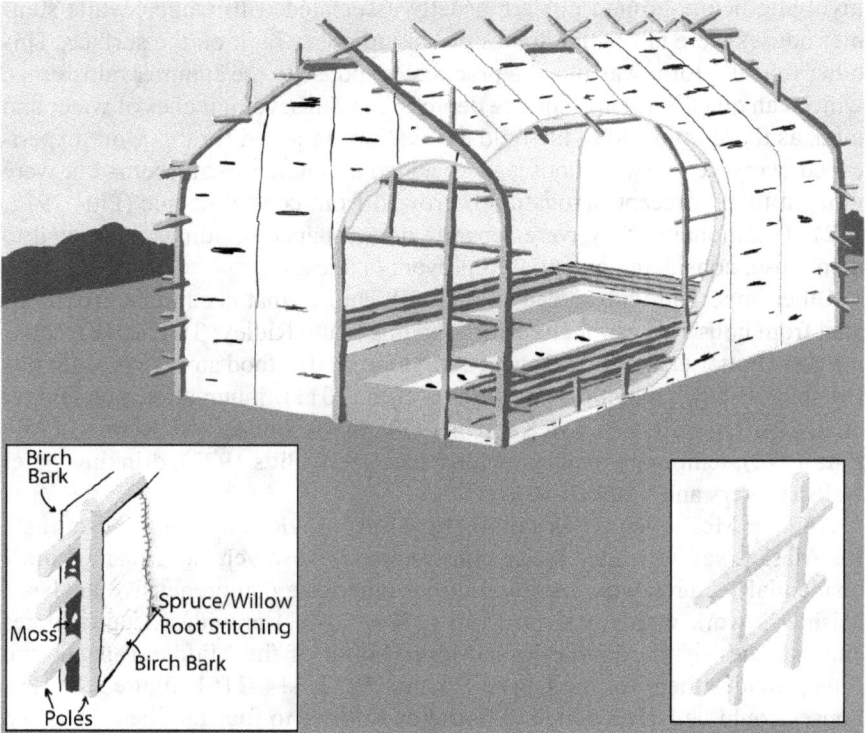

Figure 2.8. The traditional double-walled semi-subterranean *dlaat shyex* bark house at Pickupsticks and the late nineteenth century Goodpaster village (based on Mishler 1986: 29–34).

usually just a hide. Data concerning windows are conflicting; for some house types, they were not part of the construction, but during funeral rites, the cremated ashes of a person were passed through the house via windows. It was quite important, or *'engii* (bad luck, taboo), that the ashes did not pass through the doorway because women used the doorway for entrance and exits (Kirsteatter 2000). If windows were not considered part of the household construction, they might have been specially created only upon the need for the funeral rites. Houses were often burned once the owner's funeral potlatch was concluded with their ashes placed inside. This is important; both John Cook and Robert McKennan faced local Native criticism for "opening graves" at the Healy Lake Village Site and Dixthada Village Site (Mishler and Simeone 2006, xxv). However, both Cook and McKennan were convinced they were only excavating house pits, as their excavations proved. Here, Kirsteatter indicates that abandoned housepits might also commonly be expected to be

Figure 2.9. Reconstructed single-walled spruce-bark house from Chena Indian Village, an interpretive visitor installment near Fairbanks, Alaska. Photos by Mary Wolff 1990.

also the graves of their occupants, indicating researchers should consider treating housepits as potential gravesites.

Inside, two benches faced each other along the house's length, with a doorway opening between them and a centrally shared hearth. Ideally, the house was shared by two monogamous unrelated natal families of opposite moieties, whose seating positions in the house mirrored each other (figure 2.10). Children were not allowed on the benches, and women were restricted from sitting on the bench portions where the males slept, or in some cases, from using the benches entirely. The husbands would be joined in a lifelong economic partnership. Sleeping occurred on top of benches for men and young boys and below the benches for women and children. Seating and sleeping placement on the benches were rigidly enforced by gender and age-grade, a practice shared with people in the Lower Copper River (Shinkwin 1974, 1979), Cook Inlet (Kari and Fall 2016), and Lower Koyukuk (Loyens 1966, 59–60; McFadyen Clark 1996, 145). During waking hours, women's activities tended to occur toward the front of the house nearer to the door, while the back of the house was reserved for the elderly, widows, or unmarried adults (i.e., young men) (Pitts 1972, 112). Men were restricted to the benches while inside the home. Women's activities were directed in front of the males toward the center or rear of the residence (Loyens 1966). Male activities were generally reserved for outdoor areas.

The house was constructed as such: first, a pit was dug using sharpened sticks and wooden shovels. Second, a pole frame was built over the pit and covered in birchbark sewn together with spruce roots or willow lashings. Third, a layer of dirt and moss was placed over the bark for insulation. Some houses included an outer layer of birchbark, called a "double-wall," as it required a second construction framework. Benches were then constructed and lined with caribou hide. A smoke hole was placed in the roof, and a doorway was simply a hide covering but dug halfway into the ground. The framework was often decorated with geometric red ochre and charcoal grease-based painted designs.

The houses could be built with the intent of lifetime use by the village's head person or might be created only for the singular occasion of the potlatch. A family might move into one after the potlatch was completed, or it might be abandoned immediately after as part of the gift consumption process. A large structure was built in Kechumstuk in 1919 for just such an occasion and abandoned soon after (Andrews 1980, 6–8). Sometimes a flat roof was used; other times, a pitched roof was part of the construction, or a rounded roof/wall construction was employed, similar to a modern-day Quonset hut. House size depended on social status resulting from how many extended family members were brought into the residence, but dimensions

Tikaan
Wolf Moiety side

Ch'ezhenn'
Eagle Moiety side

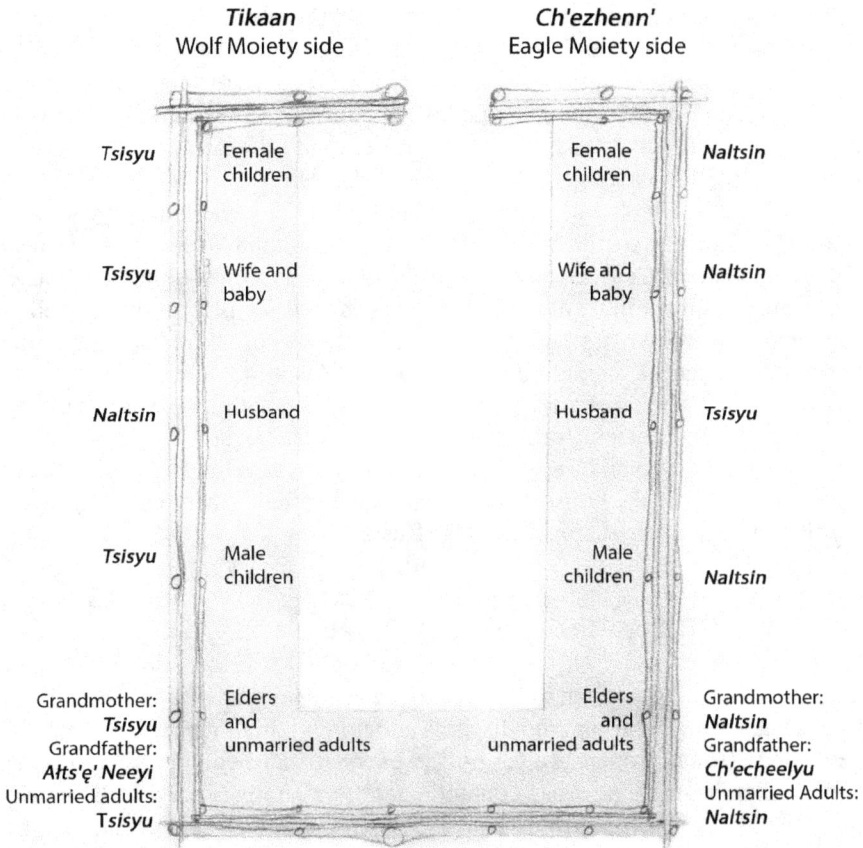

Tsisyu	Female children	Female children	*Naltsin*
Tsisyu	Wife and baby	Wife and baby	*Naltsin*
Naltsin	Husband	Husband	*Tsisyu*
Tsisyu	Male children	Male children	*Naltsin*
Grandmother: *Tsisyu* Grandfather: *Ałts'ę' Neeyi* Unmarried adults: *Tsisyu*	Elders and unmarried adults	Elders and unmarried adults	Grandmother: *Naltsin* Grandfather: *Ch'echeelyu* Unmarried Adults: *Naltsin*

Figure 2.10. **Traditional seating arrangement in a shared dual-family house observed at Goodpaster village, incorporating the floorplan from the Pickupsticks site structural feature (see chapter 7). In this traditional arrangement, a Naltsin family from the Crow Moiety has joined in a hunting partnership with a Tsisyu family from the Seagull Moiety. Only two elders from each family have moved in (seating data based on McFadyen Clark 1996, 145).**

typically ranged from 20x10x10 feet (occupied by two natal families) to 40x25x10 feet.

Historic log-cabin-style residences were initially supported in the traditional manner by upright poles rather than corner notching, influenced by Cook Inlet construction styles. They became gradually adopted in Alaska after the 1860s as iron and steel axes became available through the trade networks. Corner-notched log cabins became the prevalent form only after the 1890s, diffusing from the Klondike goldfields. For a brief period around the time of historical contact, rooms were attached to the back of the house for use as first menstrual seclusion or were built as a separate detached smaller house.

Residence designs similar to these traditional forms are shared throughout the Tanana Valley. The dome/beehive-shaped version is shared with the Hän on the Yukon River drainages to the northeast and the Ahtna and Dena'ina to the south. Rectangular Dene houses, also referred to sometimes as a Plank House in Łingít and interior British Columbia Dene lands, are widely shared across Dene societies and were found as far south as the Pacific Coast Dene in Northern California (Baumhoff 1958). The domed skin/bark house, menstrual and birth huts, domed sweat lodges, and simple hunting/traveling shelters are shared across a much larger region. They are found among all the Alaska Dene people, including the Mackenzie Basin to the east. The simpler residence forms being shared extensively extra-regionally suggests that they represent a more ancient form than the rectangular houses, as suggested by oral history (Gordon and Savage 1974; Pilon 1991). It is likely that the shared cultural aspects of the house form, village design, and kinship system likely facilitated each other's adoption and diffusion.

SOCIAL AGE CLASSES, GENDER ROLES, AND TECHNOLOGY

Additional rules applying to *'engii*-enforced behaviors also patterned the proper disposal of tool-making discards and minimizing interpersonal contact between personal property (e.g., tools, weapons, and medicine bag) in order to keep them from being cross-contaminated from another individuals' potential *'engii*. These expectations enabled the standardized household seating patterns to be maintained across space and time. The result was that villages and individuals attempted to maintain a form of hyper-cleanliness and respect for personal space, which was similarly practiced and patterned throughout the Dene cultural region. Individuals and households who deviated from the patterned cultural norm could be considered dangerous and faced ostracism. States of purification from negative *'engii* could be re-obtained for individuals through ritualized use of heat, fire, ashes, and water.

Social roles were primarily achieved through individual merit. Secondarily, they were achieved through age-determined classes. Thirdly, they were determined through gender roles. Important age classes were prepubescent children who had little to no formally structured responsibilities. Next were unmarried young adults who were past puberty. Puberty initiated a series of rites and gender-specific craft and task production. These generally were defined by biological sex but seem to have also been responsive to personal identity choice if strong-willed younger persons chose to identify with behaviors associated with the opposite sex. Mastering these led to the next stage, married life, which typically occurred during the middle teenage years for females and middle twenties for males. Married adults were tasked with the upkeep of households and the care for elder and younger generations. The final most respected age class was reserved for elders. Attaining the role of elder was a loose term generally determined when one's children had married and thus taken on the burden of household management. These age-graded classes conferred specific *'engii*-regulated duties that were further defined by gender roles. Elders who were childless, widowed adults, post-menopause women, or those who chose not to take on leadership roles could be expected to be safely released from the structures of *'engii.*

The final process of corporeal life was death. Abortion, infanticide, and geronticide were considered acceptable in cases when it improved the community's chances of survival in times of resource stress. Infanticide and abortions were generally avoided in cases where adoption by childless couples was an option. Banishment was typically utilized instead of capital punishment in cases of crimes within the community, as revenge killings were expected. In those cases, the cycle of revenge killings between clans could be broken if a specific potlatch was given in the place of a killing. All other forms of killing except for war casualties were considered murder (Andrews 1975, 117). Death was not the end of life, and after leaving the body, one's spirit traveled through the universe before returning to this existence. Deceased individuals were expected to return to their families to be reborn, although some reincarnated as different animal or natural forms, or did not return at all, a sign that their personal journey had finally achieved fulfillment (Cannon 2021).

Extensive descriptions of the role that gender-related *'engii* taboos played in association with hunting practices and hunting implements help to frame the details to which male hunting implements and behaviors could be affected through female contact, especially during a young woman's first menstruation period (Andrews 1975, 118–120; Luke 1998; O'Brien 2011; Thomas 2005). While Tanana society seems to have been structured to favor male leadership and labor ease, the gendered avoidance regarding hunting weapons should not be understood in a negative sense. Instead, it was considered that the deep life-creating magic inherent within all women between puberty and menopause would cancel out the death-bringing luck that any favored hunting weapon might possess. Thus, in the presence of women of menstruating age, activities became "gendered" as individuals who did not identify with those roles would naturally attempt to keep their activity areas free of accidental *'engii* contamination. In a women-only camp or household, all technology and labor forms would expect to be present but not gendered; and similarly, in male-only camps. Tasks become gender-ascribed only in the presence of multiple gendered identities and age grades at the same place. This pattern is expected to facilitate forms of age-graded sexual divisions of labor and the gendered forms of knowledge learning for prepubescent children.

Individuals who did not ascribe to the gender or sexual identities into which they were born, were an accepted part of society, although they were not afforded a formalized third gender category. Opportunities to discuss the lives of those individuals within the constructs of Dene identity does not seem to have occurred with early anthropologists. Perhaps, like individuals who found themselves belonging to the middle moiety, transcending the duties of either moiety, these individuals could transcend the gender-identity roles as needed.

The taboos enforced the association of large-game hunting and adult male behaviors in Dene society as a heavy emphasis was placed on the association of hunting success and leadership roles. Thus, the avoidance of contact between hunting weapons and women of childbearing age was widely practiced, the consequences of which were considered dire and could cost the hunter his life (McKennan 1959; Thomas 2005, 2). These taboos were not applicable for girls who had not reached menarche or for women past menopause (Vitt 1971, 126). Gendered roles were culturally enforced; however, it did not necessarily follow personal sexual orientation or biological sex and were flexible depending on the situation at hand. Plenty of accounts exist of Dene women of child-bearing age also being primary providers of large game meat within a family unit (cf. Kari and Fall 2016, 240). Gender identities were considered equal, and social hierarchies were enhanced largely through both descent and personal merit (Olson 1968, 113).

Woodworking may have had a gendered component; birchbark crafting was often associated with women's skillsets, while spruce woodcraft was associated with the male gender. Men's wood-crafting always occurred outdoors, while women's sewing occurred inside residences. The male curation of hunting weapons is often overemphasized in ethnographic work. Men often slept with their weapons and tools, as it was 'engii for women to come into contact with them. However, both genders were involved in their curation, as babiche for bowstrings and any leather sewing and beaded decoration (i.e., for quivers) was done by women (Vitt 1971, 84). Crafting produced snowshoes, toboggans, canoes, and rafts, jointly using wood and faunal materials produced explicitly by women and men, although men often put together their final forms. It should be noted that most gendered or age-structured 'engii restrictions relating to hunting/hunting weaponry were suspended during communal hunts, which were seasonal occurrences, where everyone who was physically capable was expected to help in the capture, kill, and butchery of game as they could.

Personal toolkits for both men and women were carried on the body and were not considered communal property. Toolkits were overwhelmingly dominated by the use of wood, bone, antler, and copper. The use of stone as a technological component in the nineteenth century was minimal compared to earlier periods, except in the realm of hide-work where children were encouraged to assist (Hanson 2008, 122–123). Copper was a highly desired item for knives and awls that were used both for big game, fur-bearing animals, and bird hunting. Composite arrows, using detachable long, barbed bone or antler points, sometimes with stone or copper end blades (e.g., Thomas et al. 2020), were used both before rifles became available in the 1860s and alongside them well into the 1930s (McKennan 1959). The composite arrows were designed for the shaft's recovery after a successful shot, which after impact, fell out of the animal, leaving the dart tip mechanism inside the victim. Caribou antler and moose long bones were desirable for the multi-inch long arrowheads. Compound arrows designed for black bear, moose, caribou, and beaver were created so that the hind shaft could detach from the fore shaft upon impact (McKennan 1959, 55; Rainey 1939b; Vitt 1971, 80). Sheep hunting arrows may have been preferred to be constructed as a single shaft, designed to stay in the animal. Bear spears were topped by either a removable bone point or copper dagger (figure 2.11). Bone knives were kept sharp through the use of a whetstone. Knife blades were ideally created from moose or lynx ribs. Stone adzes were used to cut down larger trees (usually during the winter for ease of chopping). Stone mauls were used for various hammering tasks, especially for house and fish weir construction and for copper preparation and tool formation. Muzzle-loading rifles were introduced to coastal Alaska Natives who traded them inland in the early nineteenth th century. They apparently were only used for warfare as a prestige tactic until technology regarding firing efficiency and accuracy had sufficiently advanced beyond the bow and atlatl in the late nineteenth century (Townsend 1983).

Drills were handheld using one's mouth and made with bits made of copper, tooth, or stone. Awls were of copper or bone, and ulus were used by women and made of copper or thin slate. Fire was made using a corded mouth drill or flint and pyrites (e.g., Gómez Coutouly et al. 2015). The personal fire kit included flint, pyrite, tinder, and birch fungus, held in a moosehide bag. Flint contains carbon and pyrite sulfur. The birch fungus contains nitrates, which, when combined with wood ash containing potassium and water, produce potassium nitrate salts, basically a crude, mild form of gunpowder. The fire kit was considered so important that it was burned with its owner upon the cremation pyre. A long, smoldering birch log could also be carried between camps. Smokeless fires were used in emergency cases where

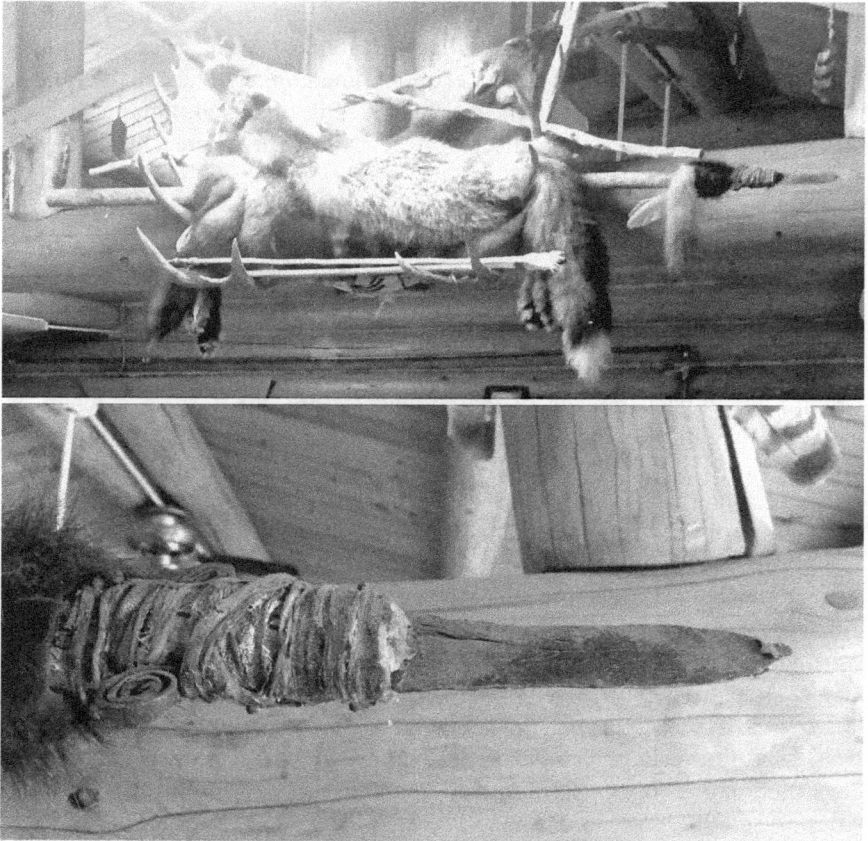

Figure 2.11.   Traditional copper bear spear at Healy Lake Tribal Hall.

snowdrift shelters were used, possibly indicating that marrow grease and bones were curated for this purpose (Vitt 1971, 97–99).

Women's toolkits typically included a snowshoe needle, sewing awl, knife, skin scrapers, and sinew for thread. Men's toolkits included a crooked knife, awl, drill, lancet, and a small bag of ochre (McKennan 1959). For personal decoration, blue or red ochre was powdered and mixed with animal grease for paint. Ochre was considered an expensive item and could be used as a trade medium. It needed to be purchased from the earth by leaving behind gifts when it was taken, similar to leaving gifts for mice and squirrels if their cache contents were used for human sustenance. Ochre was powdered and rolled into large balls with fat and sap, used to color wood and for body paint (Anderson 1957, 1; Mishler 1986, 41; Thomas 2005, 148–150). Bone ornaments fashioned to resemble hollow cylindrical dentalium shells were created from large mammal long bones, and the similarly shaped porcupine quills were also valued. Art was individualized and restricted mainly to personal adornment, displaying prestige and prowess (Vitt 1971, 86). Tanana men were expected to excel at woodcraft and women with leathercraft. Both skills were essential to master, especially with artistic ascetics, ensuring a career to barter for food and necessary items in a person's old age if one could not depend on any grown children for care. Personal clothing and bodily decoration (and, by extension, tools and household decoration) illustrate the ritualized act of reciprocity. Beautiful adornment was created and gifted by women to their men. Just as it emphasized and enhanced the prestige and luck of the wearer at social gatherings, it was expected to be worn during the hunt, enticing game animals to "fall in love with the hunter" and gift themselves willingly as a food sacrifice to a handsomely dressed pursuer (Easton 2005, 101). Hide scrapers may have been part of the personal toolkit for men and women, being gifted from elders to children (Hanson 2008).

Copper objects were sought as prestige items. These were primarily produced by the Lower Ahtna people along the Chitina River. They were also produced to a lesser extent by other groups surrounding the Wrangell Mountains (Cooper 2012), and a source may have been known on the Copper Creek, a tributary of the Charley River to the northeast of Shaw Creek (Kari 2011a). This product was only consumed by the Middle Tanana people and not produced in their territory. Copper knives for men were especially sought as both an item marking wealth, social status, and also for practical use as both a knife, dagger, and lance head for bear spears (Noguchi and Kondo 2019). Copper awls were valued for hide work, and copper sheet arrowheads or end blades were used as well (Dixon et al. 2005; Hanson 1999, 2008; Thomas et al. 2020; VanderHoek et al. 2012; Workman 1976). Copper was also fashioned into small objects for bodily and clothing adornments (Cooper 2012; Shinkwin 1979) and was also a useful medium for trade (Hayden 1998).

THE SEASONAL ROUND

The seasons were observed to revolve repetitiously. Life, death, and rebirth cycled in and out of the yearly cycles, which were embedded in the great century-long cyclical periods of game population expansions and crashes. Cycles were expected, but it was understood that new and unique factors could be present with each, requiring an attitude of openness to adaptation and innovation to them. The annual cycle, or seasonal round, for nineteenth-century Middle Tanana groups was focused on a village that was centrally located between seasonally available key resource exploitation areas (Shinkwin et al. 1980). Mishler (1986, 15) suggests that a dual-centralized village system was occasionally used. In this case, instead of a group always returning seasonally to a single centralized location, they might instead maintain two villages that were located close, only several miles apart, possibly on opposing sides of the Tanana River. They might be occupied simultaneously or one at a time, depending on resource availability and demographic pressure (Mishler 1986, 15).

The year was divided two general seasons, winter and summer, which were further divided into twelve to thirteen months of different resource availability periods, rather than fixed solar or lunar periods. The year began around September/October, as freeze-up occurred. The twelve month-periods for the *Salcheege* were *Ninchuundeeghi* "Bull Moose Rutting Time (September), *Unenh Taanzeexdeghe* "Slush Ice Moves Downstream" (October/ November), *Unenh Tatedetiigi* "Month It Starts to Freeze" (November), *Saa Tsidl* "Small Sun" (December), *Unen Saa Noch'eteedlchaax* "Month the Sun Starts to Get Larger" (January), *Ch'eyaan' Zaa'* "Eagle Sun" (February), *Ch'etthaa Zaa'* "Hawk Sun" (March), *Unenh Xwluu Dezeeghi* "Month the Snow Becomes Soft" (April), *Ch'et'qq' Zaa'* "Leaves Sun" (May), *Unenh Ch'edegaayi* "[Animal] Birthing Month" (June), *Unenh Ch'eleghi* "Fish [King Salmon] Run Month" (July), and *Ch'et'qq' Tsiik Saa'* "Leaves Are Becoming Yellow Sun" (August) (Kari n.d.; Andrews provides slightly different names/translations: 1975, 69–75). The thirteenth month was only referred to through circumlocution.

Martin Gutolski (2002) suggested plausible interpretations for some of the pictographs recorded by Giddings (1941) at Moose Creek Bluff (*Ddhel Edeeniileni*) near *Salcheege*. One image showed five figures in a high-prowed boat with four tally marks above, and the other associated imaged depicted six images in a similar shaped boat with eight tally marks above. Gutolski drew connections to an origin story of the seasons as inscribed with similar imagery on a Dene song staff from the central Yukon Territory. The associated legend told that the summer and winter worlds were once divided from each other by the sky. The winter animals who inhabited our world made a hole in the sky, allowing the summer world to descend into ours, perhaps recalling the end of the Pleistocene; however, the sky's weather continues to keep the two from mixing. The story stick associates the six anthropomorphic figures in one boat as representing winter, and the boat with five figures as representing summer (Cruikshank 1991). The tallies above the figures are perhaps indicative of the number of months associated with the warm and cold seasons.

In September, bands moved to the caribou fences for upkeep and maintenance in anticipation of the migrations. Moose could also be taken in the fences. A late anadromous fish run was capitalized on in October, a unique event for the Middle Tanana (Vitt 1971). During this time, freshwater fish retreated from smaller upland streams into the deep-water lowland rivers and lakes for the winter. In November, group dispersal followed, where people left in small family groups to find fresh winter meat, including recently hibernating bears. This dispersal was organized by the band chief and shaman (if they were different individuals). Each of the local ungulate species had distinct ecological needs and migration routes, and the herd abundance of these three species often dictated where and how groups would disperse. A risk mitigation strategy of assigning specific families to specific ungulate species at different places on the landscape may have been practiced. Families shared their planned destinations with each other in case of shortfalls; families in need could travel to other families' locations to reduce the chances of malnourishment or starvation.

Groups coalesced again near the winter solstice for a lengthy period of festivities and feasting. January, the coldest month, was usually spent in the villages with people using stored foods. Only during this period would the long cycle of creation myths involving the dual cultural motifs of the narcissistic creator-trickster Raven, *Dotrotsela,* and the moral transformer-hero Traveler, *Saatedlech'eeghe,* be recited, possibly also due to the optimal visibility of the stars (Cannon et al. 2020; Easton 2005, 14–26; McKennan 1959, 175–195; Thompson 1990, 140; Thornton et al. 2019). Families might disperse again in February. March was the most critical period of potential annual starvation; moose hunting was typically participated in as the month waned. Crusted snow allowed hunters and dogs to take moose who broke through the snow and could not move quickly. April, May, and June brought freshwater fishing and small game hunting, including endemic birds such as ptarmigan and spruce hen. These activities may have occurred at a separate spring camp, and some also moved later into the uplands to intercept caribou returning to calve in June.

As plants came out of winter dormancy, the new growth was used for fish trap maintenance in anticipation of the salmon season. Migratory birds played a vital food role during the warmer months and were actively hunted with special blunted arrows (Haynes and Simeone 2007) and snares. Women and children played an important role in collecting birds and eggs. Midsummer fish camps were placed near the mouths of streams where clear running water entered the muddy, silt-laden Tanana or could be several miles upstream at their intersection with smaller streams. Fish were caught using both dipnets and large woven conical willow traps, where fish were funneled via log weirs.

Late summer was devoted to preparing the fish and gathering edible fruit, vegetable, and rootstock. Rabbit drives also occurred at this time. Salmon runs were negligible farther upstream from the Volkmar River on the Tanana, and groups upriver focused instead on lacustrine fish species and oriented those harvests differently.

Small fur-bearing mammals were sought throughout the year between massive game migrations, but children could not come into contact with their remains, though they could help with their hunts. Often, the oldest band members, youngest members, and women with small children could be left in villages and fish camps to cure food and harvest small game and plants during times of necessary extended mobility.

Trading could happen when a meeting could be anticipated at any time of year, and a trade partnership between two male individuals was considered lifelong. While a trade partner was only encountered rarely during the year, maintaining this relationship was just as important as the hunting partner. Conducting trade without a partner appears to have been quite challenging to practice, likely due to the cultural expectations of positive/balanced reciprocity when items changed hands (Easton 2005, 126). In order to conduct trade, make a profit, and not be held in the future of expectations to return that value to the purchaser, a sort of "blind trade" needed to be established, where the actors could not know the identity of the other. The person who had goods to trade would shut themselves within a house and hang a long pole outside the door with a rattle. The rattle would allow a trade exchange to occur through affirmation or denial. It would allow for the option of identities to be hidden if desired so that value could be exchanged without the expectation of immediate or future return (Paul 1957, 7–8; see also Mauss [1925] 2016, 75).

ANIMAL AND PLANT USE

Many game and vegetable types were commonly used, but two animals were considered to have a particular sacred place: salmon and moose. While caribou was considered the most critical animal economically, it does not seem to have had any additional sacred practices or taboos attached. Salmon and moose were entered formally into the naming of the months. The salmon ceremony, where the first salmon caught of the season was considered sacred and consumed communally by all village members (Loyens 1966, 37), was necessary for all Dene cultures dependent on this seasonal resource. However, the ceremony seems to have been abandoned soon after the widespread adoption of fishwheels by Native families, when it quickly became apparent that it was impossible to identify which fish was the actual first one caught.

Moose still retains its symbolically sacred place today (Simeone 1995). It is still ritually sought for the potlatch ceremony, where the moose-nose stew is considered to be of particular importance. The rest of the animal is also prepared and consumed, but not with the ritual overtones of the stew. The stew is cooked only with neutral-tasting vegetables that do not detract from the taste of the game. While salt and pepper are provided, their use is frowned upon by elders. The experience of the taste and texture of the seared moose meat is particularly essential, being the focal point of the meal. Today the uniquely yellow-colored moose leather is preferred for traditional regalia, shifting from the older preference for the lighter gray caribou hide.

Bear fat was a highly prized commodity. Bears seem to have been sought, especially when they were beginning to den when their body fat reserves were at their best. Songs were required to be sung upon their death in the village. One was always expected to avoid mentioning them by name (ANLC0881b 1983). Women needed to avoid all contact with bear meat during their childbearing years, and the spirit of the bear was especially feared and respected. However, the fat could be consumed by anyone. If men treated women improperly in any way, they would be cursed with terrible bear encounters. Among the Koyukon, bear hides could only be tanned by men (McFadyen Clark 1996, 6).

Otters were considered powerful and actively avoided as their spirit could cause sickness or death; (McKennan 1959; Vitt 1971, 125). The otter taboos were extensive, comparable to those for bears (Haynes and Simeone 2007, 73), but the reasons are unspecified. Franz Boas ([1916] 2016, 170–171) records an origin story, perhaps related, from the Tsimshian people of central British Columbia, which discusses that Otter was responsible for gifting aquatic food to people and therefore must not be killed. Since the otter taboo is similar to the bear taboo, it may suggest that the otter, being aquatic, carried similar power for this realm that bears carried for the terrestrial world (it was *'engii* to mix aquatic and terrestrial foods in a meal). In one tale, Traveler meets brown bear and shapeshifts into an otter to escape, suggesting they are equivalent power creatures (de Laguna and DeArmond 1995, 154).

If they had to be killed, specific purification rights needed to be followed, such as discarding the tools used to kill and process the carcass. Other fur-bearing animals were actively sought for meat and clothing. Foxes, wolves, and wolverines were taboo to eat but could be used for fur, though wolf-hunting or killing seems to have been avoided (McKennan 1959; Vitt 1971). Wolverines, foxes, wolves, dogs, and otters were all considered to have descended from the mythic *Cet'aeni*, the tailed-people who had lived in the Alaska Range prior to the arrival of the Dene (Vitt 1971, 118; Wright 1977, 38–39). The fur-bearing mink, weasel, marten, and ermine were descended from the otter. Coyotes are a recent newcomer to Alaska (Hody and Kays

2018) but fell under the canid taboo. Mice were considered to be a harbinger of evil and always killed.

Dogs were especially revered and used for hunting and transport, and their blood was used in women's medicine (Andrews 1975). They were only killed during starvation periods and otherwise considered taboo as food (Brucks and Lovick 2019). Dogs were valued as pack animals and fitted with packsacks, as people typically pulled sledges until the historic period's introduction of the dogsled. They were also used in lynx, porcupine, bear, and moose hunting. Their tails were always docked, and they were valued as companions and for protection. Dog behavior appears to have been left for puppies to learn from older dogs (Vitt 1971, 93–94). Dogs could not consume ungulate heads or many of the fur-bearing animals, requiring them to be cached in trees (only men could consume game heads).

The use of ravens and cranes was avoided, and a taboo similar to otters was also attached to loons. Eagle pinions were preferred for arrow fletching, but hawk and swan feathers were also acceptable. Goose feathers were only used as a last resort (Vitt 1971, 77).

If an *'engii* animal was killed for any reason, negative *'engii* could be averted by tying willow twigs to the animal's joints, and the knife used needed to be immediately discarded. Women should not consume fresh meat, and if a carcass was butchered in the camp, any blood on the ground must be disposed of (Vitt 1971, 127). Squirrels, marten, and muskrat could be hunted (often by women and children) for dog food, and their skins were used for women and children's parkas. Lynx, beaver, porcupine, and muskrat were fairly *'engii*-free and actively hunted by all and welcomed for their taste.

Caribou and sheepskins were preferred for clothing for their optimal weight, warmth, and durability (Vitt 1971, 70). Rabbit, fox, marten, and ground squirrel hides were used for caps. Moosehides were preferred for tents and outer moccasin soles, and rabbit skin was used for inner soles and mitten linings. Moose was preferred for creating babiche; however, bear or caribou were also acceptable (McClellan 1975, 266). Thick moosehide was preferred for quivers. These rules are generally identical to those of the Ahtna (Simeone 2018, 72–79).

LANDSCAPE CULTIVATION PRACTICES

While a seasonally migrating forager paradigm dominated these lifeways, it is also necessary to point out some food and resource cultivation practices. Fish and fishery cultivation were necessary for places beyond the reach of significant salmon migrations. The Upper Susitna, just southwest of the study area on the other side of the Alaska Range, was an area where this practice has been documented. There, ponds would be artificially dammed with rock stacks during the early summer flood season, maintaining the higher lake levels during drier summer periods when river levels had dropped. This practice promoted fish growth. The dams would then be released in the autumn, and the fish would be washed into weirs and nets placed below the outlets (Andrews 1980, 47; Street 1995). This practice was never documented explicitly for the Upper or Middle Tanana; however, prospector Carl Tweiten (1990) credited the Native people with this idea when he utilized it on the upper Goodpaster River in the 1930s, suggesting it may have been known and used regionally.

Practices of plant modification by the Middle and Upper Tanana groups were focused on trees. A tradition of cultivating living trees as part of the extensive caribou fence networks was performed throughout the region. Tree growth was promoted within the fences to help guide ungulates to gaps where snares were set to capture moose or corrals designed to capture caribou. Live trees would occasionally be cut or bent just enough to turn them into desired angles to support the fences and tree blinds (Andrews 1980). They may have also been modified as way markers or place markers (figure 2.12) (Duer et al. 2020); trails could also be marked by upright poles or charcoal pictographs on blazes (Powell 1909, 286–287). Trees were also cultivated for craft items. If a birch tree (*Betula*) was to be used for creating bows, the tree needed to be dead and seasoned, at least five inches in diameter, and have no knots to be harvested.

Figure 2.12. Two views of a potential Culturally Modified Tree at the northwest base of the hill Swan Point is located on. The knot is approximately 2.5 m above ground.

Several bows could be split from a single log if the wood was of good quality. Birch stands and individual trees could be curated in such a way to facilitate the desired conditions to be achieved at harvest by stripping them of lower branches when young (Vitt 1971, 73). Bows were tailored to the individual and were only passed to others as gifts, trade items, or through inheritance (usually uncle to sister's son). Their use life typically extended to about two years.

With the assistance of adzes and the crooked knife, fire was utilized in the bow creation. Fresh willow bark could be wrapped around the bow in such a way as to produce a decorative coloring during the firing process. Older men who had mastered the craft were valued community members who used this skill to trade for food when they could no longer hunt for themselves and their families. Spruce trees were curated for creating arrows. Their curation required debranching at a young age, then later debarked and left standing for three years to season appropriately before being cut down. Logs could be anywhere between 1–8 inches in diameter, being split after for arrow creation. Green (fresh with sap running) spruce logs, about two inches in diameter, were desired for bear spears, and spear points could be made from moose and caribou long bones. Caribou antlers were straightened using water, fire, and fat to create spear points measuring three feet long were used for brown bear lances (Vitt 1971, 88). Spears were a summer crafting item, while bows and arrows tended to be crafted in the fall.

Finally, fire was also used as a tool to clear brush around villages and clear and enhance new growth in desired hunting areas. Fire cultivation in traditional land-use practices has been documented extensively worldwide, but only briefly for the Tanacross people. This practical use of fire in the region was documented by Roy Mitchell (Johnson 1981). He concluded from his informants that a widespread tradition of fire ecology was practiced throughout the Tanana, reducing wildfire danger to villages and enhance the landscape productivity of moose, furbearers, and edible plants. His informants emphasized the practical nature of the exercise, which was repressed after the construction of the ALCAN Highway. Alan Boraas extensively described the symbolic purification nature that fire and burning held for the Kenaitze Dena'ina, ideas that may have been shared by the Tanana and may have influenced practices involving the ritual abandonment of village sites (Boraas and Kalifornsky 1991; Lutz 1959).

CULTURAL IMPLICATIONS

The cultural summary above provides a rough outline of the proper path a Dene person of the Middle Tanana would have followed to ensure the

cyclical return of food and goods to their families. The process of reciprocal gift exchange between non-kin and natural entities, proper treatment of
foraged animals, and their ritual consumption (eating and disposal) ensured
future annual and generational returns of abundance. This worldview was
upended entirely during the twentieth century when direct observation of
Euro-American disregard for the sacred *'engii* practices and their treatment
of nature and non-kin as purely extraction commodities did not cause an
immediate collapse of the natural world.

Alan Boraas has described this paradigmatic change as akin to the Enlightenment when the Europeans' traditional Christian cosmology was similarly
overturned (Boraas and Peter 2008). The result is an experience of cultural
discord, where a number of ideas of traditional spirituality, Euro-American
Christian practices, adherence to secular state and federal laws, and understanding scientific natural philosophy constructs compete within the individual for primacy in creating a clear path for constructing a successful life
on a personal and community level. This sense of internal disorder continues
to have substantial ramifications, informing current perceptions of individual
health, sense of community, and cultural dissolution. It is currently significantly heightened through two forms: the earth's ecosystem's current observable slow, dangerous trend toward impending collapse and the abnormally
high rates of social problems such as violence, substance abuse, and suicide.
The first is experienced through the increasingly disruptive seasonal climate
changes, the rise of dangerous invasive species, and the negative impacts on
native animals. Modern extinction is unique to past extinction events and is
conceptualized as the result of animals refusing to return to this world due to
their mistreatment by humanity. The second form, social collapse, is experienced by losing community and family members to violence, trauma, abuse,
and neglect. Both forms are considered closely tied to each other, and working to heal one will heal the other.

Today's long-proven connection between these social and environmental
impacts and Euro-American industrial-consumer behaviors heavily informs
traditional Native rights activism. The path toward the future requires heal-
ing individuals, communities, and the natural world through interconnected
efforts. Making sense of a holistic, healthy present requires a clear understanding of the past.

ARCHAEOLOGICAL IMPLICATIONS

This ethnographic summary presents the cultural expectations as codified
through the sacred Dene practices of reciprocity and *'engii* in the Tanana

Valley. Reciprocity bound all entities in the universe together from the basic to most complex levels through cause and effect. The ability to manipulate this process through powerful individuals' activities and ceremonies was recognized. Thus, the conscious decision by a person to engage in these behaviors required the realization that they were interacting with the fabric of the universe; thus, it is here described as a theory of deep reciprocity.

This reconstruction presents a sort of perfect ideological image of how the past should look. In reality, the archaeological record will likely produce a picture that both supports and deviates from this ideal, instead reflecting a palimpsest of everyday practicality. McFadyen Clark noted this problem when she conducted a similar ethnoarchaeological study of three nineteenth-century traditional Dene houses on the Koyukuk River. Artifact discard patterns sometimes conformed to the expected social rules, and other times did not (1991, 204–206). Deviation from the predicted pattern could be explained by the presence of sleep doctors who were extraordinarily powerful and could manipulate the natural order of the world (therefore, were not affected by the rules of 'engii), the presence of elders who were no longer expected to conform to the cultural rules of 'engii or of elders who lived alone without children, households who might have a house dog, male-only households (often partnerships between younger men who had not yet built the wealth or skills needed to be considered acceptable for marriage), female-only households (often partnerships between older women who chose not to or could not remarry, Wallis 2004), nontraditional Dene (i.e., people who felt the need to evade the social charter), poor housekeepers, or households maintained during deprivation times.

Household archaeology encompasses all the behaviors that occurred before, during, and after a site or residence occupation. This period can be quite extensive. Discarded artifact movements at residential sites are predicted to be deposited in relation to the direct activities that produced them, which the presence of household features should structure. Discarded artifacts might be moved about on the floor through trampling, kicking (especially in the relative indoor darkness), or scavenging, and finally, their further movement during attempts to clean the house. Residence construction may disturb earlier buried components, especially given the desire to occupy a semi-subterranean dwelling during the winter.

Acknowledging these problems, we can move forward with a series of predictions of how this cultural system of deep reciprocity and proper behavior should have symbolically imprinted a pattern on the archaeological record. First, food resources were seasonally patterned. Consumption of them was also seasonally constrained, but storage technology weakened these constraints. Technology, being dependent on resources, was likely seasonally patterned but was probably generalized to be multi-functional across resources as much as possible. Personalized hunting technology may likely reflect materials that the individual could directly acquire before manufacture. The growing preference for organic raw materials over stone may reflect this belief system. Certain high-quality raw materials that might only be acquired through long-distance trade might be avoided for everyday personal hunting use. Copper reflects ideas of wealth, luck, and social prestige. The concepts of hunting luck should be reflected as personal adornment items inadvertently lost at kill and carcass processing sites. Toolkits and their raw materials should reflect gendered divisions of labor. It may have been more acceptable to use raw materials that had come into contact with multiple individuals for carcass processing toolkits. Increased crafting tools in a village site may reflect the age divisions of labor, where elderly individuals may have been crafting tools as a livelihood, and children and apprentices may have been practicing manufacturing skills. Hearths could represent both crafting and food preparation behaviors.

Symbolic behaviors should result in visible archaeological patterning in predictable ways. Archaeological patterning should be reflective of the practice of *'engii*. Cultural purification rights should be observable, and zooarchaeological remains are expected to reflect reciprocity/sharing. The concepts of *'engii* should be reflected in technological life histories and labor divisions by gender and age class. Zooarchaeological patterning should reflect the avoidance of certain animals and the absence of specific anatomical sections based on adequate transportation and consumption practices. The concept of possible impurity through interpersonal contact should pattern on raw material acquisition; trade materials might only be used for more generalized tasks, while materials found within territories might be more valued for personal technological use.

Resource acquisition and processing were divided by gender and age class, and technology and band movements may reflect this. Bands should be increasingly observed through time to use local resources more intensively within principal watersheds through time, with exotic resources becoming rarer. Resources found outside those watersheds should become considered more exotic as band movements become more constricted. As mobility decreases and sedentism rises, more time should be invested in technology and material culture that does not need to be adapted to a highly mobile lifestyle. Increased social cooperation means technological investment by an increased variety of actors and increased variety of trade items. It should be symbolically recognized as codified distribution behaviors and expectations of reciprocity.

WT was facilitated by a logistic mobility system that funneled resources within watersheds to centralized seasonal villages. Resource rights to these stream-based territories were typically extended to outsiders only through kinship ties. The Moiety kinship system affected residential house and village construction strategies; larger villages should be identified through the presence of unique, differentiated, great houses, reflecting the expectations of non-kin lifelong partnerships, the need to shelter extended family members, symbolic rules of deep reciprocity, and the expectation to host potlatches. The large, rectangular houses were likely an innovation created in response to the non-kin lifelong partnership. They could be a proxy for the antiquity of the practice of the dual moiety system. Multiple house forms were used, and many of the other forms, being more straightforward and practical in style, likely predate this social charter.

Clan reorganization along Moiety sides was a nonviolent stress response to growing populations and migrations. It should be recognized as increased demographic pressure, resulting in decreased mobility and intensification of local resources. Potlatching and wealth aggrandizement via reciprocal gift exchange should be represented in the need for storage and large communal buildings. Large quantities of faunal remains and storage facilities may reflect extensive social cooperation. Not all pit features indicate food caching. Pit features can indicate a wide variety of behaviors, including residences, food processing, food storage, hearths, births, burials, and other behaviors. Burning events at village sites may reflect seasonal landscape clearing or ritual village abandonment, rather than being a sign of interpersonal violence.

CONCLUSION

This ethnographic summary represents an idealized picture of how the Middle Tanana people interacted with the world, with each other, and how the spheres of various animals and spirits were expected to respond in return. Everything about an individual's life was framed within the dual context of deep reciprocity codified through *'engii. 'Engii* could affect group dynamics and governed all aspects of everyday life. One knew they had achieved the place of perfection, *hutlaane* (KY), through the sense of *ch'eghwtsen'* (LT), when the great love that bound all of creation was personally experienced (MT reconstruction uncertain). This experience produced a sense of true belief (Boraas and Peter 2008). The practical application of this personal path is expected to leave recognizable symbolic signatures in the archaeological record. It is important to note that this ethnographic reconstruction brings together information from a wide geographic range. While some cultural practices were indeed widely shared across the region, others likely differed from village to village, a proposition challenging to control for.

By definition, an ideology is simply a Platonic form that can never be perfectly achieved. In actual, everyday life, not all people in a given society will live up to their expected social charter. The dual concepts of *'engii* and positive reciprocity provided a guide that each individual and group was supposed to use, informing all decisions, gender roles, identity-appropriate behaviors, and their intersection with the universe. There were likely plenty of instances where individuals did not make a culturally defined optimal choice.

Tying this into the theoretical constructs of this text, risk-averse choices that would result in a full belly, perceived safety for oneself and family, and confidence that resources would remain available and accessible throughout the year was considered optimal. Optimality was informed through the sacred fulfillment of *'engii*: to take nothing more than necessary unless one planned to gift the surplus or conduct trade. Gifting back to the realms of nature that had produced goods and to people considered competitors ensured a benevolent future. Identifying and quantifying optimality in the archaeological record is explored in the following chapter.

The Dene recognized that even given the best planning, the universe was unpredictable, and all contingencies could not be planned for. Social mechanisms were developed as a contingency. These included cultural values for innovation and, more importantly, the development of extensive kinship networks throughout the region, dictated by the moiety system, and a social mechanism for binding non-kin together for life. These social networks should assist in the diffusion of technology, ideology, and genetics. The potlatch system eased social tensions due to unequal socially determined access to resources or widespread ecological resource shortfall. Marrying sons out to other villages ensured access to neighboring resource areas if needed through newly formed kinship rights. Spreading out kin across the region locked down extensive landscape knowledge. Ecosystem engineering was minimal but practiced through landscape burning, tree cultivation, and seasonal fish farming. The Dene fundamentally believed that resources were reciprocally enhanced positively. If they treated the environment and animals with respect and gratitude, the landscape would be obliged to gift them back whatever they needed in abundance.

Chapter Three

Complexity and Optimality in the Archaeological Record

In August of 2014, myself and five other archaeologists were conducting surveys in the Middle Susitna Valley, one of the few places in southcentral Alaska that has remained relatively untouched by Euro-American material culture during the Territorial and Statehood periods. The surveys were in response to a proposed major hydroelectric project, and each day our two crews would be ferried by Robinson R44 helicopters from our basecamp at Stephan Lake to our research locations. As our small three-person crews were mapping sites or searching landforms for cultural remains, we would often encounter wildlife, that was generally unaccustomed to humans. Some days bull caribou would run circles around our crew, both curious and scared at our unexpected presence; at one moment running up close to us and quickly veering off. We interpreted their behavior as being curious about our unique presence in a land otherwise devoid of humans; but perhaps as the traditions said, they were indeed offering us their bodies, running off insulted that we turned down their personal sacrificial gift of food.

On later flights, we watched as disparate groups of caribou began to coalesce. On those flights, the caribou could be hard to distinguish from the surrounding underbrush unless they were moving, but finally, one morning I looked below us and saw a group appear that seemed to have no outer boundaries to the herd. Thousands of animals had come together, milling about on a prominent plateau. Later wildlife population estimates suggested that the herd numbered over 46,000 animals then (ADF&G 2020), and for the following three days smaller groups began splintering off, moving east following their ancient migrations across the southern Alaska Range foothills. Their drive to migrate was so strong that they would move through our survey locations, generally unbothered by our presence even when we found ourselves face to face in the thick spruce forest. Finally, after those three days were over, not a single caribou remained in the basin. In the space of a week the 100 mi² landscape had gone from a region full of large-game food options to one completely devoid of that food staple, and the experience left a lasting impression on me of how that must have felt to the ancestral Ahtna families of the valley.

For decades, archaeologists have worked out difficult statistical methods for understanding how people of the past experienced food security, made dietary choices, and tried to foresee and forestall future caloric shortfalls. These are informed through recent wildlife and ethnographic observations, which help us to construct models that link disparate facts about past diet economies into a coherent representation, and are especially helpful for learning how past periods of stress were mitigated.

The previous chapter provided a comprehensive summary of Middle Tanana culture, providing an internal theoretical framework for how that should have affected the regional archaeological record. That is an example of the basis of the direct historical approach, used by North American archaeologists since the 1920s to interpret the recent precolonial record just preceding a region's historical documentation through ethnohistoric comparisons. It can lose interpretive efficacy as one excavates deeper back in time, where chances of cultural change continue to increase. Since then, archaeologists have developed methods and theories to guide data collection and interpretation for past cultures that do not have any recent analogs.

This chapter provides a quick summary of external academic theories currently used to guide archaeological interpretations. Using these frameworks derived from both Alaska Native and Western observational and experimental sciences together should provide a holistic path toward understanding the past. The latter portion of this book will focus on two archaeological sites from the Middle Tanana, Swan Point and Pickupsticks. The excavations of them have recovered upward of 100,000 artifacts collected over thirty years. The site was located on lands owned by the State of Alaska and was recovered by projects sponsored by the Alaska State Office of History and Archaeology (OHA). The recovered artifacts were curated by Dr. Holmes at the OHA laboratory in Anchorage, slowly being added to each year. By the time this work commenced, the collection had filled over thirty boxes and several shelves of artifact trays.

Why are theoretical structures so important? Each artifact contains an infinite number of quantifiable facts; thus, no researcher can measure them all. Every researcher who has investigated the collection has first decided what small subset of facts (known as variables) they will measure and collect. The variables needed are identified through research models, which are used to derive predictive conclusions depending on how well they support the modeled hypotheses. Facts are organized through models, and models are organized through theoretical paradigms, which are responsive to philosophical critique.

A vast number of national resources have been dedicated worldwide toward uncovering, understanding, and capitalizing on the reconstructed past. In a globalized market-driven political economy, the past is considered a non-renewable resource that can be exploited for any number of reasons. As such, a wide variety of theoretical perspectives, models, and methods have arisen and are available for interpretive use. In such an environment, there can be no "pure" theoretical approach. Just as cultural sharing occurs naturally between neighboring groups, these academic camps also borrow from each other's strengths and highlight each's weaknesses. In such an intellectual climate, the following work should be considered a merging of themes and valuable methods and models. It reflects the investigator's formal North American education and builds upon the processual tradition of structuring hypothetico-deductive investigative concepts regarding economic resource production, flow, and consumption (Binford 1978). The settlement features explored here provide a glimpse into households. Subsequently, post-processual ideas about the division of labor by gender and age-graded identities (Conkey and Spector 1984), the culture-specific entangled life histories of things and people (Hodder 2011), inform a discussion of Neo-Marxist explorations into the concepts of power, group membership, and social mechanisms designed to ease tensions arising from these situations (Moore 1986; Tringham 2012, 83–85), and an anarchist/collective action-influenced perspective on the reflexive agencies between social elites and community members who wield power collectively (e.g., Furholt et al. 2020). These behavioral interpretations are bolstered through investigations of site formation processes (i.e., Schiffer 1987).

The data sets used here focus on the later years between about 8,000–70 cal BP of the Holocene Epoch, which began with dramatic global warming conditions around 11,700 cal BP. A significant portion of it is primarily devoted to the past 3,000 years. It is argued that the archaeological remains at these two sites relate directly to the ancestors of the regional Alaska Natives that were historically encountered by Euro-Americans in the Middle Tanana region, justifying the linguistic and ethnohistoric-informed interpretive lenses (Steward 1942), further informed through the perspective of intersectionality (Leone et al. 2005). The primary archaeological data used here was collected by myself and Dr. Holmes and represents a dataset likely biased by both natural taphonomy and cultural behaviors. We cannot fully reconstruct the original conditions (such as time of year, resource availability, stress from neighboring groups, group health, etc.) that influenced the cultural, linguistic, and artifact assemblages referenced here. In order to minimize as many spurious or circular inferences as possible, the following theoretical paradigms and models are used to structure this study. Further models are referenced as necessary later.

OPTIMAL FORAGING THEORY

One of the theoretical approaches used here is grounded in Human Behavioral Ecology (HBE) derived from Optimal Foraging Theory (OFT). HBE focuses on identifying environmental and economic situations conducive for humans to optimize their energy capture (Bettinger 2009; Surovell 2003, 2009). This energy is encapsulated in all material forms (sunlight, atmosphere, minerals, plants, animals) and the states of energetic transfer between them. It attempts to understand the types of cultural, economic, and ecological states (qualitative character/structure) and conditions (quantitative composition/amount) that structure those transferal circumstances. Two outcomes are generally predicted. Either immediate survival choices may be considered rational and risk-averse, or long-term energy optimization on a system at the expense of the short-term capture is considered the rational choice. It recognizes that environment and economy exist as a complex system where multiple factors are in a constant state of independent and dependent flux (Reiches et al. 2009; Tucker and Taylor 2007).

Actors then are predicted to read their economic system within which they live, and over time consume it in a rational, optimal, risk-averse way. Biologists and anthropologists have operationalized these OFT models since the 1960s by making observations in living communities. Their data provide the laboratory from which paleontologists and archaeologists create inferences about the past. When applied to archaeology, proxies identified for measuring optimization are determined from modeling faunal and technological assemblages as diet consistency problems and mobility (e.g., Byers and Ugan 2005; Yesner 1981; Zeanah et al. 1995). Archaeologists generally only apply OFT models heuristically as an explanatory mechanism for observed, *post hoc* processes.

HBE models are designed to produce deterministic linear outcomes, enhancing their predictive power and utility. Linear processes and behaviors are relatively easily modeled. As it measures adaptation to resource equilibria, it is most appropriate to use in cases where long-term economic/environmental health is evident and predictable. In these cases, cultural behaviors and technology adapting to the system have likely entered a stasis-like innovation state, and new optimizations are generally not expected to occur.

HBE assumes that persons act as rational actors (Cosmides and Tooby 1994), in the same vein as most traditional economic theory models (Bicchieri 2003; Hollis and Nell 1975). However, "rational" is a subjective term that cannot be consistently defined cross-culturally or even between persons within similar social groups. Some actors find success by capitalizing on high-risk situations, and cultural values can support these behaviors. Economists have responded to that problem and the difficulty of modeling the increased unpredictability of such situations by building upon psychological models (Becker 1962; Godelier 2012; Tirol 2002). These models attempt to measure how much the rational actor's role in decision-making processes occurs within a given time frame (Femenia 2000; Richardson 2010; Yamagishi et al. 2009). The studies suggest that risk mitigation concepts evenly inform our internal decision-making processes between the rational actor (i.e., behaviors informed through long-term experiences) and the emotional actor (i.e., nonrational behavioral decisions informed through spur-of-the-moment needs; 'fight or flight') decisions.

OFT excited the processualist archaeology movement. It provided robust mathematical models with which to test behavioral models and link middle range theory to high-range theory (see Winterhalder and Smith 1981). Anthropological and archaeological studies extensively explored OFT applications during the 1980s. Their conclusions suggested that when a long-term predictable and stable economic system was present, humans working within that system would show adaptive tendencies toward energetic optimization by using conservative, economizing behaviors regarding energy expenditure and capture practices (Kaplan and Hill 1985; Whitehead and Hope 1991). However, this was inconsistently documented across social groups. It became understood that OFT models were challenging to operationalize for human social systems for several reasons. These were our broad, omnivorous diets, complex culturally informed consumption mechanisms, and differing culturally specific interpretations of success given similar environmental conditions. Economic choices mirror dietary choices, and both are informed through cultural values. Due to this and the difficulty quantifying past independent environmental variables, archaeologists can generally only use OFT models for exploratory and explanatory qualitative thought exercises. OFT's strength is that it can highlight adaptive, conservative behaviors, and from there, suggest periods of increased cultural stability. Its weakness is that it cannot inform observed adaptive responses to periods of instability through any comparative analysis.

COMPLEXITY THEORY

In order to understand what happens when cultural, economic, and environmental systems are in a state of dynamic change, we also need to utilize a different body of theory that informs nonlinear patterns and models. At any given time, the local environment contains a finite potential quantity of energy in the form of sunlight, atmosphere, minerals, plants, and animals. When the local energy sink potential is relatively increased, and those new forms become a long-term event, humans can learn to adapt to it, consuming and conserving it. Periodically, however, every energy system will eventually collapse or be subsumed within another (Turner and Sabloff 2012). In these economically shifting situations, humans may adapt by resorting to non-conservative risk-prone behaviors that provide immediate, rather than long-term, benefits. Recognizing this, humans have successfully adapted culturally and biologically to both situational long-term energy conservation and short-term risk-mitigation strategies. Modeling these behaviors requires both linear and nonlinear theoretical constructs (Bettinger 2009).

Until the time comes that the global ecosystem on this planet exceeds the annual solar energy capture, there remains the potential for energy systems to continue to evolve in complexity utilizing the excess energy input. Organisms and cultural systems are expected to respond by evolving and increasing or decreasing their behavioral and cultural repertoires in response to the energetic systems they exploit. Chaotic systems are then considered to be far more necessary than long-term stable periods for evolutionary novelties to develop. More complex energetic states will drive human response trends toward increasingly complex biological, cultural, and technological systems and might signal behaviors that favor innovation over conservation (Berkes and Jolly 2001). If cultural systems are demonstrated to be supporting conservativism and a lack of innovation, systemic energy trends have likely been stable over a significant period of time and space.

Complexity Theory models the universe as a series of interlocking systems throughout which energy is continuously flowing and ebbing. In the absence of new energy inputs, all energetic or economic systems will eventually lose energy and dissipate. A balance will attempt to be achieved between the driving force and the constant rate of thermodynamic loss. This balance is termed an attractor (or critical) state. This attractor state will facilitate the survival of systems within it, favoring their energy balance and conservation (Chekrouna et al. 2011). Eventually, the resulting near-equilibrium state, given enough energy loss, shifts to a repeller state, as the constant loss of energy will cause the system's inevitable failure. Subsequently, without a new energy influx, the sub-systems dependent on it become extinct. A new injection of energy (characteristic of dissipative systems) will result in a spontaneous, chaotic structure, where a predictable outcome is no longer a possibility. When a state reaches this phase, a host of new potential equilibrium states then becomes possible (see also Butzer 1980, 1996). Each time an equilibrium state is achieved, it is inherently unique and different from those previous and all those after (Philipson and Schuster 2009; Brogliato et al. 2007).

HBE then provides models appropriate for predicting behavioral optimality within the human cultural states approaching energetic equilibrium, but not the chaotic transitional states between them. Actors experiencing a life dominated by a near-equilibrium state would be remiss not to capitalize on the system's predictability, increasing the likelihood of linear behaviors, rational decisions, minimized technological innovation, and promotion of conservative and risk-averse economics. Here, energy is being gradually lost from the system, not gained. Therefore, any organism dependent on the system would predictably optimize and conserve their use of the remaining gross energy, increase their fitness, slow the thermodynamic loss rate, and forestall the coming inevitable unstable repeller state. New energy sources are sought for acquisition during the repeller state, and the previous near-stable economic, ecological, energetic, cultural, and behavioral systems are thrown into chaos.

Chaotic systems, whose outcomes are fundamentally unpredictable, favor adaptive behavioral strategies that focus on immediate payoff. Short-term energy optimization is unattainable. It is a highly variable, unstable state. Those who can adapt best to the immediate shifting stressors will survive long enough to see the attractor state become an eventual equilibrium state. Small initial fluctuations, such as population reduction or expansion of a critical food species; group migration into a neighboring area, can have dramatic long-term results in adaptive cultural or behavioral trends. An initial shift in diet breadth may trigger a long-term technological change. For example, a group may transition to intensified, time-consuming, but energy-efficient, group-oriented net and weir fishing as opposed to individualized, less-efficient leister/spearfishing. Thus, their diet and culture may begin to reflect these values. Or, one group's migration into a neighboring drainage might set off a cascade of additional domino-effect further migrations if other band movements are likewise disrupted. Alternatively, settlement strategies might shift as both groups seek agreement on socio-cultural innovations that utilize the same space and resources.

Long-term changes are those being low in frequency, incremental, directional, and cumulative at a regional to global scale (such as climate change) (Dincauze 2000, 70–71). They usually correlate with trending shifts of landscape use, cultural and technological changes, and biophysical changes and are often interpreted as the "human response." The smallest unit of chronological measurement for these events is usually measured by the decade, century, or even millennium. While observable through statistical trends, the human response is rarely directly observable as those changes occur in real-time, and is potentially visible only through the use of trans-generational memory aids, that is, oral history. Human responses to long-term system changes can also have measurable effects on feedback mechanisms.

Responses to short-term system changes resulting in visible shifts in technology, land-use strategies, or even one that elicits a biophysical expression are predicted to be rare, unique, but not impossible or unknown. Responses to long-term system changes are much more likely to produce these visible trends. Many cultural changes were likely a response to internal social stress caused by undesirable external ecological or social factors. They were probably negatively perceived and only conservatively adapted to after-the-fact, as external conditions persisted or worsened. Therefore, their visibility may be affected by lag time (Butzer 1982; Dincauze 2000, 77). Humans are uniquely adapted to succeeding in both systems. They will use conservative behaviors to adapt to systems that are in long-term stasis and risk-prone behaviors to adapt to systems that are in unstable, chaotic states (Byrne and Callaghan 2014; Elliott and Kiel 2004; Thaler 2015; Waldrop 1992; Wiessner 1982).

NICHE CONSTRUCTION THEORY

Being a species well-adapted to both extremes of ordered and chaotic states suggests that we can inherently recognize when energy systems are approaching instability and find innovative cultural, economic, and biological adaptations to ease those shifts and promote energetic equilibria. Our species' internal and external ability to adapt to environmental fluctuations, extreme states, and periodic uncertainty is well documented (e.g., Richerson and Boyd 2008). Niche Construction Theory (NCT) is designed to study how organisms alter their local environments in ways that improve their survival and reproduction (Odling-Smee et al. 1996). Organisms exchange energy with their ecological systems by consuming food and emitting waste as they interact with their environment and respond to physical changes within a surrounding landscape. The transfer of energy can have positive, negative, and benign effects on the environment, with measurable properties (both intended and unintended) that enhance that specific organism's survival and reproduction rate (Odling-Smee et al. 2003, 419).

There are two primary responses that organisms use when faced with selective pressures within a system. The first being relocation, which can be both short-term and long-term, cyclical or permanent. The second being perturbation, when an organism responds by staying in place and changing one or more internal behaviors or external things within their immediate ecosystem (Odling-Smee et al. 2003). These situational responses can be either inceptive, where an organism initiates the relocation/perturbation response, or counteractive, where an organism attempts to negate *in situ* the environmental change that is or has already occurred.

NCT integrates evolutionary studies of ecosystem creation, facilitation, and maintenance by organisms (Smith 2007a). It explores how species modify their environments in such a way that they can facilitate another's survival (Odling-Smee et al. 2003). NCT was introduced to evolutionary biology in the early 1980s (Lewontin 1982, 1983) and is also referred to as ecosystem engineering (Jones et al. 1994 and 1997a). It is explanatory for cases where animals respond to natural selection stimuli by actively modifying their environments, leading to both immediate and long-term benefits (Bleed 2006). This process creates a participant feedback system where some independent environmental pressures combine with the organism's characteristics and facilitate stability. The NCT methods have been demonstrated as having specific evolutionary consequences, facilitating cross-species co-evolution, and remain controversial (Boni and Feldman 2007; Day et al. 2003; Laland and O'Brien 2010).

The bulk of NCT research is often focused on studying a given scenario's feedback mechanism and is rarely concerned with the initial causal factor's development (Broughton et al. 2010; Donahue 2005; Laland and O'Brien 2010). It has been conceived as a component of the extended human phenotype (Dawkins 1990). NCT provides a basic model for beginning to understand predator/prey facilitation and may be useful for generating hypotheses of plant and animal domestication processes (Kylafis and Loreau 2008; Smith 2007b; Zeder 2016) and demographics (Borenstein et al. 2005; Ihara and Feldman 2004; Lehmann 2007; Sterelny 2007). However, it can be limited and fall short of providing a mechanism for species succession, resource depletion, and competition (Jones et al. 1997b; Kylafis and Loreau 2010; Laland et al. 1999).

SOCIAL COMPLEXITY

As the previous theoretical frameworks indicate, human societies are dependent upon their resource extraction networks designed for energy consumption and conservation. Therefore, over time, the principle of energy conservation is reflected in the complexity of those social and economic networks. Energy networks capture and transform raw energy from its state in the environment (demonstrated through OFT and NCT models) to humans and their settlement strategies (e.g., Rappaport 1971). As net energy capture increases, its output should be reflected in increased complexity of energy processing networks (i.e., technology), increased adaptive mechanisms to store and preserve that extra energy, and increased adaptive social complexity (Barton 2013; Binford 2001; Oswalt 1976). The intensification of niche resources through agricultural development and maintenance has historically provided many societies the net gain in energy needed for high social complexity to arise. It represents a single vector in a multifactorial problem. Social complexity represents a complicated spectrum, and agriculture, statehood, industrialization, and capitalism should not be considered the final determining products of long-term net energy gains (Bleed and Matsui 2010; Smith 2011).

Increased social complexity consumes energy at a higher rate, and if the system persists over time, it will lend itself toward conservative behaviors that sustain this complexity. This process should be especially evident in cultural learning mechanisms. As complexity increases, more time must be invested in either maintaining or innovating their behaviors and social relationships (Mills 2017; Mills et al. 2018). Maintained or conserved cultural expressions may be preserved long after their favorable initial energy costs become negligible. A change in the behavioral system may require a substantial internal energy investment. Learning networks should reflect complexity through increased standardization and specialization across space and time. Raw material extraction and processing should become more complex, and maintenance should become standardized. Increased complexity and time maintaining trade networks should be recognized by standardization of routes, meeting times, and trade relationships. It should also favor specialists who seek to increase their own wealth and status through the ritualized production, acquisition, and consumption of prestige objects beyond the typical consumer/producer goods flow (Earle and Spriggs 2015). Technological complexity, coupled with any demographic expansion, is expected to give rise initially to a wide variety of localized forms, and standardization of that complexity will follow, representing conservation of complexity; applicable to migration and colonization scenarios (Costin and Hagstrum 1995; Kline and Boyd 2010). It should reflect time-since-adoption, selective pressures, and level of extra-group interaction (Kline and Boyd 2010). Therefore, it should be observable as a regional spread, increased technological investment in specialized tools, rules of reciprocity, clothing, transportation forms, and residential structures, analogous to genetic drift (Neiman 1995; Shennan 2001). If demographic pressure is low but isolated populations are actively interacting, all forms should trend toward increasing complexity and decreased localized differentiation given widespread regional adoption

(Powell et al. 2009). High demographic pressure and active intergroup inter-action tend to produce localized distinctions as competitive adaptive traits (Henrich 2004, 2006).

HOUSEHOLD ARCHAEOLOGY

The post-processual reaction to the processualist's normative approach of stitching facts together into a single cohesive theory about the past recog-nized the necessity for understanding cultural systems as an equally crucial interpretive framework that can inform taphonomic bias. In this paradigm, the built medium becomes a passive yet symbolic backdrop that informs and inspires the social activities that took place there (Briz i Godino and Madella 2013). It also heavily underscored the need to understand the pres-ervation bias of archaeological remains and how this informs interpretations (Hodder 1999). Therefore, within the context of household archaeology, the microlevel of investigation (e.g., micromorphology, isotope, phytolith, pol-len, and residue analyses) vitally informs site-specific taphonomic studies, spatial variation of activity areas, and reconstructions of the deposition and life-history of places (Briz I Godino et al. 2011; Lancelotti and Madella 2012; Weiner 2010; Zurro et al. 2009).

Household archaeology represents an outgrowth of processualist archaeol-ogy that began its development during the 1970s (Ashmore and Wilk 1988; Wilk and Rathje 1982). It filled the needed function of a small-scale observa-tion of the fundamental social location where activities happened: the home (Bourdieu 1970). Lewis Binford (1980) modeled resources as being directed toward this sphere and being processed along the way. The alternative to that logistic mobility model was his residential mobility model, where the household unit traveled to these extraction locales. In either scenario, the domestic space, where child-rearing, food provisioning, and elder care occur, was considered the focal point of human activity (Conkey and Gero 1991; Kuhn and Stiner 2019).

As initially constructed, current cultural-historic frameworks consist of models of power and social functions typically from a traditional Western (Euro-American) top-down approach. They focus on authoritative frame-works as the drivers of social mobilization and cultural change via models of power, ideology, and social structure. When frameworks of feminist theory (Hendon 1996), gender archaeology (Moore 1986), Neo-Marxism (Frankel and Webb 2006; Tringham 1990), and anarchism (Furholt et al. 2020) were incorporated to highlight agency, identity, and inequality, the average house-hold, rather than authoritarian figureheads, became the focal unit where social agency and mechanisms of cultural transformation were actively negotiated (such as ideology, identity, class, and gender roles). On a small scale, social changes reflect and affect social changes at a large scale (Furholt et al. 2020; Moore 1986).

Household archaeology highlights the intersectionality of gender and age-graded identity roles. Gender studies have been criticized as emphasizing dualistic masculine/feminine perspectives built on a projection of traditional Euro-American ideals (e.g., Geller 2009). Problems can arise when utilizing the direct historic approach for ethnographic reconstructions of non-male behaviors. Many original ethnographies were produced before developing and applying feminist and queer theory and can reflect emphasized Victorian-Era ideals of social cisgender spheres (Fulkerson 2017, 3). Queer archaeology emphasizes the reality of additional nonbinary gender roles or nonconformity to defined roles (e.g., Alberti 2013). Representations of the intersection of these identities and their social functions have to be carefully approached to ensure that interpretation reflects past cultural realities.

The basic social construct of the human family is one aspect that marks our species as fundamentally unique from others (Kuhn and Stiner 2019). The level of effort expended through behaviors and energy dedicated to the natal family's success is what marks these as exceptional, as they are not wholly exclusive to our species. Their premise builds upon three earlier themes (Isaac 1978; Lovejoy 1981): resource sharing, role specialization, male assistance in raising children, and a fourth, which I posit is equally essential: care of adults (infirm or elderly).

These themes are held as a necessity due to the extremely long time it takes for human children to develop physically, culturally, and psychologically into an adult (Kuhn and Stiner 2019, 307). Healthy child development requires a cohesive, cooperating, temporally stable community. For a foraging society, the base camp becomes the focal point of safety, shelter, resources, socialization, and work. Individual stress is significantly mitigated when all individuals in the group agree on their social charter, the basis of which is cooperation. Cooperating behaviors, economic arrangements, and social activities are fundamentally signaled in the archaeological record by sharing food and non-food resources. This cooperation and care are extended to adults who benefit from care for short or long-term infirmities or old age.

Male provisioning behaviors might better be framed as a risk-mitigation strategy designed to increase cooperation beyond the natal family (defined as sexual partners and their offspring), especially when considering the vast energetic and social expenditures needed to raise a well-adjusted child. Male provisioning behaviors are often viewed as fundamentally selfish, being a useful activity in which one can increase personal prestige and gain more mating rights (e.g., Hawkes 1991; Hawkes and Bliege-Bird 2002). While this statement certainly carries truth, it may be more informative to frame higher-risk male provisioning strategies as designed to promote social cooperation across multiple natal families, non-related individuals, and various persons who cannot provision themselves (e.g., children and the elderly). In this sense, it becomes a necessary strategy to promote cooperation and mitigate social stress both within the community and between communities.

Household behavior patterns should not only be equated with architecture, familial reconstructions, or even the domestic sphere (Blanton 1994; Hendon 1996; Kent 1990; Stanish 1989). Instead, they represent the remains of all social activities that happened in that specific space and environment. These encompass the time in space from preconstruction to abandonment and subsequent taphonomic occurrences. Households can also inhabit multiple structures and extended areas (Sulas and Madella 2012) and should not be assumed as fully representative of that sphere. They are part of a more extensive socio-technological system structured to reflect planning and contingency decision making within a broader social network.

CONCLUSION

When applied to the study of human cultural systems, the HBE paradigm has been both rewarding and problematic. The body of research has proven most useful in studying specialization and conservative behaviors. Generalist foraging and opportunistic behaviors tend to complicate the models, though researchers still find utility with them. When applied to humans, the utility of the models is increasingly challenging to operationalize, given the increasing complexity of human and environmental systems. However, they continue to be informative, especially in ethnographic applications, providing a framework of simplistic economic hypothesis construction and testing. Their utility lessens, however, when they are applied to the past human artifact record. The framework that HBE provides has been the most useful for conceiving archaeological hypotheses for reasons of adaptation, change, and stasis in the record. HBE has not solved the ever-elusive, high-range theory sought by processualists. It does provide utility for generating hypotheses and when used in conjunction with other models, especially when considering NCT.

OFT models can provide optimization mechanisms to resource abundance. NCT provides a mechanism for understanding cultural systems' responses during present or future times of resource stress, thereby generating interesting frameworks of study for archaeological problems. NCT provides us with a mechanism for understanding how human systems adapt to and survive unforeseen chaotic events that upend system equilibria, such as extinction, climate and ecological change, and demographic shifts. Social complexity frames the processes within social relationships that led to and sustained complex, energy-consuming behaviors across individuals whose adaptive utility is beyond the simplistic OFT models. It provides mechanisms for operationalizing CT discussion into human behavioral contexts. Household archaeology (analysis and interpretation of residential features) can provide a glimpse into the fundamental social interactions of the past. The analysis and interpretation of residential features through this lens can offer a glimpse into the fundamental social and natural interactions of the past. Within the Neo-Marxist perspective, these places become the nexus of cultural change and represent a reflection of their societies as a whole.

Chapter Four

The Traditional Place Names and Language of the Middle Tanana Dene

I climbed up the steep hill, which had been partially dug away for highway quarry material. The steep, south-facing slopes along the central Tanana River support a unique micro-ecosystem of steppe tundra: flowering dryland sedges and grasses that are reminiscent of the high sagebrush prairies of southwestern Montana, where I grew up. These are considered to be analogs for the dominant early Holocene ecosystem, which supported herds of wapiti and bison in the Tanana prior to the expansion of the thick spruce taiga 6,000 years ago. I walked toward the top of the bluff and found the old excavations of a site called Broken Mammoth by the Euro-American archaeologists. This site was one of the first important Pleistocene sites found that marked Shaw Creek Valley as important for archaeologists.

Broken Mammoth also has preserved cultural components dating through-out the Holocene into the recent past, not surprising given its beautiful vantage overlook of the Middle Tanana Valley. Its original Middle Tanana name was *Daats'ehwt'ee Denh Ddhele'* (we have elevated place mountain [Kari 2015]). From it, one could see the mighty *Tene Naa* (trail river: the Tanana River) and where it begins at the high rocky knolls of *Tthehwnaneede'aani* (rock that stands up) and *Xwteth Cheeg Ddhele'* (pass mouth mountain) at the mouth of the *Xwteth Cheeg Na'* (pass mouth stream: the Delta River). Just below the bluff I stood on was the Shaw Creek boat launch where a protohistoric village or trade fair site of the *Debedee Na' Iin* (Sheep Creek People) once was. Looking to the southwest was a ridge called *Ttheech'el* (broken rock), a name also shared with a ridge to the east overlooking *Ttheech'el Menn'* (broken rock lake: Quartz Lake). At the base of *Ttheech'el* was the village site of *Takon' Ndiig Cheeg* (clear water mouth). The families of this village utilized the watershed of *Niidhaayh Na* (gravel stream: Dry Delta Creek), which flowed south to north to meet the *Tene Naa* (trail water: Tanana River).

A mile north was another site, Mead, which also has preserved terminal Pleistocene and Holocene cultural components but no elicited traditional name. The extensive wetlands throughout the lower valley are an important stop for seasonal migrating waterfowl. In mid-May, the cacophony from these flocks is thunderous and difficult to sleep through at night. From there, a person can look to the northeast up the Shaw Creek Valley and see several glittering lakes known as *Ch'etthįį' Bene'* (meat lake). Close to them is the Swan Point site, whose reconstructed traditional name might be *Ch'etthįį' Denh* or *Ch'etthįį' Ddhele'* (meat place or meat hill). In the distance, one can see the valley of *Udzih Ndiig* (caribou stream, whose meaning has been borrowed into the English name: Caribou Creek). The stream flows within a mile of the Pickupsticks site, another ancestral village site of the Shaw Creek people, with no specific elicited or reconstructed traditional name.

This chapter explores aspects of historical linguistics (language change), lexicography (dictionary compilation), and etymology (word origins and the historical development of their meanings) of traditional place names in order to gain an understanding of the linguistic antiquity of the Dene in the Tanana Valley. It is informed by Dr. Jim Kari's lifetime of work in the ongoing production of several language-specific dictionaries (Ahtna, Dena'ina, Koyukon, Lower Tanana, Middle Tanana, with lesser work in the other Alaska Dene languages). These dictionaries, produced using the software program Lexware, have recently standardized the orthography across these languages. They are cross-referenced by topical and grammatical themes that have influenced the development of analyzable place names lists and robust reconstructions of Proto-Dene. The reconstructed lists and proto-language have developed in tandem with the dictionary work and are a secondary reflection of the former. One significant development from this decades-long lexicographic reconstruction has culminated in the proposed Proto-Dene geolinguistic theory termed the Proto Dene Lex Loci (PDLL: "word/law of location"). It represents "a theory of Dene prehistory that is a composite of geographic information (in Dene place names networks) and Dene lexicographic-etymological information" (Kari 2019b, 44). This chapter focuses on applying the PDLL theory to the Middle Tanana place names and generating comparative insights for cultural-historical frameworks.

In order to understand the cultural time depth of these place names, a correlation model between their language and the archaeological record is explored in subsequent chapters. Constructing and interpreting a sense of connection across archaeological assemblages is a robust process demonstrating causal relationships between temporal, spatial, cultural, and ecological patterns of data and deriving concepts of value and utility (e.g., Binford 1962). Causal mechanisms between language and artifacts can only be shown with great care (Anthony 2007; Hemphill and Mallory 2004; Menk 1980). Genetics, languages, and technology, while they can facilitate each other's dispersal, cannot always be assumed to be deterministically linked (Posth et al. 2018). Therefore, the regional diffusion of archaeological technocomplexes should not be expected to necessarily equate with gene flow or language spread, although they can undoubtedly facilitate each other's success. Aspects of culture, language, and DNA are always shared and borrowed between neighboring groups. If this is strongly demonstrable, proxies for them can be established with some degree of confidence. However, since language is not necessarily a determinant of technological culture or genetic haplotypes, we cannot assume that correlations exist without additional solid evidence.

For the past six decades, the processual approach of Americanist archaeology has driven much of North American archaeological investigatory frameworks, stressing the correlation of constructs of meaning between archaeological assemblages and their original ecosystems and regional traditions. These cultural-historical constructs can also be further enhanced by studying linguistic toponymy (Jones 2016; Klejn et al. 2017; Mayor 2007). Studying traditional place names is one method that allows us a unique temporal, spatial, and culturally bounded glimpse into the ancient past (Barrett and Ko 2016; Kari 2005). Therefore, a study of traditional Middle Tanana toponyms is considered an integral dataset needed to understand the regional archaeological record (Burenhult and Levinson 2008; Levinson 1996). As linguistic artifacts, place names can provide culture-specific regional information of settlement and land-use systems, resource procurement, and travel routes, and some can indicate time depth as well (Kari and Fall 2016, 144).

Defining ancient precolonial ethnolinguistic boundaries using material cultural proxies is complex and can be problematic (Ardener 1989; Craig et al. 2004; Just 1989; Sherratt and Sherratt 1997; Whittle 1996). Speculative work has been done in Alaska with some general success correlating the Arctic Small Tool tradition (ASTt: ~5,000–3,000 cal BP) and other regional coastal-oriented archaeological technocomplexes with the Proto-Eskimo language family. The term Eskimo is widely recognized as a negative ethnonym, and in Canada, it is appropriate to use the term Proto-Inuit. In Alaska, however, the Proto-Eskimo are considered ancestral to Inuit, Yup'ik, Unangan, and Alutiiq people, and also significantly contributed ancestral genetic haplotypes to the Alaska Dene; thus, an appropriate name encompassing them has not yet been put forth (Flegontov et al. 2019). Similar studies correlate the Riverine and Marine Kachemak tradition of southcentral Alaska (~3,300–800 cal BP [Reger and Boraas 1996]) with Proto-Yup'ik-speaking groups (contested by Leer 1991, and recently by Anna Berge, who suggests connections to the proto-Aleut language (personal communication)). The Northern Archaic and

Athabascan traditions have been long been linked with Proto-Dene-speaking groups (Boraas 2002, 2007; Burch 1988; de Laguna 2000 [1947]; Kari 1988, 2005). However, more recent ideas consider an alternative idea that Proto-Dene language might instead be associated with ASTt and its migration from Chukotka (Dumond 2010; Vajda 2018, 2019). A necessary but potentially problematic assumption for these models is that each technocomplex correlates with a singular linguistic entity, a model that is easy to construct as a thought exercise but difficult to find direct evidence for, since none of these languages left written artifacts to confirm presence and antiquity.

THE PROTO DENE LEX LOCI THEORY

From the Dene perspective, people belong to the land, rather than the opposing Euro-American concept that land belongs to the people. Place names tie people, economy, and cosmology together. Naming a place imbues it with meaning and power and allows an individual to participate within that construct. This chapter aims to explore and present the evidence for Middle Tanana linguistic antiquity in Alaska using time-perspective models in a manner that can be consumed and used by archaeologists. The goals here are to (1) present the status of the place name dataset, (2) frame the argument for toponym conservation and observed mechanisms of change, (3) explore the Proto-Dene Lex Loci theory through a geospatial demonstration, and (4) demonstrate how this theoretical approach informs a temporal model of the diffusion of the proto-language into Alaska and its seriation through time.

Today English, part of the Indo-European language family, dominates the Tanana Valley as the primary language used. This dominance is the result of centuries-long trends of global colonial geopolitics and capitalist economics. Prior to this, the Na-Dene language family (also more appropriately known as Athabascan-Eyek-Tlingit (AET) as Haida is now considered unrelated) was the only language family present in the Valley. It was also the most geographically widespread language family in North America, comprising fifty-three languages and encompassing over 1,500,000 miles^2 (Kari 2011b). Na-Dene was primarily represented in today's western Canada and interior Alaska but had also diffused into more southern areas of the Oregon and California Pacific Coast and the American Southwest. This vast spread is considered to be the result of multi-factorial trends over the last 1,200 years, which effectively expanded the prior geolinguistic reach by a factor of 2 or 3 (Matson and Magne 2007; Potter 2010). The point of greatest linguistic diversity within Na-Dene has been documented in northern British Columbia and southern Yukon Territory. That localized diversity presents strong evidence for an ancient proto-language core being centered there, currently called Proto-Dene (termed Proto-Athapaskan in earlier literature) (figure 4.1).

Within Alaska, the Na-Dene language family represents the greatest geographic spread compared to the other Native language families there. By the end of the nineteenth century, it was characterized by twelve languages.

Figure 4.1.   Proto-Dene homeland.

Once vibrantly alive prior to the 1930s, today, these languages struggle for functional survival and are often primarily spoken and understood only by a handful of community elders. However, efforts continue on multiple fronts to ensure their survival. The process of defining these languages was complicated, as they are not clearly distinguished from each other (Krauss and Golla 1981) and are better characterized as dialectical continuums (McKennan 1981, 563). Recent lexicography work has now confirmed that Middle Tanana qualifies as a separate twelfth language and not merely a dialect of Lower Tanana as it has been classified previously. Middle Tanana is defined by the absence of definitive tones found in the neighboring Lower Tanana and Tanacross languages (Holton 2010; Kari 2015). It exhibits a distinct vowel system, syllable structure, and unique morphophonemics.

Nearly a generation of federal and religious-supported efforts to stamp out the Alaskan Native languages occurred before academic and local Indigenous efforts began in the 1970s to document, study, and revitalize those traditional languages. These early studies and insights into Alaska's traditional languages and place names continue to be valued and actively consumed by many regional archaeologists, assisting in understanding the past.

Historical linguistics provides comparative methodologies that study similarities in languages to identify (1) phonological and morphological relatedness in words and grammatical structure that indicates a common origin, and (2) similarities in words that indicate borrowings from one language to another (Bloomfield 1984; Sapir 1916). These allow for reconstructed relationships between these closely related languages and their ancestral form, Proto-Dene.

To clarify what Proto-Dene is, it represents a reconstructed lexicography of vernacular language. Reconstructed Proto-Dene root words used here are indicated by a preceding asterisk. At the turn of the twentieth century, Alaskan Dene languages had at least two spoken forms, one form for everyday use and one sacred form reserved for ceremonial and shamanic use. Additional gender/career-restricted forms such as midwife speech may have been utilized as well. The ritual form was also traditionally believed to be an older language form. In Gwich'in, it has been posited that the early Anglican missionaries coopted the shamanic form for Christian theological use and translations in the Tukudh Bible (Raboff 2020).

Today, an English dictionary does not represent any single identity group's living parlance but is instead a comprehensive corpus of formal words, archaisms, patois, jargon, and abandoned words. It represents words used by some groups but not others. No English speaker has a full grasp of it, and individuals make common use of words that are not yet recognized by it. Proto-Dene should be understood in the same way; it represents a reconstructed lexicographical language. While the reconstructions are robust, as a whole, it represents words that were spoken in different eras and in different places by differing groups. It represents logical or regular reconstructions but cannot reconstruct irregularly produced words that may have been in use in the past. Therefore, it should not be expected to have ever been a singular body of active speech, any more than an English dictionary is today.

Three groups of traits form the cohesive network in Kari's PDLL theory (Kari and Fall 2016, 144–147) and allow for extensive comparison and analysis in Dene place name networks. The first group is locational, overt, and/or contextual information. These names either convey information overtly through their name or additional contextual information tied to the toponym (e.g., themes of myth, history, tenure, land-use, etc.). The second group is composed of Watershed Tenure (WT) devices. These are pragmatic patterns that enhance the memorization of landscapes and features. The third group is Dene historical linguistic traits. These are grammatical irregularities, irregular morpheme themes, linguistic substrates, opaque semantics, and so on.

The first group emphasizes the rule-driven features of Dene place naming. Some of this information can be overtly obvious from the name's translation (as in one of the Middle Tanana names for the Tanana River below its confluence with the Delta River mouth: *Tene Naa*: (trail water). Some of this information is metonymically implied. For example, all streams have both a mouth and headwaters area, but if "stream mouth" is formally incorporated into a place name (as in the village name *Takon' Ndiig Cheeg* [clear stream mouth]), it implies that a regularly used site was present nearby. Places named "clear water" indicate locations where weirs were commonly constructed to capture migrating anadromous fish runs. If "headwaters" is incorporated into a toponym (as in the name of the upper Shaw Creek stream area *Debe Deendiig Tl'aat* [sheep horn stream headwaters]), it implies that the area was utilized habitually as an autumn hunting ground. When mouth and headwaters are not elicited in a name, those areas would not be expected to have been habitually utilized. Morphologically complex riverine directionals were also incorporated into place names, used for orienting or guiding the observer on typical travels through the landscape. These were especially useful if the country is otherwise unknown to the traveler. Essentially, the place names, when given as a travel narrative, become a culturally bounded cognitive wayfinding or navigation system (O'Meara et al. 2020, 291). Other themes often can only be accounted for if the traditional stories attached to those landscape features are also known.

The second group focuses on naming and grammatical themes. Cross-language comparison of grammatical traits can be problematic if orthographies are not standardized. These orthographic inconsistencies have been minimized in recent corrective cross-language lexicographical work (Kari 2019a). The standardized dictionaries allow for a systematic comparison of linguistic elements across languages and have allowed for a robust reconstruction of Proto-Dene. Within the Northwestern American region traditionally used by all Dene groups, long-term stable regional use of landscapes is evident across languages through WT-patterned use of formalized hydronyms, oronyms, and shared boundary names (Kari 1996a, 1996b).

The Proto-Dene toponymic stem seriation model discussed later focuses on the bipartite elements (sign+generic) used to construct typical Dene place names. The "generic" element is a descriptor that is unique to the individual geographic feature type, such as the stems for -lake, -river, or -mountain (Kari 1996a, 1996b), and the "sign" element distinguishes each feature individually. For example, the Middle Tanana name for Shaw Creek: *Debedee Na'*: the first word *"Debedee"* (sheep horn) refers to the sign element, and the second word *"Na'"* (river) refers to the generic stem (Kari 2015).

The heavily systematic nature of the sign+generic elements within traditional Alaskan Dene toponyms could be patterned mnemonically as themed generative geography, where local features within a specific watershed would often share the sign descriptor, facilitating their memorization. This mnemonic device also demonstrates their development from a person-specific system to a regional cross-community shared symbolic system (Harris and Holton 2019; Kari 2011b, 245–248). The symbolic system is auto-instructional and resulted in increased retention of a greater geographic region by individuals, spatially expanding the shared regions of toponyms, or place name networks among communities. The strain of memorizing the unique names of a locale is thus eased when one needs only to know the themed generic element and the expected metonymic extensions (i.e., the thing of which a place is named for or closely associated with (e.g., Thornton 2008, 93)). It is primarily a practical method of passing on a mental geographic template to persons who had not yet been to a specific region (Kari 2010a) and maintaining local history. This concept was emphasized by Edward J. Glave in 1890 (in Cruikshank 1991, 113) while exploring the Yukon interior:

> Throughout my letter I have retained the native names of geographical points wherever I could learn them. In my opinion, this should always be studied. The Indian names of mountains, lakes and rivers are natural landmarks for the traveler, whoever he may be; to destroy these by substituting words of a foreign tongue is to destroy the natural guides. . . . Another very good reason why these names should be preserved is that some tradition of tribal importance is always connected with them. These people have no written language, but the retention of their native names is an excellent medium through which to learn their history.

Prior to historical record keeping, place name survival was entirely dependent on a shared cultural memory system. The Alaskan Dene utilized no written or pictographic symbolic systems to promote their maintenance. Therefore, as temporal distance increases into the past from the point of recorded documentation, the chance of toponymic shifts occurring also increases unless a mechanism is in place to ensure conservation. An additional stressor on toponym retention is the limit on how many can be memorized, especially in low-demographic regions. Five hundred place names tend to be a universal plateau for memorized toponym retention; informant Shem Pete himself contributed around six hundred in Dena'ina (Hunn 1994; Kari and Fall 2016; Thornton 2008, 72).

Place names were both an intensively personal and a shared community experience, as identity becomes tied with the home landscape. It is essentially a culture-bound sense of space (i.e., O'Meara et al. 2020, 291). Toponyms were also shared inter-communally as members left one band and joined another through marriage or other socioeconomic mechanisms (McKennan 1969). McKennan's (1959) description of lifelong male hunting partnerships emphasized relationships across generations and between different members of different village backgrounds. These formalized relationships could facilitate sharing cultural landscape knowledge about extraterritorial regions and conferred landscape use rights for additional communities. By becoming a shared symbolic, culture-wide mnemonic device, toponyms became actively conserved and maintained independently by numerous actors across vast geography and dispersed across multiple cultures and languages, resistant to change concerning distance and time.

The shared symbolic toponymic system facilitated the conservation of landscape naming, reducing the risk of place name changes or loss through time, ensuring their trend toward long-term conservation and antiquity across a broad, regional swath of consecutive memories. This conservative, symbolic system appears to have been shared multilingually, appearing in all the documented Dene languages of Alaska (Kari 2010b). Conservativism in Dene languages is signaled by the level of analyzability, functionality, and generative geography rules, suggesting it originated within the early history of Dene languages.

The third group focuses on a small percentage of names that can offer clues to potentially founding or otherwise ancient behaviors. The lexicographic and etymological analysis has identified some unique irregularities in the otherwise high degree of semantic analyzability of Dene names. Unique patterns can additionally arise with how landscape feature names are shared, borrowed, or duplicated, across languages (Kari 2019b, 59). Occasionally, the meaning of the names appears to be deliberately obscure, coded as opaque semantics

(Kari and Fall 2016, 144–147). Sometimes, place names also retain the archaic form of a word, such as in the untranslatable name for Salcha village *Sah Cheeget*. Sometimes, the toponyms appear in neighboring languages as a cognate, where both languages share identical meanings within the place names.

Sometimes, the original name provenance (coining location) can be detected. Consider the traditional name for Mt. Hayes; *Xosrotl'odi* (Lower Tanana, who lived northwest of the mountain) and *Xasatl'aadi* (Ahtna, who lived south of the mountain): meaning in both languages "the one with upward (i.e., rising) sun at headwaters" (Kari 2013; Kari 2019b, 59; Kari et al. 2012). The name makes overt geographic provenance sense only from the Lower Tanana's perspective near Fairbanks, where the winter sun rises behind the mountain for several months. This perspective is completely lost from the Copper River Valley Ahtna viewpoint, who, despite that fact, still used the Lower Tanana's perspective in the name (see Kari 2019b, 55 and table S1).

METHODOLOGY: DATABASE CONSTRUCTION

Between 2013 and 2020, I worked closely with Dr. James Kari cataloging and mapping his disparate place name lists. Currently, we have mapped over 12,500 traditional names in the twelve Dene languages across the state. Of importance to this book are the Middle Tanana place names. Those toponyms were incorporated into a single digital platform, an ArcGIS geodatabase, along with place names from the other eleven Alaska Dene languages. Kari's curation methods allowed for systematic editorial control concerning their collection, spelling, editing, and translation. Occasionally, other researcher's work was incorporated to fill geographic data gaps as needed. The file geodatabases were published on Esri's website ArcGIS Online and on a series of online web maps, which were then embedded in a user-restricted website, The Web Atlas of Alaska Dene Place Names (Kari and Smith 2017). The web atlas allows for users' remote access, easing the editing process and facilitating public outreach and education, and are continually updated.

This toponym work represents a small, secondary subset of Kari's overall lexicographical work developing primary cross-analyzable digital dictionaries in several of these languages (Kari 2017). Kari's primary dictionary work in Middle Tanana, Lower Tanana, Koyukon, and Ahtna, demonstrates deep Dene antiquity in interior Alaska, demonstrated by the near-complete lack of any non-Dene loanword borrowings in these core regions and very few candidates for substrates. Other neighboring languages such as Dena'ina exhibit more, a function of historic and precolonial cultural interactions unique to that region. The lack of virtually any loanwords or borrowings regarding terminology for animals, technology, or places, indicates that the languages were not preceded by, nor displace, any other cultural or linguistic knowledge set in the Tanana or Copper River regions, and instead determined singular, innovative names for those natural subjects.

THE MIDDLE TANANA TOPONYMS

A summary of the Middle Tanana toponym list is detailed in table 4.1. The list represents a reconstruction, and some names were produced based on the rules of integrated elements (structure, content, distribution, and networks [Kari 2011b, 242]). Names given by informants to researchers were only passed on with the understanding that they had been learned from previous generations and not coined (Kari 2011b). As such, the orally maintained lists often exhibit confirmational redundancies. For example, it was estimated that around 80 percecnt of the Ahtna place names corpus to the south had been elicited by at least two different speakers (Kari 2011b, 242). Territorial boundaries of previous researchers (e.g., Krauss et al. 2011) were also refined using the toponyms as initial points of reference.

Table 4.1. Middle Tanana Multi-Lingual Place Name Totals

Borrowed Toponyms	Total Shared Feature Names	Divergent Feature Names	Cognate Feature Names	Calque Feature Names
Between English and Middle Tanana	116	86	20	10
Between Middle Tanana and other Dene	117	11	106	n/a

Sources: Kari 2015; Kari and Smith 2017.

Over 12,500 traditional place names in the twelve Alaskan Dene languages have been reconstructed and mapped to date. They describe a landscape covering about 785,000 km² (~303,000 mi²), or roughly an area in size between the Republics of Mozambique and Turkey, the thirty-fifth and thirty-sixth largest nations by landmass in 2020. In the Middle Tanana language, 361 place names have been elicited or reconstructed (262 within their WT territory), describing a landscape covering about 23,100 km² (~14,300 mi²),

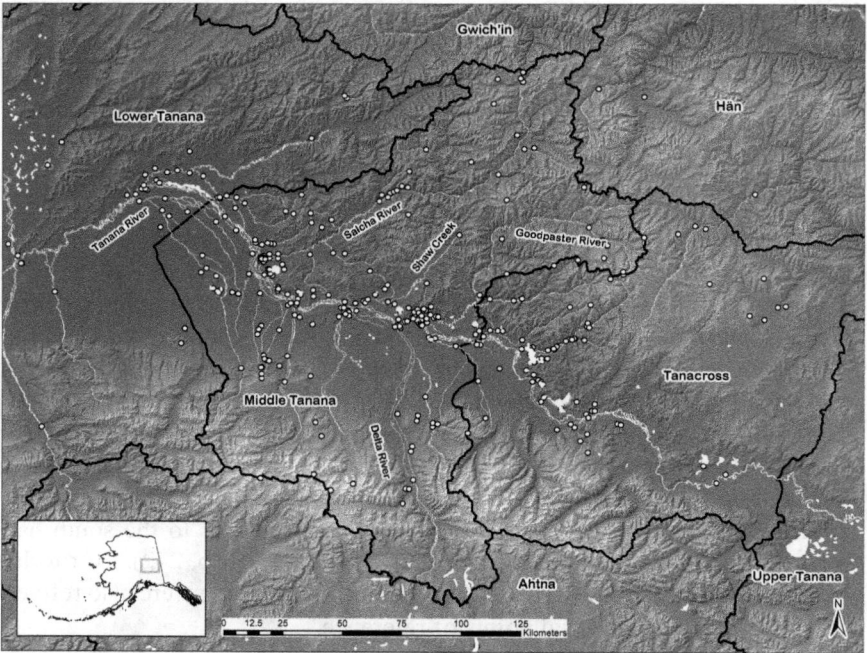

Figure 4.2. Middle Tanana traditional place names.

or roughly an area in size between the Republic of Djibouti and Belize, the 146th and 147th largest nations by landmass in 2020 (out of 194 recognized) (figure 4.2). The names tend to cluster more in the Tanana Valley flats rather than the uplands when compared to the neighboring Lower Tanana and Tanacross corpora to the east and west, respectively. This patterning difference may reflect the fact that many of the Middle Tanana place names were provided by women, Bessie Barnabas and Eva Moffit, whose personal land use may have differed from traditional male foraging patterns.

In the Middle Tanana list, 117 (32.4 percent) names are attested to in at least one other Dene language. The shared toponyms primarily exist along the frontiers of the Middle Tanana language territory or are significant features visible from great distances or shared by multiple territories. Almost all of these shared names are lexical cognates due to both common etymological origins and reconstructive efforts (Kari 2019a, 76), and rarely divergent (table 4.2). The paucity of distinct or autonomous cross-lingual place name-sharing suggests that conservation of toponyms was of critical collective importance to all groups involved in sharing the landscape and superseded any deep-seated intergroup antagonism. In other words, different bands almost never carried unique, divergent names for the same landscape feature. This pattern suggests that Dene culture promoted the conservation of place names rather than innovation, lending support to the hypothesis that the names represent an ancient naming pattern rather than a recent pattern.

Table 4.2.   Middle Tanana Multi-Lingual Place Name Percentages

Borrowed Toponyms	% Total Shared Feature Names	% Divergent Feature Names	% Cognate Feature Names	% Calque Feature Names
Between English and Middle Tanana	32.1	23.8	5.5	2.8
Between Middle Tanana and other Dene	32.4	3.0	29.3	n/a

Sources: Kari 2015; Kari and Smith 2017.

DATABASE DISCUSSION

The Middle Tanana toponym list is one of twelve created and curated as part of a more significant effort to build a comprehensive Alaska Dene traditional atlas. The lists used here were largely curated at the Alaska Native Language Center Archives at the University of Alaska Fairbanks. Kari and others initially curated the various place names through first-hand interviews, and historical documents analysis (Allen 1985; Kari and Tuttle 1996; Kari 2015; Mishler 1986), with reconstructions based on the PDLL-themed geography theory. These lists are curated in various digital formats, usually as PDFs, Microsoft Excel and Access datasheets, and several ArcGIS shapefiles. I created a standardized ArcGIS geodatabase and incorporated each languages' place name lists into it as individual feature classes. These toponyms were matched with an official United States Geologic Survey (USGS) name, a Geographic Names Information System (GNIS) name, or Canadian Board of Geographic Names (CBGN) identifier, or even unofficial colloquial English names when applicable.

Following categories created by Kari, the language-specific feature classes were also given standardized individual fields recording any alternative name, literal translation, feature type, semantic type, latitude, and longitude. For the English and Dene shared or borrowed names, each was also coded as a loanword (calque, cognate, or divergent) to demonstrate the curation preference type. The hydronyms and oronyms were also coded for generic stem category and relative seriation age following Kari (1996a), and all names were also given their elicited sequence number.

Toponym lists strongly reflect the drainage-based travel system. The sequence number for each name indicates the sequential order by drainage that names are given in both singular and merged travel narratives and lists. The process of correlating Native Alaskan toponyms with their correct landscape features is complicated as traditional Dene mental mapping templates are both vista-based from a perspective of standing on the land and travel-narrative-based, from a perspective of moving through the land. Travel narratives encompass one of the five main types of traditional Dene narrative genres (Kari 2010a, ix–xv). In the elite travel narratives, where toponyms were provided with a high level of detail, place names were given in "arrays" as the speaker re-imagined traveling through the countryside (Hays et al. 2014 and Kari and Fall 2016, 231–234). Thus, maintaining the relative sequence of names given orally becomes vitally essential for matching the names to actual features. For example, if three names are provided in a specified traveling sequence, but only the first and the third name are applied to a known feature, the second name's unknown location can be estimated with a degree of certainty as it can logically only belong to a feature that exists within the line-of-sight path of the most likely travel corridor between the two known points.

The names do not reflect or correlate well with travel routes as defined by twentieth-century modes. That includes mechanized travel by both on-road and off-road vehicles, motorboats, aircraft, or land ownership/management restrictive influences of the historic (twentieth-century) period. Instead, they strongly reflect precolonial tenure patterns and regular foot-travel routes through landscape, which was primarily ordered by drainage systems (Kari 2010a, 2011b). The traditional pattern is due to the unique ecological pressures that the northern boreal forest had on human use, resulting in difficult landscape vistas, seasonal travel restrictions due to extensive muskeg bogs, and thick vegetation that is difficult to penetrate on foot. Secondarily, they reflect travel modes by boat, but only in those places where unmechanized boat travel could occur (Kari 2010a). Finally, while their patterning strongly reflects precolonial travel routes and tenure, their survival has also been a function of twentieth-century settlement locations.

The western concept of mapping typically requires a theoretical sky-based observation point, requiring the user to simultaneously imagine the landscape from both an aerial view and ground perspective, and extensive enculturation to develop that mental template. That model requires a specific type of geospatial learning and extensive practice with reinterpreting on-the-ground aspects with imagined aerial views. The aerial orientation of standard map perspectives can be confusing for informants who have only experienced the perspective of place names from a land-based perspective by traveling through it. Named features can appear prominent when encountering them on foot but appear relatively small when depicted on a map.

The importance of maintaining place name relativity and drainage organization was recognized and utilized by Kari early on and incorporated into almost all his toponym work. The current Dene place name network represents a reconstruction in varying levels of detail. The datasets indicate the systemic, auto-instructional nature of the names and reveal millennia-long stability. Each toponym's sequence number is subject to change as new names are elicited and incorporated and are therefore unique to each language and publication date. Not all researchers have maintained a sequential drainage identifier for their lists (e.g., Juneby and Ritter 1978). When this happens, unlocated place names lose their relative approximation regarding other names, and it becomes all but impossible to estimate a mappable location for them.

Memorizing and maintaining the proper relative order of place names allowed a traveler to move about in an unknown landscape with relative ease. The names are often embedded with basic descriptions of features, sometimes including a directional element that could indicate the orientation of the observer's viewpoint, the expected direction of travel, and thus produce a spatially oriented template in the observer's mind. The travel narratives could be given from one person to another, memorized, and used with precision by people passing through an unknown country without local guides or traveling through a landscape otherwise not seen for decades (Kari 2010a). Thus, the names do not merely provide a unique feature identifier as modern American place names typically do. They can also provide seasonal predictors of band movements, potential seasonal camp locations, predictable resource use areas, and seasonal travel orientations (e.g., Jarvenpa and Brumbach 2016).

This concept is vitally important; the place names were not merely reflections of the landscape, but cultural resource knowledge and traditional land use were actively coded within the place names (Afable and Beeler 1996). Thus, the toponyms act as a survival or resilience mechanism for a culture entirely dependent on the landscape for their existence (see Kari 2010a for examples and discussions of the narratives). The names were held in such regard that their knowledge was at least on one occasion, used in a funeral song to "sing" a young man's recently deceased's spirit through the landscape (Coray 2007, 55–60).

Finally, traditional place names also often incorporate circumlocution and only rarely directly reference beliefs. Their association with places considered sacred or *'engii* due to recent events, past events, mythological events, or vision quests associated with Traveler's trail is not overtly coded in the names but can only be inferred from the stories and oral histories associated

with the places, illustrating the importance of experiencing the ancient traditions as one moved about the landscape as a young person. It was up to each
individual to remember the oral histories and integrate them as a personal
experience of the sacred and mundane as they moved from place to place.
In a sense, the toponymic system acts like a cosmic metanarrative. Like the
comprehensive star maps (Cannon et al. 2020), this grand overarching cultural system described and defined the Dene people's lifeways on personal,
community, and historic levels and was lived and experienced on a daily basis
prior to the gradual relocation to today's urban environments.

COMPARING THE ENGLISH AND
DENE TOPONYMIC SYSTEMS

Perceiving the landscape toponyms as a shared symbolic system allows us
to add the fourth conceptual dimension, time, to our observation of an otherwise three-dimensional geographic system (Anthony 2007; Tilley 1994). The
study of traditional Middle Tanana Dene geography is at once a snapshot
of the landscape as it appeared in tandem with their informants' lives and
the lives of their immediate elders from whom they had learned the corpus.
Traditional Alaskan toponyms were learned through shared life experiences
of the community within the landscape. Therefore, in the most conservative sense, the place names depict a cognitive Dene landscape spanning
the eighteenth to mid-twentieth centuries, being the living memory of the
protohistoric landscape. Using Kari's PDLL analysis, we can begin to tease
out the elements that allow us to gain time perspectives embedded within the
place name system and understand which names were coined recently and
which were devised centuries or even millennia ago (as demonstrated in Kari
2019b). Further, Kari has developed a relative dating system to systematically
observe linguistic dispersal and seriation events, which should have predictable archaeological correlations.

During the Historic Period, the Middle Tanana and Euro-American populations interacted with the same Alaskan landscape in fundamentally different
ways. These alternative culturally informed interactions are evident in the
patterned choice of named topographic features. In English, not all streams,
mountains, or other topographical reliefs present in Alaska have been named,
and the same is true of Dene (e.g., Thornton 2008, 103–104). During the fur
trade era, as traplines became a primary source of income in the nineteeth
and early twentieth centuries, personal names of Alaska Natives became
incorporated in the traditional landscape corpus, representing the new concept of individual rather than communal land tenure. Throughout Alaska,

Native landscape features also began to integrate new English, Russian, and occasional Chinook loanwords, borrowings, or themes, often contracted with the Dene generic element. Occasionally, some traditional Dene place names simply shifted to their meaning in English within Native communities as that language became the new first language (Smith 2020a, 104–106).

Dene toponyms favor culturally significant topography, emphasizing the perceptive value of resource-rich areas (i.e., Traditional Ecological Knowledge) and travel routes in each language. While a large number of place names are cataloged throughout the Middle Tanana territory (427 English and 262 Dene), only seventy-one places share both a Dene and an officially registered English toponym. The remaining names are uniquely named geographic features which do not share a name in the other language. This pattern demonstrates the fundamentally different ways both cultures have interacted with the same landscape and its perceived cultural value (e.g., Thornton 2008, 26). Undoubtedly some Indigenous names have been lost (the other Tanana Valley languages show a much higher density). The degree of features that share an English and Dene place name may have been increased if a similar survey had been undertaken a century ago.

Donald Orth, who oversaw the initial federal survey of Alaskan place names in the 1960s, noticed this pattern as well, describing the following:

> Eskimo, Aleut, and Indian names, like those of the Europeans, are generally commonplace and descriptive. Native naming habits, however, have two characteristic differences. The natives tend to name many small, even minute, landmark features and ignore those that are large. Few mountains were named unless they stood alone and had some peculiar characteristic. For foot, boat, or sled travel, there was no need to name large and vague features. In addition, the natives commonly applied several names to one feature, based on the characteristics of its particular parts. Many streams, even short ones, had various names along their lengths. Many of the native names now appearing on published maps are long and unpronounceable by the average English-speaking person. Geographic names evolve historically, their origins and form being closely associated with the languages of the peoples who successively occupy the area. Thus, many Native names are changed or altered in form due to adjusting to the new language, English. This is a universal process. However altered, many of these names have become or will become firmly established as part of the Native heritage of the Alaska landscape. (Orth 1971, 5)

While noting the significant contribution of the earlier, traditional toponyms to the new English place name registry, Orth did not attempt to quantify that contribution.

Focusing on the shared toponyms between English and Middle Tanana, only six of the seventy-one (11.8 percent) shared names appear to represent the borrowing by English of a preexisting Dene name as a cognate, as in one of the Middle Tanana names for the community of Salcha: *Sał Cheeget* (Kari 2015), illustrating the attempt (perhaps unrealized) at preserving the auditory integrity of the Dene languages. English speakers also occasionally borrowed the meaning of the names (a calque: a loan translation); eight (8.9 percent) English names preserve the older Dene as a calque. An example of that is a stream near the study area, Caribou Creek; in Middle Tanana, it is *Udzih Ndiig*, meaning "caribou stream" (Kari 2015).

The low number of Middle Tanana-origin toponyms in the USGS list (3 percent) is reflective of field efforts by the USGS personnel. By the 1960s, when their surveys took place, the Middle Tanana communities had long since dissolved, with only a few individuals remaining in the Salcha area. The nature of the documented place name borrowings suggests that English names that recall animals and natural objects or phenomena (e.g., Clearwater Creek, Eagle Creek) may actually be forgotten Indigenous borrowings.

RENAMING ALASKA

Naming the landscape was and is a community effort; everyone using the corpus of names must come to an agreement on what those names are and their preservation to avoid confusion, especially in the absence of written records. They are maintained through the cultural awareness of their users. Maintaining multiple names for similar features is inefficient and increases the risk of communicative confusion between social actors and was strongly avoided by the Dene. Divergent names of singular landscape features are unique and rare.

The Middle Tanana place names corpus remains markedly less dense, especially in upland regions, when compared against the downstream language of the Lower Tanana and the upstream language of the Tanacross. How were so many Middle Tanana place names lost, especially when there wasn't a concerted effort to remove the Middle Tanana Natives from their ancestral lands, as happened in so many other places of the continent? The answer is a story of multiple historical factors, including the previously discussed factors of early community dissolution, pandemic depopulation, and enforced language suppression.

As explored earlier, between the U.S. purchase of the Territory of Alaska in 1867 and passage of the Alaska Native Land Claims Settlement Act in 1971, the Dene territory was unorganized in a Western legal sense (Hensley 2009). The prior eighteenth and nineteenth centuries had been a period of massive economic and cultural upheavals. Throughout the territory, the fur trade had shifted the balance of local economic trade consumption power from interior

Alaska to the external coastal-based colonial Russian trade sphere and the riverine-based British and American colonial powers' trade sphere (Boraas 2007). The result was a period of intensified intertribal warfare, which dramatically reshaped Alaska's linguistic map during the nineteenth century prior to the arrival of the Euro-Americans. Despite this cultural trauma, most Native place names seem to have survived, attesting to the conservative power of the Dene landscape naming system (Andrews 1975; Burch 1974; Fienup-Riordan 2016; Kari and Fall 2016; Raboff 2001; Pratt 2019).

After the 1890s, the massive influx of Euro-American prospectors and trappers, some of whom ultimately became permanent settlers, brought territorial law to the region. It was based on the US judicial system's tradition of common law, and imposed a new moral code emphasized by the subsequent missionary-teachers who quickly dispersed throughout the territory (Jackson 1903). The new population swamped the old by a factor of 4–1, and English and Euro-American cultural traditions quickly became dominant.

The Alaska Native languages were not abruptly removed from the interior Alaskan landscape, nor did the Euro-Americans move into an empty territory, as had happened in so many other places on the continent. The new population moved into a landscape that was vibrantly alive with descriptive, useful toponyms, and the immigrants and Native peoples found innovative ways of peaceful coexistence. However, for Alaska Natives who permanently moved into Euro-American communities, they often experienced economic and cultural disenfranchisement (Stebing 2009). The new religious and secular education systems also heavily encouraged (sometimes through traumatic and violent means) English literacy and the active repression of Indigenous languages (Charles 2009; Napoleon 2009; Williams 2009). The trauma experienced by youths in the boarding schools facilitated the loss of the Indigenous languages, some of which are currently functionally extinct (such as Middle Tanana) and many of which are highly endangered. The loss of these languages represents a tremendous loss of traditional knowledge, far more than is reconstructed here (e.g., Nader 2018, 2).

The actions of marginalizing the preexisting cultures by the immigrant population in the territory did not stop at the erasure of spoken Native language and practiced culture. Place names themselves became either anglicized or wholly renamed. The history of naming and renaming the Alaskan landscape by the Russian, British, French Canadian, Spanish, and United States colonial powers was extensively documented by Donald Orth (1971, 1–43). Orth incorporated Native toponyms in cases where those were in everyday use. He oversaw official consolidation of the Alaskan geographic toponyms throughout the 1960s in response to official statehood in 1959 and the federal governments' requirement to maintain uniform geographic names

(Public Law 80–242). By the early 1970s, Orth's team ultimately cataloged 25,876 place names across the state. The effort was not conclusive and remains ongoing, and as of December 2017, the official place name registry of Alaska contains 34,337 toponyms (GNIS 2017; USGS 2015).

The modern corpus of English USGS names has required a vast amount of energy to produce. It has involved numerous military and corporate-financed expeditions of five colonial empires spanning two hundred years, resulting in skirmishes, battles, starvation, and death for many non-Native members involved. Orth (1971) devotes forty-three pages briefly but comprehensively detailing these numerous expeditions. I emphasize it here to illustrate the vast energy expenditure spent to produce the Americanized landscape that we have collectively inherited today. The enormous energy expenditure of renaming the landscape demonstrates the conservative utility in preserving any previous toponyms. Less energy is required to conserve preexisting toponyms than will be expended by renaming them. Therefore, a pattern of toponymic stability will be naturally facilitated in any cultural system given enough time. Selective forces should favor the optimization and conservation of an existing place name system, and less energy expended toward innovation should eventually occur.

COMPARING THE RECONSTRUCTED DENE TOPONYM SETS

Investigating the ways that Middle Tanana place names have been borrowed into English provides a model of examining the possibility that Proto-Dene may have encountered another prior unrelated language in the valley. All place names are fully analyzable through Dene grammatical rules; no evidence of any place names being preserved from other non-related languages exists. This pattern is also reflected in the dictionaries, where no loanwords or substrates from non-European or non-Dene are evident.

Within the Middle Tanana dataset (n=361), 112 toponyms (31.0 percent) are elicited in other Dene languages. While some of these represent reconstructions, most were elicited firsthand. Most of these are found along the protohistoric borderlands and travel corridors between cultural-linguistic groups. As Orth noticed, multiple names are occasionally noted for similar features, and 98 (27.1 percent) of the toponyms carry an alternative name. Of the 361 names, 110 (30.4 percent) are shared cognates (table 4.2). An example is in the Dene names for Mt. Wrangell: MT: *K'ełt'een*, UT: *K'ełt'iin*, AT: *K'ełt'aeni*, (Kari 2019b: 52). All are difficult to translate into English, and it becomes something like "on it, the one [God] actively causes/creates."

Two names (0.5 percent) appear to be divergent; an example of one is the is the traditional Middle Tanana names for the Upper Tanana River (upstream from the Delta River): *Tth'itu'* (straight water) or, downstream from the Delta River, *Tene Naa* (trail river). The Koyukon, Gwich'in, and Lower Tanana have cognates with the downstream name "trail river," and Lower Tanana, Tanacross, and Upper Tanana have cognates with the upstream name "straight water." Meanwhile, in Ahtna, it is uniquely called *Ba'aaxe Tuu'* (outside water) (Kari and Smith 2017). In this, the Dene showed a preference for the practical maintenance of the place name's cognates. In contrast, the opposite was true for first-language English speakers who preferred to use loanwords or calques when incorporating Native toponyms. The value difference reflects the internal grammatical structure of each language; English grammar can readily absorb borrowed words while complex nouns in Dene follow strict rules of incorporating aspect, theme, pronoun, and mode onto a root word, restricting innovation and the incorporation of unrelated loanwords.

NAMES AS SIGNS: THE PRECOLONIAL MODEL OF DENE LINGUISTIC RADIATION THROUGHOUT ALASKA

In the mid-1990s, Kari (1996a, 1996b; see also Bender 1998) published a linguistic model of systematic language seriation and dispersal based on three unique geographical identifiers that are generally attached to place names as generic stems. It presented the argument detailing how the seriated root words for -stream, -lake, and -mountain, embedded in most toponyms, were uniquely patterned spatially on the Dene landscape. The spatial patterning demonstrated that the minute consonant and vowel shifts within those stem seriations indicate a common, traceable origin point for the Alaskan Dene languages to the southern Yukon/northern British Columbia region (figure 4.3). The systemic seriation pattern can be relatively dated and can be modeled chronologically when coupled with archaeological data. The typology of time-perspective traits allows for detecting general regional and subregional patterning among geolinguistic cognates and lexical or grammatical diffusions (using adjacent root/morpheme dictionaries). It is best demonstrated through the riverine stem seriation pattern described here.

The geographically patterned seriation of stem shifts suggested a clear, relatively dated pattern of dispersal. Originally, the model was presented as a comparative, qualitative analysis, and time perspective and seriations of sets of names were suggested for the spread. This current study seeks to depict the relative position of Middle Tanana toponyms within that model. The

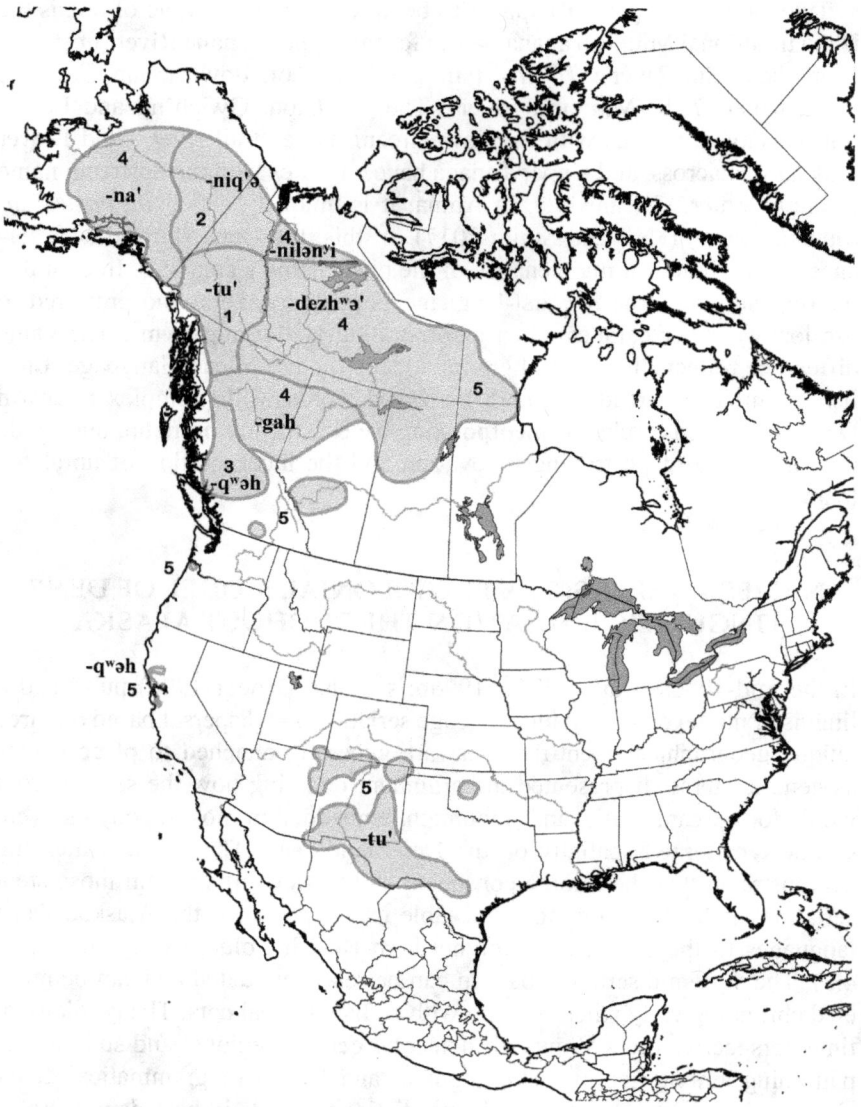

Figure 4.3. James Kari's model of hydronymic districts and numbered relative riverine stem seriation (1996a, 1996b).

following quantitative and spatial model is informed by the mapping efforts of Kari and myself, initially published in 2017.

THE RELATIVE MODEL OF PROTO-DENE DISPERSAL AND DIFFERENTIATION USING GENERIC ELEMENTS AS A PROXY STREAM GENERIC ELEMENTS

The oldest relatively dated generic element used to describe stream names in the Na-Dene languages represents sound change variations based on the stem -*tu*. This fundamental term simply means "water" in Proto Dene (Kari 1996b, 2021). This generic element is expressed as -*tú'ə* in Tagish (Sydney 1980), -*tu'ə* in Kaska (in Kari 1996b), and -*tu'ən* in Tahltan (Hargus and Kari 1988; see also Moore 2019), and it was commonly used as the generic forms of "stream" and "lake" in the traditional place names of norther British Columbia and Southern Yukon. Three of the six largest rivers in the Alaskan Dene traditional territory carry this stem: the Yukon, Tanana, and lower Copper Rivers, suggesting that the linguistic tenure of these eastern areas is older than in central and western Alaska, where comparable-sized rivers (the Susitna, Kuskokwim, and Koyukuk) do not. The subsequently derived generic element -*chù* is found in Southern Tutchone (Tom 1987, in Kari 1996b), and -*chú*, -*chúa* is found in Northern Tutchone (Tom 1987). It is also found in a small minority of Hän stream stems (Kari 1996b). The stem -*chu* is found in Gwich'in, suggesting this language may represent some of the earliest of the Alaskan seriations. The use of -*tu'ə* as a stem in Alaska is rare, but where used, it may indicate places of greater antiquity in use. A small cluster of more significant hydrologic features bearing these stems is found in the Lower Tanana region, especially toward the Alaska Range. This important stem provides an idea of the earliest geographic spread of Proto-Dene, incorporating the Upper Yukon, and Tanana Rivers, with some knowledge of the Copper River. The stem is absent from the region of the Susitna, Kuskokwim, and Koyukuk drainages suggesting significant linguistic seriation from Proto-Dene had already occurred by the time these areas were settled.

As the ancestral Gwich'in mapped on to their northern territory, it became necessary to create specific, differentiated terminology for streams. *Kǫǫ*, for example, denotes a fish-bearing stream. Thus, the next relatively oldest stream stem in Alaska represented a unique innovation and became the preferred generic naming stem. From that stem, almost all other Alaskan stem seriations are derived: -*njik*. It is occasionally retained in several Upper

Tanana, Tanacross, and Northern Tutchone streams. The stem is also occasionally found in the neighboring Koyukon language as a preserved cognate (*-ndzik*), likely a product of nineteenth-century Koyukon movements into western Gwich'in territory and borrowing the preexisting place names. Subsequently, the closest seriation of that stem is found in the Hän language to the southwest and upstream on the Yukon: *-ndek* (Kari 1996a, 1996b; Ritter and Johnson 1978). Thus, the territories of the Gwich'in, Hän, Upper Tanana, and Tanacross are considered to represent the most ancient Dene language tenure in Alaska. The archaeological record of the Gwich'in and Hän territories remain quite understudied, while the archaeological record of the Upper Tanana region is generally referred by proxy to the cultural sequence at Healy Lake (Cook 1969), where Cook interpreted Dene antiquity into the middle Holocene, with evidence of cultural continuity into the earlier Holocene and Terminal Pleistocene levels as well.

The following series of streams represent stem seriations throughout the Tanana Valley. The oldest are found in upstream regions and the youngest downstream. These represent a unique pattern not observable along any other major Alaskan river. The Copper, Susitna, and Koyukuk River drainages all employ singular stems, and the Kuskokwim drainage employs two stem patterns. The Yukon drainage also employs multiple, but remains unique from the Tanana due to its far greater length and the multiple ecosystems it crosses through. The fact that the Tanana Valley employs all six primary Alaskan Dene riverine stems within its singular ecosystem and relatively shorter length suggests that this region was the core area for much of the Proto-Dene linguistic seriation in the state. The earliest seriations are the stem *-nign*, which is most dominant in the Upper Tanana language, and *-ndig* found in the Tanacross language. The seriation of these two likely occurred after the Upper Tanana settlement, not prior since they are not found outside this region. The Upper Tanana stem is retained in several stream names by the Tanacross, while the converse does not occur.

A subsequent downstream directional was coined in Proto Dene: **ni·q'ə*, literally "on the upstream." The divergent stem element *-niq'ə* is found in various surviving forms in several Dene languages (Kari 1996b, 261). In Alaska, the innovation is used in Gwich'in, Hän, Upper Tanana, and Tanacross. It becomes a generalized, generic stem in the languages found west and south of central Yukon and Upper Tanana, with the boundary of this use running just east of the Delta and Goodpaster Rivers in the Tanana Valley, marked by the prominent Donnelly Dome (*Łuu Tadzeey*). This basic widespread cross-linguistic pattern suggests to Kari that this may represent a long-standing ancient linguistic sign of marking feature importance. Further, it indicates that the regions where stream names are found that bear the stem *-niq'ə* were visited much earlier before becoming permanently settled by the Proto-Dene speakers of the Yukon Flats and Upper Tanana Valley. This indicates that from a linguistic perspective, the Tanana Valley above Big Delta was inhabited by the ancestral Dene for far longer than the region downstream from there.

In the central Tanana Valley, the next relative stem seriation is found in Tanacross and Middle Tanana: *-nda'*. This stem is retained in both languages and is considered a unique archaism, and is employed as a riverine stem reversal because it is not the only generic form used by the Middle Tanana, but was used alongside the final seriation form: *na'*. When the languages made specific use of two unique stems, the reversal is likely marking important streams for reasons unknown today (e.g., Kari 2019a, 78). The generic element *-nda'* only survives north of the Alaska Range, embedded in sixteen riverine names, roughly correlating with the *-niq'ə* linguistic boundary.

As a generalized stream stem, *-niq'ə* is unique and does not cluster dominantly in any present-day language. Thus, it may represent an ancient, Proto Dene dispersal into the region stretching from Beaver Creek in the Yukon Flats down the Kuskokwim River valley toward Bristol Bay, which occurred long after the dispersal in the eastern Brooks Range and Upper Tanana. In the Brooks Range, it is only found on the name *Tlaakk'oł Neekk'e* of the Middle Fork Koyukuk River. It is only found west of the central Alaska Range and is absent from any names south of the Alaska Range in Ahtna or Dena'ina territory on Cook Inlet (Kari 1996a, 1996b).

The earlier stems mentioned here tend to cluster in core groups, typical of a logistically mobile land-tenure system where resources are extracted from the landscape in a systemic staged process, ultimately funneling them toward the cultural settlement cores (Binford 1980). The *-niq'ə* generic stem group is patterned so that only the major rivers in the western Alaskan region appear to carry it. At the same time, minor streams use alternative stems derived from **noʔ*. The unique geospatial pattern of two riverine stems used simultaneously is also a highly significant reverse hydronym pattern. Kari has suggested that this may have operated as ancient watershed-tenured boundary signals for the initial bands dispersing into Central-Western Alaska.

The final major Dene stream stem seriation was the **noʔ* hydronym. It appears as an abrupt boundary scored in the Middle Tanana Valley in the Delta and Goodpaster River area. The distinct regional naming signal suggests that it correlates with the earliest or "vanguard" Dene names there. It represents the most widespread Alaska hydronym, recorded orthographically as *-na'*, *-no'*, and *-nu'* but are pronounced the same. These became the dominant riverine stems found today in south-central and western-central Alaska. The stems **noʔ* are centered along three major Alaskan tributaries, the middle and lower Tanana, Copper, Susitna, Koyukuk, and Kuskokwim Rivers, the Cook Inlet area, and Lake Iliamna regions. The stem is related to the term "moving nomadically," providing an additional behavioral reference of mobility by those forefront naming groups (Kari 1996a), which, if the cultural sequence at *Minchu Mina'* (UK), or Lake Minchumina, can be held as a regional proxy, does not predate about 3500 cal BP (Holmes 1986). The stem shift **noʔ* is found interspersed on the landscape on smaller streams where the older stem -**niqʼə* is applied to more significant streams, suggesting their initial use was mutual. The stem **noʔ* is also found in Middle Tanana. The retention of the stem **noʔ* on the middle-lower Yukon is evidence that they represent the initial naming conventions for early Proto Dene speakers there, but only after that form was in formal use.

Of particular importance is the singular presence of **noʔ* as the only utilized riverine stem employed by the Ahtna of the Copper and upper-middle Susitna River drainages. Ahtna and Dena'ina are the only Dene languages present south of the Alaska Range, and Dena'ina is considered to be a recent arrival from the west, between 1,000 and 500 years ago (Reger and Boraas 1996). Ahtna, meanwhile, appears to represent an ancient culture *in situ* with minor hints in the place name corpus of an ancient linguistic origin in the central Tanana Valley (Kari 2019b). The language exhibits no substrates or ancient candidate loanwords; in other words, it exhibits no evidence for previous language displacement or interaction. In their traditional territory of the middle Susitna Valley, the unbroken documented 6,500-year radiocarbon and cultural chronology is strong evidence for an ancestral homeland of the Proto-Ahtna (Dixon et al. 1985; Hays et al. 2014). Since the Ahtna language retains virtually no substrates or candidate loanwords from neighboring languages present prior to the historic period, and the place names show no additional generic stem forms such as documented throughout the Tanana, I am in agreement with Dr. Kari that the proto-Dene form that dispersed with the Northern Archaic tradition into the valley represents the seriation after **noʔ* came into common use, and the archaeological record provides a deep, time perspective proxy for that seriation. Further anecdotal place name evidence indicating the antiquity of the Ahtna language comes from the Upper Kuskokwim toponym list. At the headwaters of the Tonzona River (*Ch'idotl'uł No'*: braided string stream) is found a hill with and above a Pleistocene terminal moraine called *Tsis Ti*. The meaning of the name is opaque in the Upper Kuskokowim language, but remains translatable in the Ahtna language located over 100 miles to the east: "among the rocks."

This evidence suggests that the ancestral Ahtna language has been in this region for a similarly proposed time depth of the Yeniseian languages and their representative Syalakh Culture in central Siberia (Vajda 2018,

278–281). Given the relative seriation model above, the middle and Upper Tanana and middle and upper Yukon linguistic and cultural occupations are inferred to be much earlier, a middle to early Holocene phenomena.

In the Middle Tanana stream stem corpus (n=95), two use the stem *-tu'*, seventeen use *-ndíg*, four use *-nda'*, four use *-niq'ə*, and sixty-one use the stem *-na'*. This pattern of such a variety of riverine stems being preserved by a single language is unique. It illustrates the conservative preference by the Dene for preserving ancient toponyms in their original form rather than shifting their stems to the most recent or dominant innovation. It further situates the Middle Tanana area as a core region of ancient linguistic differentiation instead of the Upper Tanana, where the riverine stems pattern more singularly.

CONCLUSION

Kari's hydronymic districts and relative dispersal hypothesis is a robust mechanism for understanding the Dene language family's radiation through Yukon and into Alaska. Linguistic models today generally have little efficacy for studying linguistic change beyond a few thousand years; and yet, the PDLL theory helps us to understand for more ancient linguistic patterns in this region. No single riverine stem is unique to the Middle Tanana language. Instead, it reflects knowledge of larger regional patterns independent of language boundaries. The oldest hypothetical WT areas, such as the Tanacross and Upper Tanana, appear to use more distinct and geographically bounded riverine stems and languages that seriated later, such as the Middle and Lower Tanana, to make use of multiple stems for the same geographic feature type. The stems themselves tend to pattern in geographic clusters; therefore, they do not only reflect active cultural living patterns but, more importantly, reflect ancient linguistic seriation patterns (Kari 1988, 1996a, 1996b, 2005).

Chapter Five

Understanding Archaeological Research

I pulled the copper bar from the open forge, holding it tight in a pair of tongs, laid it on the anvil, and began to pound it out, drawing the ends out and beginning to give its blade a recognizable shape, before placing it back over the open coal fire. I repeated the process until my arm was tired, then handed it over to Evie. We switched places, Evie heating and pounding the piece into shape and I tending the fire, keeping the coal heated and burning.

The Middle and Upper Tanana people also maintained ancient family ties throughout the central and upper Copper River area. These ties brought copper-objects and the knowledge of traditional copper metallurgy into this area centuries ago. As Kory Cooper has extensively documented, the Ahtna copper smithing tradition was a deeply sacred, closely guarded, and highly valued secret. I had always been fascinated by it, and Evie had been a practicing blacksmith for over a decade. Finally, we combined our efforts and began to see if we could produce something similar to a traditional voluted dagger.

It's easy to write what is known about the *chaîne opératoire*, or the technical and social processes involved in the step-by-step production, use, and disposal of artifacts. It is another thing to attempt to recreate that process, a field of study called experimental archaeology. When we began, we started with a small, homemade forge that Evie had cobbled together from parts designed from a YouTube tutorial. In those years, neither of us had much money, and we spent months saving up for and buying the copper stock and coal. About every four months we would be able to get together for a night of forging.

We quickly learned that despite reading everything that had been recorded about the smithing process, some information appeared to be overemphasized or out of context, leading to conclusions about copper behavior that didn't hold up to reality. We used different stock, and different pre-smithing stock shapes. We tried cold hammering, hot hammering, and even several attempts at melting in crucibles. I had been trained in the old western traditions of leathercraft, and found that heated copper could be worked similarly to wet leather. Evie, used to working with steel, found it to be oddly soft, malleable, and forgivable. We wore out one forge, eventually building a bigger one, and, after a windstorm knocked down several spruce trees around her cabin, we build a toolshed with the salvaged timber. This was a painstakingly slow process that took years; months passed between each individual forging experiment.

In the third year of our experiments, we had reconstructed the process enough that we were able to start producing copper knives that were shaped like the few that had survived in museum and private collections. Despite being crudely shaped compared to the surviving specimens, they were recognizable. Evie showed them to relatives, who in turn told us of several elder men who still remembered and had practiced the art of their creation. Sometimes, we were given small pieces of remembered information that had never been recorded, and the implementation of that information greatly eased our work. We still have a long way to go before we produce a blade that we feel truly encompasses the traditional creative process.

Culture is a multi-faceted phenomenon. Thus far, this book has summarized those aspects of it related to the Middle Tanana people's history, ideology, and language. The cultural ideology of the Middle Tanana explored here provides a framework through which the facts of the archaeological record can be knit together to form a meaningful narrative. Frameworks are subject to cultural constructs; in other words, facts will be construed to form different narratives depending on the observers' background, training, and expectations. The interpretations here are designed to explore the uncovered archaeological facts through traditional Dene constructs in addition to current archaeological paradigms, as far as a non-Native person can.

The many Dene languages are verb heavy, where compound words are formed from root bases by affixing aspect, verb theme, pronouns, and modes (Holton 2009). The result is speech patterns that are actively coding persons and their actions within common parlance. In other words, most discussions pertaining to a thing require a descriptive degree of animacy. Thus, discussing subjects or objects that have physical or spiritual power or subjects who have or can cause great harm or disruption are both perceptually and grammatically perceived as dangerous. Therefore, circumlocution (avoidance speech) was the way to draw attention to a dangerous topic without speaking forth that power and causing trauma (Jetté 1911). Today, if a subject comes up in conversation and is dismissed as a "small thing" by a knowledgeable elder who becomes silent or changes the subject, one is expected to infer *'engii* about the topic and follow suit, and pay attention to the proper times and circumstances for such a conversation. When anthropologist Cornelius Osgood found that Deg Hit'an and Upper Kuskokwim community members were extremely reticent to share their local history with him, he seems to have erroneously concluded that they placed no value on such memories of the past (Osgood 1959, 76).

In Dene traditions, the past had a power like any other aspect of the cosmos. In addressing the past, one focused its power dangerously on themselves in the present, just as one would when speaking of any other large, dangerous being (such as bears or mountains). Handling the physical remains of the past, and even speaking of certain past events and past persons could be quite *'engii*, and thus could only occur through proper training, and then could only occur by practitioners at specific times and events, such as the midwinter festival or other potlatch events (Cannon et al. 2020). Thus, archaeological work, when conducted, discussed, and warehoused improperly and without the blessing of the community, can be viewed as both dangerous to interact with and dangerous for community integrity. It is helpful to behave as if the past activities and behaviors that produced artifacts and sites are quantumly entangled with our present interactions with those same artifacts and sites.

So, if it is culturally insensitive or inappropriate to conduct archaeological work or speak of the Dene people's archaeological past, why is it done? Presently in the globalized world, the past has become a resource that the market economy can harness to structure the flow of monetary resources and political power. That political power, being an imperial and colonial legacy, has a strong record of denying Native agency of their own history (i.e., claiming non-Native origins of pre-Columbian archaeology to further socio-political gains, or teaching it only from a western perspective), denying Native control of their past (i.e., denying Native Americans' control of resources on ancestral lands and their own development of an education curriculum), or questioning ancestral connection to specific geographic regions. These are processes not unique to the past but continue to be widespread in the United States and Canada today.

UNDERSTANDING SCIENCE AS TRADITIONAL EURO-AMERICAN KNOWLEDGE CREATION

Currently, scientific archaeological conclusions carry more weight than traditional customary knowledge in civil structures. Therefore, it is both an appropriate and necessary tool to study the past in this invasive manner and discuss the findings. It is a powerful tool that can be used to either empower or disempower descendant communities, depending on the goals of the investigation team, level of outreach, and community research partnerships (Atalay 2012; Tuhiwai Smith 2012).

First, to avoid confusion, it is essential to highlight the fundamental differences between oral tradition, history, and archaeology. History is the study of the past primarily through the written word. It is often focused on events and people considered to have directly affected its course. Oral traditions are typically focused on the important aspects of the past that have moral consequences for the present. Archaeology is the study of material items and their own use history or life history. From the life history of discarded items, we can infer human behaviors. The study of human remains and ancient DNA in archaeological contexts is usually the realm of biological anthropology or bioarcheology, requiring archaeologists to be familiar with the ethics and methodology of that subfield. The scientific study of the material past and its inferences on human behavior is quite robust and will often highlight different patterns and phenomena than studies restricted to oral or written history may not be concerned with. Thus, each should be considered to be a unique method providing an alternative perspective on the past. Each ultimately has unique goals; sometimes, they will easily confirm each other, sometimes not, but because the objectives of each are alien to each other, they should not be expected to always be in agreement. It is up to the consumer to decipher the meaning of where their conclusions intersect and what to do with that understanding.

Second, we must understand that the archaeological sciences are a fundamentally Western cultural knowledge-production tool (Trigger 2009). Archaeology uses the scientific method to design its research process and produce conclusions. The scientific method is an ancient, customarily acceptable way to produce accurate knowledge about the physical universe for western societies. Therefore, it is helpful to think of the scientific process as a traditional customary knowledge path of the western world. That exercise also helps to balance the way we compartmentalize Native American and Euro-American knowledge networks.

Part of the goal of this book is to explore the cross-cultural intersection of knowledge production; therefore, we must first ask: what is western traditional knowledge production, and why is it traditionally structured the way it is? To summarize, the goal of science is to reveal the facts and minute building blocks of the universe and its working mechanisms. It is tasked with preserving, advancing, and creating all human knowledge. In traditional western philosophy, the world cannot be understood at face value. Instead, its constituent parts must be learned to be read; and if one can read them, one has access to a deeper truth about the nature of reality. The process of learning to understand the hidden nature of reality is considered to have been codified five centuries ago by Sir Francis Bacon through the Scientific Method: one constructs a question that can be tested and then forms further testable conclusions around those results. Thus, the quest for the hidden truth of the universe is never conclusive and always generates more study topics. It is also fundamentally positivist; entirely dependent on the material world to provide answers for the structure of reality. Reality, however, is forever changing as new questions are formulated. This concept was not a novel development of the European Scientific Revolution; their use of inductive and deductive reasoning methods was an ancient, widespread, respected tradition of western philosophers.

Bacon and his philosophical cohorts throughout Europe were convinced that through a thorough comprehension of the material world, called "the Book of Nature," they could then "read it" and understand the true nature of God, as creation was thought to be an accurate reflection of the Creator (Harrison 2001; Pedersen 1992). The Book of Nature was a construct of medieval European thinkers, based upon the earlier classical Greek traditions of metaphysics, whose traditions held that the deepest truth behind the physical world's structure was *Logos* or pure conscious thought.

The idea that a deeper truth was hidden beneath the trappings of the physical world, and that one could comprehend that truth through carefully controlled introspection of their own sensory perceptions was shared by both the ancient Greek philosophers and the Brahmin philosopher-rulers of ancient India (Collins 1998). Perhaps these ideas resulted from ancient cultural borrowings that traveled back and forth across the trade routes of the Persian Empire of Cyrus the Great. Perhaps they originated even deeper in time through shared Indo-European ancestry with the horse-riding chalcolithic cultures of the Central Asian steppes. Either way, the concept that a person should study the physical world in all its intricacies is a near-sacred tradition of great antiquity in European and Middle Eastern philosophy. By doing so, the underlying truth of a thing could be understood through philosophically guided thinking.

Thus, philosophically guided thought is the acceptable path to producing truth. For the meta-physicists, pure thought was considered a greater reality than the physical universe. This idea is why today, Euro-American culture considers their constructs of the past to be equal to or even more important than the physical remains of the past. It is also why those constructs must be formed through the most careful studies of those physical remains so that they reflect the greatest probability of truth about them. This concept remains the traditional path of enlightenment for many, and for scientists and science enthusiasts, it is considered the traditionally appropriate way to produce and explore knowledge.

The traditional way to learn the nature of reality for Western culture is originally described in Plato's Republic (Bloom 1968), where the ancient Greek philosopher Aristotle provides the famous allegory of the cave. In this ancient, 2,400-year-old story, all persons are allegorically born in the darkness at the back of a cave, chained to a wall. Above and behind them is a fire they cannot see; all they know is the reflection of that fire's light on the wall in front of them. Between the prisoner's backs and the distant fire are persons making shapes in the light. All the prisoners can see are the shadow images on the wall, which is the only reality they know. In the story, some prisoners seek to break free and do so. They crawl around the wall to which they were once chained and see the fire. At first, they are blinded by it, but then learn by studying it how it produces light and how the other figures manipulate that light to produce the shadow plays cast on the cave wall for the prisoners to observe.

At this level, the shadow puppeteers are allegories for social teachers, such as parents, educators, religious teachers, political leaders, and any conveyor of information. The freed prisoners' learning process here is an allegory of mastering the natural sciences; they understand now how the world's physical properties work and that the shadows are simply a pale reflection of it. At this level, the puppeteers appear to the neophyte philosophers as liars, as they are manipulating the light to produce a version of reality for the prisoners that is not true. The next step for the freed prisoners occurs when some perceive that the shadow puppets and fire may instead actually be pale reflections of truths not yet perceived, and through the use of inductive, deductive, and mathematical reasoning, find their way outside of the cave into the blinding sunlight, where they must learn to understand the greater reality of the outside world. At this level, the philosopher realizes that if they return and describe this higher truth in frank terms to the prisoners chained in the back of the cave, those prisoners will have no frame of reference for understanding that reality as it is entirely beyond their experience and perception. They will mock or even kill the philosopher who returns. The philosophers then realize that the role of the shadow puppeteers in conveying those truths in an understandable medium is essential; that medium can be used to either benevolently convey the truth of the outside world or manipulate the prisoners into accepting their darkened cave reality as the only one there is.

Scientific research and primary scientific publications continue to follow this model; they will begin by explaining the factual nature of the thing being studied and then provide the supporting and dissenting evidence for it, followed by their methods for detecting the studied phenomenon. Then they will present their qualitative or quantitative methodology and data used to produce new conclusions. Thus, scientific analyses represent an ancient respected traditional way to produce knowledge and understanding, and this is the formulae through which excavation results will be explored here. The final step of statistical analyses, however, is left to the primary literature.

LEGACIES OF ARCHAEOLOGICAL THOUGHT

The archaeological insights here represent the continuing legacy of past generations of archaeological research paradigms. Artifacts and features that share similar forms and functions were used to create one of the earliest investigative constructs: typologies, which are used as proxies for cultural continuity and development. Typological constructs are a research relic of early twentieth-century Americanist normative cultural historians exploring the form of a thing over space and time. Typologies continue to retain utility today; in their older iterations, they relied on identifying a singular form of an object that was supposed to represent the most perfect physical aspects of the object in question; often, however, that type-form was generally determined by the first place, or the first artifact found that described the thing in question. Today, we often rely on that mental template backed by statistical measurements to confirm the reality of any proposed form (Anderson 2008, 170). Presently, the physical artifact type and type-site concept have generally fallen into disuse for producing new Americanist research avenues and find most of their utility in the realm of private and bureaucratic archaeological investigations.

An early archaeological interpretive paradigm that developed in the 1940s whose utility continues today is called the *direct historical approach* (Steward 1977). Archaeologists recognized that similar patterns between the regional ethnohistoric and recent precolonial typologies usually indicated cultural continuity and used these patterns to demonstrate recognizable cultural roots back through time. The focus of it is to highlight technological forms of change and stasis through time. If radical breaks or changes are observed in the material cultural record, it was assumed that a cultural disruption event has occurred (criticized by Willey and Phillips 1958, 49–50; but see Carr 1995 and Clark 2001, 12–22).

As the material culture typologies were further refined, they were used to inform cultural-historic frameworks of traditions and cultures of objects. Material-cultural constructs then became inferred proxies for ethnolinguistic constructs, a problematic endeavor when we understand that ethnic groups can wholly and quickly shift their resource and technological base in the face of social or environmental factors while maintaining language and identity. In an attempt to control for spurious ethnohistoric correlations, Matson and

Magne (2007, 6–8) suggest using the *parallel direct historical approach*, where the cultural-historic frameworks of at least two different adjacent regions are compared to understand which technological constructs shift boundaries and which can be held as a constant for more informed ethnic proxies. Matson and Magne's approach is more difficult to apply to the Middle Tanana study region because the major riverine drainage systems surrounding the Tanana Valley have also been occupied by other Dene groups with similar or identical material cultural history. This approach is more efficaciously used by Alaskan archaeologists when comparing the material cultural remains of perceived inland-vs-coastal economically oriented groups (Friesen and Mason 2016a, 12; Tremayne 2018), but not within or among interior groups themselves (but see Anderson 1988 and Holmes 1986).

Since those early studies into artifact form and function, investigations blossomed into studying mechanisms for technological evolution or abandonment. In the Alaskan interior, topics of environmental catastrophism (usually attributed to volcanism) and ecological determinism were mid-century themes that continue to underlie some popular theoretical constructs (Anderson 1984; Derry 1975; Holly 2002). These have developed into ideas of ecological systems as either outside destructive, sustaining, or productive forces of cultural systems that continue to find positive explanative utility (Giddings 1963; Mason and Bigelow 2008). Over the first two decades of the twenty-first century, research in the Tanana Valley has been guided along the lines of exploring sociocultural, seasonal, geographic, and economic networks of land-use patterns and subsistence economies (Potter 2008a, 2008b, 2008c; Smith 2012). Post-processual methods critiquing or exploring the subjective nature of these interpretations and emphasizing gender or age-graded roles remain underemphasized (Heppner 2017). Today, portions of all of these paradigms retain mixed utility. Their terminology tends to persist as useful conveyors of information, even after the research paradigms that produced them have lost their efficiency. Unfortunately, their use can also carry a legacy of outmoded arguments (Anderson 2008).

Today, the bulk of archaeological exploration in Alaska currently occurs through the largely privatized vocation of Cultural Resource Management (CRM), a pattern that began with the construction of the Trans-Alaska Pipeline System in 1975. The CRM industry is principally driven and funded as a legal compliance management industry motivated mainly by the interaction of any development (planned or otherwise) that occurs on federal, state, and tribal lands. That process can also peripherally affect other privately held properties. The development and perpetuation of this industry is a response to over a century of principle US legislation included in the Antiquities Act (1906: Public Law 59-209; U.S.C. 431–433), Historic Sites Act (1935:

Public Law 89-249; 16 U.S.C. 461–467), the National Historic Preservation Act (1966: Public Law 89-665; 16 U.S.C. 470), the National Environmental Preservation Act (1969: Pubic Law 91-190; 42 U.S.C. 4321–4347), the Archaeological Resources Protection Act (1979: Public Law 96-95; 16 U.S.C. 470aa-mm), the Native American Graves Protection and Repatriation Act (1990: Public Law 101-601; 25 U.S.C. 3001–3013), and their subsequent amendments.

These laws also require that persons applying for archaeological research permits meet basic education requirements of an accredited master's degree in an appropriate field of study. This requirement ensures that the most up-to-date methodology is employed. Researchers are expected to have a basic knowledge of cross-cultural relationships with descendant Alaska Native communities and are trained to disseminate their findings professionally and publicly. That last bit is important; any archaeological resource that is not on private lands is considered part of the public domain and generally cannot be collected for private use or sale. Much of the funding for research is provided through tax-funded grants and salaries. Therefore, the public has a vested interest and a right to access the findings, which are provided through museum repositories and publication venues.

The practical interpretation of these federal laws and their interaction with similar state, municipal, and tribal laws have developed an industry partnership between federal, state, and private CRM entities that currently focuses on statutory compliance through archaeological survey and mitigation. In this system, sites are identified and tested for just enough information to assess their relative regional importance and are otherwise preserved intact and only excavated when they are in danger of destruction. Their interpretation has resulted in creating state-specific inventories that include all the research into these sites and management strategies that support their protection and study based on their relative value to the American public (NPS 1995). Value and protection are best informed through a site's comprehensive comparison against all known sites, driving the perpetual need for additional surveys. Despite the decades-long practical application of these laws, inventories remain far from complete, continuing to direct most funding toward initial survey and only basic recording of this aspect of precolonial archaeology.

In the absence of a detailed, comprehensive analysis of all known sites in a given area, most agencies default to protecting all cultural resources equally through a management strategy that is as least invasive into known sites as possible. It usually falls to mitigating CRM efforts and academic archaeologists who are usually further funded through various state salaries and federal grants to take the time for careful, quality investigations of known sites. However, archaeologists in other industrial sectors often find creative ways to fund and publish their research. As such, the majority of archaeological remains in Alaska remain only cursorily described. Initial explorations, often referred to as "Phase 1" explorations, simply have to confirm the presence of cultural items. This basic confirmation can be a single flake, a single feature, or even just an informed story. When cultural surface depressions are encountered, they are often assumed to either be house pits or cache pits and may be described as such without further analysis.

BACKGROUND OF THE HOLOCENE ARCHAEOLOGY OF SHAW CREEK VALLEY

There are two principal archaeological sites that this book focuses on, Swan Point and Pickupsticks. The Swan Point Archaeological Site was discovered in 1991 by Richard VanderHoek and Thomas Dilley. Dr. Charles Holmes had directed them to explore an isolated hill while excavations were beginning at the nearby site of Broken Mammoth (Holmes et al. 1996). Within a decade, both Broken Mammoth and Swan Point became widely known for their unique insights into Terminal Pleistocene human behaviors. The Shaw Creek basin where they are situated has become widely recognized for its remarkable preservation of several other Terminal Pleistocene assemblages stretching human occupation back over 14,000 years. This unique look into confirmed pre-Clovis behaviors has provided impetus and funding for a number of regional investigations, and a related survey in 2010 resulted in the discovery of the Pickupsticks site by Charles Holmes and Randy Tedore, named because a recent wildfire had toppled many spruce trees across the site (Holmes 2012).

The Swan Point site is located about 6 km northeast of the middle Tanana River, on an isolated bedrock knoll on the northwestern edge of the Shaw Creek Flats in central Alaska. The Pickupsticks site is located at the top of a similarly isolated hill northwest of Caribou Creek at the north end of the basin, approximately 5 miles to the east from Swan Point. The Flats are broadly characterized as a black-spruce bog interspersed with small lakes, creeks, and birch stands, with the current vegetative regime holding stable throughout the middle Holocene. Swan Point's locale is relatively well-drained, with mature stands of white spruce and birch (Reuther et al. 2016). Before 2010, the ecological setting of Pickupsticks was similar; that year, a localized wildfire reset the vegetative regime. The discovery of the site occurred in the same season, just after the wildfire had ceased. While the fire's intensity toppled many of the trees on the site, its effect on the artifact and feature record seems to have been minimal.

Between 1991 and 2019, multiple excavation crews have returned to Swan Point for nineteen field seasons under Dr. Holmes's direct supervision. Most of these excavations were conducted with volunteer crews sponsored by the Alaska Office of History and Archaeology. Two field schools were sponsored through the University of Wisconsin Oshkosh (2005 and 2006), and three by myself with the University of Alaska Fairbanks (UAF) (2017–2019). While the work at Swan Point has yet to be comprehensively summarized in a single volume, multiple specific aspects of its analysis have been completed and discussed in many key conference papers, posters, published papers, and several PhD dissertations. At Pickupsticks, test excavations took place in 2011, 2014, 2015, and 2017 by Charles Holmes and were directed by myself with Holmes in 2019 (summarized in Smith et al. 2020).

The overall purpose of this study was to investigate the origins and antiquity of Alaskan Dene culture in this region through the household perspective. The domestic sphere is significant; it represents the focal point where a society's cultural values are symbolically intensified and reassessed daily. Therefore, village sites are considered an integral part of the archaeological focus of this endeavor. Distinct research gaps exist concerning them in the Alaskan interior. In the Tanana Valley, the Dixthada village site (MT: *Dithaade*: somewhat distant/ancient) at Mansfield Lake (MT: *Dihthaade Menn'*: somewhat distant/ancient lake) represents the only other detailed precolonial household archaeological study in the Upper Tanana Valley watershed (Rainey 1939a; Shinkwin 1979). In the lower Tanana Valley, the only household archaeological studies have been at Lake Minchumina by Ed Hosley, Charles West, and Charles Holmes (summarized in Holmes 1986). In the central Tanana, the Terminal Pleistocene summer residence at *Xaasaa Na'* (upward-going sun stream) remains the only described residential feature (Potter et al. 2011).

The house pit at Swan Point is located at a secondary locus downhill from the main excavation area. It was initially discovered and tested in 2002 and 2005, which confirmed the presence of material cultural remains (Holmes 2008). Later excavations were conducted in 2017 and 2018, which ultimately revealed the extent of the feature and the immediate area. The house pit at Pickupsticks was discovered and tested in 2010, 2011, 2014, and 2015 by an irregular-shaped trench. In 2019, the entire feature was excavated, including a limited exploration of the immediate area outside the feature. Due to the relatively small size of these features, it is recognized that many, if not most, past activities that occurred within the domestic sphere were outdoors. Thus, the domestic sphere is not equated or limited to being the residence feature. However, due to time constraints, available personnel, remote location, and loss of the final planned field season in 2020 due to the global SARS-CoV-2 pandemic, further exploration of these "outdoor" areas at Swan Point and Pickupsticks remain limited. Finally, to explore additional site-specific behaviors, the excavated assemblage from the main locus at Swan Point was included.

SPATIAL MAPPING SUMMARY

When rendering digitized artifact density maps, they can either be generated by cumulative artifact count (Esdale 2009; Potter 2005; Potter et al. 2018), artifact weight (Potter 2005), or artifact size. All potentially can generate very different spatial organization maps, depending on the desired investigation. A map produced by artifact count will be biased by total artifact numbers and their locations. High amounts of small artifacts will influence a map where any post-depositional artifact movements will likely be highlighted. A map produced by artifact weight will be biased toward artifact size and number. It will be influenced by material types that are denser and heavier and, therefore, less likely to be affected by post-depositional events than others. A map produced by artifact size will be biased by material types that are not curated as much as others (Surovell 2003).

Lewis Binford considered the third option to reflect original site behaviors as most likely, informed by his "Working Around a Hearth" model developed from ethnographic observations at Anaktuvuk Pass in north-central Alaska (1983, 153) (figure 5.1). In this model, workers seated near a fire will generally not face it directly (avoiding light-blindness). A drop zone of smaller debris will form in direct association with their location. Few pieces of this debris will make it into the fire, although a toss zone of larger artifacts may

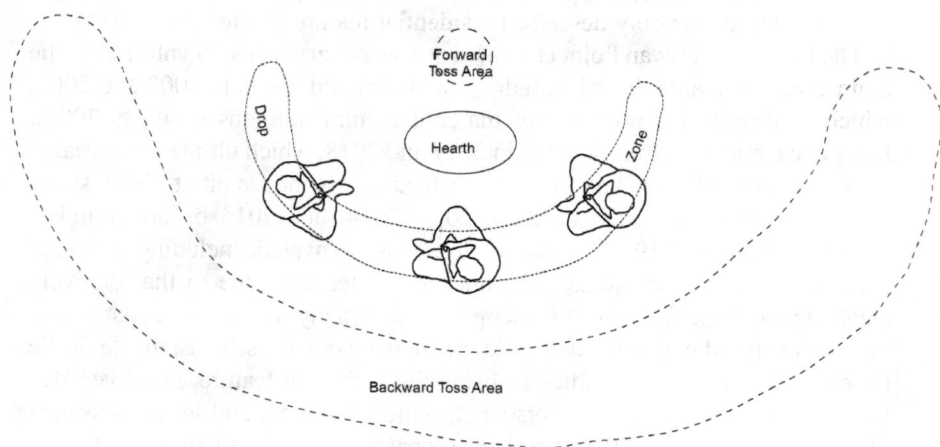

Figure 5.1.   Adaptation of Binford's "Working Around a Hearth" model (1983: 153).

collect on the opposite side of the worker's hearth. A backward toss zone of the larger objects will form an arc behind the workers. Informed by this model, it is considered that rendering density maps by artifact size is more likely to minimize post-depositional taphonomic effects and will be more likely to represent original site behaviors.

GEOARCHAEOLOGICAL SUMMARY

Interpreting soil formation processes at a site is integral for informing local and regional environmental contexts. These help to inform the behavioral interpretations implied from the artifact scatter patterns (Gladfelter 1977). Two separate loci were excavated at Swan Point: the main locus is at the southeast tip of the knoll. It is characterized by 0.7 to 1 m of aeolian sand and wind-blown silt (loess) deposition overlying a highly degraded outcrop of mica-rich schistic bedrock being primarily of felsic gneiss, locally termed Birch Creek Schist (Dilley 1998, 147). The stratigraphy and archaeological deposits at the main locus are relatively undisturbed by annual freezing and thawing of sediments (cryoturbation) or other post-depositional non-cultural mixing processes, such as bioturbation, except for a few krotovinas and invasive precolonial cultural pits (Dilley 1998; Holmes 2001; Kielhofer et al. 2020). Floral turbation is present, but its effects are minimal. Krotovinas and tree roots were encountered in the cultural layers, but their impacts on the archaeosediments have been minimal and easily tracked.

The Protohistoric/Historic zone is assumed to be primarily observed on the surface and in the sod layer: the A/O horizon (Munsell [2017] color code 10YR 2/1). It represents the organic-rich sediment layer and the root mat. Below surface measurements began at the base of the sod and top of mineral soil. The top 35 cm of cultural remains almost entirely corresponds with the Bw horizon layer (fine silt). The Bw horizon (10YR 3/3) represents a very fine aeolian silt loam with some interspersed organics. It generally transitions to a C horizon (fine silt) below. The C horizon (10YR 4/6) represents a very fine, organic-poor aeolian silt; very thin (<1 cm thick) organic-rich "stingers", often generalized as paleosols, are also evident (see Kielhofer et al. 2020, 1–2). Levels 1–6 (each being 5 cm thick) tend to be within the Bw horizon, while the transition between the Bw and C horizons tend to occur across the site in Level 7. At the bottom of the C horizon, a thin layer of highly degraded, discontinuous, schistic rubble and aeolian sands marks the Late Pleistocene stratigraphy (Dilley 1998; Holmes et al. 1996) (figure 5.2).

CZ1a (725–1530 cal BP) is vertically assumed to encompass the top four levels, or 20 cm, of sediment. Horizontally, the radiocarbon samples suggest

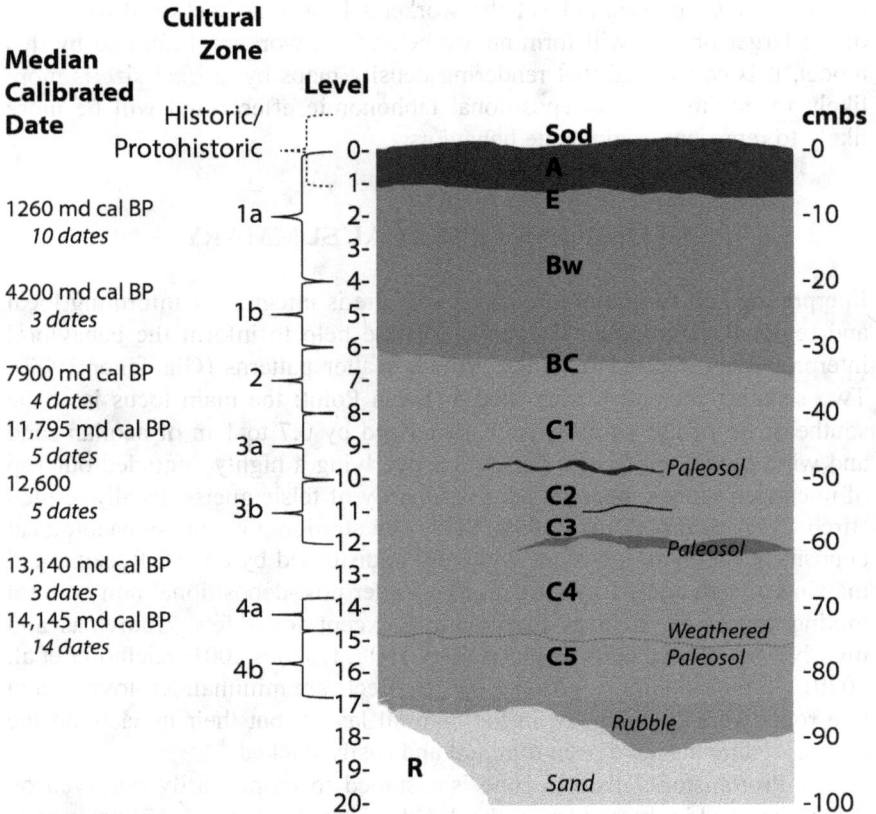

Figure 5.2. Generalized sediment profile of the main locus at Swan Point (adapted from Holmes 2006).

that this component may be separated into a northern, older component and a southern, younger component. CZ1b (4800–5525 cal BP) is assumed to encompass the next lower two levels (or 10 cm) of sediment. CZ2 (7500–8200 cal BP) represents the following two deeper levels (10 cm). The early Holocene components are constrained to Levels 8–12 (~40–60 cmbs), and the Terminal Pleistocene components to Levels 14–17 (~70–85 cmbs). These arbitrary vertical groupings are informed through dated hearth features, faunal remains, and formal lithic classifications.

Even though the vertical displacement of artifacts appears limited, it was considered necessary to conduct a comprehensive analysis of all within the upper eight layers (top 40 cm of the stratigraphic column) to provide data confirming that observation. Initially, this project was limited to analyzing only CZ1a as it corresponded closest in time to the house pit occupations at

Swan Point and Pickupsticks. However, because there was no stratigraphic separation between the artifacts in these three components, it was soon recognized that the inclusion of CZ1b and 2 would allow for a systematic comparison of raw material and activity behaviors across time. Additionally, it would provide a more informed idea if any vertical artifact displacement occurred within the top 40 cm of deposition. CZ3a, 3b, 4a, and 4b date to the earliest Holocene and beyond into the late Pleistocene over 14,000 years old. These components are beyond the scope of this book.

The natural taphonomic processes at Locus 2 are quite similar to the upper locus. CZ1a1 (795–925 cal BP) is represented by a single artifact, an unmodified moose talus, in the top two levels. CZ1a2 (1810–2115 cal BP) is represented in levels 2–4, or the Bw horizon. CZ1b (2535–3600 cal BP) is represented by two pit features whose origin may not be anthropogenic. CZ2 (7850–7975 cal BP) in levels 5–12, primarily the C horizon, and CZ3a is represented at the base, only by a single artifact, a spiral-fractured wapiti humerus fragment. At Locus 2, CZ3a is represented in the three levels above the rubble layer (figure 5.3).

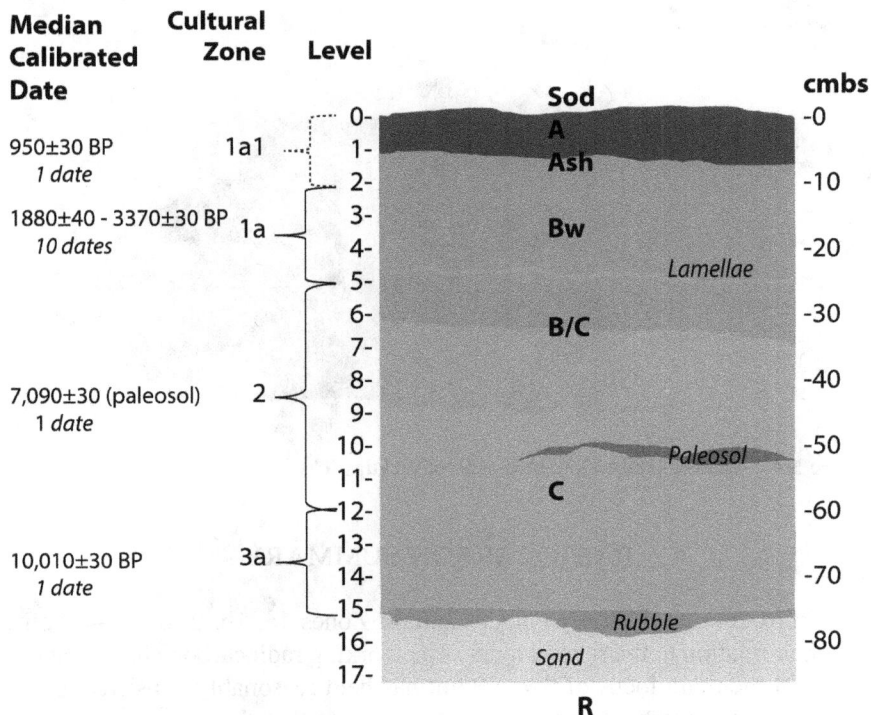

Figure 5.3. Generalized sediment profile of the second locus at Swan Point.

The Pickupsticks site depicts similar formation processes to those observed at Swan Point, but with a few crucial differences. It is located at the top of a smaller knoll, about 50 meters above the surrounding valley, with expansive views toward the Tanana Valley to the southwest. It is characterized by 0.3 to 1 m of aeolian sand and wind-blown silt (loess) deposition overlying a highly degraded outcrop of mica-rich schistic bedrock, being primarily of felsic gneiss just as with Swan Point. However, sediment accumulation has been minimal on the knoll's southern and central areas, typically less than 30 cm deep. It gradually grows thicker toward the north (lee) side of the hill. Due to the shallow nature of the sediments, a relatively thicker Bw horizon has formed, and the C horizon is minimally defined.

Additionally, a thicker layer of very fine, well-sorted aeolian sand exists to the northern end of the hill. The difference in the processes between the two sites may be due to a higher aeolian-energy environment. Only a single cultural occupation (785–1530 cal BP) has been described at the site, similar in time to Swan Point CZ1. The artifacts are generally restricted to the top 45 cm in the Bw horizon (figure 5.4).

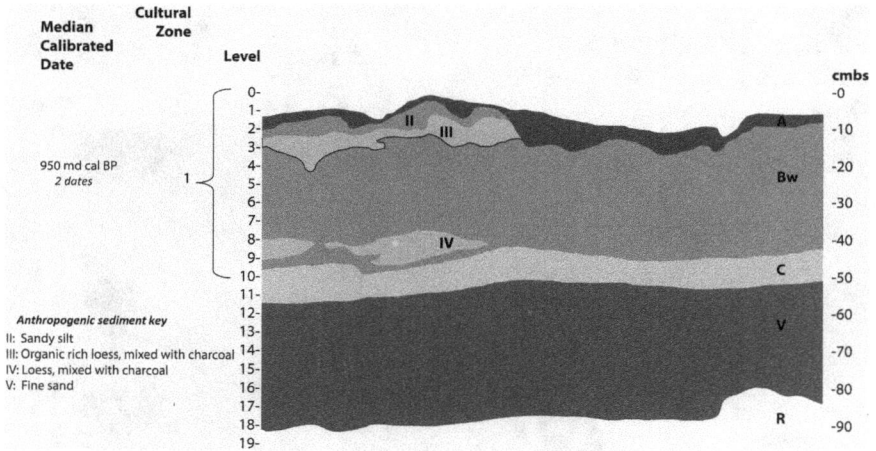

Figure 5.4.   Generalized sediment profile of Pickupsticks.

RADIOCARBON SUMMARY

This book focuses on the younger Cultural Zones 1a, 1b, 2, of Swan Point and their relation to the second locus. The working radiocarbon chronological model at the main locus of Swan Point has held reasonably consistent since 2006. The radiocarbon record strongly suggests that the upper eight 5-cm levels at the main locus are associated with these three components. The working vertical model indicates that this pattern is relatively uniform across that area.

Laboratories used for assay analysis were Beta-Analytic USA, the University of Georgia Center for Applied Isotope Studies, Washington State University Radiocarbon Laboratory, and the University of Arizona AMS Laboratory. The online OxCal version 4.4.2 program and Bayesian phase analysis (Bronk Ramsey and Lee 2013) was used to produce the calibrated dates published here (these used the IntCal20 atmospheric curve [Heaton et al. 2020; Reimer et al. 2020]).

CZ1a (Levels 1–4) is split into two radiocarbon clusters, a younger zone (CZ1a1 ~725–1,150 cal BP) and an older one (CZ1a2 ~1,450–2,115 cal BP). Most of the older dates cluster in the northeastern half of the excavation area, while all of the younger dates cluster in the southwestern half. Artifacts relating to these two events cannot be reliably segregated horizontally or vertically; they will be discussed together only as CZ1a. CZ1b (Levels 5–6) has dates beginning around 2600 but more tightly clusters between around 4,800–5,525 cal BP, likely representing multiple occupation events. CZ2 (Levels 7–8) spans 7,500–8,200 cal BP, illustrating several occupational events that span a very unique and relatively unstudied period in the ancient Alaskan past, the transition between the American Paleoarctic and Northern Archaic traditions (Holmes 2008) (figure 5.5, table 5.1).

Excavations at Swan Point Locus 2 have concluded that the features and assemblage most likely represented two occupations, one associated with the house pit and an earlier artifact component that had been disturbed by its construction. The recovery of two ungulate bones, a moose talus from Level 4 and a wapiti humerus fragment from just above the rubble horizon, suggest that other cultural components are ephemerally represented (equivalent to CZ1a1 and 3a at the main locus). Thirteen organic samples were chosen to provide dates of the natural stratigraphy, the numerous anthropogenic features visible in the sediments, and other cultural events.

Given the close proximity of the two loci at Swan Point (~50 meters) and between the Swan Point and Pickupsticks sites (~5 miles), it is quite likely, given the ethnographic summary, that the same band utilized all three areas. Many of the radiocarbon dates appear to overlap in time, strengthening this expectation. The work at Swan Point and Pickupsticks suggest three broad cultural zones are present representing the precolonial period for this research, between 8,000 and 700 cal BP (Holmes 2008; Hirasawa and Holmes 2017).

In summary, the radiocarbon record from both sites suggests an almost continuous use of the landscape based on overlapping assay probabilities from about 725–2,115 cal BP (CZ1a), about 2,535–5,530 cal BP (CZ1b), and

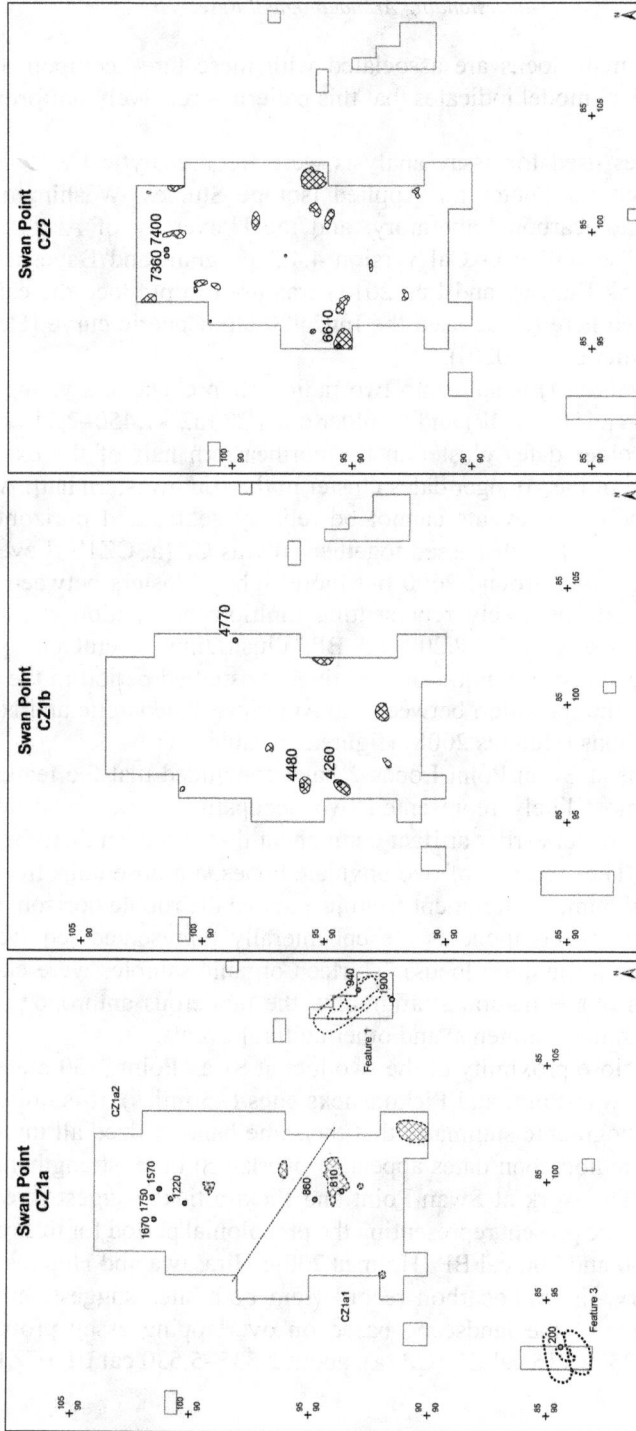

Figure 5.5. Mean uncalibrated radiocarbon locations and hearth features for Swan Point CZ1a, 1b, and 2.

Table 5.1. Radiocarbon Assays and Interpretations

ID	FS ID	Material	Site/Locus	Context	¹⁴C BP	±	IntCal20 Cal BP 2σ	Swan Point Cultural Zone	Tradition	Generalized Ecological Events
Beta 340993	75	Charcoal	Main Locus Block	Hearth	810	30	675-772	1a1	(Athabascan tradition)	Medieval Warm Period
Beta 223302	40	Charcoal	Main Locus Block	Hearth	860	40	681-904	1a1		
AA 109204	202	Collagen	Main Locus Block	B Horizon	880	20	730-897	1a1		
UGAMS 47575	1641	Birchbark	Pickupsticks Housepit	Bark on top of precolonial excavation into bedrock, base of modern excavation	930	25	776-917	1a1		
UGAMS 43503	1620	Charcoal	Feature 1	Base of Feature 1	940	20	791-913	1a1		
UGAMS 22416	UA2015-252-0018	Burned twig	Pickupsticks Housepit	50 cmbs, Base of Stratum III	950	25	791-919	1a1		
Beta 486532	33	Collagen, moose talus	*Locus 2*	B Horizon	950	30	788-923	1a1		

(continued)

Table 5.1. (continued)

ID	FS ID	Material	Site/Locus	Context	¹⁴C BP	±	IntCal20 Cal BP 2σ	Swan Point Cultural Zone	Tradition	Generalized Ecological Events
WSU 4523	112	Charcoal	Main Locus Block	Charcoal, possible root	1,220	70	1,003-1,296	1a1	(Transitional Athabascan tradition)	White River Ash East: 1,095-1,170
WSU 4524	150	Charcoal/Wood	Main Locus Block	Hearth, charcoal and burnt bone	1,570	70	1,310-1,588	1a2		White River Ash North: 1,560-1,689
UGAMS 47576	373	Collagen	Pickupsticks, Disturbed	10-15 cmbs, moose tibia fragment, B Horizon, within housepit feature	1,580	25	1,400-1,527	1a2		
WSU 4522	57	Charcoal	Main Locus Block	Charcoal	1,670	60	1,410-1,702	1a2		
WSU 4521	79	Charcoal/Wood/Resin	Main Locus Block	Hearth, charcoal associated with burnt bone	1,750	80	1,420-1,791	1a2		Devil tephra 1,625-1,825
Beta 401123	219	Charcoal	Main Locus Block	Hearth	1,860	30	1,706-1,816	1a2		
Beta 215326	110	Charcoal	Feature 2	Roof Sod	1,880	40	1,706-1,917	1a2		
UGAMS 43501	1514	Charcoal	Feature 1	Hearth, F2019-2	1,900	20	1,731-1,818	1a2		
UGAMS 41457	1253	Charcoal	Feature 2	Interior Hearth F2018-13	1,910	20	1,742-1,881	1a2		Stable Late/Middle Holocene Boreal Ecosystem
Beta 215325	109	Charcoal	Feature 2	Living Floor	1,910	50	1,712-1,975	1a2		
UGAMS 41458	1254	Charcoal	Feature 2	Interior Hearth F2018-14	1,950	30	1,750-1,986	1a2		
Beta 215327	113	Charcoal	Feature 2	Living Floor	2,090	40	1,941-2,290	1a2		

Table 5.1. *(continued)*

Lab ID	No.	Material	Locus	Provenience	Age	±	Cal range (2σ)	Tradition	Event
UGAMS 41454	301	Charcoal	*Locus 2*	Pit 1	2,460	25	2,366–2,705 1b	(Northern Archaic tradition)	
Beta 486530	300	Charcoal	*Locus 2*	Pit 1	2,460	30	2,365–2,707 1b		
UGAMS 43636	30	Charcoal	Main Locus Block	From base of B horizon near flakes	2,800	20	2,850–2,960 1b		Major Tanana flooding event ~3,000
Beta 401124	92	Charcoal	Main Locus Block	*Picea* assc. w/ calcined bone	3,060	30	3,425–3,466 1b		*Watana tephras* 3,360–4,400
UGAMS 41456	873	Charcoal	*Locus 2*	Pit 2	3,090	20	3,239–3,368 1b		
UGAMS 41455	872	Charcoal	*Locus 2*	Pit 2	3,370	30	3,491–3,692 1b		
Beta 190580	140	Charcoal	Main Locus Block	Hearth	4,260	40	4,644–4,959 1b		Stable Late/Middle Holocene Boreal Ecosystem
Beta 401125	107	Charcoal	Main Locus Block	*Larix* hearth	4,480	30	4,977–5,286 1b		
UGAMS 30767	168	Charcoal	Main Locus Block	Hearth, Feature 17-01	4,770	25	5,471–5,585 1b		
Beta 209886	87	Charcoal	Main Locus Block	Hearth?	6,610	40	7,429–7,570 2	(Transitional Northern Archaic tradition)	*Oshetna tephra* 6,570–7,970
UGAMS 47573	694	Charcoal	*Locus 2*	Paleosol	7,090	30	7,842–7,975 2		*Mt. Mazama* ~7,700
UGAMS 43638	82	Charcoal	Main Locus Block	B/C Horizon	7,360	25	8,032–8,297 2		Increased aridity
WSU 4426	1751	Charcoal	Main Locus Block	B/C Horizon	7,400	80	8,033–8,365 2		

Sources: Abbott et al. 2000; Broecker 2001; Davies et al. 2016; Harris 2005; Hirasawa and Holmes 2017; Mulliken 2016; Reuther et al. 2019; Smith 2020a; Wooller et al 2012.

the earliest from around 7,500–8,200 cal BP (CZ2). Cultural Zone 2 is associated with hearth features only. Cultural Zone 1b is associated with hearth features. Artifact scatters suggesting tent-like features were present and are also associated with two small, buried pit-like features of unknown origin or purpose from Locus 2. Cultural Zone 1a2 is associated with the house pit at Swan Point Locus 2 and several outdoor hearths at the main locus, and the earlier moose element at Pickupsticks. The youngest phase, Cultural Zone 1a1, is associated with the Pickupsticks house pit, the large Feature 1 surface pit at Swan Point, and several outdoor hearths.

Excavations at Swan Point Locus 2 have concluded that the features and assemblage most likely represented two occupations, one associated with the house pit and an earlier artifact component that had been disturbed by its construction. The recovery of two ungulate bones, a moose talus from Level 4 and a wapiti humerus fragment from just above the rubble horizon suggest that other cultural components are ephemerally represented (equivalent to CZ1a1 and 3a at the main locus).

Chapter Six

The Holocene Environmental Context of the Middle Tanana

Our plane lifted off from Talkeetna. It was the middle of April, and the streets were filled with mud from the melted winter snows and the boot prints of climbers hoping to make an early ascent of Denali, towering to the north. We were flying east, deep into the middle Susitna Valley, to extract lake sediment cores for paleoecological reconstructions. The Middle Susitna region lies southwest of the Middle Tanana region and has a similar climate. Much of it lies at about 2,000 feet (600 meters) in elevation, while the Middle Tanana is much lower. In contrast, the Shaw Creek Flats lie at about 1,000 feet (300 meters) in elevation. These two basins are divided by the Alaska Range and the Monahan Flats basin where the Nenana and Susitna River headwaters form.

As we flew into the Talkeetna Mountains, we left behind a springtime climate, and entered a world covered in several feet of snow and of frozen lakes and rivers. The Nelchina caribou herd was dispersed across the landscape in small bands preparing to birth a new generation in the upcoming weeks, and bears were coming out of their dens, foraging for the scarce food that early spring provides.

Our K2 Aviation's de Havilland Otter landed on the first of our lakes, and we positioned our ice augers and began drilling access holes through the two-meter-thick ice. Next, our small crew prepared our Bolivia and Livingstone corers for driving by hand into the sediments deep below. Lakes form natural sinks where sediments from the surrounding watershed are deposited, and if the basin is deep enough, these typically remain undisturbed, maintaining a record of flora and faunal fossil residues preserved in the sediments that slowly formed over the top of them, annual layer by annual layer. For this study (Bigelow et al. 2019), the investigators were particularly interested in extracting (among other things) pollen, radioisotopes, and tephra samples, which were used to reconstruct paleoecological chronologies of the region.

These chronologies were incredibly important for providing information about the Holocene landscape within which Dene ancestors had made a living for thousands of years (Bigelow et al. 2019). The investigators have spent decades throughout the Alaskan interior collecting and analyzing these core samples; each providing a unique glimpse of ecological stasis and change since the Terminal Pleistocene.

The Middle Susitna is particularly important for its series of preserved tephras across the landscape, which are almost entirely absent from the Tanana Valley to the north. These tephras became incredibly important to Alaska archaeologists, who, between 1978 and 1984, also conducted a widespread survey in response to two proposed hydroelectric dams that were never built. Hundreds of precolonial sites representing a variety of site-specific behaviors were identified then. Many of these were subsurface, with artifacts preserved above and below these tephras. The tephras were dated by several laboratories using the most precise radioisotope-counting methodologies of the day. Once their probable deposition periods were known, they were used to relatively date artifacts deposited by humans above, below, and within those layers, providing an inexpensive way to date hundreds of site components.

This provided James Dixon with a bulk of regional data to construct a working chronology for lithic technological forms, demonstrating when they changed and how long they remained unchanged in the area. This chronology for south-central Alaska helped to inform the much older record of the Tanana Valley, providing a level of comparative, analogous details for the middle and late Holocene that was otherwise absent. Between 2012 and 2014, plans for another hydroelectric power plant were again revitalized, prompting a new survey that recovered over one hundred new sites and reanalyzed the dates of those volcanic tephra deposits, providing higher precision on those events. The current interpretation of them, and their relationship with human activities is summarized next.

LATE HOLOCENE ECOLOGY

Presently, the Tanana Valley is characterized by silty glacial rivers and streams flowing northward from the central Alaska Range. Clear streams tend to flow south from the rolling northern Yukon Tanana uplands into the Tanana River, often interrupted by large lakes along the Tanana Flats' northern margins. Other streams, occasional non-glacial-fed, flow north and northwest into the Tanana River from the foothills of the Alaska Range to the south. This ecological setting provided the basis of the economy of the ancient Dene cultural system. In cases where humans invest less energy into modifying their local environments to enhance resource return (niche construction), they are increasingly at the mercy of local ecological and environmental shifts that affect those resources. Understanding those past changes help us to recognize potential cultural resilience mechanisms.

Different small-scale ecological shifts punctuate the last few millennia in this region, and this signature is evident in lichen growth patterns. Evidence from lichen growth on moraine deposits suggests periodic glacial advances reached standstills in the Coastal and Brooks Ranges at 850, 650, 500, 300, and 100 lichenometry years BP, with the final advance correlating with the Little Ice Age (Evison et al. 1996; see also Calkin 1988 and Wiles et al. 2010). Increased glacial activity can correlate with cooling periods marked by decreased solar irradiance (Wiles et al. 2004). The end of the last cooling period correlates with an increase in solar irradiance, decreased volcanic activity, a shift in natural feedback mechanisms facilitating ecological change, and anthropogenic activities contributing to a greenhouse effect (Overpeck et al. 1997). The cooling episodes prior to that have recently been correlated with the colonial genocide of the fifteenth and sixteenth centuries, when an estimated 56 million indigenous persons perished across the Americas due to European actions. The unfathomable loss of such a population sector (estimated to have been 90 percent of the pre-Columbian population) led to the abandonment of over 50 million hectares of agricultural land to forest succession. The resulting sequestration of carbon in the new forest expansion dramatically cooled the planet, with the authors concluding that this became a primary factor driving the development of the Little Ice Age (Koch et al. 2019).

Prior to the global anthropogenic ecological shifts of the past 500 years were important climatic fluctuations that occurred about 1,000 years ago. These correspond with important human behavioral, settlement strategies, and widespread migrations in North America. During that period in the southern Yukon, Kuhn et al. (2010) have highlighted a shift in caribou mitochondrial DNA, suggesting a pulse of new, outside lineages were integrated around 1,000 cal BP and correlates with two important ecological interruptions. The first being the long-term global Medieval Warm Period (1,200–700 cal BP [Broecker 2001]), which may have placed faunal populations under stress through decreased fodder availability and increased seasonal temperatures. Large game populations seem to have shifted to more southern locales as a response (Perry 1980). The second was the younger eruption of Mt. Churchill located on the southern border of Alaska and Yukon (1,170–1,095 cal BP

[Davies et al. 2016]). This genomic signal may be localized to the southern Yukon territory; no significant genetic change has been observed for caribou herds farther east in the Mackenzie and Selwyn Mountains for the last 4,000 years (Letts et al. 2012) or to the west in Alaska.

The Medieval Warm Period (~1,200–700 cal BP) correlates with a time of increased salmonid population density across the North American Pacific Rim (Mann et al. 1998), corresponding with the period of intensified human use of their migratory paths, a need for large-scale storage of the harvest product of these species, and their rise in cultural and spiritual importance in the cultures that subsisted on them (Boraas 2007). The development or intensified use of a salmon storage-based economy during this time revolutionized the cultures of the Pacific Coast from Alaska to California. It increased the carrying capacity of local landscapes by up to six times (Croes and Hackenberger 1988; Matson and Coupland 1995), resulting in an increased number of individual villages, village population sizes, and cultural diversity, and may have been one of the catalysts for the development of key aspects differentiating the Athabascan technological tradition from the earlier preceding Northern Archaic tradition.

THE ROLE OF VOLCANISM IN REGIONAL CULTURAL CHANGE

Complexity theory focuses on understanding how energy inputs into open systems can bring about unpredictable, long-term changes to that system. One example of a predictable energy input mechanism is changes in the earth's axial tilt or orbit, which shifts the energy input from the sun toward or away from arctic regions, resulting in widespread changes in the ecology (Mason and Bigelow 2008). An unpredictable but repetitive interrupter of the Alaskan Holocene ecological system is volcanism. During the Holocene, several volcanic events led to varying degrees of widespread ashfall events, possibly as few as thirty-nine (Mulliken et al. 2018) or as many as seventy (Riehle 1985). These mainly affected southcentral Alaska and the Cook Inlet region, and few left any traceable effects in the Tanana Valley.

These tephra events' consequences for past human populations are complex and should not be modeled as linear events. In other words, human responses to each event were likely unique to varying degrees. Essential variables to consider include the depth of ashfall, affected solar insolation, atmospheric cooling, plant response, precipitation needed for floral recolonization, the terrestrial faunal response, aquatic response, marine response, season of ashfall, human perception of the negative effect the ashfall had on resources, degree of impact ashfall has on necessary seasonal mobility strate-gies, external population pressure affecting migration pathways away from the event, and re-dispersal into the altered landscape by humans and or other faunal species. Each tephra event and its effects on the archaeological record should be considered an exclusive event with distinct responses (Begét et al. 1991; Reger et al. 1993).

Several events were of sufficient magnitude that they have captured the interests of archaeologists. Of particular interest is the latest eruption of Mt. Churchill (1,170–1,095 cal BP [Davies et al. 2016]) located on the southern boundary between Alaska and Yukon. Its eruption's explosivity value is estimated to have been a VEI 6, similar to the 1883 Krakatoa, 1912 Novarupata, and 1991 Pinatubo eruptions. It resulted in a massive ash cloud, called the White River Ash East tephra, that spread over 1,000 km eastward. This massive eruption may have occurred during the winter season (Clague et al. 1995; seasonal hypotheses discussed in MacIntosh n.d.; Workman 1979; West and Donaldson 2000). In response to the eruption, a large-scale Dene exodus from the region was proposed by David Derry (1975). Wil-liam Workman (1974, 1979) observed significant typological changes in the local precolonial record of southern Yukon at the same time, which seemed to support that hypothesis and developed a model of population expanding east and south from southern Yukon in response to the volcanic event, suggesting a domino effect where each out-migrating group pushed into another's territory and caused further migrations. This model continues to find utility and efficacy for explaining the disruptions observed in the cultural record of northwestern Canada during that time. Gregory Hare et al. (2012) further suggest that the typological shift regarding dart/arrow manu-facture and associated technology changes signals a human behavioral stress response, ultimately lasting between 1,000 and 500 cal BP. During that period, upland hunting activities increased in southern Yukon, and caribou numbers decreased. Kristensen et al. (2019) demonstrate that activity regard-ing obsidian-use trade networks also intensified between southern Yukon and British Columbia after. These shifts in landscape use may have been a response due to significantly increased lacustrine stress associated with the tephra fall (Hughes et al. 2013; Lacourse and Gajewski 2000).

Investigations have since focused on whether this event affected Alaska or not. The regional typological shifts observed approximately a thousand years ago, discussed in the following chapter, correlate temporally with the event, but definitive markers indicating any population migrations into Alaska from the east at this time remain elusive. A possible depopulation was proposed to explain a dearth of radiocarbon-dated sites in the affected area of the Upper Tanana after the eruption (Mullen 2012). A small survey in the Upper

Tanana by Joshua Lynch et al. (2018) also indicated a lack of regional site visibility for several centuries after the eruption, suggests a regional drop in demographic pressure. They proposed a territorial population expansion in the Upper Tanana may have taken place after this, during the last 500 years (also modeled by Mullen 2012). However, this pattern of low demographic pressure has been shown to span both sides of the time of volcanism (Potter 2008a), and may have begun much earlier, suggesting volcanism was not the original culprit but may have instead prolonged any human population rebounds. The demonstrated pattern of low population density and high mobility for this period have suggested to some that it is unlikely that any long-term or permanent population replacements occurred (Gordon 2012). A recent regional survey indicated a pattern of resource intensification focused on river locales may have occurred after the tephra fall (Doering et al. 2020). Recent work regarding the question of cultural hiatus in response to the White River Ash East ashfall was conducted at the Fortymile site on the confluence of the Fortymile and Yukon Rivers (Smith 2020b). Findings there suggest the direct effects of the ashfall in the area surrounding the site suppressed regional pollen production for around five years with continuous human occupation throughout this period of stress. Comparisons of faunal assemblages before and after the event document a long-term widening diet breadth occurring post-eruption, a potential signal for a human population stressed for food resources (Smith 2020b, 84–89).

The oral ethnogenesis stories describing volcanic-like events originate entirely from the eastern Canadian Dene people. The Mountain, *Tłı̨chǫ*, *K'ashó Gòt'ine*, and South Slavey people of Northwestern Canada, on the eastern front of the Mackenzie Mountains, consider volcanic events to be closely tied with their ethnolinguistic origins (Fast 2008; Moodie et al. 1992). No explicit stories of volcanism have yet been curated from oral traditions for the Tanana people. However, stories do persist in the Upper Tanana describing one or a series of years without a summer, where rivers remained frozen through the warm months and food was difficult to obtain, all recognizable effects that regional and global volcanism can have on local climate (Fast 2008).

Several other later-Holocene tephra events also hold interest to precolonial archaeologists of interior Alaska. One volcanic episode that directly impacted the Upper and Middle Tanana Valley was Mt. Churchill's earlier, smaller eruption, known as the White River Ash North ashfall event (Hanson 1965; McGimsey et al. 1990). Evidence suggests this eruption occurred during the summer season (Lerbekmo et al. 1975), estimated at 1,560–1,689 cal BP (Reuther et al. 2019). A possible outmigration away from the ashfall area was also suggested through a regional radiocarbon model by Mullen (2012; see also Lynch et al. 2018). Work in the Middle Tanana by Doering et al.

(2020) indicates that the period roughly between the two White River ashfalls reflects a critical point of cultural change from the earlier Northern Archaic tradition to the later Athabascan tradition. This cultural shift is indicated by greater ecological specialization in raw materials, reduction strategies, their use, a diet breadth increase, and freshwater resource intensification/specialization. Their conclusion largely follows the pattern of lowland intensification during this time identified by Potter (2008a, 2008b).

Another smaller tephra event of a similar time is described to the southwest in the Talkeetna Mountains (Dixon 1985; Dixon et al. 1985), termed the Devil Tephra. This ashfall is associated with the Hayes Volcano (DN: *Qayeh Dghelaya*: village mountain) northwest of Anchorage (recently redated to 1,625–1,825 cal BP) (Dilley 1988; Mulliken 2016). No observed cultural response has been modeled for this eruption (Dixon et al. 1985; Hays et al. 2014).

THE MIDDLE HOLOCENE ECOSYSTEM AND VOLCANIC BEHAVIOR

The regional mid-Holocene (~6,000 cal BP) pollen biomes of interior Alaska and Yukon appear almost identical to today, suggesting a recognizable and long-term stable floral landscape had become established (Edwards et al. 2000). The ecology was similar to that of the twentieth century by as early as 6,000 cal BP, with gradual cooling and increased moisture trends beginning about 5,000 cal BP, significantly affecting the summer month temperatures and increasing precipitation, with critical localized trends (Abbott et al. 2000; Calkin et al. 2001; Kaufman et al. 2016; Wooller et al. 2012). The faunal communities were recognizable to the nineteenth and twentieth centuries, with some possible small remnant communities of bison and wapiti (Potter et al. 2018).

An early significant tephra observed in the Middle Susitna Basin is the Hayes Tephra, which originated from the Hayes Volcano in the Tordrillo Mountains in the southwestern Alaska Range, dating between 3,360–4,400 cal BP (Mulliken 2016; Mulliken et al. 2018; Riehle et al. 1990). The Hayes eruption is estimated at a VEI of 5.4. Tephra spread to the east and the north, depositing most of its ash within the greater upper Cook Inlet and Susitna River watersheds (Wallace et al. 2014). These tephras have been correlated with the Jarvis tephra in the Delta River region (Begét et al. 1991) and the two Watana tephras that Dixon et al. (1985) described in the middle Susitna River area of the Talkeetna Mountains. The Hayes tephra may represent as many as seven or eight discrete deposition events (Riehle et al. 1990). It may have severely impacted human demographic pressure in southcentral Alaska, perhaps responsible for the lack of consistent human settlement in the Upper Cook Inlet region until centuries later.

The oldest significant middle Holocene volcanic event in southcentral Alaska is the Oshetna tephra, also thought to originate from the Hayes Volcano, observed throughout the Talkeetna Mountains (6,570–7,970 cal BP; Dixon et al. 1985; Mulliken 2016). The Oshetna Tephra is also potentially correlated with a southcentral Alaskan cultural hiatus, and only a few regional sites immediately predate it in the Susitna Valley. As yet, no dated components south of the Alaska Range have been demonstrated to date between 10,000 and 8,000 cal BP, providing a potential upper limit for Dene linguistic ancestry in that region. However, this research gap once existed for the Tanana Valley as well, and was eventually disproven. On the other hand, unique ecological stressors on the Copper and Susitna River valley may indicate this is a real gap; enormous proglacial lakes in the Susitna and Copper River basins decanted after 11,000 cal BP, followed by a long-term regional spike in temperatures greater than today (Smith 2019). We still do not understand when food networks became established after those events to the point that humans could successfully make a living there.

The Oshetna and Hayes tephras left easily recognizable layers in the southcentral region. Once they were accurately dated in the early 1980s, they became a proxy for relatively dating archaeological assemblages in the region. This datable stratigraphy allowed for Dr. James Dixon to work out the first detailed schematic of archaeological traditions and complexes for the Alaskan interior (Dixon 1985).

THE EARLY HOLOCENE LANDSCAPE

The earlier middle Holocene is marked by stabilizing eustatic sea levels around the Alaskan coasts (particularly the Bering and Chukchi Seas), which was mainly completed by 9,000 cal BP and had stabilized by 6,000 cal BP (Mason et al. 2001). The stabilized sea levels likely facilitated the appearance of sustained, maritime-oriented cultures on the coast a millennium later (Mason 2015). Perhaps the most visible Terminal Pleistocene/early Holocene event was the breaching of Central Beringia by the encroaching Bering and Chukchi seas (13,000–8,000 cal BP). The sea-level rise and subsequent joining of the Bering and Chukchi seas marked at the end of the Pleistocene and correlated with an increase in Alaska's ocean-induced weather patterns.

The climate prior to the middle Holocene was hotter and drier than the present. Ecologically, the period represents a long-term gradual cooling trend from the earlier Holocene Thermal Maximum (10,000–9,000 cal BP [Mason et al. 2001]) and a rise in spruce and a decline in poplar species, leading to an early loss of widespread grasslands and eventually resulting in the establishment of the boreal forest in interior Alaska by 6,000 cal BP (Bigelow 1997).

Pollen signals document a significant spread of alder from the west across northern Alaska around 9,000 cal BP (Anderson and Brubaker 1994). Alder had spread north into Yukon by 8,000 cal BP, and shortly after that, into the southern Brooks Range (Bigelow and Edwards 2001). Early spruce groves seem to have been associated with south-facing slopes during the earliest phases of the Holocene, spreading throughout the Tanana Valley until around 8,000 cal BP, when their expansion may have stalled or even retreated. With the spread of forests and parklands, a fire regime became established, requiring faunal adaptations (Mason et al. 2001; Reuther et al. 2016). A significant shift is seen in the development of a widescale forest canopy and loss of wide-ranging open grasslands around 9,000 cal BP (Bigelow 1997). Lake levels markedly increase in the interior around 9,500 cal BP, increasing the availability of the micro-ecosystems for widespread human cultural adaptation (Abbott et al. 2000).

White spruce expansion out of the Tanana Valley begins as early as 10,200 cal BP, facilitated by the spike in temperatures and aridity (Anderson et al. 2004; Kaufman et al. 2016), dispersing south of the Alaska Range facilitated by the earlier collapse between 11,000 and 10,000 cal BP of the large proglacial lakes Susitna and Atna (Ager 1990, 91; Smith 2019).

Across the North Slope, moisture trends generally increased between around 12,000 and 10,000 cal BP (Mann et al. 2001), sparking ecological shifts across northern Alaska, resulting in decreased grazing habitats and the widespread rise of soil paludification (Mann et al. 2013). Tundra communities expanded throughout these regions during the early and middle Holocene (Oswald et al. 2003). Eventually, as the early Holocene progressed, two generalized ecosystems became established: in northern and western Alaska, a cool, wetter maritime-influenced environment dominated, while a warmer and wetter continental system dominated in the interior (Maxwell and Barrie 1989).

The early Holocene is characterized by a single technocomplex that is widespread throughout the state, the Denali complex. The Denali complex, belonging to the American Paleo-Arctic tradition, tends to be ecologically associated with the upland birch/spruce parklands that developed during this period and hunting large game that had also adapted to it. Bison, wapiti, moose, caribou, and sheep were all available and associated with these parkland areas, although not uniformly dispersed (Guthrie 2006; Krasinski and Haynes 2010). There is considerable debate surrounding the origins and interpretation of the complex. Still, at face value, the earliest dates for the complex are associated with the central Alaska Range, especially the Tangle Lakes region (West et al. 1996a, 1996b, 1996c).

There appears to be an inverse correlation between the later decline of the Denali complex and the rise of the spruce boglands across the Tanana Flats. During this period, much of the early Holocene rich and regionally variable Pleistocene flora and fauna became gradually extirpated by about 6,000 cal BP. Today, one can find steep southfacing treeless slopes throughout the Tanana Valley which host a restricted, subarctic steppe plant community (Lloyd et al. 1994). These communities provide analogues for the Pleistocene ecosystem, which was likely a variable complex mosaic of steppe tundra with some minimal tree communities, though it is not well understood yet.

Due to the far more variable floral community that the early Holocene people faced, relative to the middle Holocene vegetation, many Denali complex assemblages may represent a relatively stronger regional and seasonally variable multipart toolkit, focused on large game acquisition, availability, and variation in upland areas within a logistic system (Coffman 2011; Potter 2008a). As the early Holocene progressed, the floral responses to increased temperatures and moisture greatly stressed those unique Terminal Pleistocene faunal communities, resulting in localized extirpations, decreased body sizes, and overall reduction in population numbers. As a result, the regional variations in the early Denali complex became increasingly generalized as the middle Holocene approached (Heidenreich 2012; Wygal 2009). These events became encoded in the story of the origin of the seasons. In this tale recorded by Julie Cruikshank for the Dene of the upper Yukon, the Distant Time world was once only inhabited by winter and its animals. The animals created a hole in the sky, allowing the animals and season of summer to come into this one. They never mix, ebbing and flowing with the weather (1991).

In the Middle Tanana, the Swan Point assemblages dating to this later period of technological generalization were locally termed the Transitional Period, between 8,000 and 6,000 cal BP. It represents a poorly understood period in Alaskan archaeology, where the earlier Denali complex technology transitions to the later Northern Archaic toolkit. The lack of understanding may be due to a lack of data represented in the interior Alaskan archaeological datasets or a research bias focusing resources toward terminal Pleistocene-dated sites (Holmes 2008, 2011b; Potter 2008c).

Hypotheses discussing this temporal period suggest that the Northern Archaic tradition represents technological innovation and continuity from the previous Denali complex population as ideas diffused from elsewhere and ecology shifts occurred (Holmes 2008; Potter 2008a). Alternatively, the Northern Archaic tradition may represent a new population adapted to the boreal forest constraints arriving from the southeast, either displacing Denali peoples or migrating into an already abandoned landscape (Anderson 1968; Workman 1978).

The earliest assemblages resembling the Northern Archaic tradition are found in northwestern Alaska (RBS-8110, Last Day 8900, XHP-550 9000, and Nogahabara 10,780 cal BP [Esdale 2008, 2009]). Three of these sites (excluding the Nogahabara site; Odess and Rasic 2007) are found in the Noatak River Basin, suggesting to some a northwestern origin (Mason and Bigelow 2008). However, the association of the early dates at Nogahabara with the cultural materials should be considered cautiously (Holmes et al. 2008), and most Northern Archaic sites date between 6,000 and 4,200 cal BP (Esdale 2008). Notched bifaces also appear at the eastern end of the continent in Newfoundland at 8,300 cal BP (Sanger and Renouf 2006) but are no older than 6,500 cal BP in the Yukon and Northwest Territories (Clark et al. 1999; Gordon 1996, 199; Hare 1995).

The geographic gap of the oldest Northern Archaic sites in Northwestern Alaska being located so far from similar assemblages elsewhere on the continent, as well as the widespread continuation of many elements of the Denali technocomplex within the later Northern Archaic components (Cook 1969), has inspired some researchers to propose that they be lumped together; the "Denali/Northern Archaic" cultures (Pearson and Powers 2001). Canadian perspectives also tend to support the idea that the Northern Archaic developed largely out of the former complexes (Betts 1987; Clark et al. 1999; Dumond 1977). Both traditions encompass a similar geographic region (Potter 2016, 540), and novel technological elements may have diffused west from the Canadian Shield Archaic tradition (Workman 1979). Perhaps the *-niq'ə* linguistic boundary that Dr. Kari has documented informs Dr. Holmes's early Holocene Transitional Period of the Middle Tanana, and will help us make sense of the different patterning of Denali, Nenana, and Chindadn complexes observed throughout the length of the Tanana Valley, as well as the genetic haplotype differences between the population who interred their children at *Xaasaa Na'* and the ancestral Dene (Flegontov et al. 2019; Moreno-Mayar et al. 2018). However, analyzing those questions are beyond the temporal scope of this book.

Finally, one major event occurred far to the south, which induced a massive widespread human response; the eruption of Mt. Mazama (Crater Lake) around 7,700 cal BP in southern Oregon (Harris 2005; Zdanowicz et al. 1999). This massive eruption (VEI=7) produced a tephra cloud that spread northeast, covering much of Washington, northwestern parts of Montana, southwestern Alberta, and the Fraser River region in southern British Columbia. The event has been proposed as a mechanism for diffusion patterns observed west across the American Great Plains and documented as far to the northwest as Manitoba (Matz 1987; Pettipas 1981, 1–15). It remains speculative to discuss a causal connection between the Northern Archaic origins and Mt. Mazama's eruption. However, the possibility that demographic pressure due to outmigration may have created a cascade of cause and effects that influenced this technology's northward spread through the boreal forest should be considered.

CONCLUSION

The Holocene Epoch, an 11,700-year-long interglacial period, is regionally marked by significant shifts of the environment, climate, geography, and ecology from the far colder and drier Pleistocene to the increasingly warmer and wetter period that is recognizable in Alaska and Yukon today. The ecological history of the Tanana Valley has remained stable for over 6,000 years, with few external events providing recognizable stressors. It is punctuated by some regional cooling and warming events; however, human response appears to be limited to the increasing abundance of salmon in the ecosystem beginning during the Medieval Warming Period, which affected the entire Northern Hemisphere. The ecology of the Upper Tanana is marked by two enormous volcanic events from the same volcano, Mt. Churchill. The last likely occurred in the winter season between 1,170–1,095 cal BP and the earlier during the summer season between 1,560 and 1,689 cal BP. The later eruption left a strong cultural mark on the technological chronology remains of the people of the Yukon headwaters country, and the earlier left a muted mark on the radiocarbon chronology of the Upper Tanana.

How these events might have impacted human populations? In the southern Yukon, the events disrupted food webs and raw materials flows, and seems to have spurred an eastward moving human migration. In the Upper Tanana, stressed demographics are somewhat associated with the older eruption and appear to be the only marked human response to either eruption. Important volcanic stressors are also observed south of the Alaska Range that forms the southern boundary of the Tanana Valley. These are periodic volcanic events occurring throughout the middle and later Holocene. While they may have been a barrier for human settlement during the middle Holocene in the upper Cook Inlet, the technological patterns in the Middle Susitna Valley appear to be generally unaffected by those events, suggesting human population continuity.

The earlier Holocene (11,700–6,000 cal BP) was marked by variable climate temperatures, and shifting flora and fauna communities, unlike the more stable middle and later Holocene system. The human cultural response to this more stressed, energetic, fluctuating system is reflected in the long-term change of the Denali Complex into the Northern Archaic tradition, and the earlier regional differences observed between the Denali, Nenana, and Chin-dadn complexes. Many successful Alaskan species experienced reduced body sizes, diet changes, and extirpation. This critical period provides analogues that many of the elements of the mythic journey that the transformer-hero *Saatedlech'eeghe* (Traveler) preserved, and suggests that during this critical time period, the initial cultural elements or ethnogenesis of the northern Dene people, were formed.

Chapter Seven

The Middle Tanana Dene and the Archaeological Traditions of the Taiga

The first summer I arrived in Alaska as an archaeologist, I began working on the cultural resource crews at Fort Greely near Delta Junction. That year we were tasked with mitigating numerous archaeological sites located along an old esker separating Jarvis and Sawmill Creeks (*Banadee'endedzi* [gravel stream] and *Baach'eltl'egi Niige* [something migrates to it stream]). Those sites represented all the ancient cultural periods of the region, from the early Pleistocene Chindadn complexes to the latest copper points of the Athabascan tradition. That summer we excavated in all kinds of inclement continental weather. I became used to the infamous Delta Wind, which whipped through the passes of the Alaska Range that towered over us to the south, rising great loess clouds off the Delta River and depositing them throughout the Valley, slowly deepening the sediments covering these ancient sites.

The Middle Tanana Valley is situated in the geographic core of the Alaska Dene's vast regional linguistic and material cultural area. Currently, the over 14,000 years of documented human occupancy there is summarized as five consecutive material-cultural traditions with evidence of technological continuity between them. The genetic reconstructive history suggests that three significant periods of genetic introgressions have occurred during the late, middle, and early Holocene, each of which contributed to Dene ancestry. Today's Indigenous Alaska Dene languages retain no evidence of contact with any other precolonial language in either the Tanana or Copper River basins. Their traditional place names and their geographic patterning support innovative coining, reuse of old place names to familiarize novel landscapes, and no evidence of borrowing (table 7.1). The focus of this chapter discusses the region's final two archaeological traditions: the Northern Archaic and the Athabascan traditions and their origins over the past 8,000 years, in order to illuminate the unique development and antiquity of Dene history here.

Table 7.1. Middle Tanana Cultural, Ecological, and Genetic Periods

Holocene Period (cal BP)	Local Archaeological tradition	Genetic Population	Interior Ecological Trends	Shaw Creek Period
70-0	Modern	Northern North American/ Multi-Regional	Increased Anthropogenic trends	Modern
0-50	Historic	Introgressions	Post-Little Ice Age warming trend	Historic
50-1,000	Athabascan	Northern North American	Cooler, stable climate, punctuated by minor warming and cooling trends. Interior boreal forest ecosystem	Late Taiga
1,000-2,000	Transitional Athabascan			
2,000-3,500	Late Northern Archaic	Northern North American/ Paleo-Eskimo		
3,500-5,000	Early (Classic) Northern Archaic			Middle Taiga
5,000-6,000		Northern North American		
6,000-8,000	Transitional Northern Archaic	Transitional Genetic Period	Warming maximum (drier and warmer than present), expansion of parkland forests	Early Taiga
8,000-9,000	American Paleo-Arctic (Denali complex)	Ancient Beringian	Cooling trend increased local moisture (drier than present), grasslands	
9,000-10,000			Possible hotter, drier climate, but quite variable and localized	
10,000-11,700			Warming trend (highly variable moisture and temperature)	Transitional Period

Source: Holmes 2008

INSIGHTS FROM COMPARATIVE REGIONAL
ATHABASCAN TRADITION ASSEMBLAGES

Multiple researchers have documented material cultural correlates of the Dene in archaeological context in order to demonstrate their origin and antiquity in place (reviewed in Potter 2016; see also Ives 2008). The result is a complex story; the diffusion of aspects of oral history, material culture, language, and genetics certainly facilitate each other's regional visibility. However, deterministic arguments correlating them can often become over-simplified and ignore problems of equifinality. In other words, any given interpretive scenario contributing to the ethnogenesis of the Dene people in an open cultural-ecological system might be reached by several different and unrelated series of events. Studying multiple hypotheses of how each of these realms may interact with each other clarifies that research.

The youngest precolonial archaeological tradition in the Tanana Valley is the Athabascan tradition (table 7.1), assumed to represent the recognizable material cultural record as manifested by the Tanana Valley Dene at the point of contact with Euro-Americans (Cook and McKennan 1970; Rainey 1940). Due to boreal forest soil taphonomy and precolonial technological constraints in this region, lithic technological remains represent the most easily recognizable aspect of the archaeological record, so much so that interpreting their meaning still forms the bulk of the archaeological research produced (Potter 2016). That research and taphonomy bias means other avenues of thought must be devoted to the latest, 1,000-year-long Athabascan tradition, which documents a growing influence and preference for alternatives to lithic technology forms, emphasizing instead a growing reliance on bone (MT: *tth'en*), antler (*ch'edee*), wood (*duuł*), bark (*ch'elaat*), copper (*ts'itsiy t'eex*), and ceramics (no specific term) as preferred raw materials. At the point of historical contact, stone technology had become restricted to forms mainly useful for cooking, steam baths, hide scraping, and woodwork (Dixon 1985; Holmes 1975; Potter 2010; Workman 1978).

The tradition is marked by other widespread technological shifts, including the early adoption and use of bow-and-arrow (*tth'ełtįį, k'a'*) technology, although some researchers argue that this technology has been previously periodically incorporated into and abandoned in earlier Alaskan toolkits (Dixon 2013; Maschner and Mason 2013). Ceramics are rare in the Tanana but present in some later artifact assemblages at the sites of Dixthada (*Dithaade*: nearby place) (Shinkwin 1979), Cripple Creek (LT: *Dradlaya Nik'a Donga'*: round whitefish stream uplands) (Smith 2012), and Nenana River Gorge (Plaskett 1977); the closest ethnographically known utilized clay source-quarry is near Rampart (LT: *Toch'iltthwxde*: where they color something (moose) brown), on the Yukon (Rainey 1940).

The southern Yukon ice-patch artifact record provides an unparalleled preservation record of organic implements not observable in the lower elevation sites. There, evidence of an abrupt and complete technological shift in these upland contexts from the earlier atlatl darts, which had been otherwise in use since the early Holocene, to bow-and-arrow technology around 1,300 cal BP (Hare et al. 2004, 2012) is documented. With this change, a preferential shift from birch (*k'iiyh*) (a hardwood) use in dart shafts to the usage of spruce (*ts'ebe*) (a softwood) for arrow shafts also occurred (Alix et al. 2012). Bow-and-arrow technology was used alongside rifles until the World War II era, well into the Historic period (McKennan 1959; O'Brien 2011).

In the ice patch record of the southern Yukon, the abrupt shift to arrows also signals a shift to the preferred use of bone and antler (with the occasional copper end-blade inset) instead of stone for projectile tips (Hare et al. 2004, 2012; Thomas et al. 2020). In the Copper River Valley and other drainages of the Wrangell Mountains to the north and east, the use of copper in a wide array of objects appears to have become widespread during this period, especially in the past few centuries. Its widespread use but limited appearance in the archaeological record is evidence supporting the oral traditions attesting that it was a coveted prestige item (Smith and Combs 2020; Franklin et al. 1981). Copper (both annealed and cold-hammered) became useful for various tools and personal adornment during the Athabascan tradition. Copper use by the northern Dene begins between 1,800 and 1,250 cal BP (Cooper 2012, table 2) and appears in the Alaska Range perhaps as early as 1,270 cal BP (Dixon et al. 2005, 137).

The last of the regional curated stone projectile technologies include the unique, five-sided, shouldered Kavik Points (named after the Kavik River (Iñupiaq: *qavviq*: wolverine [MacLean 2011] near where they were documented, which appear in Alaska and Yukon between around 600 cal BP and 200 cal BP. Kavik Points are a simple projectile point often shaped by bifacial pressure flaking of larger flakes into a smaller usable form. At the Klo-Kut site (GW: *Tl'oo Kat*: on grass) on the upper Porcupine River (GW: *Ch'oodèenjik*: quill stream), the Athabascan tradition was characterized by two cultural phases (Morlan 1973; Cinq-Mars 1974). Stone Kavik/Klo-Kut points dominated the younger phase (600 cal BP to nineteenth century CE), while antler and bone projectile points dominated the early phase (1,200–600 cal BP). This pattern of an abrupt, rapid transition to a complete osseous projectile point and a later shift back to the lithic points is an important pattern that may inform the Tanana Valley assemblages. Taphonomic bias there favors stone preservation due to the acidic boreal forest soils of the Tanana Valley. It may severely constrain the archaeological visibility of bow-and-arrow technology between 1,200 and 600 cal BP. Thus, their absence in assemblages during this time may not reflect actual absence from the toolkit (Doering et al. 2020, 379). While not as robust as the southern Yukon ice patch record, the Alaskan ice patch record suggests a similar chronological pattern of the arrow and osseous tool adoption. Preserved artifacts suggest regional bow and arrow technology stretches back at least a thousand years and osseous projectile points for five centuries prior (VandeHoek et al. 2012, 157–158). Kavik/Klo-Kut points (associated with bow and arrows) have been recorded across Alaska, Yukon, and British Columbia (Derry 1975; Matson and Magne 2007; Morlan 1970, 29; Smith 2012; Workman 1978). They are absent from the southern Yukon ice-patch record (Christian Thomas, personal communication 2019), possibly an indicator that they represent a specialized hunting technique not used in restricted upland contexts. In northern Alaska and British Columbia, they are considered a proxy for ancestral Dene presence in regions that unrelated ethnic groups also used (Matson and Magne 2007, but see cautions raised by Ives 2008).

In the Tanana Valley, the use of the ancient microblade technology, a mainstay since the late Pleistocene, was gradually phased out early in the tradition between 900 and 500 cal BP. Usually, their late contextual occurrence in a site is questionable, and some are only represented by minimal artifacts numbers. Important microblade-bearing components dating to the Athabascan tradition in this region have been recorded at the Healy Lake Garden Site (*Teyh Ch'ets'edze'*: kidney hill) (1,050 cal BP; Cook 1969, 271), Swan Point CZ1a (866 cal BP; Hirasawa and Holmes 2017), Healy Lake Village Level 1 (673 cal BP; Cook 1969, 245). US Creek CZ2 (673 and 630 cal BP; Smith 2012, 117), and the Klein Site Lower Locus at Quartz Lake (529 cal BP; Doering et al. 2020). Burin technology also appears to be dropped in tandem with core-and-blade technology in the later Holocene (Holmes 2008, 77).

The Klein Site, adjacent to the Shaw Creek Flats, is located on the northern bank of Quartz Lake (*Ttheech'el Menn'*). Both the Upper Locus (1,080–1,280 cal BP) and the Lower Locus (520–560 cal BP) exhibit bifacial and core-and-blade lithic reduction strategies that are dominated by the use of local materials (Doering et al. 2020, 480; Reuther 2013, 21). However, of note are the early remains of a copper bipoint and sheet fragments associated with the Upper Locus, documenting the early import of this prestigious item.

Precolonial Dene settlement systems were dominated by the network of riverine and lake systems. Winter villages and fish camps tended to be centrally located between multiple stable, seasonally available resources. They were found at the juncture of larger and smaller streams and lakes, places ideal for fishing and storing food and orienting oneself on the landscape (Craft LeFebre 1956; Potter 2008a; Rainey 1939a; Shinkwin et al. 1980). The presence of house features and food storage pits suggests that the seasonal sedentism pattern described ethnographically can be extended across the past millennium. Research by Ketz (1982), Smith (2012), and Yesner (1980, 1989) at Paxon Lake have confirmed the economic importance of caribou, and David Plaskett (1977) has confirmed the use of sheep at the Nenana River Gorge. Initially, moose remains appeared to be elusive, but later work (Potter 2008a) has demonstrated that their use was second only to caribou in assemblage variability.

Relatively little in-depth research has been devoted to late-precolonial residential features in the Tanana Valley. Most sites have been recorded only by surface recognition with minimal subsurface testing. Many known village sites are on Alaska Native patented lands and have not needed any legal mitigation, remaining understudied. Regional academic interest and funding have mainly reflected public interest, focusing on the terminal Pleistocene's earliest sites and cultural periods. Anne Shinkwin's (1979) extensive investigations at the Dixthada site near Lake Mansfield (*Dihthaade Menn'*: not far lake) remains a definitive work on precolonial residences (400–600 cal BP) in the valley. Another excavation of an Upper Tanana protohistoric residence comes from the Tok Terrace site (TNX-00033) (Sheppard 2001). A recent survey was also published of residential features dating to the past few centuries along the Middle Fork Fortymile River (*Ts'eyh K'eetl'aa Ndiig*: canoe bottom stream) (Coffman et al. 2018). This region is to the east of the study area is considered an ancestral use area for the Healy Lake band. In the Shaw Creek basin, the Gilles Creek site may also contain the remains of either a protohistoric rectangular residential feature or large cache pit, which dates to 200±40 BP (Yarborough 2003, 5). Data on the precolonial Tanana Valley residential features remains too sparse to produce a robust idea for either the antiquity or settlement patterns of household features, thus providing an impetus for this study.

In the Copper River basin to the south, Doug Reger's (1985) survey of Tazlina Lake (*Bendiil Bene'*: lake flows-lake) revealed a pattern of village and residences also dating to the last few centuries, similar to the findings at the Ringling Site at Gulkana (*C'uul C'ena'*: tearing stream) (Cooper 2012; Hanson 1999, 2008). Late precolonial village sites along the Tyone River (*Nilben Na'*: water surges stream), particularly at its mouth (*Nilben Caek'e*: water surges mouth) (TLM-00009) and Crosswind Lake (GUL-00033: *K'estsiik'eden*: elevation comes up lake), are located upland from the Copper River bottom. Several late precolonial house features were also described in the middle Susitna valley, with one possibly a 1,300-year-old candidate at site TLM-00215 (Dixon et al. 1985; Hays et al. 2014).

It is rare to document residence features older than 500 years in the Alaskan interior. Charles Holmes's work at Lake Minchumina (*Benh Chwx Bene'*: large lake-lake) in central Alaska was important in documenting their continuity into the earlier late Northern Archaic tradition investigated residential features. Holmes's (1986) cultural sequences demonstrate that a distinct shift in residential feature shape occurred there around 950 cal BP, coinciding with the Athabascan tradition technological changes, occurring between the Spruce Gum Phase (beginning around 950 cal BP to present) and the earlier Minchumina tradition (a localized variant of the Northern Archaic tradition) (2,600–950 cal BP). At least one undated late Holocene Dene residential feature (and possibly a few others) was described at the Tuktu site (*Sehno' Hutl'ot*: black bear stream headwaters) in the Brooks Range (Campbell 1961). Dena'ina residences are considered periphery to this study, as they appear to be heavily influenced by neighboring non-Dene groups and are omitted (see O'Leary et al. 2020 for a recent survey).

Several other recognizable large nonresidential feature types described in historical and ethnographic documents include stone iñuksuk (*tthee chiił*) (Spencer 1959), wooden ungulate drivelines (*tthik*), and fish weirs (*hwtsith*) (Osgood [1940] 1970). These features facilitated communal strategies involving mass kill and storage of large game and fish to ensure against seasonal resource scarcity, which appears alongside bow-and-arrow adoption after 1,300 cal BP (Arndt 1977). Ungulate and fish fences necessitated extensive social networks and cooperation for their maintenance. They facilitated food capture for a large number of people (Ives 1990), and Boraas (2007) hypothesized that, along with cache pits (*tsaa k'ee*), they could be seen as an archaeological proxy for observing extended kinship complexity in the past (see also Potter 1997). Overall, the precolonial expansion in the use of seasonal residences suggests an increasing trend toward a stronger seasonal-based logistic mobility pattern where task-oriented groups extracted resources and funneled them toward a centralized residential site using spike camps ,where those were further processed for transport. This pattern expanded during the past millennium, significantly intensifying during the past 500 years (Potter 2008a, 2016, 548). For the millennium prior (2,000–1,000 cal BP), a pattern of intensified use of lowland riverine and lacustrine ecosystems is observed in the Tanana Valley, being early precursors of this land use practice (Potter 2008a; Doering et al. 2020). To understand these unique lifeways, this chapter will focus especially on the features and artifacts of Pickupsticks and Swan Point in the Shaw Creek basin.

THE PICKUPSTICKS CEREMONIAL SITE

The excavations at the Pickupsticks site revealed a component approximately 850 years old. The sediments at the site preserved a complex soil profile within the residential feature. The sediment structure is the result of natural eolian processes, a precolonial excavation that dug a rectangular pit into the soft bedrock, and the collapsed associated wall and ceiling structure into the pit feature (figure 7.1). The structural remains appear to have been constructed in a rectangular form based on the sunken floor construction. Scorched and unburned timber fragments and chunks were recovered in situ, suggesting a construction method involving attaching small-diameter (5–10 cm diameter) logs at intersecting at 90-degree angles to each other.

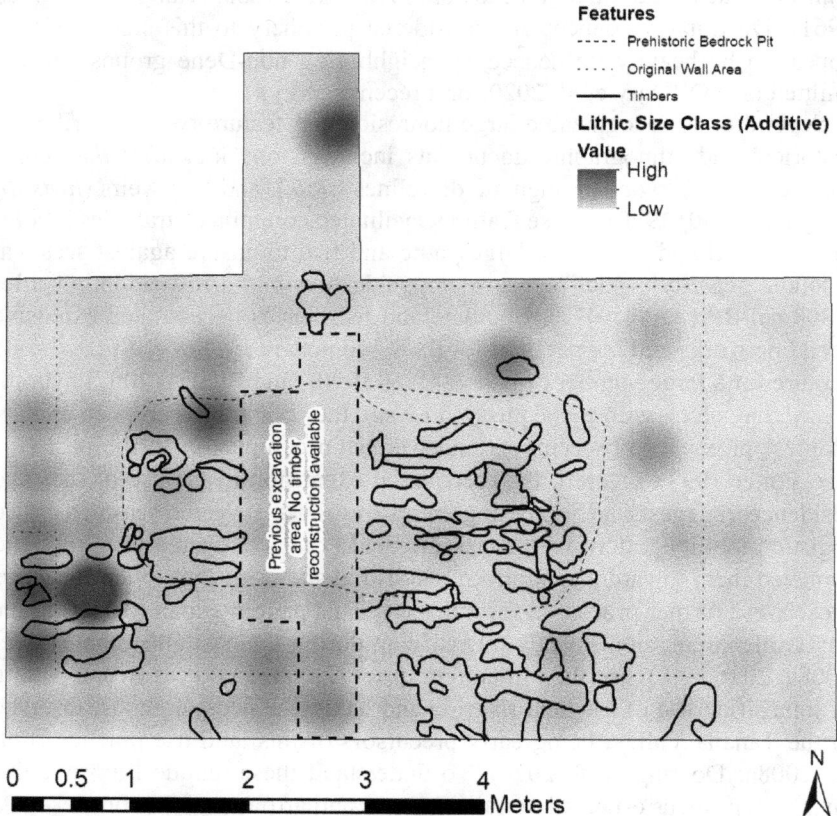

Features

- - - - -   Prehistoric Bedrock Pit

· · · · · ·   Original Wall Area

————   Timbers

Lithic Size Class (Additive)

Value

High

Low

Previous excavation area. No timber reconstruction available

0   0.5   1   2   3   4

Meters

N

Figure 7.1. Debitage and features associated with Pickupsticks. The background is a kernel density map (10 cm) based on additive debitage size class.

Small pockets of poorly sorted sandy silt were noted to be in stratigraphic association with the timber fragments but not above or below, suggesting an association with the timbers. Pieces of birchbark were also recovered in association with the timber remains. They are interpreted to be the remains of the bark-lined walls. Some internal structural post remains, which likely supported a central beam, were recovered in the eastern end of the excavation. The protohistoric bark houses described at nearby Goodpaster village were constructed similarly: a rectangular frame of small-diameter logs, covered in birchbark with an internal layer of insulating packed sod built over an oval pit dug several feet into the sediment (Mishler 1986, 29–35; Pitts 1972, 107–120).

Fragments of birchbark were found *in situ* lying along the floor within the bedrock pit, held there with at least one wooden peg that was still in place. No distinct hearth could be detected, but an enhanced area of ash mixed with sediment toward the central-front area of the feature, just above the regolith, hints of a possible candidate. The lack of a hearth may indicate the remnants of rake-out and trampling activity (Kovács 2013, 191). However, very little reddened soil is associated with the ash deposit, and it may be related to a post-occupational burning episode. Other site excavations have suggested that internal hearths were lined with stones or logs, which were not observed at Pickupsticks (McFadyen Clark 1996, 70–71, 101, 104; see also Shinkwin 1979, 41, 44). Additionally, the presence of birchbark flooring, which is highly flammable, advocates against the presence of an internal hearth.

The feature likely represents a rectangular single-room dwelling. No evidence of any additional rooms was observed. The horizontal layers within the feature were uncompacted, probably due to structural collapse with little post-depositional trampling (Gé et al. 1993; Courty et al. 1994; Matthews 1995; Matthews et al. 1994; Milek 2012). Based on the berms' location and the stratigraphic profiles, the original walls likely extended several feet wider and longer than the outline of the sunken section of the floor, and sandy disturbance areas suggest this was the case. If the original construction included the wall benches described in so many ethnohistoric accounts, they likely ended at or near the bedrock feature. A hint of a faint depression leading to the west suggests the entranceway's presence was there. The floor space is roughly 3.5 m × 5.5 m, or about 19.25 m². These measurements are smaller than those reported for the later average Ahtna houses (5.1 ± 1.2 m × 5.6 ± 1.4, 29.9 ± 13.4 m²; O'Leary et al. 2021, 84; Potter 1997) and Dena'ina houses (5.6 × 6.7 m; O'Leary et al. 2021, 71–77).

The collapsed wall construction materials and birchbark are scorched, and some charcoal is mixed within what is considered sod that was packed into the original walls. Very little ash is observed within this. The scorch pattern appears to indicate that the structure had collapsed before a later burning epi-sode. The collapse may have been a slow one over time due to abandonment, and the scorch marks on the wood might be due to a later wildfire. Discrete units of poorly sorted sand, quartz pebbles, loess, and charcoal are consid-ered to have an anthropogenic origin. They are likely the result of sediments packed into the roof and wall as insulation.

The majority of nineteenth-century household residences were built and maintained for an extended period. The HBE-derived Technological Invest-ment Model suggests that when considerable amounts of labor are invested in the creation and maintenance of an object, an adequate trade-off for long-term utility is expected (Neiman 1995; Shennan 2001). The primary traditional purpose of these kinds of residences here was to offer a family a centralized shelter to return to during the winter season annually, which were either aban-doned or burned upon the death of the family head.

The lack of a thick packed earth floor suggests further evidence for a short-term occupation, like the absence of internal hearths. The soft regolith, which was dug into as part of the original construction, was still observed to be in sharp relief in 2019. It was so soft that it had to be protected during the excavation, as it was soon noticed that repeated trampling wear was quickly crushing some of its edges. These pieces of evidence suggest that the feature likely represents a short-term occupation, perhaps not related to household residency behaviors. Occasionally buildings such as this could be built for the express purpose of a short-term potlatch ceremony as an external gifting signal, such as was built at Kechumstuk (*Saa Ges Cheeg*: sun fork mouth) and Healy Lake (*Teyh Ch'ets'edze'*: kidney hill) in the early twentieth century. In this case, the payoff for the labor investment is the future positive reciproc-ity expectations of the giftees and goodwill ties forged between otherwise competitive families.

One sample was a twig recovered from near the base of the mixed strata within the feature and dated in 2015 to provide a preliminary age. It closely matched with an assay recovered from the birchbark fragments recovered from the floor. The two nearly identical dates that cluster together at a median age of 851 cal BP (784–918 cal BP) are considered to have a solid contextual relationship with the precolonial building's construction.

Lithic technology can provide data on site-specific behaviors. Expedient tools, often crafted onsite, tend to be curated for immediate use. Debitage, the byproducts of tool use and curation, provides data on preferred material types, basic technology production at a site (useful if tools were made at one location but not discarded there), and ideas of raw material origins. More for-mal bifacial technology tends to reflect inter-site behaviors. The material type can either suggest or provide detailed provenance data concerning quarry origins. Bifaces often experience a landscape-wide life history, as they tend to be designed and curated for several use events. Their life history begins as a blank chipped initially in a form maximizing weight and utility at the quarry site, followed by options employed to haft it into a projectile weapon or knife, which can then be used for activities at a kill or butchery site. After use, the tool may be recovered and retooled into a more diminutive form for similar reuse. These activities may occur at a different workshop site and be repeated until it is discarded due to either loss or its small size is no longer considered useful for further needs. In material cultural remains dominated by the preservation of lithic products, they remain an inexpensive top producer of landscape behavioral modeling proxies. Therefore, while many lithic tool types were found at Pickupsticks and Swan Point, bifacial artifacts will be specifically summarized here.

Seven bifaces have been recovered from Pickupsticks, five in association with the housepit. Three broken distal biface sections and one basal fragment were recovered from the house's forward section, and one larger base was recovered toward the back of the house. All had evidence of usewear. One complete notched biface was recovered from an excavation unit separate from the block at the housepit. Notched bifaces may be more strongly associated with atlatl darts than bow and arrows, which appear to have preferred to utilized osseous points (Hare et al. 2004, 2012). Four scrapers were also recovered. Only a single artifact has been classified as a microblade, and five larger definitive blades were described (one retouched and one with usewear). An irregular core that might be associated with microblade production was also recovered, all suggesting that microblade production if it occurred here, was minimal to nonexistent at the site.

Most of the lithic byproducts recovered were found deposited near the front southwest corner of the house (figure 7.1). According to the universal rules governing Dene household seating arrangements, this area is where unmarried girls and mothers would be expected to work. It is unique that the pattern only tends to be seen on one side of the long axis. If this was a dual-family residence, evidence of work should be expected to be equally distributed throughout the forward section. Faunal discards also cluster toward the front of the house, with much of the identified fragmentary remains in the front center.

The recovered lithic artifacts are finely crafted, related to butchery (unifaces), hunting and meat package reduction (broken bifaces), and utilized blades and burin spalls. Unused quartz debitage and rocks were also heavily represented within the Pickupsticks feature, but not outside of it. These quartz pieces, potentially manuports, were also directly associated with the wall remains, suggesting they were somehow associated. Monty Rogers

(2015, 59–60, and chapter 5) extensively discusses the association of quartz and Dena'ina house features. His work concluded that quartz had general, multi-purpose utility based upon its hardness (for crushing) ability to hold an irregular edge, utility as a heating stone, and also for producing black ochre. Copper-bearing quartz was a source of black paint, needing to be crushed and fired in order to be utilized (2015, 89). All types of mineral pigments were considered to be deeply powerful (Thomas 2005).

When faunal remains are found in abundance at a site, they can provide important ecological data concerning predation strategies by humans, human diet breadth, individual and population health and demographics, ecosystems that were targeted, and distances traveled to fulfill dietary consumption needs. Unfortunately, the Holocene faunal data from both Pickupsticks and Swan Point is minimal and can only prove answers regarding the presence of species in an assemblage, and not behaviors regarding their use. About 13 percent of the faunal remains could be identified at Pickupsticks; species identified include moose (*Deniige: Alces alces*), wolf or domesticated dog (*Tikaan: Canis lupus* or *Łii: Canis lupus familiaris*), coyote or domesticated dog (*Tikaan gay: Canis latrans* or *Łii: Canis lupus familiaris*), river otter (*Uziiy': Lutra canadensis*), muskrat or hare (*Dzenh: Ondatra zibethicus* or *Gah: Lepus othus*), red squirrel (*Dlik: Tamiasciurus hudsonicus*), and unidentified bird (*Tsuuye: Aves*). Most of the specimens (97.5 percent) exhibit evidence of burning. All specimens were incomplete (fragmented) and weathered to varying extents. In all cases, bone lengths were incomplete. Thus, these identifications are used with caution. All were visually examined for evidence of human and nonhuman animal modifications, but very little was observed (gnaw marks, cutting, tool use, digestion, Binford 1981; Lyman 1994; Stiner et al. 1995).

The faunal items present there, while fragmentary and often singular, appear to represent possible consumption behaviors and use of animals considered in the early twentieth century as 'engii (sacred/taboo), especially in the case of the otter remains (one calcined distal left tibia). Otters were considered a powerful creature, and the only culturally appropriate handling of these animals was traditionally reserved for especially strong sleep doctors. As outlined earlier, the fur-bearing animals and canid remains were important but had extensive regulatory customs pertaining to them. The moose remains are ambiguous, as one fragment dates several centuries earlier than the house construction. It is considered intrusive and suggests an earlier group of behaviors is evident in the unexcavated areas outside the residence.

Moose was represented by several forelimb, hindlimb, and teeth fragments. At least one tibia fragment dated to 1,580±25 BP (1,400–1,527 cal BP), predating the house pit. The date could indicate the remains of two cultural components or the presence of an older item curated for use during the final occupation. River otter, muskrat or hare, and red squirrel were all represented through fragments of limb elements. For these smaller mammals, classifications remain tentative, as definitive identification can be influenced by complete long-bone element length and more identified remains. Concerning the canid remains, the wolf was identified through a rib fragment and dog or coyote through a femur fragment. Coyotes are currently understood to have arrived likely in the early twentieth or late nineteenth century (Hody and Kays 2018). Their expansion across North America is strongly correlated with the wolf's extirpation (Ballard et al. 2003). Coyotes tend to avoid wolf-dominated areas, a pattern that seems to be valid throughout the Holocene (Fuller and Keith 1981; Nowak 2003). Therefore, the apparent presence of these canid remains is more likely domesticated dog remains.

The presence of fur-bearing animals and bird remains may indicate a fall occupation, as this was the best time of the year for fur harvest when new hair growth was optimal and activities were not consumed by fishing. Most of these species present at Pickupsticks are within the expected faunal assemblage remains for late Holocene interior assemblages (Potter 2008a, 2008b), although taboos concerning canids and otters should be remembered. All animal types present here were typically acquired through the use of snares and projectile weaponry (table 7.2).

Table 7.2. Faunal Presence at Pickupsticks

Middle Tanana Name	English Species Name	Average Mass (lbs.)	Used for Food?	Hunting Technology
Deniige	Moose	1,100	Yes	Snare/Projectile
Tikaan	Wolf	130	Avoided, used for fur	Avoided
Tikaan gaay	Coyote	30	Avoided, used for fur	Avoided
Łii	Dog	20-100	Avoided, used for packing, hunting, protection	Assisted hunting
Uziiy'	River Otter	18	Avoided	Avoided
Gah, Gex	Hare	11	Yes	Snare
Dzenh	Muskrat	3	Yes	Snare
Tsuuye	Bird	n/a	Yes	Snare/Projectile
Dlik	Red Squirrel	1	Yes	Snare

Source: Andrews 1975; Kari n.d.; McKennan 1969; Mishler 1986; Vitt 1971.

SWAN POINT CZ1A

Swan Point exhibits several punctuated cultural zones throughout the Holocene and transitioning across the protohistoric/historic period. The youngest
occupation transitioning the protohistoric/historic periods remains under
analysis and will not be discussed in depth here. The next older occupation
at Swan Point is called Cultural Zone (CZ) 1a. It encompasses the top four
5-cm levels, or 20 cm of the mineral horizon at the main locus, and the top
five levels (25 cm) at Locus 2. It can be subdivided into a younger series of
occupations (CZ1a1) that is similar in age to Pickupsticks, and a series of
occupations several centuries older (CZ1a2).

Eight hearth-like features were observed at the main locus; these include
descriptions of charcoal, soot, ashy soil, or reddened sediment concentra-
tions (Matthews et al. 1994; Shahack-Gross et al. 2004). Hearths with
younger radiocarbon dates (CZ1a1) cluster toward the north of the excavated
area, and hearth features with older dates cluster toward the south (CZ1a2).
However, they are at similar depths below the surface, so they cannot be
stratigraphically isolated. Radiocarbon assays from one surface depression
at the main locus, Feature 1, suggest it is associated with CZ1a1. A small
hearth located near the southern end of the feature is associated with the
older CZ1a2. At Locus 2 is a larger surface depression, Feature 2, whose
radiocarbon assays are associated with CZ1a2. Due to the close proximity
of both loci, it is likely that activities at both places are closely related, but
cannot be considered spatially discrete. Feature 1 at the Swan Point main
locus represents an ovoid surface depression roughly 2 m x 1 m long, oriented SE/NW. It is capped by about 10 cm of undisturbed sediment and is an
intrusive pit dug through all of the Holocene sediments and into the lowest
Pleistocene sand layer.

The presence of scraper discards and fragments suggests that hide-working
processes were present. They are scattered across the whole block, with little
patterning between the north and south halves. The random pattern extends
to the expedient flake tools and burin spalls. Two unique artifacts of note are
a copper bipoint, located via metal detection, perhaps associated with CZ1a1,
and broken pieces of a large basalt adze, situated in the older CZ1a2. Bipoints
were commonly utilized both as awls and also part of one of four known
copper arrowhead or end blade manufacture sequences. In this technique, the
bipoint formed a central spine, and a separate sheet of copper was hammered
around it to form the blades (Franklin et al. 1981, 29–30; see also Cooper
2012). Microblades and their associated cores, tablets, and larger blades are
fairly evenly distributed about the locus. They cluster ubiquitously, appearing
throughout CZ1a levels.

Thirty-five biface pieces are associated with the northern half of the main locus block, arguably associated with CZ1a2 (figure 7.2). Eighteen of them are basal sections, dominated by chert (n=13), then rhyolite (n=3), basalt (n=1), and quartzite (n=1). Six biface tip sections cluster along the northeast margin of the block. Biface tips are suggestive of breaks that occur during use, either as a cutting or piercing action. Three of these have observable edge wear, indicative of knife use. Five medial and two edge fragments are also scattered randomly, as well as five complete bifaces; two exhibit edgewear, and two have impact fractures. Of the complete bifaces, five had hafting wear, three had impact fractures, two had edge wear, and two had heat treatment evidence. Of the proximal biface bases (n=26): six were thermally altered, sixteen had hafting wear, ten had edge grinding, four had edge wear, and two had impact fractures. Of the distal biface tips (n=10): one was thermally altered, five had edge wear, and one had impact fractures. These summaries are import, as utilized broken biface tips can be indicative of hunting behaviors that happened off site, being transported to the site in meat packages, then discovered and discarded during further butchery or consumption activities. Biface bases can represent onsite discards produced during weapon refurbishment.

Fractured distal and medial osseous arrow sections were dated around 675 cal BP (ID no. 22344 and 22345). Two lithic bifaces from Level 3 CZ1a were also likely intended for use as arrowheads. Both are similar in form to Kavik/Klo-Kut points (Smith 2012), which again become visible in the regional archaeological record generally between 600 and 200 cal BP. Other broken biface sections are found in every level of Swan Point CZ1a, but their use as either dart points, arrow points, or knife blades are obscured. These different projectile point technologies may have been utilized side by side or belong to different occupations; If the Klo-Kut site on the Yukon to the north can be used as a proxy, it suggests that a preference for osseous arrows existed between 1,200 and 600 cal BP and stone-tipped arrows after that. Additional evidence for regional arrow manufacture and use in the Central Alaskan Range spanning the past 1,000–1,200 years BP is detailed in the Alaskan ice patch recoveries (VanderHoek et al. 2012, table 1 and figure 5). Several small stone projectile points identified as arrowheads were also recovered from a precolonial house floor at the East Cove Site (MMK-012) at Lake Minchumina, dating between 1050 and 1540 cal BP (Holmes 1986). Unfortunately, the central Alaska record lacks the radiocarbon resolution that the southern Yukon ice patch assemblages have provided for that region, obscuring our local understanding of technological sequences in the Tanana Valley for the Athabascan tradition.

The discard patterns in CZ1a appear to strongly resemble crafting behaviors, where hunting weapons were dismantled and refurbished, and extensive

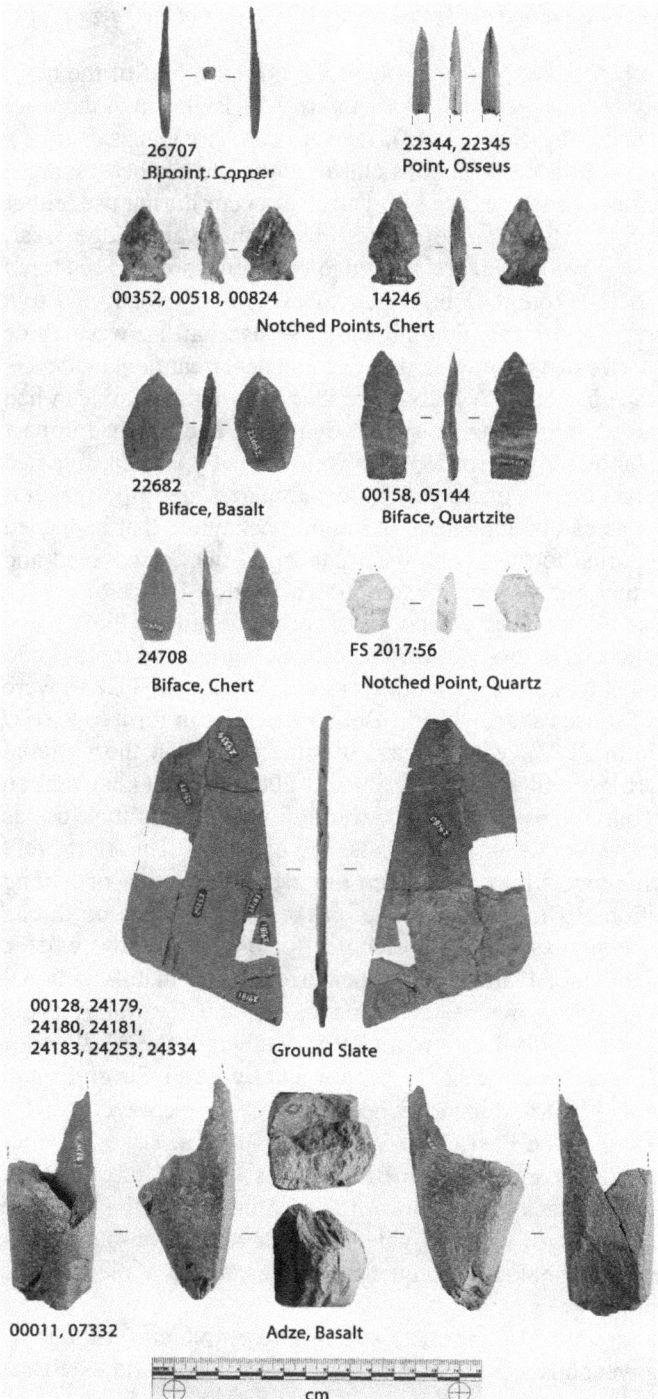

26707
Bipoint, Copper

22344, 22345
Point, Osseus

00352, 00518, 00824
14246
Notched Points, Chert

22682
Biface, Basalt

00158, 05144
Biface, Quartzite

24708
Biface, Chert

FS 2017:56
Notched Point, Quartz

00128, 24179,
24180, 24181,
24183, 24253, 24334
Ground Slate

00011, 07332
Adze, Basalt

cm

Figure 7.2. Sample of Swan Point CZ1a tools. Top left: copper bipoint, Top right: osseous point. Rows 2, 3, and 4: bifaces. Row 5: ground slate blade. Row 5: adze. Image by Eleanor Bishop.

hide and woodworking took place. They do not support the idea of much initial tool creation behaviors at this locale. The statistical results of material types by levels suggest significant differences exist between them, likely suggesting multiple episodes of use. The presence of broken biface tips and medial sections with impact damage suggest that they may have been embedded in meat packages that were transported to the site for further procession or consumption.

Using Binford's "Working Around a Hearth" model (WAHM), each level of CZ1a was mapped by lithic artifact size class and hearths (figure 7.3). Hypothetical back toss zones were informed by the density clusters that subjectively appeared as arcs. Hypothetical workers were placed in proximity between them and secondary density plots as informed by Binford's model. Comparing each of these levels, the lithic density map of Level 0 and 1 is far more different from Levels 2–4. While differences exist between Levels 2–4, similar patterns also run between them, suggesting that homogenizing processes have affected these levels more than the uppermost one. Additionally, it indicates that the lithic assemblage of Levels 0/1 may represent an undated occupation between the Historic/Protohistoric occupation (~1,800–1,915 AD) and CZ1a1 (725–1,150 cal BP). The combination most informs the final, generalized reconstructed WAHM of Levels 2–4.

Surface depressions that have a confirmed precolonial cultural origin can be the result of a number of past behaviors. They can be the remains of house pits (Mishler 1986; Rainey 1939a), birthing pits (Ruth Ridley: TCC 2018), cache pits (Fair 1997; Lanoë 2018; Lanoë et al. 2019a; Mishler 1986; Rogers 2015; Smith 2012), cooking pits (Potter et al. 2011), cremation pits (Potter et al. 2011), inhumation pits (Potter et al. 2014), pitfall traps (McKennan 1959), smokehouses (Pitts 1972), first menstrual huts (Anderson 1957), sweat baths (McKennan 1959), temporary shelters (McKennan 1959), drinking water wells (Rogers and Stone 2010).

No evidence in the stratigraphy suggested that Feature 1 has been extensively disturbed since its initial construction. Beneath the surface, Feature 1 was recognized in the northwest end of the excavation as charcoal-rich fine silt, bifurcated by the Bw horizon. The southwestern section of the buried feature, a portion of which remains in situ, was apparent as a poorly sorted matrix of sandy gravels (absent in the northeastern section) and charcoal. The majority of charcoal was observed near the base of the buried feature.

The difference in sediment composition between the northwest and southeastern ends of the feature is telling, indicating a more complicated construction profile. The southeastern end appears to represent the original pit feature. The northwest end appears to have been purposely dug out as well but is not as wide or deep and is filled with fine loess. It also has a thick deposit

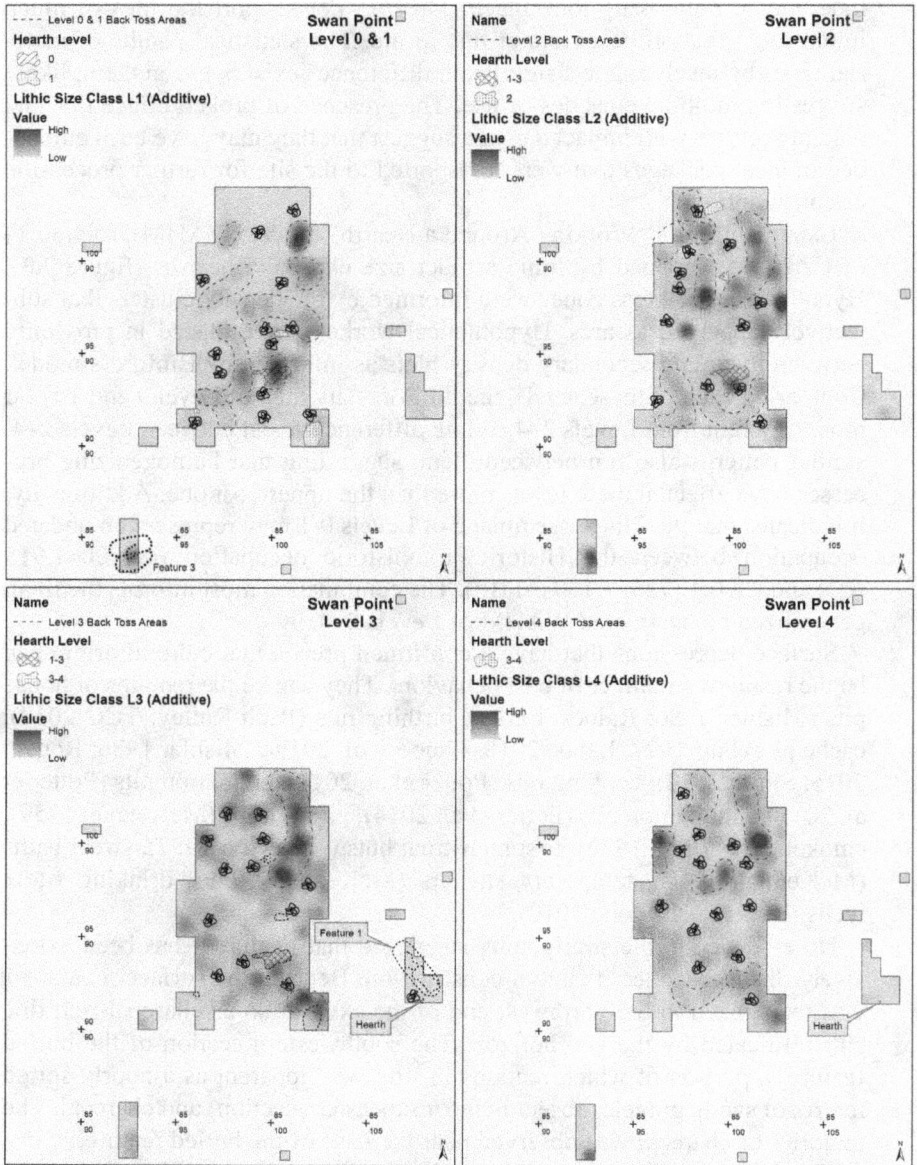

Figure 7.3. Comparison of hypothetical "Working Around a Hearth" models by CZ1a levels (Binford 1983). The background is a kernel density map (10 cm) of debitage size class.

of charcoal suggesting a hearth, complicating interpretation. The southeast end is filled with poorly sorted sandy rubble and is clearly demarcated from the surrounding undisturbed sediment. The southeastern base of the feature had several layers of preserved burned material below the rubble fill. In the northwest, it was a single thin layer of charcoal that could be traced extending beyond the feature to the south in the west profile, likely on an old living surface. The horizontal border of the pit was clearly discernable, suggesting that the digging mechanism may have been through a punching-and-loosening method with an object like a sharpened pole.

A pattern of displaced B horizon sediment and interspersed B/C sediments in the northwest end suggests that part of the feature may have experienced a complicated period of crushing, trampling, or mixing; a detailed future micromorphological study could shed future light on this. Perhaps it indicates a nonhuman intrusion into a buried cache. The feature appears to have experienced minor use wear in the southeast, as indicated by the sharply contrasted disturbed/undisturbed sediment contact, and extensive use life toward the northwest. The complicated nature of interpreting this feature may suggest that several independent reuse events may have occurred. If it was a dwelling, it is perhaps a candidate for a short-term, single-person dwelling. However, the sharp stratigraphic change in the horizontal walls between the disturbed and undisturbed layers suggests that it was not occupied as a long-term domestic feature of any kind and likely instead represents the remains of a cache pit. Few artifacts are present to inform any further conclusions.

THE SWAN POINT LOCUS 2 RESIDENCE

The second cultural locus at Swan Point exhibits a separate assemblage of artifacts and features whose radiocarbon dates fall within those recorded for the Late Taiga Period's CZ1a2 (Hirasawa and Holmes 2017, 108; Holmes 2001, 158; Holmes 2008, 71). The second locus is downslope from the main area, approximately 50 m south-southwest, along the south-facing slope. The area demonstrates a confined space of subsurface precolonial cultural disturbance, including a residence feature, surrounded by soil stratigraphy similar to the main locus, exhibiting limited disturbance and mixing.

Seven discrete stratigraphic layers are defined here. The uppermost O/A horizon is an organic mat with a thin layer of mixed humified organics and mineral matter (10YR2/1; black) that is devoid of artifacts. Below it is a deposit of fine-grained silt loam that caps the entire feature. This silt loam (Bw horizon) has a reddish-brown coloration near the top (10YR4/3) but trends toward a dark yellowish-brown (10YR3/4) at the bottom. An intermittent layer of ash and charcoal was found dispersed throughout the locus between the upper two strata and is interpreted to not be of anthropogenic origin, likely representing the remains of at least one precolonial wildfire at the surface of the Bw horizon. The lower portion is artifact bearing. The C horizon is fine-grained silt, interpreted to be the naturally deposited loessic sediment into which the housepit was dug (10YR3/2; very dark grayish brown). The regolith is heavily weathered schist bedrock underlying the entire site and is easily dug through. Intermittent layers of rubble and sand lie over the bedrock (figure 7.4).

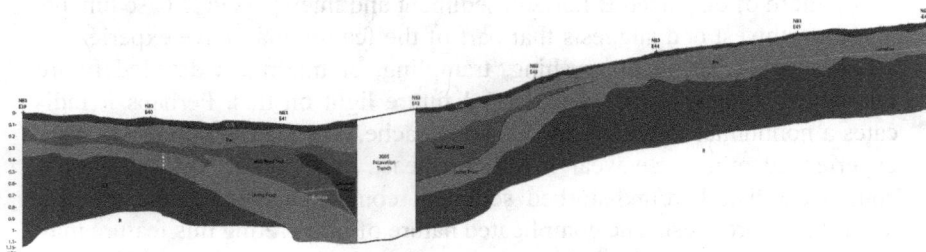

Figure 7.4.   Stratigraphic profile (north wall) along, bisecting the housepit feature and 2005 trench on a grid east/west axis.

Between the Bw and C horizons is Stratum III, a charcoal matrix, which is an anthropogenic mixture of charcoal and loess restricted to the pit feature's confines. It is interpreted to be the burned remains of the wooden structure that formed the original domicile construction. Within the confines of the pit feature is Stratum IV, a horizon composed of poorly sorted gravel, sand, and silt that is devoid of noticeable organics except for some charcoal. It is interpreted to be the remains of moss/sod insulation. Similar sediment matrices have been observed on sod used on historic cabin roofs (Mobley 2008). The interpretation was bolstered by my own personal experience examining and excavating historic log-and-sod structures, particularly a historic cabin destroyed by a wildfire at Uhler Creek (EAG-00468) (work reported in Mills 2010). In the context of the subarctic boreal forest, usable "sod" is dominated by moss and poorly sorted sandy loess, with little organic soil development as seen in well-drained loessic soils. Mossy sod like this is not typically found on the hill where the site is itself but is observed throughout the surrounding poorly drained low-lying areas (figure 7.4).

Below these levels is Stratum V (10YR4/6; dark yellowish-brown), a compacted loess that forms the interior living floor and remaining wall structure

Figure 7.5. Digital photomodel image of the Swan Point footprint. Image by Ted Parsons.

and, intermittently, the outdoor living surface. A human footprint was found embedded into the top of this horizon (figure 7.5). Strata III-V, capped by the Bw horizon and underlain by the C horizon, are interpreted as anthropogenic units, and all are artifact bearing.

An entrance tunnel or deeply-incised pathway leaves the house at a 135-degree angle off the long axis on its eastern corner. Two post molds were observed on the southern corner, and their shape resembles a gnarled root ball located at the base of many black spruce trees. A third post mold was observed along the southwestern wall. The feature's sub-rounded nature and embedded small lithic and faunal fragments suggest discard patterns, floor maintenance, and sweeping behaviors (Matthews 1995; Matthews et al. 1997). Small charcoal pieces were observed in the roof layer in horizontal lines running along the house's long axis, suggesting a construction similar to the lattice-like framework documented by Pitts (1972, 143) for the traditional dome-shaped winter house. Two superimposed hearths were found forward of the house's center, closer to the door. These two hearths indicate the presence of reuse of the house over two separate seasons. A reconstruction based on these feature interpretations and Roger Pitts's (1972, 115) descriptions of similar construction types is included in figure 7.6. The regolith was observed to have been culturally disturbed in ancient times, and an earthen floor was likely prepared on the foundational surface (Kovács 2013, 190). The floor space is roughly 2 m x 4 m or ~8 m² (figure 7.7).

The living floor was observed to be lower than the surrounding outdoor living surface, a process that could be produced by purposeful digging, as if to create a heat trap inside the house, or from passive trampling as members entered and exited the residence regularly. The entrance tunnel was observed to be infilled by a layer of poorly mixed rubble, sand, and silt. This layer (Stratum IV) was observed to be thickly deposited on top of the floor elsewhere throughout the house. It was more ephemerally dispersed to the northeast and southeast outside of the residence but not to the west. It likely represents the remains of a sod roof, and its relatively thicker deposit over the tunnel in contrast to the living surface directly to the north and south suggests that this sod extended over a long entranceway as well. See McFadyen Clark 1996, 145–168, for further examples of similar structures.

The remains of a small shod human footprint were also identified in 2017. These findings were reported in Smith et al. 2019. Laboratory analysis suggested that a footprint of its dimensions is typically left behind by an eight- or nine-year-old person with an average height of 137 cm (4 ft. 6 in.) and a healthy body mass of 35.5 kg (78 lbs.). The footprint was located on the top of the outdoor living surface horizon, just beyond the outer edge of the house pit feature. Because it is so well preserved, it is considered most likely related to the end of the residential occupation of this locus. When elders were shown the footprint, they felt they were looking at the print of a small woman carrying a heavy load, an alternative hypothesis that also agrees with analytical results. Fibrous fragments found outside the residential structure are suggestive of possible leather or matting (figure 7.8). The material was recovered in the same level, 50 cm grid southwest of the footprint.

To preserve the print, a plaster mold was cast of the feature at Swan Point, made in the field soon after discovery. Before removing the actual footprint for museum accession, the feature's surface and sides were stabilized using Great Stuff™, a spray-on foam sealant. After the surrounding matrix with the

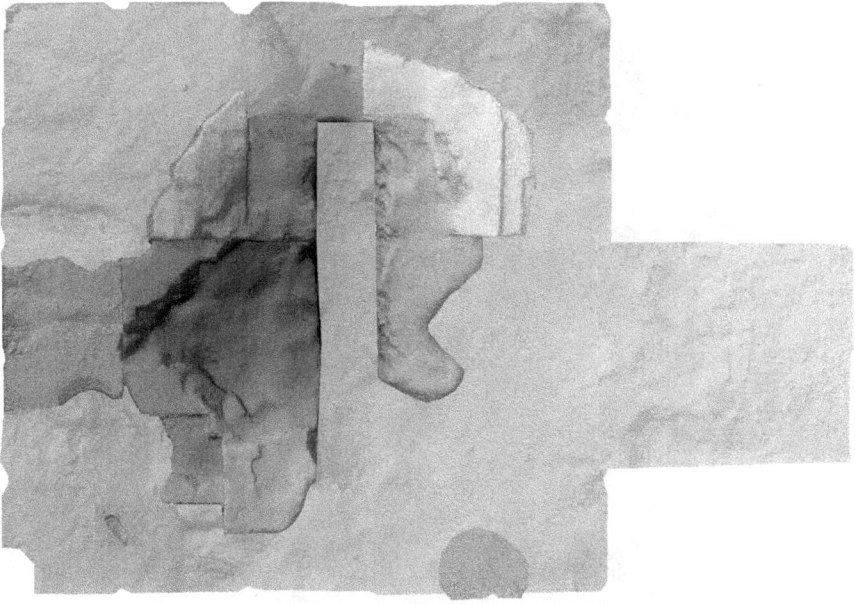

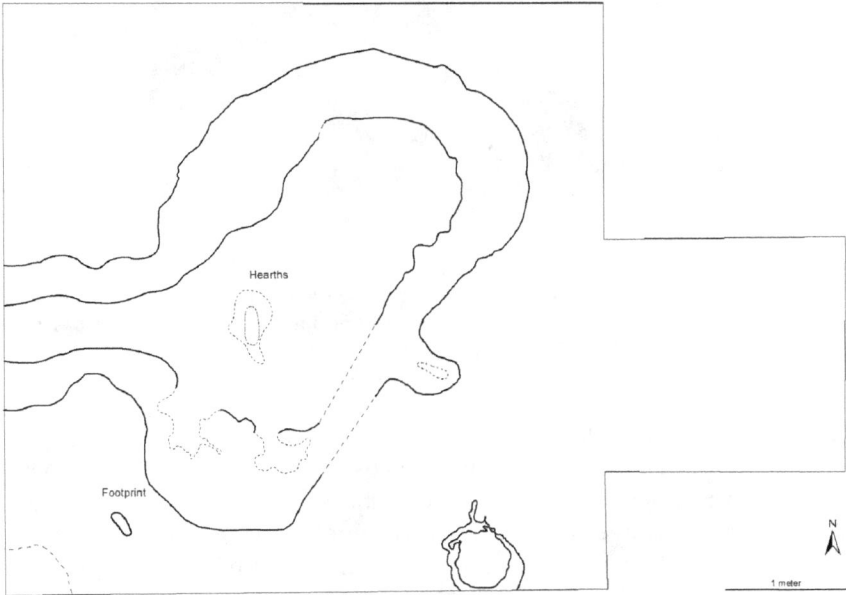

Figure 7.6.   Digital Elevation Model of the housepit floor and entrance tunnel, associated footprint, and nearby pit features on the southern excavation edge (2006 excavation trench passes through the floor and creates the gap).

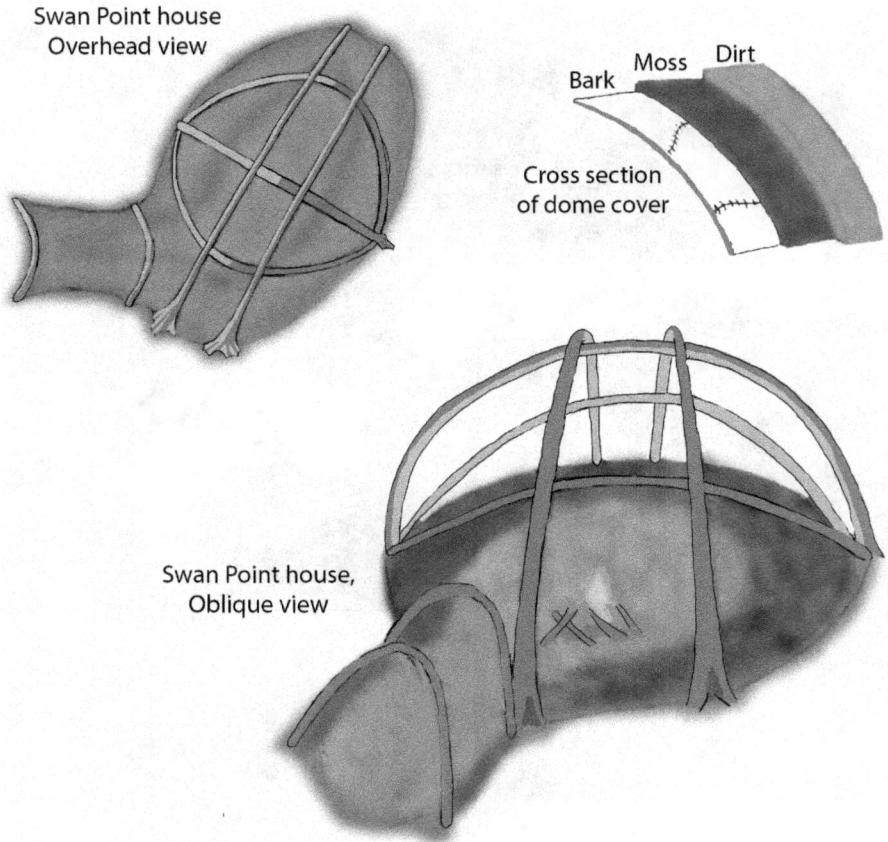

Figure 7.7. Sketch reconstruction of the framework of the Swan Point residence feature, likely covered in an insulating layer of bark, moss, and dirt. Sketch based on information from Pitts 1972: 115.

impression was excavated, a ¼-inch-thick section of plywood was slipped under the print, and the feature was removed from the site. It was taken to the Anthropology Laboratory for Cultural and Environmental Scanning laboratory at the University of Alaska Anchorage, where a wood frame was constructed. The footprint was placed within it. A base of plaster of paris was poured under the sediment of the feature and along all sides. The footprint sustained some minimal changes due to transportation, and some marginal surface damage occurred during the removal of the foam cast. The feature retained its shape during the preservation preparation process. The footprint

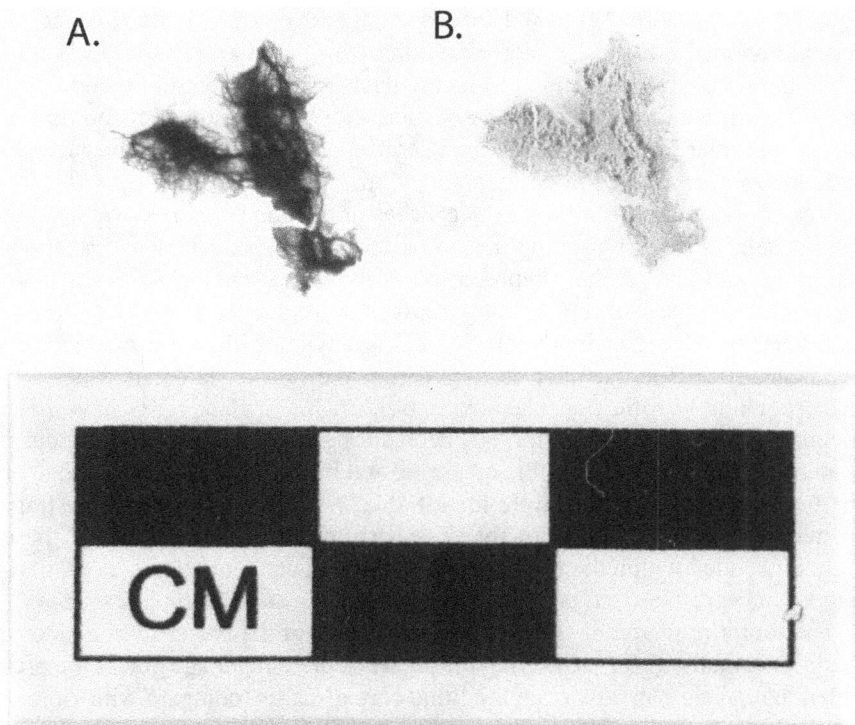

Figure 7.8. Fibrous, leather-like material associated with the footprint on the living surface at Swan Point Feature 2. A: backlit, B: front-lit. Image by Eleanor Bishop.

was then removed from the foam casing and photo modeled to document any changes to the feature that might have occurred during transport. Next, a clear resin, Super Glaze™, was poured inside and across the footprint feature's surface to preserve structural integrity. Scans with a NextEngine tabletop scanner were taken of the plaster footprint mold (scan settings: 360 degrees over twelve divisions, HD setting, neutral color, and wide range). The possibility of additional noise being added to the model due to the high division setting was not observed to be significant. Two scans of the cast were performed in different positions, and then they were aligned and fused.

Two subsurface features appeared to have once been intrusive pits along the south edge of the excavation area. Initially, these were interpreted to be household cache features, similar to the description given by Anne Shinkwin at the *Dakah De'nin's* village site (1979, 81). However, their radiocarbon dates suggest that they are both associated with earlier, isolated activities. Pit 1's radiocarbon assays averaged about 600 years earlier than the housepit

(~2,500 cal BP). Pit 2, located in the southwest corner of the excavation, dates to about 3,400 cal BP, corresponding with Swan Point CZ1b. It's possible, but it cannot be confirmed that the dates resulted from old wood being used. No artifacts were observed associated with either feature, and no further behavioral interpretations can be made concerning these features because no artifacts were recovered in direct association.

Very few formal artifacts or larger pieces of debitage were recovered from the house pit locus, suggesting that stone tool work was oriented away from the household and is likely represented in the CZ1a levels 2–4 at the main locus. One unique tool representing a bifacially retouched microblade tablet. Microblades were the dominant tool discard type, with some evidence of expedient flake use. Artifact density within the house feature is especially light, potentially reflecting cleaning activities. No artifact refits have been identified. The lithic deposition has been strongest in the back of the house. Material types of chert, rhyolite, quartzite, and basalt were preferred. None of the faunal remains (n=348) were identifiable. All represented extensive fragmentation and burning, all but five pieces were calcined, and most of these were embedded within the floor sediment. A small concentration was encountered in a nearby test pit, possibly representing a hearth-cleaning toss area.

The footprint feature is the best direct evidence of the presence of children. Additional methods for identifying the presence of younger age grades are provided in a recent paper by studying lithic core discards (compare with Gómez Coutouly et al. 2020). Their model categorizes individuals who are lithic tool creators at different skill levels: skilled (adult), apprentice (teenager), novice (pre-teens), and beginning knappers (children). These age grades are identified by recognizing less-skilled and unskilled knapping mistakes in the Swan Point CZ4 assemblage. Similar artifacts are also observable in the upper levels. The upper-most microblade core discarded in CZ1a Level 2 (ID no. 09614) represents a skilled user who abandoned a core without flaking mistakes when it became too small to use. A microblade core discard from Level 4 (ID no. FS 2017: 55) depicts a series of blade removal failures, observed as stacked step fractures across the front. These likely represent the work of a skilled practitioner who attempted to rejuvenate some flake removal mistakes that resulted in the core's premature discard (Gómez Coutouly et al. 2020, 10–11). Generally, while the biface discards in CZ1a are representative of a high level of skill, the biface discards of Levels 3 and 4 may depict varying levels of talent: ID no.'s 22682 and 00158/001544 appear to represent the biface reduction skills of an apprentice knapper. Crude bifaces and irregular flake cores on locally available materials perhaps are indicative of novice crafting. Scrapers also show a spectrum of fine crafting to crude but functional shaping, potentially indicative of experts and novices working together.

Preserved and archaeologically investigated semi-subterranean housepits are rare in the Tanana Valley. Most of our understanding about them is from features and ethnohistorical documents pertaining to the much later eighteenth and nineteenth centuries CE (see, for example, Coffman et al. 2018; McFadyen Clark 1996; Pitts 1972; Rainey 1939a; Shinkwin 1979). The presence of a precolonial house pit at Pickupsticks that is similar in morphology to the centuries-later historic Athabascan tradition-era house pits at the nearby Goodpaster River village is unique in the Alaskan and Canadian archaeological record. It dates to the Athabascan tradition's early centuries, suggesting a strong line of evidence for cultural continuity, especially for the kinship system that this construction form symbolized. The protohistoric Upper Tanana ovoid winter houses that appear similar to the Swan Point residence feature were typically constructed of an elliptical frame of small-diameter logs. This framework was then covered in birchbark or hides, and a layer of insulating sod, skin, and moss, built over an oval pit, dug several feet into the sediment (McKennan 1959; Osgood 1971; Pitts 1972). While documented for other Alaskan Dene groups such as the Dena'ina, the Swan Point House's entrance tunnel appears to have no longer been used for Tanana houses at the point of contact, suggesting this was an original construction technique that was later abandoned. The similarities of the older Swan Point residence with ethnographically documented construction techniques are also a strong line of evidence for cultural continuity in this region for the past 2,000 years.

INSIGHTS FROM COMPARATIVE NORTHERN ARCHAIC TRADITION ASSEMBLAGES

The technological precursor to the Athabascan tradition was the Northern Archaic tradition with its characteristic side-notched bifaces. It was geographically spread across Alaska, Yukon, British Columbia, and Northwest Territories. The Northern Archaic cultural signal is considered potentially to be a regional adaptation to the northern boreal forest-dominated landscape, which had become developed by about 6,000 cal BP, as their appearance correlates temporally (Gillespie 1990). However, while Northern Archaic people certainly exploited the boreal forest, they were not entirely dependent upon it, and many sites are found outside the limits of those woodlands (Anderson 1988; Betts 1987; Esdale 2008, 2009; Rasic and Slobodina 2008; Smith 2012). The Northern Archaic appears in Anaktuvuk Pass at the Tuktu Site (*Sehno' Hutl'ot:* black bear stream headwaters) early at 6,170 cal BP (Campbell 1961; Long 1965; but disputed by Anderson 2008). In the Kobuk River area, it appeared around 5,800 cal BP. In the southwest, it appears in the Ahklun Mountains and associated montane coasts, river drainages, and lakes, typologically dated to 6,000–4,000 BP, following the Onion Portage forms (Ackerman 2004). South of the Alaska Range, sites appear after 7,000 cal BP after a nearly 2,000-year hiatus (Dixon et al. 1985; Hays et al. 2014; Potter 2008c; Smith 2019).

The Northern Archaic tradition represents a widespread, long-term phenomenon in northwestern North America from which many technological elements of the Athabascan tradition trace their roots. The technocomplex has

> "side-notched projectile points; end scrapers; elongate and semilunar bifaces; boulder chip scrapers; large unifaces; notched pebbles; hammerstones; choppers; wedge-shaped, tabular, and pencil-shaped microblade cores: microblades; burins on bifaces and flakes; burin spalls; possibly burin spall artifacts microblade core tablets; end scrapers; notched, constricting base, and lanceolate projectile points." (Dixon 1985, 53)

Initially, it was described by a cultural sequence spanning 3,000 years at Onion Portage (Giddings 1967, 354) and was divided into six phases by Douglas Anderson (1968, 1984, 1988). Phase I (5,800–5,200 BP) bifaces were typified by side-notching and utilized as projectile points. The following four Phases (II–V) (5,200–4,300 BP) were typified by bifacial projectile points that exhibited a stemmed base for hafting. Phase V and Phase VI (4,300–4,100 BP) was typified by "oblanceolate" points (Anderson 1988). At the site, side-notching was far more pronounced in the earlier sequences and mostly nonexistent in the latter. A significant degree of variability regarding basal construct, notching width, and blade asymmetry was found. Microblade production was recognized by Dixon (1985) as especially visible following these later phases, so much so that he defined it as a separate complex (termed Late Denali). This designation has since fallen into disuse. Microblades and burin technology are now recognized to be used throughout this tradition (Betts 1987; Esdale 2008; Holmes 2008; Rasic and Slobodina 2008). Only a subset of these tools is found in most sites, suggesting their use is constrained by resource availability or task orientation (Potter 2008a, 2008b).

Atlatl darts were the dominant form of projectile weaponry throughout the middle Holocene (Hare et al. 2004, 2012), with a preference for composite shafts and bifacial lithics (exhibiting lanceolate, notched, and stemmed hafting forms), with a few limited organic (antler) points (stable from ~9,300 to 1,300 cal BP). Bifacial forms appear to have been similarly used for projectile points and cutting blades; variation followed function, situation, and game types (Esdale 2009; Rasic and Slobodina 2008). Dixon (1993, 2001) considers the wide variety of hafting types to be possibly associated with the development of discrete ethnic groups.

This period marks the earliest recorded large-game drivelines (Wilson and Slobodina 2007) associated with caribou hunting and large-scale food storage. Their association with the Northern Archaic signal corresponds with a specific focus on this ungulate (Yesner 1989). The earliest use of a caribou driveline is recorded at the Pond Site in southwestern Alaska, described as two generally parallel lines of stone cairns converging into a small lake, around 4,200 BP (Ackerman 2001). The growing importance of caribou in the diet and storage of large quantities of meat might signal a shift in mobility patterns, where risk-averse success meant seasonal group aggregations, after which small family units dispersed across the landscape. The caribou drive lines may signal new cooperative behaviors facilitating group assembly and planning for by up to a year in advance (Wilson and Rasic 2008). Cache pits also appear to be used in tandem with the Northern Archaic and drive lines, reflecting the need for preservation of large amounts of meat provided by the drive line hunts.

A growing increase in lakeshore use and upland use compared to both the later Holocene and the earlier Holocene suggests an increased seasonally defined land-use signal during the Northern Archaic. The signal may perhaps indicate the use of more mobile long-term task-camps or a more significant residential mobility system within expanded but predictable territories, supporting lower population and higher mobility patterns (Potter 2008a, 2008b). An increase in the archaeological visibility of caribou, fish, and hare also occurs during the middle Holocene. Conversely, there is very low visibility in bison and sheep remains, and wapiti generally disappears entirely from the archaeological record by 6,000 cal BP. However, wapiti remains have recently been identified at the Delta River Overlook site (*Łuu Tadzeey' T'aax*: beneath heart among the glaciers) at about 2,240 cal BP (Potter et al. 2018, 71). Components containing both microblades and bifaces appear in association with all faunal species; however, caribou have a stronger correlation with bifacial technology, while microblades tend to be associated with lacustrine sites (Potter 2008a; Sheppard et al. 1991, 156).

The Delta River Overlook site sits on a west-facing promontory, which juts out into the Delta River plain near Donnelly Dome (*Łuu Tadzeey'*: heart among the glaciers). For the Northern Archaic components there, Component 8b (2,240 cal BP) is interpreted to be a residential base camp, where wapiti, ground squirrel, hare, and lynx remains were identified. C8a (3,560 cal BP) remains are dominated by a small, dense cache of about fifty bifaces and uniface blanks, suggesting an abandoned toolbag. Additionally, the remains of a very large artiodactyl were recovered. C7b (4,150 cal BP) results from a short-term processing site that included bison and small mammals (Potter et al. 2018, 71).

In the Shaw Creek Valley, the Mead Site is located on a rocky bluff over-looking the Shaw Creek Flats, about a mile from the mouth of Shaw Creek. CZ1b (4,244–4,008 cal BP) is interpreted as the remains of a long-term residential base camp based on the relatively wide array of locally provenanced debitage types residence features were not apparent. The otherwise lack of bifacial technology is interpreted to be the result of their manufacture at Mead but use and discard offsite (Holmes 2001; Little 2013; Potter et al. 2011; Potter et al. 2013).

The Northern Archaic people's primary food base appears to be caribou (Clark 1994). The presence of notched cobbles suggests the adoption of nets and the growing importance of fishing (Anderson 1988) but may also represent hammer stones for processing heavy longbones (Wilson 2007). Steppe Bison (*Bison priscus*) survived in the upper Yukon drainage basin until about 5,400 years ago (Zazula et al. 2017). Bison fossils persist intermittently in Alaska almost to the Historic period, but it is not yet clear when the populations shifted from Steppe Bison to Wood Bison (*B. athabascae*) (Potter et al. 2018, 327; Stephenson et al. 2001). Joe Keeney's (2019) comprehensive summary of zooarchaeological Northern Archaic assemblages suggests they had a mixed diet breadth similar to that of the ethnographic Upper Tanana people. It incorporates caribou, moose, sheep, bison, medium mammals, birds, and fish without the aspect of salmon intensification, suggesting greatly expanded territories and mobility patterns beyond that of the later Athabascan tradition and a higher emphasis on utilizing upland settings (Potter 2008a).

Northern Archaic sites are often task-specific and tend to be small but with various tools and tool types, suggesting a residentially mobile system (Betts 1987). A pattern of a broadened resource base, technological innovation, rise in trade networks as demonstrated by more raw material sources becoming apparent across the state, reduced territory and regionalization, and increasing social complexity differentiates these sites from those of the earlier Holocene (Esdale 2008; Potter 2008a, 2008b, 2016). The Northern Archaic tradition developed innovative new hafting techniques such as strong side notching on bifaces, new hunting techniques such as mass kills typified by caribou drive lines and corrals, and meat or fish storage techniques such as the increased visibility of cache pits in the record.

South of the Alaska Range (*Łuu Ddheł*: glacier mountains), Northern Archaic sites are only associated with upland areas in the Middle Susitna Talkeetna Mountains, Clearwater Mountains, and headwaters of the Nenana (*Łuyinanest'aani Na'*: one that extends into glacier stream) and Susitna Rivers (*Tl'azii Na' Tl'aa*: [uncertain] headwaters stream). Sites predating 2,000 cal BP have not yet been described in the Copper River lowlands or along the western and southern slopes of the Wrangell Mountains (*K'ełt'iin*). A few Northern Archaic bifaces have been recovered from the Anchorage

(*Ves Dnaghiłdeq*: high bank) and upper Kenai River (*Kahtnu*: stream mouth stream) areas suggesting a brief middle Holocene incursion after 5,000 cal BP (Holmes et al. 1985, 248; Neely et al. 2016; Potter 2008c; Reger 1998).

Demographic reconstruction for the Northern Archaic is difficult; patterns of high residential mobility and low site visibility suggest a population smaller than documented at the time of contact. Ben Potter (2008a, 2008b) models a possible population expansion at around 6,000–4,000 cal BP (see also Esdale 2008, 11), correlating with dated sites doubling in visibility during this period. It is followed by a demographic crash between about 3,500 and 2,500 cal BP, and no increase until after around 500 cal BP (Potter 2008a, 96). Brian Wygal's demographic model (2011, 238) is similar, with two population peaks at 5,500–5,000 cal BP and 3,500–3,000 cal BP. Conversely, Andrew Tremayne and Bruce Winterhalder's model (2017) does not indicate much of a demographic change in the interior, with population expansions throughout the state mainly being a function of access to coastal economies and resources.

Residence constructions associated with the Northern Archaic tradition cluster in two phases, the final millennium (~2,000–1,000 cal BP) and the earlier millennium (~5,000–4,000 cal BP). Interior residence features older than the Athabascan tradition include one site, TLM-00215, in the middle Susitna that may date to nearly 1,300 years old: (Dixon 1985; Hays et al. 2014), several centuries younger than the similar feature at the Swan Point site (Holmes 2011a). These features are not distinct in form or landscape location from the later Athabascan settlement types, so they are considered here to be the earliest ancestral forms of the Athabascan house types.

The Fish Creek site (*Tsabaey Caegge*: fish mouth) comprises four excavated loci located on a small knoll near the southeastern margins of Summit Lake (*Sasnuu Bene'*: sand island lake), near Isabel Pass (*Xwteth Tęy*: pass trail) at the Gulkana River's headwaters (Cook 1977, 160, 72–180). Over 10,000 lithics of thirteen types of chert, obsidian, quartzite, slate, and basalt are represented in bifacial, core-and-blade, burin, scrapers, hammerstones, and expedient technological forms. Burned and fragmented faunal remains dominated the faunal assemblage, which included a small number of fish remains. Three conventional radiocarbon dates suggested dates between 2,100 and 3,500 cal BP, consistent with the notched bifacial technology recovered from the site. Additionally, the researchers suggested that partial-ring-like scatters of lithic debris may point to the presence of nonpermanent habitation structures.

One of the oldest sites where the rectangular house forms are found far to the south at the Paul Mason Site in Kitselas Canyon, British Columbia (~3,200–2,700 BP: Coupland 1988, 1996). Another even older representative rectangular residence form is at the Maurer Site on the upper Fraser River in British Columbia (~5,500 cal BP: Lepofsky et al. 2009; Shaepe 1998). However, just as in Alaska, most interior British Columbia and Californian traditional houses of this type date to the past six hundred years (Matson and Magne 2007, 138–145).

The early Northern Archaic residential features are unique; they seem to have no archaeological precedent. Nor do they seem to be typologically ancestral to the much later development of houses. One of these house features is at Middle Tangle Lake (*Hwdaandi K'ay' Giis Dat'aan Bene'*: downstream young willow clump is in position lake) (XMH-00035) and is dated to 4,810 cal BP (Mobley 1982), slightly older than the two or three living floors at Onion Portage (*Paatitaaq*: wild onion) around 4,100 BP (Anderson 1988, 74–75). Fifty-five tent rings were observed at Agiak Lake (*Agiaq*) in the central Brooks Range, dating to 5,600–4,900 cal BP (Wilson and Rasic 2008). Finally, ground-penetrating radar, electromagnetic induction, magnetic gradiometry, and DC electrical method surveys, conducted at the historic Slaven's Roadhouse (*Zhùr Näddhàww Juu*: wolf mountain stream) on the central Yukon River suggest that several buried circular housepit features may exist there *in situ*, estimated at 4,000–6,000 cal BP and at a depth up to 5 m (Urban et al. 2016).

Currently, the Northern Archaic tradition is conceived as a longstanding technological tradition from 6,000 to 1,000 cal BP. It incorporates technological aspects from the earlier Denali complex and passes some of these forms on to the following Athabascan tradition. There are significant, visible, and longstanding unique phases observable in the NAt. The earliest is the Classic Northern Archaic period (~6,000–4,000 cal BP), where residential features are apparent. It is followed by the Late Northern Archaic period (~4,000–2,000 cal BP), where diet breadth became much more restricted, and residential features have not been documented. Finally, the Transitional Athabascan period occurs (~2,000 and 1,000 cal BP), where cultural adaptations associated with the Dene people began to intensify and visibly alter the material cultural record.

SWAN POINT CZ1B

At Swan Point, CZ1b represents perhaps two distinct occupations of the Northern Archaic tradition in interior Alaska dating roughly 4,800–5,525 cal BP. At the site, it is represented by the artifacts in Levels 5 and 6 (20–30 cmbs, B horizon) at the main locus. Eight potential hearth-like features have been reconstructed for CZ1b.

Thirty-seven fragmented and complete bifaces are associated with CZ1b (figure 7.9). Two were basalt (one distal tip and one complete). Twenty-three were of various types of chert (fifteen broken proximal bases, one distal tip, three edge fragments, one ear, three complete). Nine were rhyolite (four

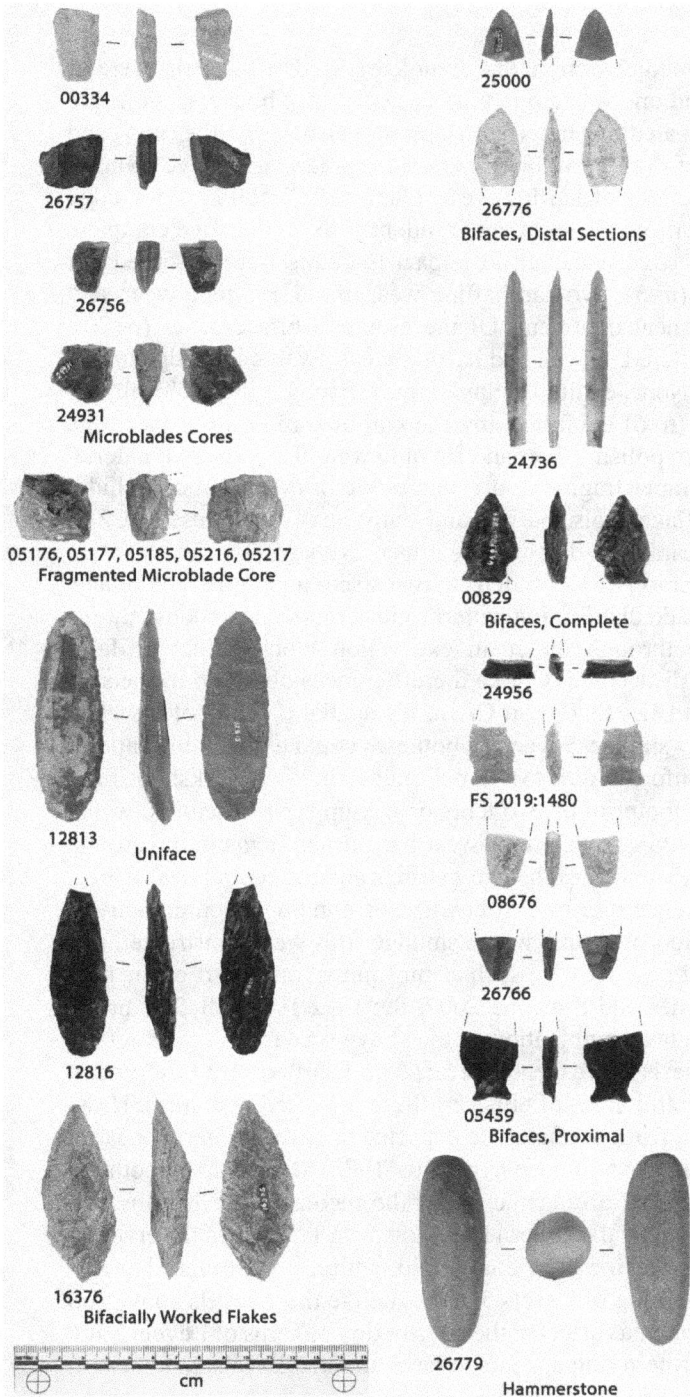

00334

26757

26756

24931
Microblades Cores

05176, 05177, 05185, 05216, 05217
Fragmented Microblade Core

12813
Uniface

12816

16376
Bifacially Worked Flakes

25000

26776
Bifaces, Distal Sections

24736

00829
Bifaces, Complete

24956

FS 2019:1480

08676

26766

05459
Bifaces, Proximal

26779
Hammerstone

cm

Figure 7.9. Sample of tools from CZ1b. Top left, rows 1-5: microblade cores. Bottom left, rows 6-8: bifacially modified flakes. Right: bifaces, bottom right, hammerstone. Image by Eleanor Bishop.

bases, three tips, one medial section, one complete). Two biface refits were of clinker (distal tip), and one was a quartzite base. Twenty biface sections are proximal bases, dominated by chert (n=15), present also is rhyolite (n=4) and quartzite (n=1). Six of these have observable edge wear, suggestive of knife use, and 10 have evidence of hafting wear. One medial section, three edge fragments, and two ears are also scattered randomly, as well as five complete bifaces; three exhibit edgewear, but no impact fractures were observed. Of the complete bifaces (n=5): two had hafting wear, three had edge wear, and two had evidence of heat treatment. Of the proximal biface bases (n=20): five were thermally altered, eleven had hafting wear, twelve had edge grinding, six edge wear. None exhibited any impact fractures, nor did any of the distal biface tips (n=6) exhibited any thermal alteration. Four had edge wear, and one had face polish. Chert and rhyolite were the preferred material types. Scraper and scraper fragments are suggestive of the presence of hideworking. Expedient flake tools, burins, and burin spalls are present. CZ1b contains the only discarded burins in these upper levels (n=9).

The spatial organization of CZ1b depicts two striking patterns: the biface, scrapers, and microblade distribution patterns cluster along a sinuous, almost backward "S" shape through the main excavation block. Other artifacts appear stochastically distributed. Unlike the differences observed in the spatial patterning between Levels 0–4 in CZ1a, the spatial patterns of Levels 5 and 6 for CZ1b is very similar. Several hypotheses could explain this pattern: (1) The pattern fits Binford's WAHM model, suggesting two workshop areas, or (2) it indicates the footprint of two tents or wikiup-type structures, where an internal pattern of living space floor-wear has pushed items in the ground and on or near the surface toward the tent margins and the central hearth area, or (3), where the presence of a ring of hearths surrounding a central activity area indicates an outdoor use zone where smudge fires were constructed in a circle to reduce insect pest activity, such as mosquitos, or as part of the hide tanning process (Haynes and Simeone 2007, 89; Lutz 1959, 18–20), or (4) potentially, it represents a combination of the above scenarios (figure 7.10).

The second hypothesis is weakened because no hearths were observed in what would be the central areas of either of these proposed tent areas. However, not all residential features should be expected to have an internal hearth, which may have been season dependent (Pitts 1972). The third hypothesis is supported by the spatial arrangement that the reconstructed hearths that cluster along the hypothetical southern ring; however, none were observed or recorded for the northern ring. The dual ovoid pattern has strongly homogenized the spatial patterning of Levels 5 and 6, unlike those levels above and below. The southern ring has affected the distribution patterns of Levels 3 and 4 above it, and the northern ring appears to have affected Levels 2–4 above it to an increasingly lesser extent (figure 7.11).

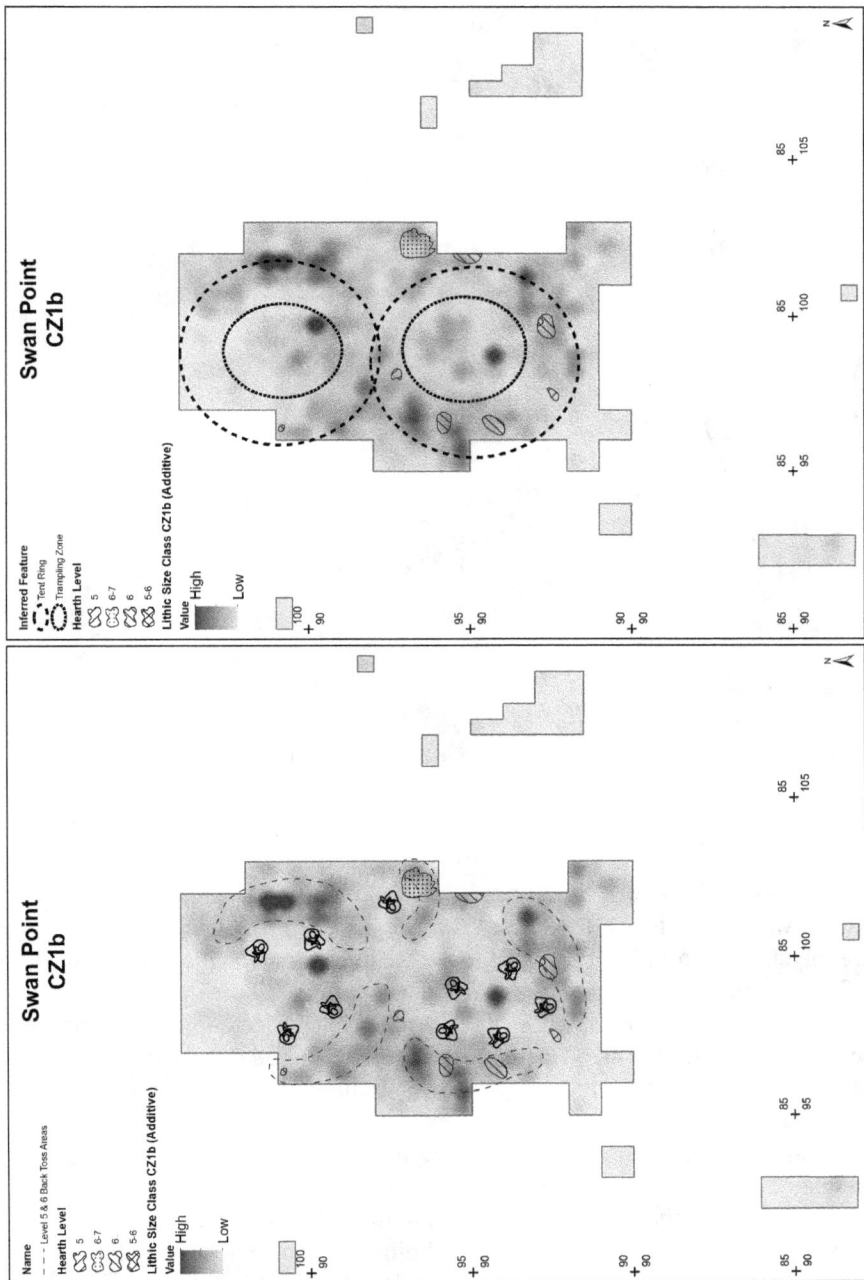

Figure 7.10. Hypothetical "Working Around a Hearth" model for CZ1b (Binford 1983) (left), and hypothetical tent ring model for CZ1b (right). Alternatively, the southern ring is explained as an activity area ringed by smudge fires designed to reduce insect activity. The background is a kernel density map (10 cm) of debitage size class.

Figure 7.11. A Niibaadl, a wikiup-type summer birchbark tent (Pitts 1972: 128) surrounded by a ring of smudge fires.

In CZ1b, a high level of craftsmanship is observed in many of the scrapers, bifaces, and microblade cores than in the younger levels. In particular, contrasting with them is the less-well-made large refit microblade core ID no. 05176, etc (figure 7.11). The angle between the core's platform and fluted face is consistently 90 degrees, less than optimal for striking consistent blades from platform to base. As a result, the fluted face depicts several microblade scars ending in step fractures. The core shattered due to improper heat application, suggesting that the core was either discarded in a hearth or the apprentice was experimenting unsuccessfully with heat treatment to attempt to improve the knappability of the core and correct the mistakes. No subpar-shaped scrapers appear in either Level 5 or 6, suggesting that if young persons were present, they were not engaged in the skinning activities. Overall, the Northern Archaic signature at Swan Point is one of butchery and tool maintenance. One uniquely shaped biface in particular exhibits a high degree of manufacturing skill with no evidence of use: ID no. 24736 (figure 7.11).

The discarded tools generally depict a high degree of skill, with some apprenticeship suggesting a social group of skilled adults and a few younger members. The hearth ring suggests summer smudge fires, either around an outdoor task area or a summer lodge. If fishing was strongly practiced during this time, the artifact patterning might indicate that missing family members (elders and small children) may explain the missing group members. The latter would have been absent at a separate fish camp locale. Otherwise, the signature suggests a task camp directed toward terrestrial game acquisition during times of the warmer months when fishing was not ideal.

INSIGHTS FROM COMPARATIVE TRANSITIONAL PERIOD REGIONAL ASSEMBLAGES

In the Middle Tanana, the approximately 8,000 cal BP component at Hollembaek's Hill (*Danige' Nuun Che'*: upland porcupine tail) (XBD-00376) near the mouth of the Gerstle River has been undergoing a series of excavations through the University of Alaska's Museum of the North. When the findings are concluded, they will provide important data pertaining to a wide breadth of faunal species use whose remains are associated with a buried anthropogenic pit feature (Lanoë 2018; Lanoë et al. 2019a; Tedor and Holmes 2011).

At the Mead site near the mouth of Shaw Creek, CZ2 (6,900 cal BP and 8,800 cal BP) is understood to be the remains of a short-term spike camp, with bifacial remains suggesting to researchers that it represented an increased period of resource stress (Holmes 2001; Little 2013; Potter et al. 2011; Potter et al. 2013).

To the south, near the base of the northern foothills of the Alaska Range, is Delta River Overlook (*Łuu Tadzeey' T'aax*). Component 6a (6,820 cal BP) represents the remains of a camp where the processing of wapiti, caribou, grouse, and several types of fur-bearing mammals occurred. The late occurrence and harvest of bison and wapiti there remains singular in the Middle Tanana Valley (Potter et al. 2018, 71).

The Banjo Lake site (6,200–7,000 cal BP) is located on the Delta Moraine, east of Jarvis Creek (*Niidhaayh Na'*: gravel stream). The assemblage represents a significant yet disturbed lithic assemblage associated with extensive expedient lithic production, as well as bifacial and core-and-blade technology. The collection is also associated with at least one, possibly two, hearths and is interpreted as the remains of a short-term camp, likely associated with prey butchery behaviors. The assemblage contains 7,000 lithics and over 12,000 unidentified faunal remains. Lithic types used included various cherts, rhyolite, basalt, obsidian, andesite, quartz, quartzite, limestone, sandstone, and slate (Esdale et al. 2015, 40).

SWAN POINT CZ2 (7,500–8,200 CAL BP)

At Swan Point, CZ2 represents an occupation during the transitional period of the final millennium of the Paleoarctic tradition, prior to the Northern Archaic tradition's full appearance in interior Alaska (Holmes 2008, 2011b). In CZ2, it is represented by the artifacts in Levels 7 and 8 (30–40 cmbs, B/C horizon) at the main locus and Levels 6–12 at the second locus. At the main locus, thirteen potential hearth-like features have been reconstructed.

Twenty-seven biface pieces are associated with these levels. One is a basalt base. Fifteen were of various types of chert (six broken proximal bases, four distal tips, two edge fragments, one ear, and two complete). Eight were made of rhyolite (four bases, two tips, one medial section, one edge fragment), one was a complete quartzite biface, and two fragments were of a worked, calcined bone reminiscent of osseous points (figure 7.12).

Eleven biface sections are proximal bases, although slightly dominated by chert (n=6), then rhyolite (n=4), and basalt (n=1). None of these have observable edge wear, but six have been edge ground, and eight have evidence of hafting wear. One exhibits impact fractures. Four medial sections, three edge fragments, and one ear are also scattered randomly, and three complete bifaces; one exhibited impact fractures, and one had evidence of hafting wear.

Of the complete bifaces (n=3), one had hafting wear, one had edge grinding, and one had evidence of heat treatment. Of the distal biface bases (n=11), one was thermally altered, eight had hafting wear, six had edge grinding, and one had impact fractures. Of the distal biface tips (n=6), two were thermally altered, one had edge wear, one had impact fractures, and one was edge ground. Chert and rhyolite were the preferred material types.

Scraper and scraper fragments suggest that a substantial amount of hide-working was conducted. Expedient flake tools, burins, and burin spalls are present. Microblades and their associated cores, tablets, and larger blades form an interesting sinuous distribution about the locus.

The spatial organization of CZ2 is strikingly different from the upper levels. While Binford's WAHM model helped reconstruct possible work areas for Levels 1–6, for Levels 7–8, it becomes challenging to observe any definitive discard arcs according to the model's predictions. A cluster of biface and biface fragments are found in the northeastern part of the excavation block, but otherwise, the remaining artifacts appear randomly scattered. One potential pattern is observed in the debitage patterning: it forms three seemingly

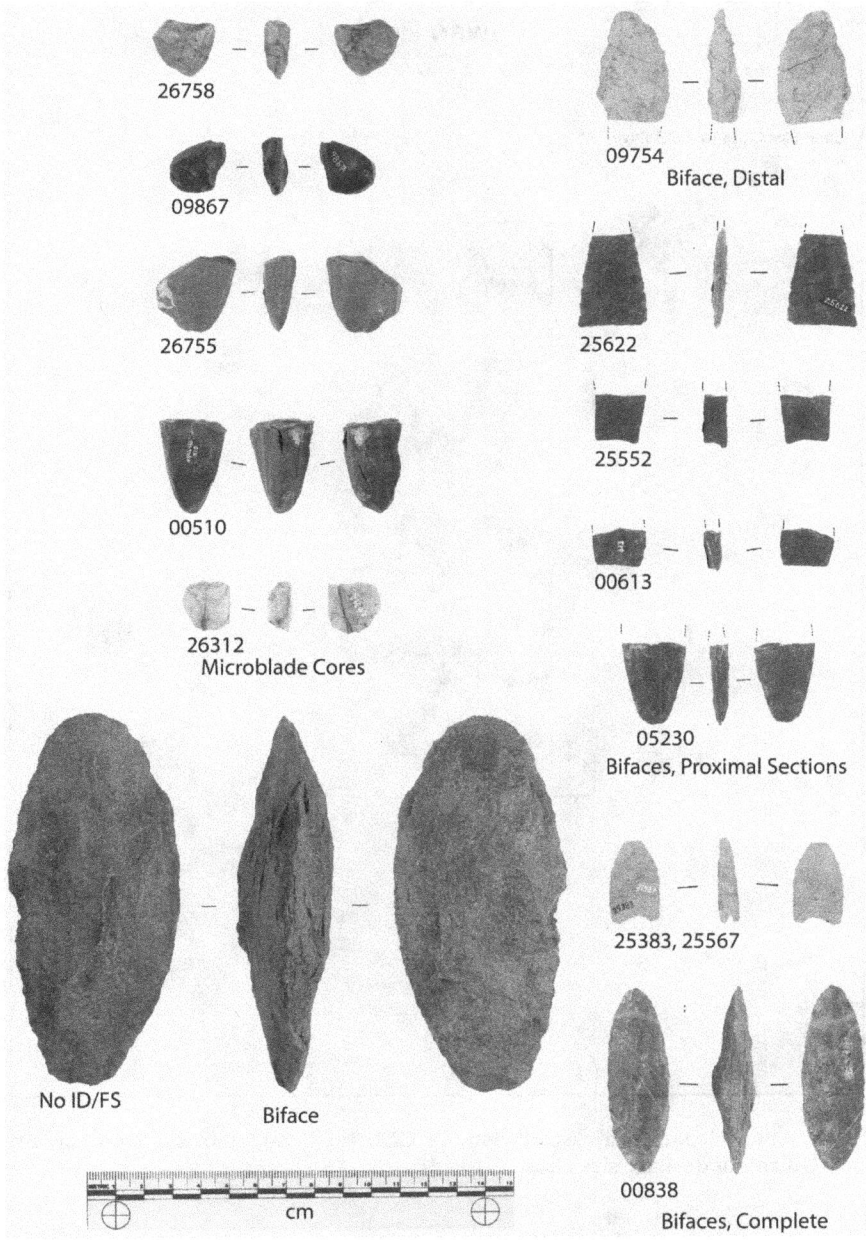

Figure 7.12. Sample of tools from Swan Point CZ2. Left, rows 1–4: microblade cores, bottom left and right column: bifaces. Image by Eleanor Bishop.

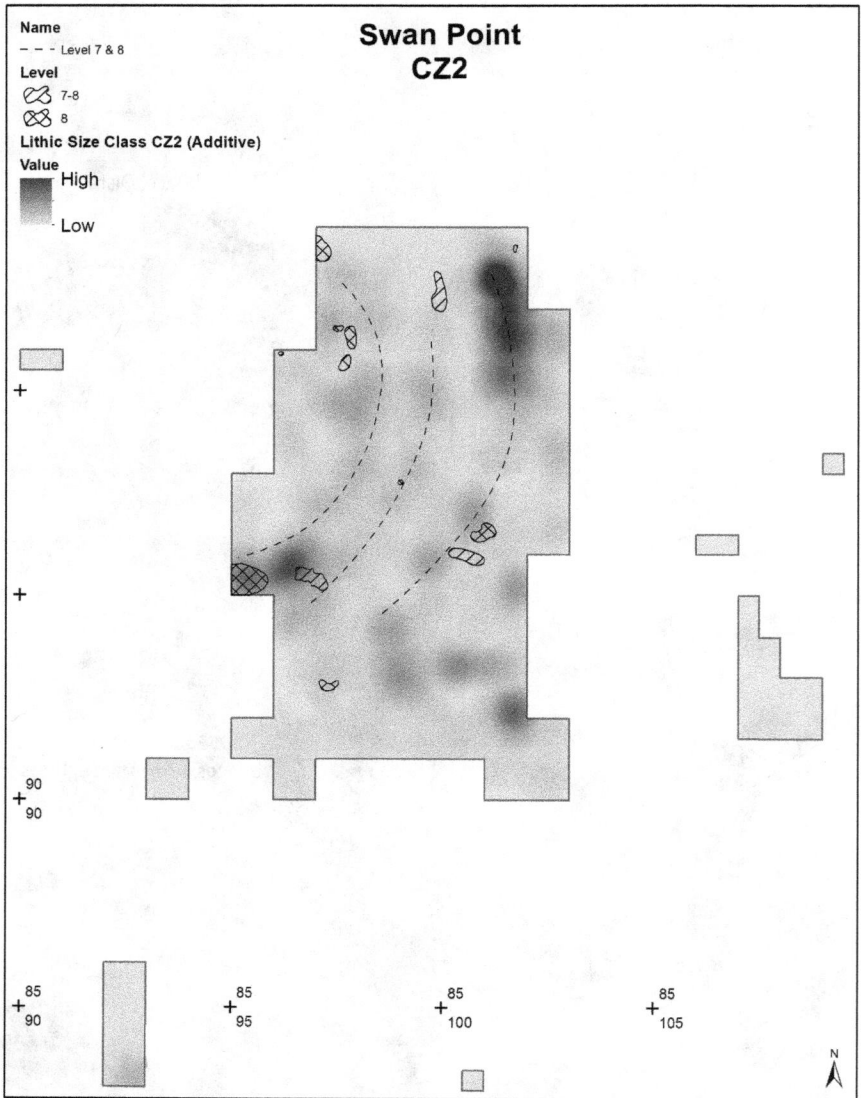

Figure 7.13. Hypothetical discard rings for CZ2. The background is a kernel density map (10 cm) of debitage size class.

concentric rings of discarded clusters (figure 7.13). It may be that these levels experienced more scattering taphonomic effects.

The CZ2 assemblage is dominated by biface forms and fragments, discarded microblade cores, and several scrapers. In CZ2, the microblade cores and bifaces all depict only a high level of craftsmanship. Few scrapers are present, possibly indicating behaviors were focused toward weapon retooling and meat processing. This component may indicate the presence of a small group of skilled adult individuals whose activities were limited to repeated short-term, task-oriented logistic camps. Throughout the Holocene at the main locus of Swan Point, activities were consistent across occupations being focused on retooling efforts and food package processing and consumption activities. Evidence of hide work increases in the younger components, along with evidence of younger members engaging in activities that affected the artifact record.

GENETIC RECONSTRUCTION SUMMARY

The reconstructed genetic history of this region is still only beginning to be understood. Remains available for ancient DNA analysis in interior Alaska currently come from only six individuals from three sites. Currently, the best summary of the available evidence suggests that a significant pulse of gene flow into the ancestral Na-Dene populations occurred between 4,500 and 2,000 years ago. Its origin is from the western Paleo-Eskimo population; a potential archaeological correlate being the Interior Norton population of the Koyukuk and Lake Minchumina regions and the earlier long-term cultural influences the Interior Norton had upon the incipient Northern Archaic traditions at Minchumina (Clark 1977; Holmes 1986; Potter 2016, 540).

The Paleo-Eskimo population originated in eastern Siberia, diffusing into coastal Western and Northern Alaska between 4,500 and 3,000 years ago. Consistent later gene flow from eastern Northern North Americans has minimized the Paleo-Eskimo genetic signature since then. Suppose there were large-scale population movements in Alaska in response to either of the White River Ash events; in that case, it might have helped minimize the later expression of Paleo-Eskimo ancestry in current Na-Dene people. However, no significant genetic population turnover seems to have occurred in interior Alaska during the past 3,000 years. Instead, genetic flow and drift patterns suggest intensified regional relatedness among Na-Dene peoples of Alaska and northern Canada occurred. The only population-wide genetic shifts demonstrated for this period occur between the Paleo-Eskimos and later ancestral Yup'ik and Iñuit populations between 1,200 and 800 cal BP (Flegontov et al. 2019; Moreno-Mayar et al. 2018). There are minimal, if any, genetic shifts in the Aleutians occurring with the Neo-Aleut transition at the same time (summarized in Misarti and Maschner 2015). While significant technological changes occur in interior Alaska, the genetic signature appears to be primarily identical before and after this transition.

Genetically, the Dene populations share mixed descent primarily from the Ancient Beringians/First Peoples population of the Terminal Pleistocene and early Holocene, and, to a lesser extent, from the later middle Holocene Paleo-Eskimo population. They appear to be strongly associated with the earlier middle Holocene expansion of the Northern Archaic tradition people that expanded across Alaska 2,000–1,500 years prior to the appearance of the Paleo-Eskimos. The earlier Ancient Beringian genetic population (whose technological expression was the Denali complex) of Central Alaska appears to have either disappeared or transitioned as the Denali technological complex is observed to shifted into the Northern Archaic tradition between 8,000 and 6,000 cal BP in Alaska. However, our ancient DNA population models remain relatively course-grained compared to other archaeological datasets, so future research will undoubtedly provide better understanding of this history.

CONCLUSION

The Athabascan tradition, directly ancestral to the Tanana Dene people, represents a culture open to innovation. It is punctuated by several swift important technological adaptations: adoption of the bow-and-arrow, intensification of salmon harvest and storage, development of a regional copper industry, and the rising popularity in seasonal residences. Like the growing importance of organic tools, long-term trends suggest intensification and optimization of local materials that were far more accessible than earlier cultures' quality tool stone. Intensification of a resource can be thought of as an optimization behavior producing energy conservation during periods of increased territoriality and localized resource specialization (Dyson-Hudson and Smith 1978). An external source for the additional energy observed during the Athabascan period was not provided through agricultural developments or adaptation to marine resources, as in so many other places. Instead, it has been proposed that the energy needed for the sustained population growth and growing social and cultural complexity observed during the last 1,000 years was provided by the joint intensified focus on caribou and salmon. This significant, sustained energetic input at around 1,000 BP facilitated a system of punctuated nomadism, where people could centralize seasonal settlements at singular locales. The appearance of residential features during the past 2,000 years in the Alaskan interior is a crucial outgrowth of these patterns.

The discussion of the volcanic events is enlightened when one considers that the Pickupsticks residence was constructed just after the last major eruption of Mt. Churchill, and the Swan Point house was constructed just prior to the earlier one. It may be significant that the Swan Point house seems to be sized for a small family while the Pickupsticks house is intended for multi-family use. The rectangular houses were built for partnered non-kin families and their elders, which may have been an adaptation to increased resource stress that forced wider foraging ranges or perhaps even reflects the Middle Tanana people incorporating non-kin into their society as would be expected if migrating families were responded to nonviolently. The collected evidence suggests that the Pickupsticks house represents only short-term use despite the high level of the construction effort and may be instead better representative of ceremonial potlatching rather than familial residence.

There is no clear definable trait that is widely recognized by subarctic archaeologists which defines the transition between the Athabascan and Northern Archaic traditions. The accepted transition point of 1,000 cal BP is mainly used for ease of utility, but the reality is that important technological innovations, shifts in raw material emphasis, fluctuating food resource use, and changing settlement strategies are observed to represent a complex continuum of changes over the past 2,000 years. Because of this complexity, Dr. Holmes simply termed their fluorescence throughout the Shaw Creek basin the Taiga periods, a loanword brought by the Russians that describes the boreal forest. The Taiga periods describe the 9,500-year period of boreal forest's development and dominance of the Alaskan interior ecosystem, and the material cultures which adapted to it (Holmes 2008).

The Northern Archaic people appear to have been far more mobile than their Athabascan descendants. Their toolkit conserved many technological elements from the earlier Denali complex. These were sustained throughout the Holocene until the energy-maximization behaviors of the Athabascan tradition facilitated their rapid innovation. The Middle and later Northern Archaic is marked by a long-term period of gene flow from the Paleo-Eskimo expansion. This westward gene flow does not correlate with Kari's model of linguistic seriation from the east, which likely represents an even earlier event.

Throughout the Northern Archaic and Athabascan tradition components are seen tools and technological behaviors associated with big game hunting, hide preparation, and residential site occupations. Differing levels of abilities are observed in the lithic tool manufacture and curation, suggestive of activities associated with children and adolescents. The Dene ethnographic model indicates that the technological discards associated with hunting and butchering activities point to occupations where gendered activities could have taken place. The presence of high quality manufactured lithic discards and organic tool-working items should recall the roles that elders could fill using their expertise and time availability to create tools for others who were not as practiced or whose time was absorbed with the food quest.

There are earlier cultural components represented at Swan Point, which are not reviewed here, complexes that have been termed the Denali, Chindadn, Nenana, and Dyuktai, which have spurred intense research. These ancestral groups occupied the site over four further cultural zones between 14,000 and 11,000 years ago. The term "ancestral" represents a loose expression that can be defined in a variety of inclusive or exclusive ways as cultural, linguistic, genetic, or simply preexisting forebearers. These groups experienced the climatic shift from the arid, frigid Pleistocene ecological conditions to the warmer and dry early Holocene, followed by the rise of parkland forests and expansion of steppe bison and wapiti herds at the expense of the mammoths and horse herds. Finally, a cooler period of increased moisture came to characterize the Alaskan interior ecosystem that is familiar to us today, and with it the Northern Archaic presence became established as the bison and wapiti herds disappeared and the caribou, moose, fur-bearing mammals, and fish provided the new basis of the northern Dene's food economy, which lasted for millennia.

At some point during the early Holocene in the central Tanana Valley, the genetic haplotype markers of earlier *in situ* Beringian population shifted to those recognizable in the populations to the south and east of Alaska: the Northern North American lineage. How this correlates with the diffusion of Northern Archaic technological traits is not yet demonstrable. However, recognizing that something genetically and linguistically occurred in the Middle Tanana during the Denali complex of the Transitional and Early Taiga Phases (11,500–6500 cal BP) provides the best *post-hoc* genetic and archaeological proxies for Kari's stream seriation model, suggesting Proto-Dene linguistic expansion out of its homeland began to occur then.

While the Tanana languages retain no evidence of early interaction with non-Dene languages, their oral histories do describe a preexisting human-like population of *Cet'aeni* or monkey-people, meaning persons with long tails. The stories frame the events surrounding them within the genre of historical narratives rather than mythical narratives. The *Cet'aeni* lived in homes beneath the sod. Mutual strife between them and the recently arrived Dene resulted in a retaliatory attack where the Dene blocked the entrances to their underground homes with fire, suffocating the tailed-people and ultimately wiping them out (Paul 1957, 23–25). Froelich Rainey investigated several sites in the upper Tanana and upper Copper River region associated with the *Cet'aeni* stories with limited or inconclusive results (Rainey 1939a). Incidentally, since then, Beringian scientists with a research tendency toward dramatic and unrestrained ideas concerning the earliest migration and settlement of the Americas are often humorously likened to that early search for the Monkey-Man.

A significant inter-species behavioral shift in response to the increasing trends of ecological stress and is observed during the early Holocene where lions, mammoths, and horses were extirpated, bears became increasingly herbivorous, and adult large-mammal body sizes of many species began to shrink in response (Lanoë and Holmes 2016). This unique period, the first Distant Time world, was when the last of the giants, *Yaachox*, dispersed the Dene ancestors throughout the Tanana Valley, an event remembered in the Moose Creek Bluff paintings (Gutoski 2002), which was also the location where Raven created women by dressing men in female clothing (de Laguna and DeArmond 1995). The Moose Creek Bluff painting once depicted an array of creation myths, including the creation of summer, a figure interpreted to be both the image of Raven or *Yaachox*, and other figures interpreted to be within and without a house feature (Giddings 1941), possibly meant to evoke any number of myths dependent on the house motif.

The only other rock painting site in the Tanana region is at FAI-00363, found just to the southwest of Fairbanks on a rocky bluff of Chena Ridge on the northern bank of the Tanana River. There, two human figures, including one who may have a tail, are seen. The tail is not obvious, and may represent eroded paint. The paintings were associated with a village that experienced a traumatic period of death from an unknown sickness (Gutoski and Kari, personal communication). Given the interpretive association of the Moose Creek Bluff paintings with creation myths, if the anthropomorphic figure at the Chief John Heights site indeed had a tail, it might represent Traveler.

During the winter season, that world was recalled in the Dene's oral traditions as coded in the night sky, when *Saatedlech'eeghe* (Traveler) can be seen wearing a tail in his constellation form in the starry sky (Cannon et al. 2020). The tail, along with *Saatedlech'eeghe's* animal head, symbolizes his animal guide and his transformative powers. During the months and ceremonies when it was appropriate to discuss these topics, it would be recalled how Traveler, during an ancient period of cultural and ecological chaos, had transformed the archaic animals into their present behaviors, smaller bodies, static body forms, and speech (including humans), and had eradicated others considered too dangerous. During this process, he set forth the cultural rules of *'engii*, the core laws and covenants that bound the northern Dene people and the natural world together, ushering in a new world that ended with the colonial era. These traditional rules established Dene culture, guiding the ancestral Dene through the Northern Archaic, Athabascan, and Euro-American periods, shaping the archaeological record. These traditions have survived into this new chaotic world, adapting as needed to the globalized culture, informing the historic period, the current lifeways of the present, and still providing a pathway for many through the future.

Chapter Eight

Thinking about Raw Materials

We landed our helicopter above a small unnamed lake near the upper stretches of the Talkeetna River. In the cliff face above us, just before it disappeared into the clouds, was a large, light gray, thick band of rock. Our archaeology crew climbed up to the base of it. Here, we had been told by a geological reconnaissance crew that obsidian nodules would be found. Obsidian is not the most common material type found in Alaskan lithic assemblages, but is common and unique enough to provide a proxy for the movement of raw material across the landscape. Certain elemental signatures within obsidian are typically uniform enough through source deposits that artifacts can be matched to their quarry or origin area. However, not all sources identified in obsidian assemblages have yet been relocated on the geological landscape, nor were all available sources used. This place in the Talkeetna Mountains implied a new, undocumented source location.

As our crew moved up the slope, we encountered a slide of boulders that had long since broken off from the source layer. These ancient rocks were formed from a volcanic tephra and was filled with obsidian nodules. The material was uniquely colored with grey-blue swirls, but unfortunately, nothing we found was large enough to provide a nodule to craft a tool from. We took plenty of samples however; the source stretched for miles, large enough that other locations might provide larger, useful nodules. These samples we gave to Dr. Jeff Rasic at the National Park Service office in Fairbanks, who had the samples tested using their X-Ray Fluorescence (XRF) analyzer, and compared against the Alaska Obsidian Database, a comprehensive catalogue of obsidian artifact and their raw material signatures collected from all over the state. The results came back negative for cultural corelates; none of the many artifacts measured for the database had been acquired from that particular flow. Negative data is still important to research and is a good reminder that a phenomenon will not necessarily occur just because it has potential to.

The archaeological portion of this book focuses mainly on residential features and lithic artifacts. The features and the spatial patterning of artifacts were informed through ethnographic, experimental, economic, and biological analyses. This chapter will discuss the lithic landscape of the Middle Tanana, what types of stone material were used, how they were traditionally described, and where it came from. These are informed through both ethnographic reconstructions and scientific explorations. The translations were provided by an unpublished Middle Tanana Lexware dictionary file produced by Jim Kari (n.d.).

TRADITIONAL LITHIC CLASSIFICATION

Today, we make sense of precolonial lithic use through basic economic models of procurement, utility, and discard. These help to inform us of relative value of stone types, tools, and the energy expenditure needed to procure them and the energy gain their use provided (Surovell 2009). To make sense of raw material procurement strategies, it is essential first to understand both our Western culturally informed concept of geology and compare it with a reconstruction of the Tanana Dene geological constructs. The scientific study of geology represents a legacy of Earth Science in the Western European scientific tradition. It was an early outgrowth of the Enlightenment Period's Natural Philosophy and was a significant contributor in the early development of the discipline of archaeology (Goldberg and MacPhail 2006; Rapp and Hill 2006). The western perspective of geology simplifies rock types into useful categories that are typically determined by their similar physical and chemical properties and the original mechanisms that led to their formation and potential alteration.

The traditional Tanana classification method for stone types was unique, depending on color, utility type, and origin location for categorization. There are two basic unrelated terms for "rock" or "stone" found in the Middle Tanana Lexware dictionary. These are *bees* and *tthee*. The noun *bees* is a root in the likely name for "obsidian": *behts' eh*, or *bests' eh*, meaning "black stone" or " white/bright stone" and implies portability. Dene represents a group of relatively verb-heavy related languages, and complex words are formed in part by compounding verb themes onto basic root terms. The word can also refer to stones used in a steam bath. The root *ts' eh* similar is in sound to the root *ts'eł*, meaning "bright, white," such as *ts'ets'eł*, meaning "high fog, fog in the mountains." *Behts' eh* then can literally mean "bright foggy-like stone," an apt descriptor of the appearance of many types of Alaskan obsidian, and also recalls the steam rising off stones in a sauna. The term is found as the root *beets*, meaning both a portable and boiling stone, as in to cook using boiling stones. It calls back to the traditional gendered division of labor for the Tanana people, where food preparation was considered to be the purview of those identifying as female (*ts' ee*). *Beets'e'* refers to one's aunt. In traditional terms, these were women who were the ego's father's sister or mother's brother's wife (not the ego's mother's sister). Likewise, the women's ulu-like knife is called *beetseli*. The root *bees* is also found in *laabees*, describing a legendary, stationary, large, sharpened knife. Kari has reconstructed a likely Proto-Dene candidate for an obsidian term as **be·shr-tr'eʔ*, meaning literally "female stone." It is similar to the verb theme, also implying portability, and recalls how boiling stones were rotated between birchbark baskets or ceramic pots and a heating fire (Kari 2019b, 71–72), as cooking vessels (*łok*) were not typically placed in direct contact with flames. The term for coal or jet is related: *besde'*.

The second root for stone, "*tthee*," is also used to describe cooking and steambath stones as *ttheek'une'*: "stones+fire, burning" and is similar to *ttheek'on'* literally stone+fire, or steambath rocks. It appears to be a more generalized root, describing several rock types, tool stones, and landscape features. The root may reflect cultural ties with Ahtna, the Copper River people. A similar cognate for stone or possibly an unknown rock type in Ahtna is *ts'is* or *tth'ith*.

The term for ochre is *tsiik*, referring literally to yellow ochre (*tsisyu*: "ochre paint"), which appears more orange to an English speaker, or *tsiyh*: literally "ochre" (likely red). The term *tsiiyh tl'iige'* literally is "dark ochre" but refers to the color blue; it is the term used describing the paint used at the Moose Creek Bluff paintings (Giddings 1941), although surviving fragments depict pictographs using only the orange-colored ochre (UAMN n.d.). However, the surviving pieces do not match Giddings's published sketches, so both colors may have been initially present. The term for quartz is *tthee k'udli*, literally: "white rocks." This root also can be utilized as a compound to describe lithic technology: *ttheek'une' daadiidhoghe*: "stone skin scraper," *ttheek'aał*: "whetstone," or even *tthee yex*: "stone shelter." However, most tool terminology does not compound with lithic roots, reflecting the preferred use of other materials. One final odd term is *geeluu*, which is referred to as "a yellow rock." Some insight may be found in the roots *gee'*: "exact" (adjective), and *luu*: "ice". The related Lower Tanana Dictionary identifies this term with chert, chalcedony, or agate.

Four specific terms for metal are found in the dictionary; *gool* "gold" is clearly an English borrowing. The formal term for iron is *tsiy*: "iron," from the Proto-Dene *tsəy* = "move elongated." This definition appears to recall the smithing methods required to form it from its original shape into a tool. One of several terms describing Euro-Americans is *ts'iitsiy dneey*: "iron people," recalling the nineteenth-century trade origin of iron implements. The terminology for copper and iron are related: the term for copper may be derived from the former, *ts'itsiy t'eex*, which literally means "raw iron." This relationship between iron and copper terminology is similar in Iñupiaq and Sugpiaq. The term for iron *savił,haq* (Iñupiaq) *cawik* (Sugpiaq) is also synonymous with the general term for "metal," while copper *kanŋuyak* (Sugpiaq: *kanuyaq*) receives a specific identifier (Leer 1978; MacLean 2011). The last metallurgical term is unique; *ts'eyuun k'a'tthee'* literally "Stick Indian's [e.g., woodsman, or boogeyman] shells [dentalium]." *Ts'iyuun* literally means "spirit" or "ghost." It may also mean "arrowhead made of lead." Mertie Baggen recorded informant Bessie Barnabas as describing it as "black shell [i.e., dentalium], heavy, melts like gold, tender rock, shell underneath."

TRADITIONAL LITHIC PROCUREMENT PLACES

At Swan Point, some broad generalizations can be made from the raw material debitage: almost all material types identified at the site are present throughout all the individual Holocene cultural zones. Obsidian source variability increases in the younger components at Swan Point. Osseous tool crafting is directly present in CZ1a and 2, and organic tool crafting is further indirectly inferred for CZ1b through the presence of burin discards. The main locus at Swan Point was always utilized as an important workshop area, and chert, followed by rhyolite, was the preferred tool stone for bifacial, unifacial, and core and blade technology. Obsidian was generally only used in the production of microblades, scrapers, and expedient flake tools throughout the occupations. Other materials used include basalt, clinker, diorite, stibnite, hematite, quartz, quartzite, shale, and slate.

The lithic materials analyzed from these site assemblages are summarized here by their English names and Western geological typologies. The provenance can be generally inferred for most types, and for others, exact quarry or procurement locations are known. They represent primarily metamorphic materials, but igneous and sedimentary types are also present. Most of the obsidian from both sites has been geochemically characterized through the use of XRF and Neutron Activation Analysis. The two primary obsidian sources represented in these assemblages are Wiki Peak (the precise obsidian source location may likely be a smaller hill to the south, *Ttheenädi* (UT: old man rock)) in the Nutzotin Mountains (*Tthee Ddhäł* (UT: rock mountains)) to the east (Cook 1995; Patterson 2010, appendix B) and Batza Tena (*Baats'e Tene* (KY: obsidian trail)) in the central Koyukuk River Valley to the west (Clark 1995; Cook 1995).

Interestingly, the Wiki Peak obsidian source does not carry an overt obsidian signifier like Dennison Fork or the famous Batza Tena "obsidian trail" sources do. Beaver Creek, which flows along the mountain's northern flanks, is simply called *taatthee niign*: "rock [cobble] water stream." This name's general or basic nature suggests that perhaps the obsidian found in its riverine deposits was the primary regional tool stone acquired there for an ancient Dene band who did not feel the need to differentiate it from other tool stone types, such as how one might imply iron or steel by simply saying "metal" in English. Ben Potter (personal communication) noted during fieldwork there that all assemblages were heavily, if not entirely, dominated by the use of that obsidian source (see also Patterson 2010).

No place names associated with obsidian are known from within the Middle Tanana territory, but a unique material type, possibly clinker, is a glassy opaque grainy green/gray material that is likely from a nearby unknown source as it appears to be unique to the Shaw Creek assemblages. A cluster of obsidian names is regionally associated with the Prindle Volcano and Denison Fork in Upper Tanana (*mbehts'eh ndiig*: "obsidian stream"), suggesting a small outcrop may be in that vicinity. Three names surrounding the abandoned village at Kechumstuk to the east recall stone use. Diamond Mountain is called *ts'ik'aa*: "from edged stone." A small knoll to the southwest is called *mbehts'eh teyy'*, meaning "obsidian hill." The "obsidian hill" was colloquially borrowed as "flint hill" into English, suggesting that quality chert and obsidian may not have been typologically differentiated precolonially by the Dene as they are in the Euro-American geological tradition. Froelich Rainey excavated some test units on the hill finding only naturally occurring jasper (1939b). The third location was unnamed, but Abraham Luke noted that a widely known tool stone quarry was located across the Mosquito Fork from the village high atop a hill (ANLC3676a).

Most of the remaining source locations for utilized raw materials remain unknown but can be approximated. Much of the Delta River (*Xwteth Cheeg Na'*: pass mouth stream) to the southwest flows through the glacial till deposits of the Donnelly Moraines. The northern-most moraine, which borders the southern banks of the Tanana River, dates to the Last Glacial Maximum, while the youngest southern-most moraine was deposited during the terminal Pleistocene (Matmon et al. 2010; Péwé, 1975; Péwé and Holmes 1964; Péwé, and Reger 1983; Reger et al. 2008; Ten Brink 1983). A prominent, isolated hill splits these moraines, long used as an important traditional landmark, Donnelly Dome, or *Łuu Tadzeey'*: heart among the glaciers (figure 8.1). It rises 4,000 feet in elevation, 2,500 feet above the surrounding country. A mountain in its own right, it is dwarfed by the peaks of the Alaska Range immediately to the south which can rise 13,000 to 14,000 feet. The traditional name *Łuu Tadzeey'* is themed with that for the Alaska Range, *Łuu Ddheł*:

Figure 8.1.   Donnelly Dome, Łuu Tadzeey': "heart among the glaciers." The eastern Terminal Pleistocene glacial moraine can be seen in the foreground of the photograph, while the higher western lobe's glacial moraine can be seen extending from behind the right flank of the hill. The bottom sketch depicts the fleigberg as it would have appeared surrounded by glacial tongues around 14,500 cal BP.

glacier mountains (Kari 2015), and recalls the Terminal Pleistocene landscape when the great glittering Delta glacier that flowed north through the pass was split into eastern and western lobes by the tall, dark hill. Today, the Delta River originates south of the Alaska Range in the Tangle Lakes region, cutting through various bedrock formations and glacial deposits before joining the Tanana near the Shaw Creek flats, easing access to material types found within them.

Due to the ancient glacial activity, the riverbed and other streams in the region contain various material types that are potentially useful for tooling (Potter et al. 2018, 177). Chert has been noted throughout the gravels of the Quaternary till, moraines, and glacial outwash deposits within the Delta and other Middle Tanana tributaries that flow north from the central Alaska Range (Hamilton 1980; Reger and Péwé 2002; Wilson et al. 1998). A chert reduction site to the south that is relatively close to this area is located near the mouth of the Little Delta River (*Xaasaa Cheege*: upward-rising sun mouth), XMH-00167 (Potter et al. 2007), where the investigators observed chert cobbles to be in secondary glacio-fluvial deposition. Primary sources are also known in Livengood to the west (observed by myself in 2012; Proue et al. 2013, 2014); Cook 1977, 257–299), Tangle Lakes to the south (Lawler 2019; Mobley 1982), and the Kechumstuk area to the east (Rainey 1939b). Chert dominates both of the assemblages from Swan Point and Pickupsticks by number and weight.

XRF sourcing studies of rhyolite represent ongoing research. Preliminary findings suggest that known artifacts throughout the Alaskan interior represent ten distinct geochemical groups. The Groups B (likely originating from the central Alaska Range), C (likely originating from the Kuskokwim Mountains), and I (probably originating from the Nenana River Valley) are strongly represented in central Alaskan Late Precolonial and Late Holocene assemblages. Due to their proximity to Shaw Creek, these three groups are likely candidates for the types described at Swan Point and Pickupsticks (Coffman and Rasic 2015).

Copper could be obtained from several locations around the Wrangell Mountains (Cooper 2012, 571). An XRF analysis sampling the elemental composition of the recovered Swan Point bipoint confirmed that the implement was pure native copper and not the result of an industrial alloy, thus likely originating from local acquisition and production (Thompson 2016). Two potential sources for copper are also named north of the Tanana River: Copper Creek, which flows into the lower Charley River, and Molly Creek, which flows into the Middle Fork Fortymile River. Both carry names suggesting copper in the neighboring Tanacross language. These are *ttheebaa nda'*: literally "gray rock stream" (possibly copper-implied) and *ttheetsqq ndiig*: literally "rock excrement stream" (the Tanacross term for copper).

Natural copper oxide and the feces of a bear who has recently been on a diet dominated by blueberries are very similar in color ranges, hues, and shape (Cooper 2011, 258).

Ochre and lead ore/stibnite sources remain undocumented scientifically, but ethnolinguistic work summarized here indicates sources near Black Rapids Glacier (*Dałuuniideek*: ice pieces moved upward) and the Goodpaster River headwaters (*Tseyh Tl'iig Tl'aa*: shiny ochre headwaters) northeast of Healy Lake (ANLC0892a 1983; ANLC3676a 1980; Kari 2015; Mishler 1986). Stibnite, or *ts'eyuun k'a'tthee'* originated from a "mountain with lead, white rock, at head of Goodpaster; [*Labetsne*] man turned to rock up Goodpaster lead underneath, white marble on top, for rings." This material was described as being rolled into cylinders or bars and taken to trading posts or fairs. Abraham Luke described this source as high on Mt. Harper, accessible only by a pole ladder (Mishler 1986, 41). A gold prospector who spent several years in the 1930s on Tibbs Creek in the upper Goodpaster, Carl Tweiten (1990, 37), recalled that much of the gold-bearing quartz in feeder streams of the Tibbs Creek headwaters bore high amounts of stibnite. Stibnite is the principal ore of antimony, which colored the material blue; one creek in the headwaters carries the official name Antimony Creek. Tweiten (1990, 39–40) also observed molybdenum ore deposits on a divide between the South Fork Goodpaster (*Ddheł Xaxuudqą Na'*: cavity extends through mountain stream) and Healy River (*Ts'aadleey Ndiig*: least cisco whitefish stream). He discusses the extensive presence of lead in several hard rock deposits inside several mining tunnels on the creek, two of which were named the Blue Lead and Gray Lead Claims. Probably, both lead ore (galena) and the two other lead-like minerals are strong candidates for *ts'eyuun k'a'tthee'*. All three can be nearly visually indistinguishable from each other. The north side of Mt. Harper is traditionally called *Tseyh Tl'iige* "shiny ochre." It is a likely source of the shiny silver-colored ochre that is found throughout the Holocene levels at Swan Point. Geologist Theodore Chapin also described a molybdenite-bearing quartz vein high on Mt. Harper's south flank, then called Rainy Mountain, which, according to Tweiten, was a calque of the local Native place name *Tuu K'eets'en*: one on the water side. It was observed near the top of a pass to the South Fork Goodpaster River (Chapin 1919, 329).

Several local place names expound on the second root for stone. Quartz Lake and its adjoining mountain are termed *tteech'el*: "broken rock," perhaps a descriptor of the local fractured quartz observed in the bedrock. The southeastern toe of Bluff Cabin Ridge at the Goodpaster River's mouth and its associated creek are termed *tthee t'ox*: "rock nest," describing a mica-schist rock outcrop that was utilized for producing hide scrapers. McRoy Creek, east of Harding Lake, also carries the same name; mica-schist is widespread throughout the region as a bedrock material. A few miles upstream on the Tanana from Bluff Cabin Ridge is Clearwater Lake, which bears a name similar to Quartz Lake; *Ttheech'el Menn'*: torn/broken lake, where Luke recalled an extensively utilized stone quarry source once was.

The basalt found in the Shaw Creek assemblages may have originated from the Wrangell Mountains forming at the contact of lava and glacial ice. It is also found regionally in secondary deposits within glacio-fluvial gravels formed in tributaries of the Copper River (*Atna'*: beyond stream) (Richter et al. 2006; Sicard et al. 2017). The remaining material types from Swan Point and Pickupsticks likely represent locally available sources (Little 2013, 56–62; Potter 2005, 394–396). Otherwise, the Middle Tanana territory is apparently devoid of further specific lithic quarry indicators; other place names that describe stone seem to refer instead to the appearance of landforms, as in the case of the ridge at the Salcha River mouth: *Ttheech'uudegeet Ddhele'*: rock that is poked-mountain.

CONCLUSION

In the archaeological record, lithic technology had become extensively minimized during the Athabascan tradition of the past millennium. The reduced influence of stone as a multi-use essential material source appears at face value to be reflected in the lack of many formal lithic terminologies in Middle Tanana. It may be a factor of the dictionary itself; no thorough search through the other five Lexware root-morpheme dictionaries has yet been completed to see if this trend continues. If the neighboring languages are enriched with more specific lithic terminology, they could be reconstructed for Middle Tanana. If not, it lends credence to the proposal that the linguistic trend demonstrated here follows techno-cultural trends seen in the archaeological record that emphasized osseous materials over lithics throughout the past millennium and reflects the actual language as it was spoken in the nineteenth century. The dictionary is detailed in terms of non-lithic implement technology; therefore, the ancestral form spoken by the earlier Northern Archaic people likely was enriched with lithic terminology, as their toolkit emphasized it more. By the end of the nineteenth century, most technological forms that were entirely created from organic materials had incorporated lithic/metallic portions in earlier periods.

The lack of named lithic procurement areas in Middle Tanana territorial toponyms may be a factor of geology, and might be a cultural factor. Some sites elicited as quarry areas are not given proper names. Lithic procurement may also be a factor of nineteenth-century gendered landscape knowledge.

As stated earlier, a large number of place names in Middle Tanana were elicited by women (Bessie Barnabas, Eva Moffit). Young adult women were expected to interact with the landscape in a fundamentally different way than men due to the strict rule of sexual divisions of labor. While this was often not the case in real-life situations, a review of the Middle Tanana place names corpus shows that the reconstructed place names cluster more strongly with primary riverine and lacustrine environments rather than upland use areas. The pattern contrasts with that of the downriver and upriver languages. The surrounding languages have far more upland place names elicited. It is possible, then, that the adult male experience of the Middle Tanana lithic landscape is muted in the reconstruction efforts. The principal male informant, Abraham Luke, was primarily familiar with the area between Big Delta and Dot Lake, much of it within the neighboring Tanacross language area.

This exploration of lithic terminology and place names has provided several insights into primary procurement locations and cultural meanings of obsidian, ochre, copper, mica-schist, quartz, and their uses for the proto-historic population. However, it has not provided much (if any) insight into two types, rhyolite and chert, which make up 87 percent of the assemblage at Pickupsticks, and 82 percent of Swan Point CZ1a. It may be a function of their disuse: the protohistoric component at Swan Point does not use these materials. It is possible that the terminology has not yet been reconstructed, or their original names were only generalized descriptors (e.g., *red stone* or *yellow stone*, etc.). Since colors seem to be a predictor for at least some lithic differentiation, a Middle Tanana color terminology key is included in table 8.1.

Table 8.1.   Middle Tanana color terminology, with emphasis on light to dark rather than principal hues.

Middle Tanana Root	Color
kon'	Clear
tth'uų	Transparent
ts'eł	Bright/White
k'utl; giy	White
baa, bee; giyh	Gray/Off-White
beets	Tan
dząą	Murky
tthox, tthuuk	Yellow/Brown
tsiik, tsiyh	Yellow/Orange
k'il	Red/Pink
t'eł	Dark Red, Blood Red
deldiat (UT)	Blue/Green
tl'its	Blue/Black
zen	Dark/Black
t'uuts; tl'ets, tl'its	Black

A wide variety of lithic types and qualities were utilized in all the occupation levels at Swan Point and Pickupsticks. These types reflect locally available items within the central Tanana, others throughout the central Alaska Range, and farther types traveling from the Koyukuk River, Copper River, and southern Yukon territory areas. Stone terminology themes appear to have reflected gendered preference, natural appearance analogs, color, intended function, and continued utility. The terminological themes embedded in hand tool technology seems to follow the same trend. It is likely that in earlier periods when stone played a more prominent role in the necessary technology, the terms were likely much wider than is known today. This process of simplification and terminology loss is probably a function of the long trend in the emphasis on organic-based technology, as well as the reconstructed lexicographical nature of the language. Future work should analyze neighboring languages for similar trends and patterns. It may be that those language territories that had primary access to raw material sources than the Middle Tanana may be more enriched in this terminology.

Chapter Nine

Identifying Reciprocity and Meaning in the Material-Cultural Record

How does a people define itself as different from others? By common language, like the anthropologists have done in this region? By matrilineal family descent, like the Tanana Natives? By shared material culture, as the archaeologists understand it? By genetic lineages defined by the human migration specialists? By shared mythology? By place of birth? Each of these aspects contributed to the modern identity of Natives, being the reason they are all explored. Each of these topics reflect the unique developmental paths of specific cultural aspects considered crucial to the ongoing ethnogenesis of the Middle Tanana people. This book began by framing the current identities that the descendants of the Middle Tanana people utilize today and how that has been influenced by historical factors further framed during the twentieth and twenty-first centuries by Euro-American traditions of law, kinship, and land tenure. It explored the ethnographic works produced between the Depression Era and today and reconstructed the culture as it may have been in the nineteenth century, and focused on those aspects that may have influenced the archaeological record.

The regional oral traditions indicate that at an unspecified point in the precolonial past, demographic pressure originating from the Copper River basin resulted in novel forms of regional conflict in the Middle and Upper Tanana Valleys. The resolution of these tensions and conflicts are traditionally said to have been solved by the formerly endogamous bands choosing to broaden, formalize, and intensify their preexisting kinship networks, producing a shift toward exogamous marriages and binding non-related families together through economic partnerships in villages, and broadening concepts of land tenure to ease use by non-related families. The process facilitated demographic growth, seasonal sedentism, and increased territoriality. These shifting cultural ideals are reflected in seasonal household forms, as they moved from being single-family structures such as observed at Swan Point to multi-family houses such as observed at Pickupsticks, reflecting the new, inter-family partnership networks.

Residences reflect the family structure that is intended to be housed within, and symbolically represent the basic familial, social shelter (McFadyen Clark 1996). As such, they will trend toward similarity within a culture, as regional members seek to share identity concepts of social structure and comfort (Coupland 2013). Therefore, archaeologically preserved houses are much more likely to reflect their periods' common household styles, rather than being anomalies. The residential feature at Pickupsticks is identical in size, form, and construction to those historically described at the nearby Goodpaster River village. The main difference is that they were separated in time by almost 700–800 years. This temporal pattern is remarkable, suggesting that a stable aspect of one of the most fundamental units of culture, the family and household, remained constant throughout this period. The Pickupsticks house is similar in form to the homes designed to hold two non-related families in economic partnership and their respective surviving elders. They are sometimes referred to as a "four-family" house due to the inclusion of grandparents as residents. This line of evidence suggests a stable kinship and linguistic-cultural system was in place in this region throughout the Athabascan tradition of the past millennium. This proposition has been generally accepted since John Cook proposed it in 1969 from work at Healy Lake.

The residential feature at Swan Point does not readily reflect a structured, dual-family household. While it is large enough to have perhaps housed two small families, it is more likely that this feature represents a shelter for a single natal family, over at least two separate seasons. Being about 1,900 years old, the residence is dated to about a thousand years earlier than the Pickupsticks structure. If it also represented the average household of the Middle Tanana (1,810–2,115 cal BP during that period, it suggests that during the millennia separating the two, the concept of the household sustained a fundamental cultural change, moving from single family dwellings to dual family dwellings. If the spatial patterning of artifacts in Swan Point CZ1b, dating several millennia earlier, indeed are the remains of tent-like features, it is a further line of evidence of increasing technological investment through time toward more permanent and substantial residence types and the seasonal variation between them.

Being family homes, the residence features are interpreted here to be symbolic representations of the regional Dene society at different periods, seasons, and social episodes. By focusing group agency toward a residential site and actively constructing the family home environment, power was shifted from an external source to an internal one. Thus, each home would have been built as a comforting microcosm; a reminder of the communal interaction of the family with the universe. Here, the role of the extended family and their consumption patterns and renewal rites of resources took on an intensified role. The transition from single-family structures to multi-family structures between 2,000 and 1,000 years ago is observed as a local manifestation of increasing social complexity within the Middle Tanana region. It reflects a widespread socioeconomic pattern that was also especially visible in Northwest Coast societies of the same period (Angelbeck 2016; Angelbeck and Grier 2012; Grier 2003).

These residential features represent a significant investment of time and resources. The Technological Investment Model suggests that the payoff for increased energetic investment in structures should indicate an amplified sense of shelter and safety and result in longer periods of inhabitance before seasonal movements. These house features could theoretically be repetitively returned to on a seasonal basis and reused. This pattern facilitated a logistical mobility system that funneled resources toward repeated-use seasonal villages, where people capitalized on foraging resources within their watershed tenured territory enhanced using sophisticated kinship strategies. It was important that kin would be spread out in different settlements; this eased regional social tensions, and eased the utilization of extra-regional resources. Families could thus more safely move about independently in small groups in areas of relatively increased population density, and predictably find their relatives on the landscape at proposed times, no small feat in the dense subarctic boreal forest.

Investment into the arenas of extra-regional kinship maintenance and non-related family partnership households may also be a proxy for investment into potlatching and wealth aggrandizement via reciprocal gift exchange. This idea was predicted earlier to be represented in the archaeological record as the need for storage features and large communal buildings. As mobility decreases and seasonal sedentism rises, more time can be invested in technology and material culture that does not need to be transportable. The dual-family partnership system is an important proxy for potlatch behaviors, including those extending beyond the actual ritual event, such as interpersonal relationships and relationships with the natural and spiritual world. Pit features throughout the regional middle and later Holocene record suggest food storage and preservation behaviors, an important but not exclusive indicator of potlatch planning (Boraas 2007).

Wood remains at both residential features show evidence of scorching. There are several potential reasons for this: accidental household burning, arson associated with conflict, natural burning associated with forest fires, accidental incineration associated with cultural landscape burning, or purposeful burning and purification of a deceased person's house, body, and personal belongings.

The floors of both residential features are the best preserved. The Swan Point house exhibits a thick (~10 cm) anthropogenic sediment deposit that preserves the remains of small lithic debitage and crushed, calcined bones. The floor of Pickupsticks appears to have not been formed of sediment, but the actual soft, degrading regolith with a layer of birchbark on top. The presence of a sediment floor deposit over the disturbed regolith at Swan Point and the lack of any such deposit over the disturbed regolith at Pickupsticks potentially indicates relative occupational period length. The Swan Point occupation would then be considered much longer than at Pickupsticks. There is little evidence to provide a robust occupation duration of either household feature. A general lack of diversity in lithic types and forms at the Swan Point feature suggests a limited occupation; as time increases, a wider variety of lithic types and forms should have an increased opportunity to be lost in the vicinity. However, the presence of a hearth at the main locus exhibits an identical probability spread of radiocarbon dates as at the residential feature, suggests the possibility that many activities occurred there where most lithic debitage would have been deposited away from the house feature. There, an extensive variety of material types were documented (Smith 2020). The two internal hearths, buried vertically one above the other within the residence floor, exhibit identical ages, suggesting at least two separate occupations occurred, perhaps indicative of two separate cold seasons.

For the Pickupsticks residence, a greater variety in discarded lithic types and forms is present; however, the faunal remains indicate the possibility that some of the assemblage, moose remains, is a palimpsest, including a disturbed earlier occupation. The problematic moose remains were only intrusive into the southern edge of the feature, where processes related to the collapse of the original structure wall may have introduced the artifact into the house. Additionally, the assemblage pattern at the Swan Point structure indicates that these palimpsest disturbance patterns will generally only be evident outside residential features and not within them. While in the field, the regolith at both sites was observed to be quite soft and easily damaged. Due to the strong evidence that the precolonial use of the Pickupsticks residence did not wear down these cuts into the bedrock, two hypotheses emerge: the feature was used only for a minimal time, reducing the chance for wear on the floor, or construction methods were used that protected the regolith from wear.

No data was recovered that could support or refute the second hypothesis; so, it can only be noted as an untestable possibility. The first hypothesis is supported because no firm evidence of an internal hearth was observed, a necessary addition for long-term use. The presence of birchbark as used for flooring material also would be dangerous in the presence of a fire. Personal extensive experience with birchbark as kindling has shown that it is a commonly used item that can quickly and easily be lit. It burns at relatively higher temperatures for a prolonged period, thus quickly igniting larger diameter wood than other kindling items by volume. If the Pickupsticks house was not used as a long-term residence, the high level of effort and construction quality observable in it suggests that it may have been built only to display those qualities, as ethnographically documented potlatch houses were known to be, being an integral part of the gifting ceremony. Lithics were not observed to be produced and discarded ubiquitously throughout the house but are only associated with the traditional women's activity area, and even then, only on one side of the house, with artifact refits and discard piles being otherwise associated with expected seating patterns, supporting the idea that one family was primarily producing items while the other was consuming. Faunal discards are directed toward the center of the house and two outdoor "middens" near the front and back of the house. The lithic pattern of one-sided production and lack of homogenizing horizontal spread of discards throughout the feature, with faunal discards ubiquitously collecting toward the front-center, is strongly indicative of short-term use. It is revealing that only one side of a dual-occupancy designed house appeared to be producing lithic items but discarded tools are found throughout both sides, reflective of the pattern that is expected to be produced in a ceremonial potlatch situation.

The Pickupsticks house represents the built habitus, symbolizing an individual or individuals who were actively strategically maneuvering widely held fundamental Dene cultural constructs of obligating one's unrelated rivals to themselves through nonviolent means (Bourdieu 1977; Mauss [1925] 2016; Thornton 2008, 14). These behaviors are evident through the house structure that symbolizes the traditional dichotomous relatedness of the Tanana people (Bourdieu 1973) and production displays that included constructing an elaborate potlatch house the only intended use of which was to host non-related guests for a specific event. Its symbolic consumption was completed through either a final ceremonial burning, abandonment episode, or combination of the two (Mauss [1925] 2016, 115–117). It is important to remember that the Middle Tanana's kinship terminology appears to be a Proto-Dene innovation, far more ancient than the more recent precolonial inter-familial household partnership innovation. Therefore, the dual-family household form is interpreted to be an "improvement" built upon the older traditional kinship structure.

The presence of fur-bearing animal remains at Pickupsticks suggests an autumn occupation, also indicated by the fact that excavations into the sediment would have needed to occur during the warmer months when the ground was sufficiently thawed: likely June–September. It was *'engii* for children to come into contact with these creatures, indicating that the presence of younger members was absent from the building or perhaps even the site during occupation. It is the presence of the otter bones within the structure is perhaps the most intriguing; by displaying the otherwise untouchable remains, an individual was declaring their great power as a sleep doctor, displaying a magical prowess that could safely manipulate the rules of *'engii.* Handling these objects would otherwise destroy the luck, power, prestige, and intelligence of the average individual (McKennan 1959; Vitt 1971, 125). Thus, this site's purpose only becomes apparent within its social environment by understanding its cosmological and economic impacts on living Northern Dene individuals (Kristiansen 2004, 2013). Given the multiple lines of evidence supporting the presence of symbolic agency and ritualized roles, the possibility that the moose tibia fragment, which predates the building's occupation, may represent a precolonially curated item should not be discounted pending further excavation and analysis of the outdoor activity areas.

While all things held spiritual meaning and symbolism to the Middle Tanana Dene, several powerful cultural display elements of this site may be present. One is the house's placement; it was located on a hill's apex, with a wide viewshed to the southwest when trees are not present. Presumably, its location there would be more challenging to conceal. Thus, its position may have been an overt signal for its location, perhaps aided with smoke. The apparent deliberate placement of small quartz cobbles and pebbles throughout the structure's walls in the internal sod insulation may have held undefined symbolic significance. Other stones were known to possess significant spiritual power; see, for example, the Koyukon entry for obsidian/ amethystine quartz:

"baats'e, -k'ebaats'e' (n.; dene) CLU, *maats'e* L, *baasts'e* "obsidian, stone amulet, "amethyst, amethystine quartz"—JJ "The amulet is a translucent stone, which the common people cannot distinguish from an ordinary pebble, the shamans only being aware of its preternatural qualities. It has two eyes, generally not visible to common mortals. The shamans wear it hanging on a string passed around the neck, generally in a moose-skin pouch. The one used by Moglloye Tleegllesteek To' (died 1901) was about 7" long and 2 ½" thick, the sides tapering to a thin edge, and one end to a blunt point, which gave it a vague resemblance to a duck's bill. It was probably buried with him, or perhaps inherited by his wife." (b-7)—JJ "The *maats'e* constitutes the one who possesses it, under the special protection and guardianship of the spirits, and common people are generally afraid of having anything to do with it." (Jetté and Jones 2000, 85)

At Swan Point, reciprocity behaviors are also reflected in gendered and age-graded working roles where the act of rendering labor and creativity into objects that were given to others or used by the group can be observed. Earlier, I presented the cultural expectations of the archaeological expressions for gendered and age-graded divisions of labor. The presence of hide-working activity areas is indicated by the scraper discards. Skin-working is significantly associated with (but not limited to) the ethnographically documented identities of adult, married Dene women's roles. It is expected that, if younger, stronger women were present in the camp, elder women likely could focus their crafting expertise on skilled adornment, as hide preparation was incredibly taxing. Informants discussing the technology types present at the Ringling site at Gulkana (*C'uul C'ena'*) recalled that scraping hides with boulder spalls was a task often given to children (Hanson 2008, 122–123), and scraping tools were curated matrilineally (2008, 123).

Language is one key aspect of cultural identity, and chapter 4 explored how it both guided and made use of Middle Tanana Dene land-use economics. It also explored what is known about the history and dispersal of the ancestral language family into interior Alaska, the historical processes of its replacement on the landscape by Indo-European languages, and the aspects that have survived. The most robust theoretical methods point to the formation of Proto-Dene in Northern British Columbia and Southern Yukon, potentially including the Tanana River's headwaters. This formation developed after the earlier seriation from Eyak, Łingít, and Yeniseian. In this work, the development of Proto-Dene is modeled to be an early Holocene phenomenon, and the seriations from that proto-language into the recognizable Dene languages of the nineteenth century are considered to be the result of multi-factorial processes of the past 8,000 years during the middle and late Holocene, or the Northern Archaic and Athabascan archaeological traditions.

A sense of great antiquity is embedded within the structure of the place names and the languages themselves. When modeled with potential archaeological proxies, one can turn back the clock and reconstruct a precolonial narrative by correlating the linguistic and archaeological records. That exercise produced modeled *terminus ante quem* scenarios, being the latest possible date for linguistic spread through material correlates throughout the state. This relative model suggested that the presence of Proto-Dene in the Middle and Upper Tanana is at least as old as the early Holocene, likely being embedded there prior to 7,000 years ago, and subsequent seriations are associated with the later Northern Archaic and Athabascan traditions. This type of modeling cannot definitively point to the oldest appearance of the language. Still, it indicates that we should focus efforts on the unique environmental stressors of the extreme warming and extinction patterns during the millennia of ~11,000–7,000 years ago to illuminate questions of ethnolinguistic genesis.

Our limited knowledge of ancestral genetic flow and drift suggests that prior to the influx of old-world genetic haplotypes associated with Euro-American expansion of the past five centuries, an earlier pattern of unique genetic signals indicates an episode of gene flow originating from western Alaska and Northeast Asia occurring during the Middle Holocene. The signal is interpreted here to be that of a coastal-oriented population being absorbed by the preexisting ancestral Dene. Prior to this event, the Early Holocene genetic picture is one of a unique transitional population equally similar to later East Asian and Northern North American populations, possibly suggesting a pattern of genetic drift in the process of producing the dominant haplotypes we observe today. Relatively little is known about the population genetic legacy of period.

The archaeological reconstructions of chapter 7 highlight a long period throughout the Middle Holocene of material cultural stability, but one indicating initial high mobility and later resource intensification. Extensive work by Potter (2016) suggests that this is signaled by an increase in site structure variation from the earlier Denali complex components and a formal toolkit marked by decreased variation. It also indicates that more external cultural influences on interior Alaskan traditions came from the east and southeast from North America rather than to the west in Northeast Asia. It also strongly suggests ongoing technological influences from the earliest periods of settlement in Alaska.

These reconstructions serve to illustrate the dynamic, independent, and multidirectional paths that genes, language, and technological culture take to form the cultural identity of any one period. This book supports the idea that the later and middle Holocene Interior Norton tradition and Paleo-Eskimo lineage populations on the middle Yukon River were absorbed by the preexisting Northern Archaic and Athabascan tradition Northern Dene people and language through the ancient expansive Dene kinship networks. This extra-regional and extensive familial kinship system may have outcompeted any other sociopolitical system based on smaller natal family concepts if initial demographic pressure is held more or less equal. The Dene concepts of kinship support a system of competition and reciprocity designed to reduce inter-clan violence and enhance landscape sharing and interpersonal movement with non-relatives (Mauss [1925] 2016, 115–117). The long-term success of Proto-Dene as a linguistic system may have been intimately tied to their traditional kinship networks, which appear to have deep antiquity (Ives et al. 2010). There exists a theme that the clan organization may have been an adaptive nonviolent stress response to growing populations and small-scale migrations. It should be recognized as an integral success strategy originating during periods of increased demographic stress, decreased mobility, and intensification of local resources.

If the Interior Norton or earlier Paleo-Eskimos did not contribute language or kinship systems to the Dene but contributed an extensive genetic legacy, what other cultural borrowings may have occurred? Increased social cooperation indicates technological investment can be enhanced by an increased variety of actors, ideas, and a larger variety of trade items. Holmes (1986) explored the material cultural borrowings between the Interior Norton and Northern Archaic traditions surrounding Lake Minchumina, where the local Northern Archaic people made long term extensive use of borrowed material culture from the Interior Norton people. Those long-lasting technological borrowings appear to have become gradually minimized in the later Athabascan tradition there. The remaining cultural aspects may be apparent in residential use and landscape mobility patterns. The interior adaptations of the Paleo-Eskimo people are still extensively understudied. Their manifestations as the Interior Norton of western Alaska and Riverine Kachemak traditions of south-central Alaska suggest cultures that were more heavily focused on riverine and lacustrine resources than perhaps the contemporary Northern Archaic tradition (who also focused on them but to a lesser extent; Potter 2008b).

The Paleo-Eskimos may have positively influenced the trend toward using cold-season permanent residences (adopted in interior Alaska between 2,000 and 500 years ago). Still, the Athabascan housing styles and architecture are genuinely Dene, reflecting concepts of kinship and cultural ties heavily influenced by the ancient Lingít and Eyak cultural patterns on the southern coasts. The land use trends toward decreased mobility and an increased focus on freshwater resources during this time may be a subtle influence of the Interior Norton, as food preference is often heavily culturally informed (Mintz and Du Bois 2002). This idea should not be considered a unidirectional influence from the Paleo-Eskimos as these trends are also seen throughout the North American Pacific Northwest. Still, if these cultural developments were trending toward this type of land use, it may have facilitated a desire of the Alaskan Dene to incorporate both the Interior Norton and Paleo-Eskimo people into their extended kinship networks nonviolently. This new cultural influence may have brought with it novel ideas of land tenure and resource use, changes that also slowly occur during this time. These may have also been the result of adaptation requirements of the Interior ecosystem, as the middle and late Holocene saw the extirpation of bison and wapiti and the growing influence of caribou and salmon throughout the interior.

The final cultural shifts for the Middle Tanana that occurred prior to the Historic period are attested to in the local mythology. These stories documented how the endogamous bands of the Copper River and Middle and

Upper Tanana areas reorganized their landscape use to incorporate additional people peacefully. To do this, they transformed from endogamous, highly mobile territorial bands to exogamous, seasonally sedentary villages where bands joined in exogamous marriages and life-long economic partnerships. During this time, mobility became reduced, but social mechanisms for utilizing or moving into extraterritorial locales became highly developed. The kinship terminology appears to be far more ancient than this shift, indicating that existing mechanisms of traditional relationships were reimagined to facilitate this process.

This period is recognizable with the adoption of cold-season residences, which indicate a strong diffusion pattern from the Copper River area to the Middle Tanana. From the dates at Swan Point and Pickupsticks, we can suggest that the period where village life and exogamous marriage and hunting partnerships developed was the critical period between both eruptions of Mt. Churchill, roughly between 1,800 and 1,000 cal BP.

It has long been proposed that the two eruptions of Mt. Churchill had a fundamental and long-lasting effect on Dene settlement patterns and migrations. While this appears to be true in the case of the latter eruption in the southern Yukon region, in Alaska, the signal is muted, if it exists at all, and is mainly associated with the earlier eruption. The Pickupsticks house feature dates to just after Mt. Churchill's second, later eruption, and the Swan Point house dates to just prior to the first, earlier eruption. These crucial shifts in household type, then, suggest that the transformation in expanded kinship cooperation, as signaled by the change in housing types, appear to have occurred in the interim between the two eruptions, perhaps signaling a different social response to the latter eruption's ecological stressors.

Is there a correlation between residential structure styles and volcanic events? Regarding the second, more massive eruption (1,170–1,095 cal BP [Davies et al. 2016]), William Workman's original observation (1979) that material cultural change is observed in the southern Yukon records remains undisputed. Additionally, the shift from atlatl to bow-and-arrow technology also correlates strongly with the second eruption's timing. However, recent work suggests that this eruption had only minimal observable effects on Alaska population size and land-use strategies, despite the evidence of shifting technological and raw material use during this time (Lynch et al. 2018; Mullen 2012; Doering et al. 2020). Despite over forty years of work since David Derry and William Workman proposed the Athabascan Migration hypothesis into Alaska to account for these material cultural changes, no smoking guns, so to speak, have emerged in the Alaskan record.

Regarding the earlier, smaller eruption of Mt Churchill (1,560–1,689 cal BP [Reuther et al. 2019]), a stronger though not robustly demonstrated regional pattern of settlement disruption appears observable in the Upper Tanana (Lynch et al. 2018; Mullen 2012; Doering et al. 2020). The earlier, smaller eruption may have had a stronger effect on eastern interior Alaskan populations than the later, more massive eruption whose effects were felt further to the east. It may have provided a catalyst explaining the tradition of population movements north from the Copper River into the upper and Middle Tanana basin. However, what may be a likelier case is that there is no solid causal connection between the volcanic events and the cultural changes that surround them temporally. The eruptions may have simply occurred at opportune times, being useful to us today as chronological constructs for both scientific and traditional history reconstructions. Instead, what is very readily observable in the Tanana Valley archaeological record is a pattern of gradual but sustained cultural change, novel social reorganization of non-kin, and an increasing emphasis of clan exogamy over the past two millennia, within a culture that has deep *in situ* cultural ties to the early Holocene appears to be the best interpretation of Alaskan's interior record.

In the beginning of the book, I noted how households are the microcosm of a cultures' cosmology. Within it can also be seen a reflection of the typical social power structures, economic practices, familial interactions, and learning and caregiving behaviors. At Swan Point, household development is documented as at least one single family structure, with perhaps evidence of two earlier ephemeral tents. These represent the ancient singularity of the natal family. By 1,000 years ago, construction at the Pickupsticks site produced a building reflecting new ideas of Dene social organization, where clans of opposing moieties were brought together in lifelong partnership under a single roof. This practice standardized fictive kinship relationships between families who would normally be in competition or even conflict, instead focusing rivalries toward elaborate ritual gift giving ceremonies, reflected in the potlatch house at Pickupsticks. This relationship of positive reciprocity was reflected in every interaction one had with the natural, cultural, and spiritual realms. As evidenced by the dates at the two sites, these cultural ideals produced a novel socio-eco stability state that lasted over a thousand years, with ancient cultural-linguistic roots stretching back into the early Holocene.

The title of this book was specifically chosen to recall Marcel Mauss's ([1925] 2016) and Clifford Geertz's (1973) seminal works and also draw attention to how deeply the concept of reciprocal exchange permeated the Alaska Dene's daily experience with the world. After demonstrating the antiquity of this practiced behavior, we should consider that these *'engii*-structured behaviors, affected all regional Holocene cultural components in the Tanana.

The Shaw Creek basin has provided unprecedented archaeological and ecological data spanning over 14,000 years. The people of the Middle and Upper Tanana have provided and extraordinary ethnological body of knowledge. That data has enabled an unparalleled understanding of the human story, from the peopling of the Americas to the unique social complexity of the nineteenth century. For over ninety years, these datasets have been both gifted and taken by anthropologists in primary and secondary form, and those persons, including myself, have built careers and extensive prestige upon it. Few of us have yet to return that gift in equal or greater measure; we must remember that we owe an insurmountable debt to the present people, ancestors, and natural entities who provided us with this, and return that debt in abundance, bringing balance to our interpersonal, intercultural, and internatural relationships with the world.

Afterword

Evelynn Combs

I have been asked to write this afterword for Dr. Smith's book on behalf of the Healy Lake Tribal Council. We represent the present culture bearers of the ancestors discussed here, and many of our members represent the direct descendants of those communities described in it.

Anthropology has excellent potential to be a powerful tool for bringing disparate peoples and cultures together. Unfortunately, due to its present structure being created out of a long legacy of systematic racism and colonial-centric ideologies, well-intentioned researchers are often unable to break free of that legacy completely. Whether intentional or not, these systems and ideologies present real-life obstacles that we, indigenous people, have to constantly experience, and in which non-indigenous people only participate. However, many of us have been intimately aware of its methods and results for several generations, working closely with anthropologists who show strong qualities akin to our cultural values. We are the witnesses that anthropologists have also long participated in perpetuating colonist trends and behaviors; going so far as to defend and dismiss looting, graverobbing, and other dehumanizing events that we, the first people of this continent, have been subjected to for centuries.

We consider the work done to produce this book as being a historical landmark in its efforts to represent anthropology and the cultures it examines holistically. For many of our people, this is the first time an outsider has humanized our history. This book is the first time that many of us feel that our prehistory and connection to the land have been acknowledged and respected for what it is, instead of dismissed as local mythos or a romanticism of days long past.

Anthropology requires both documentation and interpretation, but interpretation without understanding is simply guesswork. Beginning with the scholars who accompanied the Spanish Conquistadors to our continent five centuries ago, foreign researchers have been comfortable creating and filling in the perceived gaps of our prehistoric and modern indigenous history, with little regard to what was told or experienced by us. How could the indigenous people already have answers to questions Euro-American academics have only thought of in the last fifty years? Having been removed from our ancestral lands, we've lost generations of people. The curation of our oral traditions has been disrupted, and our ability to live our traditional ways has been severely reduced. These factors have provided scholars with an opportunistic tool for dismissing our knowledge, experience, and interpretation of our past and present where they see fit. It's customary for anthropologists to consult with indigenous communities about work regarding their ancestral lands. It has also been customary for those non-indigenous intellectuals to reinterpret, dismiss, or completely disregard our record of history where it conflicts with the western understanding of events.

The research process that produced this book was refreshing and educational. As a descendant of the cultural groups discussed in this work, it was relieving to read a scholarly work devoid of oversimplified conclusions regarding current research paradigms concerning the perceived discrepancies of the origins of our language, culture, genetics, and technology, and placed our own perspectives about those subjects on equal theoretical footing. If there were incongruences, the research shifted to address these discrepancies. As an indigenous person, this is a considerable change in how our culture is recorded and represented. The research process was reflexive and involved many discussions of data and cross-cultural interpretations of it.

None of our elders were told they were wrong, or that somehow through our oral traditions, something was mixed up and exaggerated, or that it was easy for us to make things up about our past because being so long removed from it, we could only speak about it mythologically. If the author didn't understand something, he listened, read more of the extensive unpublished data collected and archived on our people, and returned later to discuss an altered perspective. We feel we were listened to for the first time in our history.

This book represents what anthropology strives to be. It does not idealize our history or intentionally interpret cultural material from purely a materialistic, Western-centric perspective. Instead, it speaks to the benefit of embracing perspectives that seem fundamentally different. The reflexive sections of the text are dedicated to describing the process of thought and perception breakdown, which is a complex but necessary process for good anthropology to be done. It shows how thoughts become interpretations and allows us the opportunity to understand that process without being forced to accept the conclusions at face value. This dedication to anthropological study does what many of our elders have long taught the children of my tribe: "You are mixed race, and you must learn to balance both worlds and take strength from them."

Lastly, I want to thank my good friend Gerad. The level of scholarly work gone into this text has earned him much recognition in our field, and he has humbly used it to give my people a platform to speak on our own behalf; this is a dignity and respect that most researchers would overlook. Anthropology done right has the potential to heal communities and reconnect living people to their cultural identities. It is a tragedy that this particular school of study has earned such a dark reputation among the indigenous nations, but I believe the future of anthropology is in good hands. In many ways, this work should, and has, broken generations of cyclical racism and abuse, and I am proud to have participated through it.

Evelynn Combs
Healy Lake Tribal Council

References

Abbott, Mark B., Bruce P. Finney, Mary E. Edwards, and Kerry R. Kelts. 2000. "Lake-Level Reconstructions and Paleohydrology of Birch Lake, Central Alaska, Based on Seismic Reflection Profiles and Core Transects." *Quaternary Research* 53: 154–166.

Ackerman, Robert E. 2001. "Late Tundra Tradition." In *Encyclopedia of Prehistory, vol. 2, Arctic and Subarctic,* edited by Peter N. Peregrine and Melvin Ember, 111–115. New York: Kluwer Academic/Plenum Publishers.

Ackerman, Robert E. 2004. "The Northern Archaic Tradition in Southwestern Alaska." *Arctic Anthropology* 41(2): 153–162.

Adams, Robert M. 2001. "Complexity in Archaic States." *Journal of Anthropological Archaeology* 20: 345–360. DOI:10.1006/jaar.2000.0377.

Afable, Patricia O., and Madison S. Beeler. 1996. "Place-Names." In *Handbook of North American Indians, vol. 17: Languages,* edited by Ives Goddard, pp. 185–199. Washington, D.C.: Smithsonian Institution.

Ager, Thomas A. 1990. "History of Late Pleistocene and Holocene Vegetation in the Copper River Basin." In *Late Cenozoic History of the Interior Basins of Alaska and the Yukon,* edited by L. David Carter, Thomas D. Hamilton, and John P. Galloway, 1026: 89–92. Washington, D.C.: US Geological Survey Circular.

Alaska Department of Fish and Game (ADF&G). 2020. "Nelchina Caribou Update." Retrieved from https://www.adfg.alaska.gov/static/home/library/pdfs/wildlife/nelchina_bulletin_2020.pdf. May 2021.

Alberti, Benjamin. 2013. "Queer Prehistory: Bodies, Performativity, and Matter." In *A Companion to Gender Prehistory*, edited by Diane Bolger, pp. 86–107. West Sussex, England: John Wiley & Sons.

Alix, Claire, P. Gregory Hare, Thomas D. Andrews, and Glen MacKay. 2012. "A Thousand Years of Lost Hunting Arrows: Wood Analysis of Ice Patch Remains in Northwestern Canada." *Arctic* 65(1): 95–117.

Allen, Henry T. 1985. *An Expedition to the Copper, Tanana, and Koyukuk Rivers in 1885*. Anchorage: Alaska Northwest Publishing Co.

245

Alvarez, L. W., W. Alvarez, F. Asaro, and H. V. Michel. 1980. "Extraterrestrial Cause for the Cretaceous-Tertiary Extinction–Experimental Results and Theoretical Implications." *Science* 208: 1095–1108.

Anderson, Douglas D. 1968. "A Stone Age Campsite at the Gateway to America." *Scientific American* 218(6): 24–33.

Anderson, Douglas D. 1984. "Prehistory of North Alaska." In *Handbook of North American Indians, vol. 5, Arctic,* edited by David Damas, 80–93. Washington, D.C.: Smithsonian Institution Press.

Anderson, Douglas D. 1988. "Onion Portage: The Archaeology of a Stratified Site from Kobuk River, Northwest Alaska." *Anthropological Papers of the University of Alaska* 22(1–2).

Anderson, Douglas D. 2008. "Northern Archaic Tradition Forty Years Later: Comments." *Arctic Anthropology* 45(2): 169–178.

Anderson, Douglas D., Wanni W. Anderson, Ray Bane, Richard K. Nelson, and Nita Sheldon Towarak. [1977] 1998. *Kuuvaŋmiut Subsistence: Traditional Eskimo Life in the Latter Twentieth Century.* Washington, D.C.: US Department of the Interior, National Park Service.

Anderson, Laura D. 1957. *According to Mama.* Third edition, edited by Audry Loftus. Fairbanks: St. Matthews Episcopal Guild.

Anderson, Patricia M., and Linda B. Brubaker. 1994. "Holocene Vegetation and Climate Histories of Alaska." In *Global Climates since the Last Glacial Maximum,* edited by Herbert E. Wright, John E. Kutzbach, Thompson Webb III, William E. Ruddiman, F. Alayne Street-Perrott, and Patrick J. Bartlein, 386–400. Minneapolis: University of Minnesota Press.

Anderson, Patricia M., Mary E. Edwards, and Linda B. Brubaker. 2004. "Results and Paleoclimate Implications of 35 Years of Paleoecological Research in Alaska." In *The Quaternary Period in the United States,* edited by Alan R. Gillispie, Stephen C. Porter, and Brian F. Atwater, 427–440. Amsterdam: Elsevier.

Andrews, Elizabeth. TNS 973 A1973. Saałchaege fieldnotes, 1973–1975. University of Alaska Archives.

Andrews, Elizabeth. 1975. "Salcha: An Athapaskan Band of the Tanana River and its Culture." Unpublished M.A. thesis, Department of Anthropology, University of Alaska Fairbanks.

Andrews, Elizabeth. 1980. *Native and Historic Accounts of some Historic sites in the Tanacross-Ketchumstock Area.* Fairbanks: Cemetery and Historic Sites Committee, Doyon Limited.

Angelbeck, Bill. 2016. "The Balance of Autonomy and Alliance in Anarchic Societies: The Organization of Defenses in the Coast Salish Past." *World Archaeology* 48(1): 51–69.

Angelbeck, Bill, and Colin Grier. 2012. "Anarchism and the Archaeology of Anarchic Societies: Resistance to Centralization in the Coast Salish Region of the Pacific Northwest Coast." *Current Anthropology* 53(5): 547–587.

ANLC0881b. 1983. "ANLC0881b," Alaska Native Language Archive, University of Alaska. Recording of an interview of Abraham Luke conducted by Craig Mishler, July 10, 1983, at an undisclosed location.

ANLC0882a. 1983. "ANLC0882a," Alaska Native Language Archive, University of Alaska. Recording of an interview of Abraham Luke conducted by Craig Mishler, July 10–11, 1983, at Delta Junction, Alaska.

ANLC0883a. 1983. "ANLC0883a," Alaska Native Language Archive, University of Alaska. Recording of an interview of Abraham Luke conducted by Craig Mishler, July 11, 1983, at Delta Junction, Alaska.

ANLC0892a. 1983. "ANLC0892a," Alaska Native Language Archive, University of Alaska. Recording of an interview of Abraham Luke conducted by Craig Mishler, July 7, 1983, at Dot Lake, Alaska.

ANLC0921. 1983. "ANLC0921," Alaska Native Language Archive, University of Alaska. Recording of an interview of Eva Moffit conducted by Craig Mishler, on November 11, 1983, at an undisclosed location.

ANLC0922. 1983. "ANLC0922," Alaska Native Language Archive, University of Alaska. Recording of an interview of Eva Moffit conducted by Craig Mishler, on November 11, 1983, at an undisclosed location.

ANLC0959. 1991. "ANLC0959," Alaska Native Language Archive, University of Alaska. Recording of an interview of Eva Moffit conducted by Siri Tuttle with Jim Kari, August 21, 1991, at an undisclosed location.

ANLC2874b. 1984. "ANLC2874b," Alaska Native Language Archive, University of Alaska. Recording of an interview of Abraham Luke conducted by Craig Mishler, February 8, 1984, at Dot Lake, Alaska.

ANLC3676a. 1980. "ANLC3676a," Alaska Native Language Archive, University of Alaska. Recording of an interview of Abraham Luke conducted by Elizabeth Andrews, October 20, 1980, at Dot Lake, Alaska.

Anthony, David W. 2007. *The Horse, the Wheel, and Language: How Bronze-Age Riders from the Eurasian Steppes Shaped the Modern World.* Oxford and Princeton: Princeton University Press.

Ardener, Edwin. 1989. "Language, Ethnicity, and Population." In *The Voice of Prophecy and Other Essays,* edited by Malcolm Chapman, 65–71. Oxford: Blackwell.

Arndt, Katherine L. 1977. "The Structure of Cache Pits at GUL-077, a Late Prehistoric Archaeological Site Near Gulkana, Alaska." Unpublished M.A. thesis, University of Alaska Fairbanks.

Arnold, Robert D. [1976] 1978. *Alaska Native Land Claims.* Anchorage: Alaska Native Foundation.

Ashmore, Wendy, and Richard R. Wilk. 1988. "House and Household in the Mesoamerican Past: An Introduction." In *Household and Community in the Mesoamerican Past,* edited by Richard R. Wilk and Wendy Ashmore, 1–28. Albuquerque: University of New Mexico Press.

Atalay, Sonya. 2012. *Community-Based Archaeology: Research With, By, and For Indigenous and Local Communities.* Berkeley: University of California Press.

Attla, Catherine. 1990. *K'etetaalkkaanee: The One Who Paddled among the People and Animals.* Fairbanks: Alaska Native Language Center.

Ballard, Warren B., Ludwig N. Carbyn, and Douglas W. Smith. 2003. "Wolf Interactions with Non-prey." In *Wolves: Behavior, Ecology, and Conservation,* edited by L. David Mech and Luigi Boitani, 259–271. Chicago and London: University of Chicago Press.

Barrett, John C., and Ilhong Ko. 2016. "A Phenomenology of Landscape: A Crisis in British Landscape Archaeology?" *Journal of Social Archaeology* 9(3): 275–294.

Barton, C. Michael. 2013. "Stories of the Past or Science of the Future? Archaeology and Computational Social Science." In *Computational Approaches to Archaeological Spaces,* edited by Andrew Bevan and Mark W. Lake, 151–178. Walnut Creek: Left Coast Press.

Baumhoff, Martin A. 1958. "California Athabaskan Groups." *Anthropological Records* 16(5): 157–237.

Becker, Gary S. 1962. "Irrational Behavior and Economic Theory." *Journal of Political Economy* 70(1): 1–13.

Begét, James E., Richard D. Reger, DeAnne Pinney, Tom Gillispie, and Kathy Campbell. 1991. "Correlation of the Holocene Jarvis Creek, Tangle Lakes, Cantwell, and Hayes Tephras in South-Central and Central Alaska." *Quaternary Research* 35(2): 174–189.

Bender, Barbara. 1998. *Stonehenge, Making Space*. Oxford: Berg.

Benton, Michael J. 1990. "Scientific Methodologies in Collision: The History of the Study of the Extinction of the Dinosaurs." *Evolutionary Biology*, 24: 371–400.

Berkes, Fikret, and Dyanna Jolly. 2001. "Adapting to Climate Change: Social-Ecological Resilience in a Canadian Western Arctic Community." *Conservation Ecology* 5(2): 18.

Bettinger, Robert. 2009. *Hunter-Gatherer Foraging: Five Simple Models*. Clinton Corners, New York Eliot: Werner Publications.

Betts, Matthew W. 2013. "Zooarchaeology and the Reconstruction of Ancient Human-Animal Relationships in the Arctic." In *The Oxford Handbook of the Prehistoric Arctic*, edited by T. Max Friesen and Owen K. Mason, 81–108. New York: Oxford University Press.

Betts, Robert. C. 1987. "Archaeological Investigations at Butte Lake, Alaska: A Report to the University of Alaska Museum Geist Fund." MA, Department of Anthropology, University of Alaska Fairbanks, Fairbanks.

Bicchieri, Cristina. 2003. "Rationality and Game Theory." In *The Handbook of Rationality, The Oxford Reference Library of Philosophy*, Oxford: Oxford University Press.

Bigelow, Nancy H. 1997. "Late Quaternary Vegetation and Lake Level Changes in Central Alaska." Unpublished Ph.D. dissertation, Department of Anthropology, University of Alaska Fairbanks.

Bigelow, Nancy H., and Mary E. Edwards. 2001. "A 14,000 yr Paleoenvironmental Record from Windmill Lake, Central Alaska: Late Glacial and Holocene Vegetation in the Alaska Range." *Quaternary Science Reviews* 20(1–3): 203–215.

Bigelow, Nancy H., and W. Roger Powers. 2001. "Climate, Vegetation, and Archaeology 14,000–9,000 cal yr BP in Central Alaska." *Arctic Anthropology* 38(2): 171–195.

Bigelow, Nancy H., Joshua D. Reuther, Kristi L. Wallace, Émilie Saulnier-Talbot, Katherine Mulliken, and Matthew J. Wooller. 2019. "Late-Glacial Paleoecology of the Middle Susitna Valley, Alaska: Environmental Context for Human Dispersal." *Frontiers in Earth Science* 7(43): 1–23.

Binford, Lewis. 1962. "Archaeology as Anthropology." *American Antiquity* 28(29), 217–225.

Binford, Lewis. 1978. *Nunamiut Ethnoarchaeology*. New York: Academic Press.

Binford, Lewis. 1980. "Willow Smoke and Dogs' Tails: Hunter-Gatherer Settlement Systems and Archaeological Site Formation." *American Antiquity*, 45(1): 4–20.

Binford, Lewis. 1981. *Bones: Ancient Men and Modern Myths*. New York: Academic Press.

Binford, Lewis. 1983. *In Pursuit of the Past: Decoding the Archaeological Record*. New York: Thames and Hudson.

Binford, Lewis. 2001. *Constructing Frames of Reference*. Berkeley: University of California Press.

Blanton, Richard E. 1994. *Houses and Households: A Comparative Study, Interdisciplinary Contributions to Archaeology*. New York: Plenum Press.

Bleed, Peter. 2006. "Living in the Human Niche." *Evolutionary Anthropology* 15: 8–10.

Bleed, Peter, and Akira Matsui. 2010. "Why Didn't Agriculture Develop in Japan? A Consideration of Jomon Ecological Style, Niche Construction, and the Origins of Domestication." *Journal of Archaeological Method and Theory*, 17(4): 356–370.

Bloom, Allan. 1968. *The Republic of Plato, Second Edition*. New York: Basic Books.

Bloomfield, Leonard. [1933] 1984. *Language*. Chicago: University of Chicago Press.

Boas, Franz. [1916] 2016. *Tsimshian Mythology*. Sydney: Wentworth Press.

Boni, Maciej F., and Marcus W. Feldman. 2007. "Evolution of Antibiotic Resistance by Human and Bacterial Niche Construction." *Evolution* 59(3): 477–491.

Boraas, Alan. 2002. "The Shift from Drift Net Fishing to Weir Fishing: Pre-Contact Salmon Fishing, Kenai River, Alaska." Modified from a paper presented at the Twenty-Eighth Annual Meeting of the Alaskan Anthropological Association, March 21–24, 2001. Fairbanks, Alaska.

Boraas, Alan. 2007. "Dena'ina Origins and Prehistory." In *Nanutset Ch'u Q'udi Gu, Before Our Time and Now: An Ethnohistory of Lake Clark National Park and Preserve*, edited by Karen K. Gaul, 31–40. Anchorage: United States Department of the Interior National Park Service Lake Clark National Park and Preserve.

Boraas, Alan. 2008. "The Role of *Beggesh* and *Beggesha* in Precontact Dena'ina Culture." *Alaska Journal of Anthropology* 6(1&2): 211–224.

Boraas, Alan, and Peter Kalifornsky. 1991. "Symbolic Fire and Water Transformations among the Cook Inlet, Alaska Dena'ina." Paper presented at the Eighteenth Annual Meeting of the Alaska Anthropological Association, Anchorage.

Boraas, Alan, and Donita Peter. 2008. "The True Believer Among the Kenai Peninsula Dena'ina." In *Adventures through Time: Readings in the Anthropology of Cook Inlet, Alaska: Proceedings of a Symposium*, edited by Nancy Yaw Davis and William E. Davis, 181–196. Anchorage: Cook Inlet Historical Society.

Borenstein, Elhanan, Jeremy Kendal, and Marcus W. Feldman. 2005. "Cultural Niche Construction in a Metapopulation." *Theoretical Population Biology* 70: 92–104.

Bourdieu, Pierre. 1970. "The Berber House or the World Reversed." *Social Science Information* 9(2): 151–170.

Bourdieu, Pierre. 1973. "The Berber House of the World Reversed". In *Rules and Meaning*, edited by Mary Douglas, 133–153. Harmondsworth, UK: Penguin.

Bourdieu, Pierre. 1977. *Outline of a Theory of Practice*. Cambridge: Cambridge University Press.

Boyd, Robert T. 1990. "Demographic History, 1774–1874." In *Handbook of the North American Indian, Vol. 7, Northwest Coast*, edited by Wayne Suttle, pp. 135–148. Washington, D.C.: Smithsonian Institution.

Briz i Godino, Ivan, Myrian Álvarez, Andrea Balbo, Débora Zurro, Marco Madella, Ximena Villagrán, and Charles French. 2011. "Towards High-Resolution Shell Midden Archaeology: Experimental and Ethno-Archaeology in Tierra del Fuego (Argentina)." *Quaternary International* 239(1–2): 125–134.

Briz i Godino, Ivan, and Marco Madella. 2013. "The Archaeology of Household— An Introduction." In *The Archaeology of Household*, edited by Marco Madella, Gabriella Kovács, B. Berzsényi, and Ivan Briz i Godino, 1–5. Oakwell: Oxbow Books.

Broecker, Wallace. 2001. "Was the Medieval Warm Period Global?" *Science* 291(5508): 1497.

Brogliato, Bernard, Rogelio Lozano, Bernhard Maschke, and Olav Egelan. 2007. *Dissipative Systems Analysis and Control. Theory and Applications (Second ed).* London: Springer Verlag.

Bronk Ramsey, Christopher, and Sharen Lee. 2013. "Recent and Planned Developments of the Program OxCal." *Radiocarbon* 55(2–3): 720–730.

Brooks, Alfred H. [1953] 1973. *Blazing Alaska's Trails*. The University of Alaska Press. Fairbanks.

Broughton, Jack M., Michael D. Cannon, Eric J. Bartelink. 2010. "Evolutionary Ecology, Resource Depression, and Niche Construction Theory: Applications to Central California Hunter-Gatherers and Mimbres-Mogollon Agriculturalists." *Journal of Archaeological Method and Theory* 17: 371–421.

Brucks, Caleb, and Olga Lovick. 2019. "Losing One's Way: Geographical and Moral Lessons in the Butterfly Story in Upper Tanana Athabascan." In *Language and Toponymy in Alaska and Beyond: Papers in Honor of James Kari*, edited by Gary Holton and Thomas F. Thornton, 97–120. Language Documentation and Conservation Special Publication 17. Fairbanks: Alaskan Native Language Center Press.

Burch, Ernest. 1974. "Eskimo Warfare in Northeast Alaska." *Anthropological Papers of the University of Alaska* 16(2): 1–4.

Burch, Ernest. 1988. *The Eskimos*. Norman: University of Oklahoma Press.

Burch, Ernest. 2006. *The Social Life in Northwest Alaska: The Structure of Iñupiaq Eskimo Nations*. Fairbanks: University of Alaska Press.

Burenhult, Niclas, and Stephen C. Levinson. 2008. "Language and Landscape: A Cross-linguistic Perspective." *Language Sciences* 30: 135–150.

Butzer, Karl W. 1980. "Civilizations: Organisms or Systems? Civilizations Behave as Adaptive Systems, Becoming Unstable When a Top-Heavy Bureaucracy Makes Excessive Demands on the Productive Sector; Breakdowns Result from Chance Concatenations of Mutually Reinforcing Processes, Not from Senility or Decadence." *American Scientist* 68(5): 517–523.

Butzer, Karl W. 1982. *Archaeology as Human Ecology*. Cambridge: Cambridge University Press.

Butzer, Karl W. 1996. "Ecology in the Long View: Settlement Histories, Agrosystemic Strategies, and Ecological Performance." *Journal of Field Archaeology* 23(2): 141–150.

Byers, David A., and Andrew Ugan. 2005. "Should We Expect Large Game Specialization in the Late Pleistocene? An Optimal Foraging Perspective on Early Paleoindian Prey Choice." *Journal of Archaeological Science* 32: 1624–1640.

Byrne, David, and Gill Callaghan, eds. 2014. *Complexity Theory and the Social Sciences*. New York: Routledge, Taylor, and Francis Group.

Calkin, Parker E. 1988. "Holocene Glaciation of Alaska (and Adjoining Yukon Territory, Canada)." *Quaternary Science Reviews* 7: 159–184.

Calkin, Parker E., Gregory C. Wiles, and David J. Barclay. 2001. "Holocene Coastal Glaciation of Alaska." *Quaternary Science Reviews* 20: 449–461.

Callaway, Donald G., and Constance A. Miller-Friend, eds. 2001. "Mendees Cheeg Naltsiin Keyh' An Oral History of the People of Healy Lake Village." Report prepared with a grant from the Alaska Humanities Forum and with support from the Healy Lake Traditional Council, Tetlin National Wildlife Refuge, National Park Service, and the Alaska Native Language Center at the University of Alaska Fairbanks.

Campbell, John. 1961. "The Tuktu Complex of Anaktuvuk Pass." *Anthropological papers of the University of Alaska* 9(2): 61–80.

Cannon, Chris M. 2021. "Northern Dene Astronomical and Sky-Related Knowledge: A Comparative Anthropological Study." Unpublished Ph.D. dissertation, Department of Anthropology, University of Alaska Fairbanks.

Cannon, Chris M., Wilson Justin, Paul Herbert, Charles Hubbard, and Charlie Neyelle. 2020. "Northern Dene Constellations as Worldview Projections with Case Studies from the Ahtna, Gwich'in, and Sahtúot'n." *Arctic Anthropology* 56(2): 1–26.

Carballo, David M., Paul Roscoe, and Gary M. Feinman. 2013. "Cooperation and Collective Action in the Cultural Evolution of Complex Societies." *Journal of Archaeological Method Theory* 21: 98-133. DOI:10.1007/s10816-012-9147-2.

Carbyn, Ludwig N., Sebastian M. Oosenbrug, and D. W. Anions. 1993. "Wolves, Bison and the Dynamics Related to the Peace Athabaska Delta in Canada's Wood Buffalo National Park." Circumpolar Research Series, No. 4. Canadian Circumpolar Institute, University of Alberta, Edmonton.

Carr, Christopher. 1995. "A Unified Middle Range Theory of Artifact Design." In *Style, Society, and Person: Archaeological and Ethnological Perspectives*, edited by Christopher Carr and Jill E. Neitzel, 171–258. New York: Plenum Press.

Chandler, Bruce. 2017. "Alaska's Ongoing Journey with Tuberculosis: A Brief History of Tuberculosis in Alaska and Considerations for Future Control." *State of Alaska Epidemiology Bulletin, Recommendations and Reports*: 1–8.

Chapin, Theodore. 1919. "Molybdenite Lode on Healy River." In *Mineral Resources of Alaska: Report on Progress in 1917, U.S.G.S. Bulletin 692*. Washington, D.C.: Government Printing Office.

252 References

Chapman, John W. 1921. "Tinneh Animism." *American Anthropologist*, 23(3): 298–310.

Charles, Walkie. 2009. "Qaneryaramta Egmiucia: Continuing Our Language." In *The Alaska Native Reader*, edited by Maria Shaa Tláa Williams, 85–90. London: Duke University Press.

Chekrouna, Mickaël D., Eric Simonnet, and Michael Ghil. 2011. "Stochastic Climate Dynamics: Random Attractors and Time-Dependent Invariant Measures." *Physica D* 240: 1685–1700.

Cinq-Mars, Jacques. 1974. "Preliminary Archaeological Study, Mackenzie Corridor." (Second Report). Environmental-Social Committee, Northern Pipelines, Task Force on Northern Oil Development, Report 74-11. Ottawa.

Clague, John J., Stephen G. Evans, Vernon N. Rampton, and Glenn J. Woodsworth. 1995. "Improved Age Estimates for the White River and Bridge River Tephras, Western Canada." *Canadian Journal of Earth Sciences* 32: 1172–1179.

Clark, Donald W. 1977. *Hahanudan Lake: An Ipiutak-Related Occupation of Western Interior Alaska*. National Museum of Man. Mercury Series, Archaeological Survey of Canada Paper No. 71. Ottawa: National Museum of Canada.

Clark, Donald W. 1984. "Pacific Eskimo: Historical Ethnography." In *Handbook of North American Indians, Vol. 5: Arctic*, edited by David Damas, 185–197. Washington, D.C.: Smithsonian Institution.

Clark, Donald W. 1994. "The Archaic in the Extreme Northwest of North America." *Revista de Arqueología Americana* 5: 71–99.

Clark, Donald W. 1995. "Batza Téna: The Trail to Obsidian." *Arctic Anthropology* 32(1): 82–91.

Clark, Donald W. 2001. "Microblade-Culture Systematics in the Far Interior Northwest." *Arctic Anthropology* 38(2): 64–80.

Clark, Donald W., Ruth M. Gotthardt, and P. Gregory Hare. 1999. "Microblade Complexes and Traditions in the Interior Northwest as Seen from the Kelly Creek Site, West-Central Yukon." Hudé Hudän Series. *Occasional Papers in Archaeology, 6.* Yukon Archaeology Program Publications, Cultural Services Branch Department of Tourism and Culture, Whitehorse: Government of Yukon.

Coffman, Samuel C. 2011. "Archaeology at Teklanika West (HEA-001): An Upland Archaeological Site, Central Alaska." Unpublished M.A. thesis, Department of Anthropology, University of Alaska Fairbanks.

Coffman, Samuel, C., Robin O. Mills, and Scott Shirar. 2018. "Report: Recent Archaeological Survey along the Middle Fork of the Fortymile River, Alaska." *Alaska Journal of Anthropology* 16(1): 95–106.

Coffman, Samuel C., and Jeffrey T. Rasic. 2015. "Rhyolite Characterization and Distribution in Central Alaska." *Journal of Archaeological Science* 57: 142–157.

Collins, Randall. 1998. *The Sociology of Philosophies: A Global Theory of Intellectual Change, Revised Edition*. Cambridge: Belknap Press of Harvard University Press.

Conkey, Margaret, and Joan Gero. 1991. "Tensions, Plurality, and Engendering Archaeology: An Introduction to Women and Prehistory." In *Engendering Archae-*

ology: Women and Prehistory, edited by Joan Gero and Margaret Conke, 3–30. Cambridge: Basil Blackwell.

Conkey, Margaret W., and Janet D. Spector. 1984. "Archaeology and the Study of Gender." *Advances in Archaeological Method and Theory* 7: 1–38.

Cook, John P. 1969. "Early Prehistory of Healy Lake, Alaska." Ph.D. dissertation, University of Wisconsin.

Cook, John P. 1989. "Historic Archaeology and Ethnohistory at Healy Lake, Alaska." *Arctic* 42(2): 109–118.

Cook, John P. 1995. "Characterization and Distribution of Obsidian in Alaska." *Arctic Anthropology* 32(1): 92–100.

Cook, John P., ed. 1977. *Pipeline Archaeology*. Fairbanks: The University of Alaska, Institute of Arctic Biology.

Cook, John P., and Robert A. McKennan. 1970. "The Athapaskan Tradition. A View from Healy Lake in the Yukon-Tanana Upland." Paper presented at the Tenth Annual Meeting of the Northeastern Anthropological Association, Ottawa. On File at the Office of History and Archaeology, Anchorage.

Cooper, H. Kory. 2006. "Copper and Social Complexity: Frederica de Laguna's Contribution to Our Understanding of the Role of Metals in Native Alaskan Society." *Arctic Anthropology* 43(2): 148–163.

Cooper, H. Kory. 2011. "The Life (Lives) and Times of Native Copper in Northwest North America." *World Archaeology* 43(2): 252–270.

Cooper, H. Kory. 2012. "Innovation and Prestige among the Northern Hunter-Gatherers: Late Prehistoric Native Copper Use in Alaska and Yukon." *American Antiquity* 77(3): 565–590.

Coray, Craig. 2007. *Dnaghelt'ana Qut'ana K'eli Ahdelyax (They Sing the Songs of Many People)*. Anchorage: Kijik Corporation and Lake Clark National Park and Preserve.

Cosmides, Leda, and John Tooby. 1994. "Better than Rational: Evolutionary Psychology and the Rational Hand." *The American Economic Review* 84(2): 327–332.

Costin, Cathy L., and Melissa B. Hagstrum. 1995. "Standardization, Labor Investment, Skill, and the Organization of Ceramic Production in Late Prehispanic Highland Peru." *American Antiquity* 60(4): 619–639.

Coupland, Gary. 1988. *Prehistoric Cultural Change at Kitselas Canyon. Canadian Museum of Civilization*, Mercury Series, Archaeological Survey of Canada, Paper No. 138(XVI). Ottawa: National Museum of Canada.

Coupland, Gary. 1996. "The Evolution of Multi-Family Households on the Northwest Coast of North America." In *People Who Lived in Big Houses: Archaeological Perspectives on Large Domestic Structures*, edited by Gary Coupland and Edward B. Banning, 121–130. Monographs in World Archaeology 27. Madison: Prehistory Press.

Coupland, Gary. 2013. "Household Archaeology of Complex Hunter-Gatherers on the North-west Coast of North American." In *The Archaeology of Household*, edited by Marco Madella, Gabriella Kovács, B. Berzsényi, and Ivan Briz i Godino, 45–66. Oxford: Oxbow Books.

Courty, Marie-Agnès, Paul Goldberg, and Richard Macphail. 1994. "Ancient People—Lifestyles and Cultural Patterns. Micromorphological Indicators of Anthropogenic Effects on Soils, Symposium of the Subcommission B." In *Transactions of the 15th World Congress of Soil Science*, edited by Jorge D. B. Etchevers, 250–269. Mexico DF: Sociedad Mexicana de la Ciencia del Suelo, International Society of Soil Science 6a.

Cowgill, George L. 2004. "Origins and Development of Urbanism: Archaeological Perspectives." *Annual Review of Anthropology* 33: 525–549.

Craft LeFebre, Charlene. 1956. "A Contribution to the Archaeology of the Upper Kuskokwim." *American Antiquity* 21(3): 268–274.

Craig Oliver E., John Chapman, András Figler, Pál Patay, Gillian Taylor, and Matthew J. Collins. 2004. "'Milk Jugs' and Other Myths of the Copper Age of Central Europe." *European Journal of Archaeology* 6: 249–263.

Croes, Dale R., and Steven Hackenberger. 1988. "Hoko River Archaeological Complex: Modelling Prehistoric Northwest Coast Economic Evolution." In *Research in Economic Anthropology* suppl. 3: *Prehistoric Economies of the Pacific Northwest Coast*, edited by Barry L. Isaac, 19–85. Greenwich: JAI Press.

Crosby, Alfred W. 1989. *America's Forgotten Pandemic, The Influenza of 1918. Second Edition.* New York: Cambridge University Press.

Cruikshank, Julie. 1991. *Dän Dhá Ts'edenintth'é: Reading Voices; Oral and Written Interpretations of Yukon's Past.* Vancouver, B.C.: Douglas and McIntyre.

Currier, Frederick J. 2018. *An Alaskan Adventure, A Story of Finding Gold in the Far North, From: 1894–1903.* Anchorage: Publication Consultants.

Dall, William H. 1870. *Alaska and Its Resources.* Boston: Lee and Shepard.

Davies, Lauren J., Britta J. L. Jensen, Duane G. Froese, Kristi L. Wallace. 2016. "Late Pleistocene and Holocene Tephrostratigraphy of Interior Alaska and Yukon: Key Beds and Chronologies over the Past 30,000 Years." *Quaternary Science Reviews* 146: 28–53.

Dawkins, C. Richard. 1990. *The Extended Phenotype: The Long Reach of the Gene* (new ed.). Oxford: Oxford University Press.

Day, Rachel L., Kevin N. Laland, F. John Odling-Smee. 2003. "Rethinking Adaptation: The Niche-Construction Perspective." *Perspectives in Biology and Medicine* 46(1): 80–95.

de Laguna, Frederica. [1947] 2000. *Travels among the Dena: Exploring Alaska's Yukon Valley.* Seattle: University of Washington Press.

de Laguna, Frederica, and Dale DeArmond, eds. 1995. *Tales from the Dena: Indian Stories from the Tanana, Koyukuk, and Yukon Rivers.* Seattle: University of Washington Press.

de Laguna, Frederica, and Catherine McClellan. 1981. "Ahtna." In *Handbook of North American Indians: Subarctic, volume 6,* edited by June Helm, pp. 641–663. Washington, D.C.: Smithsonian Institution.

Demit, Ellen. 2000. "Oral History 2000-02-PT.1," Wrangell-St. Elias National Park and Alaska Native Language Archive, University of Alaska. Recording of an interview of Ellen Demit conducted by Don Callaway and Connie Friend, August 16, 2000, at Healy Lake.

de Yonge, Jack. 2010. *Boom Town Boy: Coming of Age on Alaska's Lost Frontier.* Kenmore, Washington: Epicenter Press.

Derry, David E. 1975. "Later Athapaskan Prehistory: A Migration Hypothesis." *The Western Canadian Journal of Anthropology* 5(3–4): 134–147.

Dilley, Thomas E. 1988. "Holocene Tephra Stratigraphy and Pedogenesis in the Middle Susitna River Valley, Alaska." Unpublished M.A. thesis, Department of Geosciences, University of Alaska Fairbanks.

Dilley, Thomas E. 1998. "Late Quaternary Loess Stratigraphy, Soils, and Environments of the Shaw Creek Flats Paleoindian Sites, Tanana Valley, Alaska." Unpublished Ph.D. dissertation, The University of Arizona.

Dilley, Thomas E. 2013. *Arrows and Atl Atls: A Guide to the Archaeology of Beringia.* Washington, D.C.: Government Printing Office, United States Department of the Interior.

Dincauze, Dena F. 2000. *Environmental Archaeology: Principles and Practice.* Cambridge: Cambridge University Press.

Dixon, E. James. 1985. "Cultural Chronology of Central Interior Alaska." *Arctic Anthropology* 22(1): 47–66.

Dixon, E. James. 1993. *Quest for the First Americans.* University of New Mexico Press, Albuquerque.

Dixon, E. James. 2001. Human Colonization of the Americas: Timing, Technology, and Process. *Quaternary Science Reviews* 20: 277–299.

Dixon, E. James. 2013. *Arrows and Atl Atls: A Guide to the Archaeology of Beringia.* Government Printing Office, United States Department of the Interior. Washington, DC.

Dixon, E. James, George S. Smith, William Andrefsky, Becky M. Saleeby, and Charles Utermohle. 1985. "Susitna Hydroelectric Project. Cultural Resources Investigations 1979–1985: Report. Alaska Power Authority, Federal Energy Regulatory Commission Project No. 7114." On file at the University of Alaska Museum of the North, Fairbanks.

Dixon, James E., William F. Manley, and Craig M. Lee. 2005. "The Emerging Archaeology of Glaciers and Ice Patches: Examples from Alaska's Wrangell-St. Elias National Park and Preserve." *American Antiquity* 70(1): 129–143. DOI:10.2307/40035272.

Doering, Briana N., Julie A. Esdale, Joshua D. Reuther, and Senna D. Catenacci. 2020. "A Multiscalar Consideration of the Athabascan Migration." *American Antiquity* 85(3): 470–491.

Donahue, Kathleen. 2005. "Niche Construction through Phenological Plasticity: Life History Dynamics and Ecological Consequences." *The New Phytologist* 166(1): 83–92.

Duer, Douglas, Karen Evanoff, and Jamie Hebert. 2020. "Their Markers as They Go": Modified Trees as Waypoints in the Dena'ina Cultural Landscape, Alaska. *Human Ecology* 48: 317–333.

Duesenberg, H. Milton. 1994. *Alaska Highway Expeditionary Force—A Roadbuilder's Story.* Clear Lake, Iowa: H & M Industries.

Dumond, Don E. 1977. *Eskimos and Aleuts.* London: Thames and Hudson.

Dumond, Don E. 2010. "The Dene Arrival in Alaska." In *The Dene-Yeniseian Connection,* edited by James Kari and Ben A. Potter. *Anthropological Papers of the University of Alaska. New Series,* 5: 335–346. Alaska Native Language Center, Fairbanks.

Dyson-Hudson, Rada, and Eric A. Smith. 1978. "Human Territoriality: An Ecological Reassessment." *American Anthropologist* 80: 21–41.

Earle, Timothy, and Matthew Spriggs. 2015. "Political Economy in Prehistory: A Marxist Approach to Pacific Sequences." *Current Anthropology* 56(4): 515–544.

Easton, Norm A. 2005. "An Ethnohistory of the Chisana River Basin." Unpublished Manuscript, Northern Research Institute, Yukon College, Whitehorse, Yukon Territory, Canada.

Edwards, Mary E., Patricia. M. Anderson, Linda B. Brubaker, Thomas A. Ager, Andrei. A. Andreev, Nancy H. Bigelow, Les C. Cwynar, Wendy R. Eisner, Sandy P. Harrison, Fen Shang Hu, Dominique Jolly, Anatoly V. Lozhkin, Glen M. MacDonald, Cary J. Mock, Jerry C. Ritchie, Andrei V. Sher, Ray W. Spear, John W. Williams, and Gui Yu. 2000. "Pollen-Based Biomes for Beringia 18,000, 6000 and 0 14C yr BP." *Journal of Biogeography* 27: 521–554.

Elliott, Euel, and Kiel, L. Douglas. 2004. "Agent-Based Modeling in the Social and Behavioral Sciences." *Nonlinear Dynamics, Psychology, and Life Sciences* 8(2): 121–130.

Endicott, H. Wendell. 1928. *Adventures in Alaska and along the Trail.* New York: Frederick A. Stokes.

Esdale, Julie. 2008. "A Current Synthesis of the Northern Archaic." *Arctic Anthropology* 45(2): 3–38.

Esdale, Julie. 2009. "Lithic Production Sequences and Toolkit Variability: Examples from the Middle Holocene, Northwest Alaska." Unpublished Ph.D. dissertation, Department of Anthropology, Brown University.

Esdale, Julie, Aaron Robertson, and William Johnson. 2015. "Report: Banjo Lake: A Middle Holocene Site in the Tanana Valley." *Alaska Journal of Anthropology* 13(1): 35–56.

Evison, Leah H., Parker E. Calkin, and James M. Ellis. 1996. "Late-Holocene Glaciation and Twentieth-Century Retreat, Northeastern Brooks Range, Alaska." *The Holocene* 6: 17–24.

Fair, Susan W. 1997. "Story, Storage, and Symbol: Functional Cache Architecture, Cache Narratives, and Roadside Attractions." In *Perspectives in Vernacular Architecture vol. 7, Exploring Everyday Landscapes,* edited by Annmarie Adams, 167–182. Knoxville, University of Tennessee Press.

Fast, Phyllis A. 2008. "The Volcano in Athabascan Oral Narratives." *Alaska Journal of Anthropology* 6(1&2): 131–140.

Feinman, Gary M. 1998. "Scale and Social Organization: Perspectives on the Archaic State." In *Archaic States,* edited by Gary M. Feinman and Joyce Marcus, 95–133. Santa Fe: School of American Research Press.

Feinman, Gary M. 2011. "Size, Complexity, and Organizational Variation: A Comparative Approach." *Cross-Cultural Research* 45: 37–58. DOI:10.1177/1069397110383658.

Femenia, Nora. 2000. "Emotional Actor: Foreign Policy Decision-Making in the 1982 Falklands/Malvinas War." In *Social Conflicts and Collective Identities*, edited by Coy, Patrick G., and Lynne M. Woehrle, 41–65. Ithaca: Rowman & Littlefield Publishers.

Ferguson, Judy. 2002. *Parallel Destinies*. Big Delta, Alaska: Glas Publishing Company.

Ferguson, Judy. 2016. *Windows to the Land - Volume Two: Iditarod and Alaska River Trails - An Alaska Native Story*. Big Delta, Alaska: Voice of Alaska Press.

Fienup-Riordan, Ann. 2016. *Anguyiim Nalliini/Time of Warring*. Fairbanks: University of Alaska Press.

Flegontov, Pavel, N. Ezgi Altınışık, Piya Changmai, Nadin Rohland, Swapan Mallick, Nicole Adamski, Deborah A. Bolnick, Nasreen Broomandkhoshbacht, Francesca Candilio, Brendan J. Culleton, Olga Flegontova, T. Max Friesen, Choongwon Jeong, Thomas K. Harper, Denise Keating, Douglas J. Kennett, Alexander M. Kim, Thiseas C. Lamnidis, Ann Marie Lawson, Iñigo Olalde, Jonas Oppenheimer, Ben A. Potter, Jennifer Raff, Robert A. Sattler, Pontus Skoglund, Kristin Stewardson, Edward J. Vajda, Sergey Vasilyev, Elizaveta Veselovskaya, M. Geoffrey Hayes, Dennis H. O'Rourke, Johannes Krause, Ron Pinhasi, David Reich, and Stephan Schiffels. 2019. "Palaeo-Eskimo Genetic Ancestry and the Peopling of Chukotka and North America." *Nature* 570(4). DOI:10.1038/s41586-019-1251-y.

Frankel, David, and Jennifer M. Webb. 2006. "Neighbours: Negotiating Space in a Prehistoric Village." *Antiquity* 80: 287–302.

Franklin, Ursula, Ellen Badone, Ruth Cotthardt, and Brian Yorga. 1981. *An Examination of Prehistoric Copper Technology and Copper Sources in Western Arctic and Subarctic; North America*. Mercury Series. Archaeological Survey of Canada Paper, 101. Ottawa: National Museums of Canada.

Friend, Constance A., ed. 2010. *The Adventures of Yaabaa Teeshaay, as told by Ellen Demit and David Joe*. Fairbanks: Alaska Native Knowledge Network, Center for Cross Cultural Studies, University of Alaska Fairbanks.

Friesen, T. Max, and Owen K. Mason, eds. 2016a. "Introduction: Archaeology of the North American Arctic." In *The Oxford Handbook of the Prehistoric Arctic*, edited by T. Max Friesen and Owen K. Mason, 1–26. New York: Oxford University Press.

Fulkerson, Tiffany J. 2017. "Engendering the Past: The Status of Gender and Feminist Approaches to Archaeology in the Pacific Northwest and Future Directions." *Journal of Northwest Anthropology* 51(1): 1–36.

Fuller, Todd K., and Lloyd B. Keith. 1981. "Non-overlapping Ranges of Coyotes and Wolves in Northeastern Alberta." *Journal of Mammalogy* 62: 403–405.

Furholt, Martin, Colin Grier, Matthew Spriggs, and Timothy Earle. 2020. "Political Economy in the Archaeology of Emergent Complexity: A Synthesis of Bottom-Up and Top-Down Approaches." *Journal of Archaeological Method and Theory* 27: 157–191

Gé, Thierry, Marie-Agnés Courty, Wendy Matthews, and Julia Wattez. 1993. "Sedimentary Formation Processes of Occupational Surfaces." In *Formation Processes in Archaeological Context*, edited by Paul Goldberg, David T. Nash, and Michael D. Petraglia, 149–163. Monographs in World Archaeology 17. Madison: Prehistory Press.

Geertz, Clifford. 1973. "Notes on the Balinese Cockfight." In *The Interpretation of Cultures*, New York: Basic Books, Inc. Publishers.

Geller, Pamela L. 2009. "Identity and Difference: Complicating Gender in Archaeology." *Annual Review of Anthropology*, 38: 65–81.

Geographic Names Information System (GNIS). 2017. *Geographic Names Information System*. U.S. Geological Survey, Reston, Virginia. https://www.usgs.gov/u.s.-board-on-geographic-names/download-gnis-data.

Giddings, J. Louis., Jr. 1941. "Rock Paintings in Central Alaska." *American Antiquity* 7(1): 69–70.

Giddings, J. Louis., Jr. 1963. "Some Arctic Spear Points and Their Counterparts." *Anthropological Papers of the University of Alaska* 10(2): 1–12.

Giddings, J. Louis., Jr. 1967. *Ancient Men of the Arctic*. New York: A. A. Knopf.

Gillespie, Tom E. 1990. "Middle Holocene Climate and Culture Change in the Talkeetna Mountains, Alaska." Unpublished M.A. thesis, Department of Anthropology, University of Alaska Fairbanks.

Gladfelter, Bruce G. 1977. "Geoarchaeology: The Geomorphologist and Archaeology." *American Antiquity* 42(4): 519–538.

Godelier, Maurice. 2012. *Rationality and Irrationality in Economics*. New York: Verso.

Goldberg, Paul, and Richard I. Macphail. 2006. *Practical and Theoretical Geoarchaeology*. Oxford, Carlton: Blackwell Publishing, Malden.

Gómez Coutouly, Yan Axel, Angela K. Gore, Charles E. Holmes, Kelly E. Graf, and Ted Goebel. 2020. "Knapping, My Child, Is Made of Errors": Apprentice Knappers at Swan Point and Little Panguingue Creek, Two Prehistoric Sites in Central Alaska. *Lithic Technology*. DOI:10.1080/01977261.2020.1805201.

Gómez Coutouly, Yan Axel, Colas Guéret, Caroline M. Renard, Kathryn E Krasinski, Brian T Wygal. 2015." A Mid-Holocene Prehistoric Strike-A-Light from the Goodpaster Flats, Interior Alaska." *Alaska Journal of Anthropology* 13(2): 71–86.

Gordon, Bryan C., and Howard Savage. 1974. "Whirl Lake: A Stratified Indian Site near the Mackenzie Delta." *Arctic* 27(3): 175–188.

Gordon, Bryan C. 1996. *People of Sunlight, People of Starlight: Barrenland Archaeology in the Northwest Territories of Canada.* Mercury Series. Archaeological Survey of Canada Paper, 154. Hull: Canadian Museum of Civilization.

Gordon, Bryan C. 2012. "The White River Ash Fall: Migration Trigger or Localized Event?" *Revista de Arqueología Americana* 30: 91–102.

Grier, Colin. 2003. "Dimensions of Regional Interaction in the Prehistoric Gulf of Georgia." In *Emerging from the Mist: Studies in Northwest Coast Culture History*, edited by Richard G. Matson, Gary G. Coupland, and Quentin Mackie, 170–186. Vancouver: University of British Columbia Press.

Grinev, Andrei V. 1987. "Zabytaya ekspeditsiya Dmitriya Tarkhanova na Mednuyu reku [The Forgotten Expedition of Demitri Tarkhanov to the Copper River]." *Sovetskaya Etnografiya* 4: 88–100.

Grinev, Andrei V. 1993. "On the Banks of the Copper River: The Ahtna Indians and the Russians, 1783–1867." *Arctic Anthropology* 30(1): 54–66.

Grover, Margan A. 2016. "Late Precontact and Protohistoric Glass Beads of Alaska." *Arctic Anthropology* 53(2): 69–80.

Guédon, Marie-Françoise. 1974. *People of Tetlin, Why Are You Singing?* Mercury Series Paper No. 9. Ottawa, Ontario: National Museum of Man, Ethnology Division.

Guédon, Marie-Françoise. 1981. "Upper Tanana River Potlatch." In *Handbook of North American Indians, vol. 6: Subarctic*, edited by June Helm, 577–581. Washington, D.C.: Smithsonian Institution.

Guthrie, R. Dale. 2006. "New Carbon Dates Link Climate Change with Human Colonization and Pleistocene Extinctions." *Nature* 441: 207–209.

Gutoski, Martin. 2002. "Yaachox' Bluff: An Examination of a Rock Art Site in Interior Alaska and Local Oral History." Unpublished master's project, Department of Anthropology, University of Alaska Fairbanks.

Halpin, Libby. 1987. "Living off the Land: Contemporary Subsistence in Tetlin, Alaska." Technical Paper No. 149 prepared for the Alaska Department of Fish and Game Division of Subsistence, Fairbanks, Alaska.

Hamilton, Thomas D. 1980. "Quaternary Stratigraphic Sections with Radiocarbon Dates, Chandler Lake Quadrangle, Alaska." US Geological Survey Open-File Report 80–790.

Hanson, Diane K. 1999. "Interim Report of Archaeological Activities at the Ringling Material Site (MS 71-2-020-5), Gulkana, Alaska." Anchorage: Office of History and Archaeology, Division of Parks and Outdoor Recreation, Alaska Department of Natural Resources.

Hanson, Diane K. 2008. "Report: Archaeological Investigations in the 1990s at the Ringling Site, GUL-077, Near Gulkana, Alaska." *Alaska Journal of Anthropology* 6(1&2): 109–130.

Hanson, Larry W. 1965. "Size Distribution of the White River Ash, Yukon Territory." M.Sc. thesis, University of Alberta.

Hare, P. Gregory. 1995. "Holocene Occupations in the Southern Yukon: New Perspectives from the Annie Lake Site." *Hudé Hudän Series. Occasional Papers in Archaeology, 5.* Yukon Archaeology Program Publications, Cultural Services Branch, Department of Tourism and Culture, Government of Yukon, Whitehorse.

Hare, P. Gregory, Sheila Greer, Ruth Gotthardt, Richard Farnell, Vandy Bowyer, Charles Schweger, and Diane Strand. 2004. "Ethnographic and Archaeological Investigations of Alpine Ice Patches in Southwest Yukon, Canada." *Arctic* 57(3): 260–272.

Hare, P. Gregory, Christian D. Thomas, Timothy N. Topper, and Ruth M. Gotthardt. 2012. "The Archaeology of Yukon Ice Patches: New Artifacts, Observations, and Insights." *Arctic* 65(1): 118–135.

Hargus, Sharon, and James Kari. 1988. "Tahltan Fieldnotes." Unpublished Manuscript.

Harris, David Jason, and Gary Holton. 2019. "Place Naming Strategies in Lower Tanana." In *Language and Toponymy in Alaska and Beyond: Papers in Honor of James Kari*, edited by Gary Holton and Thomas F. Thornton, pp. 121–138. Language Documentation and Conservation Special Publication 17. Fairbanks: Alaskan Native Language Center Press.

Harris, Stephen L. 2005. *Fire Mountains of the West: The Cascade and Mono Lake Volcanoes* (3rd ed.). Missoula: Mountain Press Publishing Company.

Harrison, Peter. 2001. *The Bible, Protestantism, and the Rise of Natural Science*. New York: Cambridge University Press.

Hawkes, Kristen. 1991. "Showing off: Tests of a hypothesis about men's foraging goals." *Ethology and Sociobiology* 12(1): 29–54.

Hawkes, Kristen, and Rebecca Bliege-Bird. 2002. "Showing Off, Handicap Signaling, and the Evolution of Men's Work." *Evolutionary Anthropology* 11(2): 58–67.

Hayden, Brian. 1998. "Practical and Prestige Technologies: The Evolution of Material Systems." *Journal of Archaeological Method and Theory* 5(1): 1–55.

Haynes, C. Vance. 2008. "Younger Dryas "Black Mats" and the Rancholabrean Termination in North America." *Proceedings of the National Academy of Sciences U. S. A.* 105(18): 6520–6525. DOI:10.1073/pnas.0800560105.

Haynes, Terry L., and William E. Simeone. 2007. "Upper Tanana Ethnographic Overview and Assessment, Wrangell St. Elias National Park and Preserve." Technical Paper No. 325 prepared for the Department of Fish and Game Division of Subsistence, Juneau, Alaska.

Hays, Justin M., Charles M. Mobley, William E. Simeone, Patrick T. Hall, Gerad M. Smith, James E. Kari, Crystal L. Glassburn, Carol Gelvin-Reymiller, and Peter M. Bowers. 2014. "Report of the 2013 Cultural Resource Inventory for the Susitna-Watana Hydroelectric Project, Middle Susitna River, Alaska." Report prepared for the Alaska Office of History and Archaeology, Alaska State Historic Preservation Office, Alaska Division of Parks and Outdoor Recreation, Bureau of Land Management Alaska State Office, and URS Corp.

Heaton, John W. 2012. "Athabascan Village Stores: Subsistence Shopping in Interior Alaska, 1850–1950." *Western Historical Quarterly* 43: 133–155.

Heaton, Timothy J., Maarten Blaauw, Paul G. Blackwell, Christopher Bronk Ramsey, Paula J. Reimer, and E. Marian Scott. 2020. "The IntCal20 Approach to Radiocarbon Calibration Curve Construction: A New Methodology Using Bayesian Splines and Errors-In-Variables." *Radiocarbon* 1–43. DOI:10.1017/RD.C..2020.46.

Heidenreich, Stephan M. 2012. "Lithic Technologies, Functional Variability, and Settlement Systems in Late Pleistocene Beringia–New Perspectives on a Colonization Process." Unpublished Ph.D. dissertation, Philosophischen Fakultät und Fachbereich Theologie der Friedrich-Alexander-Universität Erlangen-Nürnberg.

Hemphill, Brian E., and J. P. Mallory. 2004. "Horse-Mounted Invaders from the Russo-Kazakh Steppe or Agricultural Colonists from Western Central Asia? A Craniometric Investigation of the Bronze Age Settlement of Xinjiang." *American Journal of Physical Anthropology* 125: 199–222.

Hendon, Julia A. 1996. "Archaeological Approaches to the Organization of Domestic Labor: Household Practice and Domestic Relations." *Annual Review of Anthropology* 25: 45–61.

Henrich, Joseph. 2004. "Demography and Cultural Evolution: Why Adaptive Cultural Processes Produced Maladaptive Losses in Tasmania." *American Antiquity* 69: 197–218. DOI:10.2307/4128416.

Henrich, Joseph. 2006. "Understanding Cultural Evolutionary Models: A Reply to Read's Critique." *American Antiquity* 71: 771–782.

Hensley, William. 2009. "Why the Natives of Alaska Have a Land Claim." In *The Alaska Native Reader*, edited by Maria Shaa Tláa Williams, 192–201. London: Duke University Press.

Heppner, Annalisa. 2017. "A Feminist Archaeological Approach to the Analysis of the Osseous Tool Suite from the Broken Mammoth Site, Interior Alaska." Unpublished M.A. thesis, Department of Anthropology, University of Alaska Anchorage.

Hibben, Thomas N. [1889] 2011. *Dictionary of the Chinook Jargon, or Indian Trade Language of the North Pacific Coast*. T.N. Hibben Company, Victoria, B.C. http://www.gutenberg.org/files/35492/35492-h/35492-h.htm. March 2018.

Hilmer, Hilary. 2019. "Faunal Analysis of the Historic Component at Healy Lake Village site, Interior Alaska." Unpublished M.A. thesis, Department of Anthropology, University of Alaska Fairbanks.

Hirasawa, Yu, and Charles E. Holmes. 2017. "The Relationship between Microblade morphology and Production Technology in Alaska from the Perspective of the Swan Point Site." *Quaternary International* 442: 104–117 Part B.

Hodder, Ian. 1999. *The Archaeological Process: An Introduction*. New York: Wiley-Blackwell.

Hodder, Ian. 2011. "Human-Thing Entanglement: Towards an Integrated Archaeological Perspective." *The Journal of the Royal Anthropological Institute* 17(1): 154–177.

Hody, James W., and Roland Kays. 2018. "Mapping the Expansion of Coyotes (Canis latrans) across North and Central America." *Zookeys* 759: 81–97. DOI:10.3897/zookeys.759.15149.

Hollinger, Kristy. 2003. "The Haines-Fairbanks Pipeline." Center for Environmental Management of Military Lands (CEMML), Colorado State University, Fort Collins, CO, and US Army Alaska, Fort Richardson, AK, JBER.

Hollis, Martin, and Edward J. Nell. 1975. *Rational Economic Man*. Cambridge: Cambridge University Press.

Holly, Donald H., Jr. 2002. "Subarctic "Prehistory" in the Anthropological Imagination." *Arctic Anthropology* 39(1-2): 10–26.

Holmes, Charles E. 1975. "A Northern Athapaskan Environment System in Diachronic Perspective." *The Western Canadian Journal of Anthropology* V(3-4): 92–124.

Holmes, Charles E. 1986. *Lake Minchumina Prehistory: An Archaeological Analysis*. Alaska Anthropological Association Monograph Series, Aurora 2, Fairbanks: University of Alaska Fairbanks.

Holmes, Charles E. 2001. "Tanana River Valley Archaeology Circa 14,000 to 9000 BP." *Arctic Anthropology* 38(2): 154–170.

Holmes, Charles E. 2006. "The Archaeological Sequence at Swan Point, Central Alaska." Poster presented at the 14th annual Arctic Conference, Eugene, Oregon.

Holmes, Charles E. 2008. "The Taiga Period: Holocene Archaeology of the Northern Boreal Forest, Alaska." *Alaska Journal of Anthropology* 6(1&2): 69–81.

Holmes, Charles E. 2011. "A Late Holocene "House" Feature at Swan Point Associated with Microblade Technology." Poster presented at the Thirty-Eighth Annual Meeting of the Alaska Anthropological Association. Fairbanks.

Holmes, Charles E. 2011b. "The Beringian and transitional periods in Alaska: technology of the east Beringian tradition as viewed from Swan point." In *From Yenisei to the Yukon: Interpreting Lithic Assemblage Variability in Late Pleistocene/Early Holocene Beringia*, edited by Ted Goebel and Ian Buvit, pp. 172–191. Texas A&M University Press, College Station.

Holmes, Charles E. 2012. "Field Report of Work Conducted during the 2011 Field Season at AHRS Sites XBD-156 (Swan Point) and XBD-374 (Pickup Sticks)." Report Prepared for the Alaska Office of History and Archaeology under permit #2011-04.

Holmes, Charles E., Ben A. Potter, Joshua D. Reuther, Owen K. Mason, Robert M. Thorson, and Peter M. Bowers. 2008. "Geological and Cultural Context of the Nogahabara I Site." *American Antiquity* 73(4): 781–790.

Holmes, Charles E., Douglas R. Reger, Craig Mishler, Rolfe Buzzell, Douglas Gibson, and J. David McMahan. 1985. "Progress Report, Project F-02 1-2(1 5)1 (A09812), Sterling Highway Archaeological Mitigation: Phase 1 Excavations at Four Sites on the Kenai Peninsula." Alaska Division of Geological and Geophysical Surveys Public Data File 85-04. Anchorage.

Holmes, Charles E., Richard VanderHoek, and Thomas E. Dilley. 1996. "Swan Point." In *American Beginnings: The Prehistory and Palaeoecology of Beringia*, edited by Frederick Hadleigh West, Constance F. West, Brian S. Robinson, John F. Hoffecker, Mary Lou Curran, and Robert E. Ackerman, 319–323. Chicago and London: The University of Chicago Press.

Holton, Gary. 2010. "Behind the Map: The Reification of Indigenous Language Boundaries in Alaska. Working Papers in Athabaskan Languages." *Alaska Native Language Center Working Papers* 8: 75–87.

Holton, Gary, ed. 2009. *Tanacross Learners' Dictionary: Dihthâad Xt'een Iin Aandĕg' Dínahtlǎa'*, compiled by Irene Arnold, Rick Thoman, and Gary Holton. Fairbanks: Alaska Native Language Center, University of Alaska Fairbanks.

Hughes, Paul D. M., Gunnar Mallon, Alastair D. Brown, H. J. Essex, J. D. Stanford, and S. Hotes. 2013. "The Impact of High Tephra Loading on Late-Holocene Carbon Accumulation and Vegetation Succession in Peatland Communities." *Quaternary Science Reviews* 67: 160–175.

Hunn, Eugene. 1994. "Place Names, Population Density, and the Magic Number 500." *Current Anthropology* 35(1): 81–85.

Ihara, Yasuo, and Marcus W. Feldman. 2004. "Cultural Niche Construction and the Evolution of Small Family Size." *Theoretical Population Biology* 65(1): 105–111.

Isaac, Glynn Ll. 1978. "The Food-Sharing Behavior of Protohuman Hominids." *Scientific American* 238(4): 90–108.

Ives, John W. 1990. *A Theory of Northern Athapaskan Prehistory*. Boulder, and San Francisco: Westview Press.

Ives, John W. 1998. "Developmental Processes in the Pre-Contact History of Athapaskan, Algonquian, and Numic Kin Systems." In *Transformations of Kinship*, edited by Maurice Godelier, Thomas R. Trautmann, and Franklin E. Tjon Sie Fat, 94–139. Washington, D.C.: Smithsonian Institution Press.

Ives, John W. 2008. "Review of 'Athapaskan Migrations: The Archaeology of Eagle Lake, British Columbia.'" *Canadian Journal of Archaeology* 32: 153–159.

Ives, John W., Sally Rice, and Edward J. Vajda. 2010. "Dene-Yeniseian and Processes of Deep Change in Kin Terminologies." In *The Dene-Yeniseian Connection*, edited by James Kari and Ben A. Potter. *Anthropological Papers of the University of Alaska. New Series*, 5: 223–256. Fairbanks: Alaska Native Language Center.

Jackson, Sheldon. 1903. *What Missionaries Have Done for Alaska*. Funk & Wagnalls Co. *The Missionary Review of the World*, 497–504.

Jarvenpa, Robert, and Hetty Ho Brumbach. 2016. "Initializing the Landscape: Chippewyan Construction of Meaning in a Recently Occupied Environment." In *Marking the Land: Hunter-Gatherer Creation of Meaning in Their Environment*, edited by William Lovis and Robert Whallon, 1–45. New York, NY: Routledge.

Jetté, Jules. 1911. "On the Superstitions of the Ten'a Indians (Middle Part of the Yukon Valley, Alaska)." *Anthropos* 6(1): 95–108.

Jetté, Jules, and Eliza Jones. 2000. *Koyukon Athabaskan Dictionary*, edited by James Kari. Fairbanks: Alaska Native Language Center.

John, Peter. 1996. *The Gospel According to Peter John*, edited by David J. Krupa. Fairbanks: Alaska Native Knowledge Network.

Johnson, Linda. 1985. "An Index to the Journals of Reverend Robert McDonald." On file at the Yukon Native Language Center, Whitehorse.

Johnson [Mitchell], Roy. 1981. "Upper Tanana Athapaskan Fire Ecology." Paper presented at the Eighth Annual Meeting of the Alaska Anthropological Association, Anchorage.

Jones, Clive G., John H. Lawton, and Moshe Shachak. 1994. "Organisms as Ecosystem Engineers." *Oikos*, 69, 373–386.

Jones, Clive G., John H. Lawton, and Moshe Shachak. 1997a. "Ecosystem Engineering by Organisms: Why Semantics Matters." *Trends in Ecology & Evolution*, 12, 275.

Jones, Clive G., John H. Lawton, and Moshe Shachak. 1997b. "Positive and negative effects of organisms as physical ecosystem engineers." *Ecology* 78: 1946–1957.

Jones, Richard L. C. 2016. "Responding to Modern Flooding: Old English Place-Names as a Repository of Traditional Ecological Knowledge." *Journal of Ecological Anthropology* 18(1). DOI:10.5038/2162-4593.18.1.9.

Juneby, Willy, and John T. Ritter. 1978. "Place Names of the Eagle Region." Unpublished paper on file at the Alaska Native Language Archive, Fairbanks.

Just, Roger. 1989. "Triumph of the Ethnos." In *History and Ethnicity*, edited by Elizabeth Tonkin, Maryon McDonald, and Malcolm K. Chapman, 71–88. London: Routledge.

Kaplan, Hillard, and Kim Hill. 1985. "Food Sharing among Ache Foragers: Tests of Explanatory Hypotheses." *Current Anthropology* 26(2): 223–246.

Kari, James. 1988. "Some Linguistic Insights into Dena'ina Prehistory." In *Athapaskan Linguistics: Current Perspectives on a Language Family*, edited by Eung-Do Cook and Keren D. Rice, 533–574. Berlin: Mouton de Gruyter.

Kari, James. 1996a. "Names as Signs: 'Mountain' and 'Stream' in Alaskan Athabascan Languages." In *Athabascan Language Studies, Essays in Honor of Robert W. Young*, edited by Eloise Jelinek, Sally Midgette, Keren Rice, and Leslie Saxon, 443–475. Albuquerque: University of New Mexico Press.

Kari, James. 1996b. "A Preliminary View of Hydronymic Districts in Northern Athabascan Prehistory." *Names* 44: 253–271.

Kari, James. 2005. "Language Work in Alaskan Athabascan and Its Relationship to
Alaskan Anthropology." *Alaska Journal of Anthropology* 3(1): 105–119.

Kari, James. 2010a. *Ahtna Travel Narratives*. Fairbanks: Alaska Native Language
Center.

Kari, James. 2010b. "The Concept of Geolinguistic Conservatism in Na-Dene Prehistory." In *The Dene-Yeniseian Connection*, edited by James Kari and Ben A. Potter. Anthropological Papers of the University of Alaska. New Series, 5: 194–222.
Fairbanks: Alaska Native Language Center.

Kari, James. 2011a. "Tanacross Place Names." Unpublished paper on file at the
Alaska Native Language Archive, Fairbanks.

Kari, James. 2011b. "A Case Study in Ahtna Athabascan Geographic Knowledge."
In *Landscape in Language. Transdisciplinary Perspectives,* edited by David M.
Mark, Andrew G. Turk, Niclas Burenhult, and David Stea, 239–260. Amsterdam:
John Benjamins Publishing Co.

Kari, James. 2013. *Ahtna Place Names Lists and Maps*, Version 3.1. Fairbanks:
Alaska Native Language Archive.

Kari, James. 2015. "Middle Tanana Ethnogeographic Reconstruction." Report prepared for the Tanana-Yukon Historical Society and Fort Wainwright U.S. Army,
Cultural Resources Office, Fairbanks.

Kari, James. 2017. "Advances in Dene Ethnogeographic Research." *Working Papers
in Dene Languages 2016* 13: 35–50.

Kari, James. 2019a. "Lexware, Dene Band Labels, and Recent Alaska Dene Lexicography Work." Proceedings of the 2018 Dene Languages Conference. *Alaska Native
Language Center Working Papers* 15: 71–85.

Kari, James. 2019b. "The Resilience of Dene Generative Geography, Considering
'The *Nen' Yese'* Ensemble.'" *Alaska Journal of Anthropology* 17(1&2): 44–76.

Kari, James. n.d. "Middle Tanana Dictionary." Unpublished Lexware file, version
2.4. Received March 2020.

Kari, James, and James A. Fall. 2016. *Shem Pete's Alaska: The Territory of the Upper
Cook Inlet Dena'ina*, Third Edition. Fairbanks: University of Alaska Press.

Kari, James, Gary Holton, Brett Parks, and Robert Charlie. 2012. *Lower Tanana
Athabascan Place Names*. Fairbanks: Alaska Native Language Center.

Kari, James, and Ben A. Potter. 2010. "The Dene-Yeniseian Connection: Bridging
Asia and North America." In *The Dene-Yeniseian Connection*, edited by James
Kari and Ben A. Potter. *Anthropological Papers of the University of Alaska. New
Series*, 5: 1–24. Fairbanks: Alaska Native Language Center.

Kari, James, and Gerad M. Smith. 2017. "Dene Atlas." *The Web Atlas of Alaskan
Dene Place Names, Version 1.2*. February 1. https://sites.google.com/a/alaska.edu/
denemapped/

Kari, James, and Siri G. Tuttle. 1996. Athabaskan Place Name Data. In *Archaeological Survey and Assessment of Prehistoric Cultural Resources on Eielson Air Force
Base, Alaska*. Ed. by C. Gerlach, S. Macintosh, P. Bowers, and O. Mason. Appendix V:1–18 with map. Report prepared by Northern Land Use Research.

Kari, James, and Siri G. Tuttle, eds. 2018. "Yenida'atah, Ts'utsaede, K'adiide, in Legendary Times, Ancient Times and Recent Times, an Anthology of Ahtna Narratives." Fairbanks: Alaska Native Language Center.

Kaufman, Darrell S., Yarrow L. Axford, Andrew C. G. Henderson, Nicholas P. McKay, W. Wyatt Oswald, Casey Saenger, R. Scott Anderson, Hannah L. Bailey, Benjamin Clegg, Konrad Gajewski, Feng Sheng Hu, Miriam C. Jones, Charly Massa, Cody C. Routson, Al Werner, Matthew J. Wooller, Zicheng Yu. 2016. "Holocene Climate Changes in Eastern Beringia (NW North America) - A Systematic Review of Multi-proxy Evidence." *Quaternary Science Reviews* 147(1): 312–339.

Keeney, Joseph W. 2019. "Faunal and Lithic Analysis from the Matcharak Peninsula Site (AMR-00196) Northern Archaic Context: Lake Matcharak, Central Brooks Range, Alaska." Unpublished M.A. thesis, Department of Anthropology, University of Alaska Fairbanks.

Kehoe, Alice Beck. 2013. "The Archaeology of Gender in Western North America." In *A Companion to Gender Prehistory*, edited by Diane Bolger, pp. 544–563. West Sussex, England: John Wiley & Sons.

Kent, Susan, ed. 1990. *Domestic Architecture and the Use of Space: An Interdisciplinary Cross-Cultural Study*. Cambridge: Cambridge University Press.

Ketz, James A. 1982. "Paxson Lake: Two Nineteenth Century Ahtna Sites in the Copper River Basin, Alaska." Unpublished M.A. thesis, Department of Anthropology, University of Alaska Fairbanks.

Kielhofer, Jennifer, Christopher Miller, Joshua Reuther, Charles Holmes, Ben Potter, François Lanoë, Julie Esdale, and Barbara Crass. 2020. "The Micromorphology of Loess-Paleosol Sequences in Central Alaska: A New Perspective on Soil Formation and Landscape Evolution since the Late Glacial Period (c. 16,000 cal yr BP to Present)." *Geoarchaeology* 2020: 1–28. DOI:10.1002/gea.21807.

Kirby, R. Kenneth. 2008. "Phenomenology and the Problems of Oral History." *Oral History Review*, 35(1): 22–38.

Kirsteatter, Paul. 2000. "Oral History 2000-105-03." Wrangell-St. Elias National Park and Alaska Native Language Archive, University of Alaska. Recording of an interview of Paul Kirsteatter conducted by Don Callaway and Connie Friend, August 16, 2000, at Healy Lake.

Klejn, Leo S., Wolfgang Haak, Iosif Lazaridis, Nick Patterson, David Reich, Kristian Kristiansen, Karl-Göran Sjögren, Morten Allentoft, Martin Sikora, and Eske Willerslev. 2017. "Discussion: Are the Origins of Indo-European Languages Explained by the Migration of the Yamnaya Culture to the West?" *European Journal of Archaeology* 21(1): 3–17.

Kline, Michelle A., and Robert Boyd. 2010. "Population Size Predicts Technological Complexity in Oceania." *Proceedings of the Royal Society B* 277: 2559–2564. DOI:10.1098/rspb.2010.0452.

Koch, Alexander, Chris Brierley, Mark M. Maslin, and Simon L. Lewis. 2019. "Earth System Impacts of the European Arrival and Great Dying in the Americas after 1492." *Quaternary Science Reviews* 207: 13–36.

Kovács, Gabriella. 2013. "Soil Micromorphology of the Household as Százhalombatta-Földvár Bronze Age Tell Settlement, Hungary." In *The Archaeology of Household*, edited by Marco Madella, Gabriella Kovács, B. Berzsényi, and Ivan Briz i Godino 179–216. Oakwell: Oxbow Books.

Krasinski, Kathryn E., and Gary Haynes. 2010. "The Eastern Beringian Chronology of Quaternary Extinctions: A Methodological Approach to Radiocarbon Evaluation." *Alaska Journal of Anthropology* 8(1): 39–60.

Krauss, Michael E., and Victor K. Golla. 1981. "Northern Athapaskan Languages." In *Handbook of North American Indians, vol. 6, Subarctic*, edited by June Helm, 67–85. Washington, D.C.: Smithsonian Institution.

Krauss, Michael E., Gary Holton, Jim Kerr, and Colin West. 2011. *Indigenous Peoples and Languages of Alaska*. Alaska Native Language Center, Fairbanks, University of Alaska Fairbanks.

Kristensen, Todd J., P. Gregory Hare, Ruth M. Gotthardt, Norman A. Easton, John W. Ives, Robert J. Speakman, and Jeffrey T. Rasic. 2019. "The Movement of Obsidian in Subarctic Canada: Holocene Social Relationships and Human Responses to a Large-scale Volcanic Eruption." *Journal of Anthropological Archaeology* 56: 101114.

Kristiansen, Kristian. 2004. "Institutions and Material Culture, toward an Intercontextual Archaeology." In *Rethinking Materiality. The Engagement of Mind with the Material World*, edited by Elizabeth Demarrais, Chris Gosden, and Colin Renfrew, 179–193. Cambridge, McDonald Institute Monographs.

Kristiansen, Kristian. 2013. "Households in Context. Cosmology, Economy and Long Term Change." In *The Archaeology of Household*, edited by Marco Madella, Gabriella Kovács, B. Berzsényi, and Ivan Briz i Godino, pp. 235–268. Oakwell: Oxbow Books.

Kuhn, Steven L., and Mary C. Stiner. 2019. "Hearth and Home in the Middle Pleistocene." *Journal of Anthropological Research* 75(3): 305–327.

Kuhn, Tyler S., Keri A. McFarlane, Pamela Groves, Arne Ø. Mooers, and Beth Shapiro. 2010. "Modern and Ancient DNA Reveal Recent Partial Replacement of Caribou in the Southwest Yukon." *Molecular Ecology* 19: 1312–1323.

Kunz, Michael L, and Robin O. Mills. 2021. "A Precolumbian Presence of Venetian Glass Trade Beads in Arctic Alaska." *American Antiquity*. DOI:10.1017/aaq.2020.100.

Kylafis, Grigoris, and Michael Loreau. 2008. "Ecological and Evolutionary Consequences of Niche Construction for Its Agent." *Ecology Letters* 11: 1072–1081.

Kylafis, Grigoris, and Michael Loreau. 2010. "Niche Construction in the Light of Niche Theory." *Ecology Letters* 14: 82–90.

Lacourse, Terri, and Konrad Gajewski. 2000. "Late Quaternary Vegetation History of Sulphur Lake, Southwest Yukon Territory, Canada." *Arctic* 51: 27–35.

Laland, Kevin N., and Michael J. O'Brien. 2010. "Niche Construction Theory and Archaeology." *Journal of Archaeological Method and Theory* 17(4): 303–322.

Laland, Kevin N., F. John Odling-Smee, and Marc W. Feldman. 1999. "Evolutionary Consequences of Niche Construction and Their Implications for Ecology." *Proceedings of the National Academy of Sciences* 96: 10242–10247.

Lancelotti, Carla, and Marco Madella. 2012. "The "Invisible" Product: Developing Markers for Identifying Dung in Archaeological Contexts." *Journal of Archaeological Science* 39(4): 953–963.

Lane, Albert L. 1942. "The Alcan Highway: Road Location and Construction Methods." *The Military Engineer* 34(204): 492–499.

Lanoë, François B. 2018. "Early Holocene Occupation of the Hollembaek's Hill Site, Central Alaska." Paper presented at the Forty-Sixth Meeting of the Alaska Anthropological Association, Nome, Alaska.

Lanoë, François B., and Charles E. Holmes. 2016. "Animals as Raw Material in Beringia: Insights from the Site of Swan Point CZ4B, Alaska." *American Antiquity*, 81(4): 682–696.

Lanoë, François B., Joshua D. Reuther, and Charles E. Holmes. 2019a. "Early Holocene Occupation of the Hollembaek's Hill Site, Central Alaska." Paper Presented at the Forty-Sixth Annual Meeting of the Alaska Anthropological Association, Nome, Alaska.

Lanoë, François B., Joshua D. Reuther, Charles Holmes, and Jeff Rasic. 2019b. "Environmental Change and Human Ecology in Central Alaska during the Early Holocene: Hollembaek's Hill." Poster presented at the Eighty-Forth annual Society for American Archaeology meeting, Albuquerque, New Mexico.

Lantis, Margaret. 1984. "Aleut." In *Handbook of North American Indians, Vol. 5: Arctic*, edited by David Damas, 161–184. Washington, D.C.: Smithsonian Institution.

Lawler, Brooks A. 2019. "Prehistoric Toolstone Procurement and Land Use in the Tangle Lakes Region, Central Alaska." Unpublished M.A. thesis, Department of Anthropology, University of Alaska Fairbanks.

Leer, Jeff. 1978. *A Conversational Dictionary of Kodiak Alutiiq*. The Alaska Native Language Center. Fairbanks: University of Alaska Fairbanks.

Leer, Jeff. 1991. "Evidence for a Northern Northwest Coast Language Area: Promiscuous Number Marking and Periophrastic Possessive Constructions in Haida, Eyak and Aleut." *International Journal of American Linguistics* 57: 158–193.

Lehmann, Laurent. 2007. "The Adaptive Dynamics of Niche Constructing Traits in Spatially Subdivided Populations: Evolving Posthumous Extended Phenotypes." *Evolution* 2007: 1–18.

Leone, Mark P., Cheryl Janifer LaRoche, and Jennifer J. Babiarz. 2005. "The Archaeology of Black Americans in Recent Times." *Annual Review of Anthropology* 34: 575–598.

Lepofsky, Dana, David M. Schaepe, Anthony P. Graesch, Michael Lenert, Patricia Ormerod, Keith Thor Carlson, Jeanne E. Arnold, Michael Blake, Patrick Moore, and John J. Clague. 2009. "Exploring Stó: Lō-Coast Salish Interaction and Identity in Ancient Houses and Settlements in the Fraser Valley, British Columbia." *American Antiquity*, 74(4): 595–626.

Lerbekmo, J. F., J. A. Westgate, D. G. W. Smith, and G. H. Denton. 1975. "New Data on the Character and History of the White River Volcanic Eruption, Alaska." In *Quaternary Studies,* edited by R. P. Suggate and M. M. Cresswell, 203–209. Wellington: Royal Society of New Zealand.

Letts, Brandon, Tara L. Fulton, Mathias Stiller, Thomas D. Andrews, Glen MacKay, Richard Popko, and Beth Shapiro. 2012. "Ancient DNA Reveals Genetic Continuity in Mountain Woodland Caribou of the Mackenzie and Selwyn Mountains, Northwest Territories, Canada." *Arctic* 65(1): 80–94.

Levinson, Stephen C. 1996. "Language and Space." *Annual Review of Anthropology* 25: 353–382.

Lévi-Strauss, Claude. 1963. *Structural Anthropology*. New York: Basic Books.

Lewontin, Richard C. 1982. "Organism and Environment." In *Learning, Development, and Culture*, edited by Henry C. Plotkin, pp. 151–170. New York: Wiley.

Lewontin, Richard C. 1983. "Gene, Organism, and Environment." In *Evolution from Molecules to Men*, edited by Derek S. Bendall, pp. 273–285. Cambridge: Cambridge University Press.

Little, Allison A. 2013. "Lithic Analysis at the Mead Site, Central Alaska." Unpublished M.A. thesis, Department of Anthropology, University of Alaska Fairbanks.

Lloyd, Andrea H., W. Scott Armbruster, and Mary Edwards. 1994. "Ecology of a Steppe-Tundra Gradient in Interior Alaska." *Journal of Vegetation Science* 5(6): 897–912.

Long, Austin. 1965. "Smithsonian Institution Radiocarbon Measurement 2." *Radiocarbon* 7: 245–256.

Lovejoy, C. Owen. 1981. "The Origin of Man." *Science* 211(4480): 341–50.

Loyens, William J. 1966. "The Changing Culture of the Nulato Koyukon Indians." Unpublished Ph.D. thesis, Department of Anthropology, University of Wisconsin.

Luke, Howard. 1998. *My Own Trail*, edited by Jan Jackson. Fairbanks: Alaska Native Knowledge Network.

Lutz, Harold J. 1959. "Aboriginal Man and White Men as Historical Causes of Fires in the Boreal Forest, with Particular Reference to Alaska." *Yale School of Forestry Bulletin, 65*. New Haven: Yale University Press.

Lyman, Robert L. 1994. *Vertebrate Taphonomy*. Cambridge: Cambridge University Press.

Lynch, Joshua J., Ted Goebel, Kelly E. Graf, and Jeffery T. Rasic. 2018. "Archaeology of the Uppermost Tanana: Results of a Survey of the Nabesna and Chisana Rivers, East-Central Alaska." *Alaska Journal of Anthropology* 16(1): 21–43.

MacIntosh, Gordon D. n.d. "The Calendric Dating and Seasonality of the White River Ash." Unpublished manuscript on file at the University of Alaska Museum of the North, Fairbanks, Alaska.

MacLean, Edna Ahgeak. 2011. *Iñupiatun Uqaluit Taniktun Sivunniuġutiŋit: North Slope Iñupiaq to English Dictionary*. Fairbanks: Alaska Native Languages Archives, University of Alaska Fairbanks.

Mamelund, Svenn-Erik, Lisa Sattenspiel, and Jessica Dimka. 2013. "Influenza-Associated Mortality during the 1918–1919 Influenza Pandemic in Alaska and Labrador." *Social Science History* 37(2): 177–229.

Mann, Daniel H., Aron L. Crowell, Thomas D. Hamilton, and Bruce P. Finney. 1998. "Holocene Geologic and Climatic History around the Gulf of Alaska." *Arctic Anthropology* 35(1): 112–131.

Mann, Daniel H., Pamela Groves, Michael L. Kunz, Richard E. Reanier, Benjamin V. Gaglioti. 2013. "Ice-Age Megafauna in Arctic Alaska: Extinction, Invasion, Survival." *Quaternary Science Reviews* 70: 91–108.

Mann, Daniel H., Richard E. Reanier, Dorothy M. Peteet, Michael L. Kunz, and Mark Johnson. 2001. "Environmental Change and Arctic Paleoindians." *Arctic Anthropology* 38(2): 119–138.

Maschner, Herbert D. G. 1997. "The Evolution of Northwest Coast Warfare." In *Troubled Times: Violence and Warfare in the Past*, edited by Debra L. Martin and David W. Frayer, 267–302. War and Society Series, vol. 4. Langhorn, PA: Gordon and Breach.

Maschner, Herbert D. G., and Owen K. Mason. 2013. "The Bow and Arrow in Northern North America." *Evolutionary Anthropology* 22: 133–138.

Mason, Owen. 2012. "Memories of Warfare: Archaeology and Oral History in Assessing the Conflict and Alliance Model of Ernest S. Burch." *Arctic Anthropology* 49(2): 72–93.

Mason, Owen. 2015. "Arctic Archaeology and Prehistory." In *International Encyclopedia of the Social and Behavioral Sciences, Second edition, volume 1*, edited by James D. Wright, 921–926. Oxford: Elsevier.

Mason, Owen K., and Nancy H. Bigelow. 2008. "The Crucible of Early to Mid-Holocene Climate in Northern Alaska: Does Northern Archaic Represent the People of the Spreading Forest?" *Arctic Anthropology* 45(2): 39–70.

Mason, Owen K., Peter M. Bowers, and David M. Hopkins. 2001. "The Early Holocene Milankovitch Thermal Maximum and Humans: Adverse Conditions for the Denali Complex of Eastern Beringia." *Quaternary Science Reviews* 20: 525–548.

Matmon, Ari, Jason P. Briner, Gary Carver, Paul Bierman, and Robert C. Finkel. 2010. "Moraine Chronosequence of the Donnelly Dome Region, Alaska." *Quaternary Research* 74: 63–72.

Matson, Richard G., and Gary Coupland. 1995. *The Prehistory of the Northwest Coast*. San Diego: Academic Press.

Matson, Richard G., and Martin Magne. 2007. *Athapaskan Migrations: The Archaeology of Eagle Lake, British Columbia*. Tucson: University of Arizona Press.

Matthews, Wendy. 1995. "Micromorphological Characteristics and Interpretation of Occupation Deposits and Microstratigraphic Sequences at Abu Salabikh, Iraq." In *Archaeological Sediments and Soils, Analysis, Interpretation and Management*, edited by Anthony J. Barham and Richard I. Macphail, 41–76. London: Archetype Books.

Matthews, Wendy, C. A. I. French, T. Lawrence, D. F. Cutter, and M. K. Jones. 1997. "Microstratigraphic Traces of Site Formation Processes and Human Activities." *World Archaeology* 29(2): 281–308.

Matthews, Wendy, J. Nicholas Postgate, S. Payne, M. P. Charles, and K. Dobney. 1994. "The Imprint of Living in an Early Mesopotamian City: Questions and Answers." In *Whither Environmental Archaeology?*, edited by R. Luff, and P. Rowley-Cowly, pp. 171–212. Oxbow Monography 38, Oxford.

Matz, Stephan E. 1987. "The Effects of the Mazama Tephra-Falls: A Geoarchaeological Approach." Unpublished M.A. thesis, Interdisciplinary Studies (Departments of Anthropology, Geology, and Soil Science), Oregon State University.

Mauss, Marcel. [1925] 2016. *The Gift*. Translated by Jane I. Guyer. Chicago: Hau Books.

Maxwell, J. Barrie, and Leonard A. Barrie. 1989. "Atmospheric and Climatic Change in the Arctic and Antarctic." *Ambio*, 18(1): 42–49.

Mayor, Adrienne. 2005. *Fossil Legends of the First Americans*. Princeton, New Jersey: Princeton University Press.

Mayor, Adrienne. 2007. "Place Names Describing Fossils in Oral Traditions." In *Myth and Geology*, edited by L. Piccardi and W. B. Masse, 245–261. The Geological Society of London, No. 273. London.

McClellan, Catherine. 1975. *My Old People Say: An Ethnographic Survey of Southern Yukon Territory, Part 1*. Mercury Series, Canadian Ethnology Service Paper 137 (Canadian Museum of Civilization). Ottawa: University of Ottawa Press/National Museums of Canada.

McClellan, Catherine. 1981. "Tutchone." In *Subarctic, Handbook of North American Indians. vol. 6*, edited by J. Helm, 493–513. W. Washington, D.C.: Smithsonian Institution.

McFadyen Clark, Annette. 1996. *Who Lived in This House? A Study of Koyukuk River Semisubterranean Houses*. Mercury Series, Hull: University of Ottawa Press.

McGimsey, Robert G., Donald H. Richter, Gregory D. DuBois, and T. P. Miller. 1990. "A Postulated New Source for the White River Ash, Alaska." In *Geological Studies in Alaska, 1990*, edited by Dwight C. Bradley and A. B. Ford, 212–218. United States Geological Survey, Bulletin 1999, Washington, D.C.

McKennan, Robert. 1959. *The Upper Tanana Indians*. Yale University Publications in Anthropology, Number 55. New Haven.

McKennan, Robert. 1969. "Athapaskan Groupings and Social Organization in Central Alaska." In *Contributions to Anthropology: Band Societies*, edited by David Damas, 93–115. National Museums of Canada Bulletin No. 228. Ottawa.

McKennan, Robert. 1981. "Tanana." In *Handbook of North American Indians: Subarctic, volume 6*, edited by June Helm, pp. 562–576. Washington, D.C.: Smithsonian Institution.

Meitl, Sarah J., Michael R. Yarborough, and Aubrey Morrison. 2015. "2015 Cultural Resources Report for Pogo Mine." Report prepared for the Pogo Gold Mine Project. On file at the State Historic Preservation Office, Anchorage.

Menk, Roland. 1980. "A Synopsis of the Physical Anthropology of the Corded Ware Complex on the Background of the Expansion of the Kurgan Cultures." *Journal of Indo-European Studies* 8: 361–392.

Mercier, François Xavier. 1986. *Recollections of the Youkon, Memories from the Years 1868–1885*. Alaska Historical Commission No. 188. Anchorage: The Alaska Historical Society.

Milek, Karen B. 2012. "Floor Formation Processes and the Interpretation of Site Activity Areas: An Ethnoarchaeological Study of Turf Buildings at Thverá, Northeast Iceland." *Journal of Anthropological Archaeology* 31: 119–137.

Mills, Barbara J. 2017. "Social Network Analysis in Archaeology." *Annual Review of Anthropology* 46: 379–397.

Mills, Barbara J., Matthew A. Peeples, Leslie D. Aragon, Benjamin A. Bellorado, Jeffery J. Clark, Evan Giomi, and Thomas C. Windes. 2018. "Evaluating Chaco Migration Scenarios Using Dynamic Social Network Analysis." *Antiquity* 92(364): 922–939.

Mills, Robin O. 2010. "Preliminary Excavation Report: Uhler Creek Cabin 2005-2 (EAG-00468), June 2010." Report Prepared by Robin Mills, Fairbanks, Alaska, for the Bureau of Land Management, Fairbanks District Office, Fairbanks, Alaska.

Mintz, Sidney W., and Christine M. Du Bois. 2002. "The Anthropology of Food and Eating." *Annual Review of Anthropology* 31: 99–119.

Misarti, Nicole, and Herbert D. G. Maschner. 2015. "The Paleo-Aleut to Neo-Aleut transition revisited." *Journal of Anthropological Archaeology* 37: 67–84.

Mishler, Craig W. 1986. "Report of Investigations 84-14: Born with the River: An Ethnographic History of Alaska's Goodpaster and Big Delta Indians." State of Alaska Department of Natural Resources Division of Geological and Geophysical Surveys. Anchorage.

Mishler, Craig W., and William E. Simeone, eds. 2006. *Tanana and Chandalar: The Alaska Field Journals of Robert A. McKennan.* Fairbanks: University of Alaska Press.

Mitchell, William L. 1982. *The opening of Alaska*, edited by Lyman Woodman. Anchorage: Cook Inlet Historical Society.

Mobley, Charles M. 1982. "The Landmark Gap Trail Site, Tangle Lakes, Alaska: Another Perspective on the Amphitheater Mountain Complex." *Arctic Anthropology* 19(1): 81–102.

Mobley, Charles M. 1988. *Feminism and Anthropology.* Minneapolis: University of Minnesota Press.

Mobley, Charles M. 1991. *The Campus Site: A Prehistoric Camp at Fairbanks, Alaska.* Fairbanks: University of Alaska Press.

Mobley, Charles M. 2008. "Archaeological Excavation of the Twitchell-Anderson Cabin (IDT-269), Takotna, Alaska." Report Prepared by Charles M. Mobley & Associates, Anchorage, Alaska, Under Contract to USKH Inc., Anchorage, Alaska, for the Alaska Department of Transportation and Public Facilities, Anchorage, Alaska.

Moodie, D. Wayne, A. J. W. Catchpoole, and Kerry Abel. 1992. "Northern Athapaskan Oral Traditions and the White River Volcano." *Ethnohistory* 39(2): 148–171.

Moore, Henrietta L. 1986. *Space, Text, and Gender.* Cambridge: Cambridge University Press.

Moore, Patrick. 2019. "Tagish and Tlingit Place Naming Traditions of Southwestern Yukon: Evidence of Language Shift." In *Language and Toponymy in Alaska and Beyond: Papers in Honor of James Kari*, edited by Gary Holton and Thomas F. Thornton, pp. 140–146. Language Documentation and Conservation Special Publication 17. Fairbanks: Alaskan Native Language Center Press.

Morlan, Richard E. 1970. "Toward the Definition of a Prehistoric Athabascan Culture." *Bulletin (Canadian Archaeological Association)* 2: 24–33.

Morlan, Richard E. 1973 *The Later Prehistory of the Middle Porcupine Drainage, Northern Yukon Territory.* Mercury Series: Archaeological Survey of Canada Paper, No, 10. Ottawa: National Museum of Canada.

Moreno-Mayar, J. Víctor, Ben A. Potter, Lasse Vinner, Matthias Steinrücken, Simon Rasmussen, Jonathan Terhorst, John A. Kamm, Anders Albrechtsen, Anna-Sapfo Malaspinas, Martin Sikora, Joshua D. Reuther, Joel D. Irish12, Ripan S. Malhi, Ludovic Orlando, Yun S. Song, Rasmus Nielsen, David J. Meltzer, and Eske Willerslev. 2018. "Terminal Pleistocene Alaskan Genome Reveals First Founding Population of Native Americans." *Nature* 553(7687): 203–207. DOI:10.1038/nature25173.

Mullen, Patrick O. 2012. "An Archaeological Test of the Effects of the White River Ash Eruptions." *Arctic Anthropology* 49(1): 35–44.

Mulliken, Katherine M. 2016. "Holocene Volcanism and Human Occupation in the Middle Susitna, Alaska." Unpublished M.A. thesis, Department of Anthropology, University of Alaska Fairbanks.

Mulliken, Katherine M., Janet R. Schaefer, and Cheryl E. Cameron. 2018. "Geospatial Distribution of Tephra Fall in Alaska: A Geodatabase Compilation of Published Tephra Fall Occurrences from the Pleistocene to the Present." Preliminary Report Prepared by the Alaska Division of Geological and Geophysical Surveys, Fairbanks.

Munsell Color (Firm). 2017. *Munsell Soil Color Charts: With Genuine Munsell Color Chips*. Munsell Color, Grand Rapids.

Nader, Laura. 2018. *Contrarian Anthropology: The Unwritten Rules of Academia*. New York: Berghahn.

Napoleon, Harold. 2009. "Yuuyaraq: The Way of the Human Being." In *The Alaska Native Reader*, edited by Maria Shaa Tlaa Williams, 121–143. London: Duke University Press.

National Park Service (NPS). 1995. "National Register Bulletin: Technical Information on the National Register of Historic Places: Survey, Evaluation, Registration, and Preservation." U.S. Department of the Interior National Park Service Cultural Resources. Washington, D.C.

Neely, Burr J., Patrick T. Hall, and Gerad M. Smith. 2016. "Annual Report of the 2014 Cultural Resource Inventory on Cook Inlet Regional Working Group Lands for the Susitna-Watana Hydroelectric Project, Susitna River, Alaska." Report Prepared for Alaska Energy Authority.

Neiman, Fraser D. 1995. "Stylistic Variation in Evolutionary Perspective: Inferences from Decorative Diversity and Interassemblage Distance in Illinois Woodland Ceramic Assemblages." *American Antiquity* 60, 7–36. DOI:10.2307/282074.

Noguchi, Hiroya, and Shiaki Kondo. 2019. "Hunting Tools and Prestige in Northern Athabascan Culture: Types, Distribution, Usage, and Prestige of Athabascan Daggers." *Polar Science* 21: 85–100.

Nowak, Ronald M. 2003. "Wolf Evolution and Taxonomy." In *Wolves: Behavior, Ecology, and Conservation*, edited by L. David Mech and Luigi Boitani, 239–271. Chicago and London: University of Chicago Press.

O'Brien, Thomas A. 2011. *Gwich'in Athabascan Implements: History, Manufacture, and Usage according to Reverend David Salmon*. Fairbanks: University of Alaska Press.

Odess, Daniel, and Jeffery T. Rasic. 2007. "Toolkit Composition and Assemblage Variability: The Implications of Nogahabara I, Northern Alaska." *American Antiquity* 72: 691–717.

Odling-Smee, F. John, Kevin L. Laland, and Marcus W. Feldman. 2003. *Niche Construction: The Neglected Process in Evolution*. Monographs in Population Biology 37. Princeton, NJ: Princeton University Press.

Odling-Smee, F. John, Kevin L. Laland, and Marcus W. Feldman. 1996. "Niche Construction." *The American Naturalist* 147(4): 641–648.

O'Leary, Matthew, J. David McMahan, and John B. Branson. 2021. "Mulchatna River Archeological Survey, 2000–2007," edited by Jason Rogers. Cultural Resource Report NPS/CRR-2021-2. Report prepared for the National Park Service, Anchorage.

Olson, Wallace M. 1968. "Minto, Alaska: Cultural and Historical Influences on Group Identity." Unpublished M.A. thesis, Department of Anthropology, University of Alaska Fairbanks.

O'Meara, Carolyn, Niclas Burenhult, Mikael Rothstein, and Peter Sercombe. 2020. "Representing Space and Place: Hunter-Gatherer Perspectives." *Hunter Gatherer Research* 4(3): 288–309.

Orth, Donald J. 1971. *Dictionary of Alaska Place Names*. Geological Survey Professional Paper 567. Washington, D.C.: U.S. Government Printing Office.

Osgood, Cornelius. [1937] 1966. *Ethnography of the Tanaina*. Reprint. New Haven, CT: Human Relations Area Files.

Osgood, Cornelius. [1940] 1970. *Ingalik Material Culture*. Yale University Publications in Anthropology, 22. Reprint. New Haven, CT: Human Relations Area Files.

Osgood, Cornelius. 1959. *Ingalik Mental Culture*. Yale University Publications in Anthropology 56. Department of Anthropology, New Haven: Yale University.

Osgood, Cornelius. 1971. *The Han Indians: A Compilation of Ethnographic and Historical Data on the Alaska-Yukon Boundary Area*. Yale University Publications in Anthropology 74. Department of Anthropology. New Haven: Yale University.

Oswald, W. Wyatt, Linda B. Brubaker, Feng Sheng Hu, George W. Kling. 2003. "Holocene Pollen Records from the Central Arctic Foothills, Northern Alaska: Testing the Role of Substrate in the Response of Tundra to Climate Change." *Journal of Ecology*, 91 (6): 1034–1048.

Oswalt, Wendell H. 1976. *An Anthropological Analysis of Food-Getting Technology*. New Jersey: Wiley, Hoboken.

Overpeck, Jonathan T., Konrad Hughen, Douglas Hardy, Raymond Bradley, R. Case, Marianne Douglas, Bruce Finney, K. Gajewski, G. Jacoby, Anne Jennings, Scott Lamoureux, A. Lasca, Glen MacDonald, J. Moore, Mike Retelle, Sheldon Smith, Alex Wolfe, Gregory. Zielinski. 1997. "Arctic Environmental Change of the Last Four Centuries." *Science* 278: 1251–1256.

Patterson, Jodi. 2010. "Landscape Structure and Terrain-Based Hunting Range Models: Exploring Late Prehistoric Land Use in the Nutzotin Mountains, Southcentral Alaska." Unpublished Ph.D. dissertation, Department of Anthropology, University of Alaska Fairbanks.

Paul, David. 1957. *According to Papa*, edited by Audrey Loftus. 1st printing. Fairbanks: St. Matthews Episcopal Guild.

Pearson, Georges A., and W. Roger Powers. 2001. "The Campus Site Re-Excavation: New Efforts to Unravel Its Ancient and Recent Past." *Arctic Anthropology* 38(1): 100–119.

Pedersen, Olaf. 1992. *The Book of Nature*. Notre Dame: The University of Notre Dame Press.

Perry, Richard J. 1980. "The Apachean Transition from the Subarctic to the Southwest." *Plains Anthropologist* 46: 163–193.

Peter, Evon. 2009. "Undermining Our Tribal Governments: The Stripping of Land, Resources, and Rights from Alaska Native Nations." In *The Alaska Native Reader*, edited by Maria Shaa Tlaa Williams, 178–183. London: Duke University Press.

Peterson, Steven M. 1982. "Valdez-Fairbanks Trail Roadhouses." National Architectural and Engineering Record. National Park Service, United States Department of the Interior.

Pettipas, Leo. 1981. "A Consideration of the Possible Effects of the Mt. Mazama Ash-Fall on Early Archaic Migrations into Manitoba." In *University of North Dakota Anthropological Papers, No. 3*, edited by Richard A. Fox, 1–15. Grand Forks: University of North Dakota.

Péwé, Troy L. 1975. *Quaternary Geology of Alaska*. U.S. Geological Survey Professional Paper 835. Washington, D.C.: United States Government Printing Office.

Péwé, Troy L., and George W. Holmes. 1964. "Geology of the Mt. Hayes D-4 Quadrangle, Alaska." U.S. Geological Survey. Miscellaneous Geological Investigations Map I-394. Washington, D.C.: U.S. Government Printing Office.

Péwé, Troy L., and Richard D. Reger. 1983. *Richardson and Glenn Highways, Alaska: Guidebook to Permafrost and Quaternary Geology*. Division of Geological and Geophysical Surveys. Fairbanks: Alaska Department of Natural Resources.

Philipson, Paul E., and Peter Schuster. 2009. *Modeling by Nonlinear Differential Equations: Dissipative and Conservative Processes*. Singapore: World Scientific Publishing Company.

Pilon, Jean-Luc. 1991. "Insights into the Prehistory of the Lower Mackenzie Valley, Anderson Plain Region, Northwest Territories." In *Canadian Archaeological Association Occasional Paper No. 1 "NOGAP Archaeological Project: An Integrated Archaeological Research and Management Approach,"* edited by Jacques Cinq-Mars and Jean-Luc Pilon, pp. 89–112. Canadian Museum of Civilization. Hull, Quebec

Pitts, Roger S. 1972. "The Changing Settlement Patterns and Housing Types of the Upper Tanana Indians." Unpublished M.A. thesis, Department of Anthropology, University of Alaska Fairbanks.

Plaskett, David C. 1977. "The Nenana River Gorge Site: A Late Prehistoric Athapaskan Camp Site in Central Alaska." Unpublished M.A. thesis Department of Anthropology, University of Alaska Fairbanks.

Posth Cosimo, Kathrin Nägele, Heidi Colleran, Frédérique Valentin, Stuart Bedford, Kaitip W. Kami, Richard Shing, Hallie Buckley, Rebecca Kinaston, Mary Walworth, Geoffrey R. Clark, Christian Reepmeyer, James Flexner, Tamara Maric, Johannes Moser, Julia Gresky, Lawrence Kiko, Kathryn J. Robson, Kathryn Auckland, Stephen J. Oppenheimer, Adrian V. S. Hill, Alexander J. Mentzer, Jana Zech, Fiona Petchey, Patrick Roberts, Choongwon Jeong, Russell D. Gray, Johannes Krause, and Adam Powell. 2018. "Language continuity despite population replacement in Remote Oceania." *Nature, Ecology, and Evolution*. 2(4): 731–740.

Potter, Ben A. 1997. "A First Approximation of Ahtna Region Archaeology." Unpublished M.A. thesis, Department of Anthropology, University of Alaska Fairbanks.

Potter, Ben A. 2005. "Site Structure and Organization in Central Alaska." Unpublished Ph.D. dissertation, Department of Anthropology, University of Alaska Fairbanks.

Potter, Ben A. 2008a. "A First Approximation of Holocene Inter-Assemblage Variability in Central Alaska." *Arctic Anthropology* 45(1): 89–113.

Potter, Ben A. 2008b. "Exploratory Models of Intersite Variability in Mid to Late Holocene Central Alaska." *Arctic* 61(4): 407–425.

Potter, Ben A. 2008c. "Radiocarbon Chronology of Central Alaska: Technological Continuity and Economic Change." *Radiocarbon* 50(2): 181–204.

Potter, Ben A. 2010. "Archaeological Patterning in Northeast Asia and Northwest North America: An Examination of the Dene-Yeniseian Hypothesis." In *The Dene-Yeniseian Connection*, edited by James M. Kari and Ben A. Potter 5: 138–167. Fairbanks: Alaska Native Language Center.

Potter, Ben A. 2016. "Holocene Prehistory of the Northwestern Subarctic." In *The Oxford Handbook of the Prehistoric Arctic*, edited by T. Max Friesen and Owen K. Mason, 537–562. New York: Oxford University Press.

Potter, Ben A., Peter M. Bowers, Joshua D. Reuther, and Owen K. Mason. 2007. "Holocene Assemblage Variability in the Tanana Basin: NLUR Archaeological Research, 1994–2004." *Alaska Journal of Anthropology* 5: 1–20.

Potter, Ben A., Charles E. Holmes, and David R. Yesner. 2013. "Technology and Economy among the Earliest Prehistoric Foragers in Interior Eastern Beringia." In *Paleoamerican Odyssey*, edited by Kelly E. Graf, Caroline V. Ketron, and Michael R. Waters, 81–104. Center for the Study of First Americans. College Station: Texas A&M University Press.

Potter, Ben A., Julie A. Esdale, Joshua D. Reuther, Holly J. McKinney, Charles E. Holmes, Caitlin R. Holloway, and Crystal L. Glassburn. 2018. "Archaeological Investigations at Delta River Overlook, central Alaska." Archaeology GIS Laboratory, Report #7. University of Alaska Fairbanks, Fairbanks.

Potter, Ben A., Joel D. Irish, Joshua D. Reuther, Carol Gelvin-Reymiller, and Vance T. Holliday. 2011. "A Terminal Pleistocene Child Cremation and Residential Structure from Eastern Beringia." *Science* 331: 1058-1062. DOI:10.1126/science.1201581.

Potter, Ben A., Joel D. Irish, Joshua D. Reuther, and Holly J. McKinney. 2014. "New Insights into Eastern Beringian Mortuary Behavior: A Terminal Pleistocene Double Infant Burial at Upward Sun River." *Proceedings of the National Academy of Sciences* 111(48): 17060–17065.

Powell, Adam, Stephen Shennan, and Mark G. Thomas. 2009. "Demography, Skill Accumulation, and the Origins of Behavioural Modernity." *Science* 324: 1298–1301. DOI:10.1126/science.1170165.

Powell, Addison M. 1909. *Trailing and Camping in Alaska*. A. New York: Wessels.

Pratt, Kenneth L. 2019. "From This Point . . . the River Changes Its Name Again": Lavrentiy Zagoskin's Contributions to the Study of Alaska Native Place Names." In *Language and Toponymy in Alaska and Beyond: Papers in Honor of James Kari*, edited by Gary Holton and Thomas F. Thornton, 9–38. Language Documentation and Conservation Special Publication 17. Fairbanks: Alaskan Native Language Center press.

Pratt, Kenneth L., ed. 2009. *Chasing the Dark: Perspectives on Place, History and Alaska Native Land Claims*. Anchorage: United States Department of the Interior,

Bureau of Indian Affairs, Alaska Region, Division of Environmental and Cultural Resources Management, ANCSA Office.

Proue, Molly, Hayley E. Brown, Sarah McGowan, and Andrew Higgs. 2013. "2011 and 2012 Cultural Resources Survey for the Tower Hill Mines Livengood Tieline Project." Report prepared for Tower Hill Mines, by Northern Land Use Research, Inc., Fairbanks.

Proue, Molly, Andrew Higgs, Hayley E. Brown, and Sarah McGowan. 2014. "2012 Cultural Resources Survey Report for the Tower Hill Mines Livengood Project." Report prepared for Tower Hill Mines, by Northern Land Use Research, Inc., Fairbanks.

Raboff, Adeline Peter. 2001. *Inuksuk: Northern Koyukon, Gwich'in, and Lower Tanana, 1800–1901*. Fairbanks, Alaska: Alaska Native Knowledge Network.

Raboff, Adeline Peter. 2020. "Gwich'in Shamanic and Sexual Vocabulary." Paper presented at the 47th annual meeting of the Alaska Anthropological Association, Fairbanks, Alaska, February 26–29, 2020.

Rainey, Froelich G. 1939a. "Archaeology in Central Alaska." *Anthropological Papers of the American Museum of Natural History* XXXVI(IV): 351–405.

Rainey, Froelich G. 1939b. "Diary-Upper Tanana." Froelich Rainey Collection, Box 1, Folder 25. Alaska and Polar Regions Department, Rasmuson Library Archives, University of Alaska Fairbanks, Fairbanks.

Rainey, Froelich G. 1940. "Archaeological Investigation in Central Alaska." *American Antiquity* 5(4): 299–308.

Rapp, George (Rip), and Christopher L. Hill. 2006. *Geoarchaeology: The Earth-Science Approach to Archaeological Interpretation*. New Haven: Yale University Press.

Rappaport, Roy A. 1971. "The Flow of Energy in an Agricultural Society." *Scientific American* 224(3): 117–132.

Rasic, Jeffery T. and Natalia S. Slobodina. 2008. "Weapon Systems and Assemblage Variability during the Northern Archaic Period in Northern Alaska." *Arctic Anthropology* 45(1): 71–88.

Reckord, Holly. 1983. "Where Raven Stood: Cultural Resources of the Ahtna Region." *Occasional Paper No. 35*. Fairbanks: Cooperative Park Studies Unit.

Reger, Douglas R. 1998. "Archaeology of the Northern Kenai Peninsula and Upper Cook Inlet." *Arctic Anthropology*, 35(1): 160–171.

Reger, Douglas, and Alan Boraas. 1996. "An Overview of the Radiocarbon Chronology in Cook Inlet." In *Adventures through Time: Readings in the Anthropology of Cook Inlet, Alaska*, edited by Nancy Yaw Davis and William E. Davis, 155–171. Anchorage: Cook Inlet Historical Society.

Reger, Douglas R., Al G. Sturmann, and James E. Begét. 1993. "Dating Holocene Moraines of Black Rapids Glacier, Delta River Valley, Central Alaska Range." In *Short Notes on Alaskan Geology 1993*, edited by Diana N. Solie and Fran Tannian, Professional Report 113: 51–59. Fairbanks: State of Alaska Division of Geological and Geophysical Surveys.

Reger, Richard D., and Troy L. Péwé. 2002. "Geologic Map of the Bog Delta A-4 Quadrangle, Alaska." Report of Investigations 2002-2. Alaska Division of Geological and Geophysical Surveys, Fairbanks.

Reger, Richard D., De Anne S. P. Stevens, and Diana N. Solie. 2008. "Surficial Geology of the Alaska Highway Corridor, Delta Junction to Dot Lake, Alaska." Alaska Division of Geological and Geophysical Surveys, State of Alaska, Department of Natural Resources.

Reiches, Meredith W., Peter T. Ellison, Susan F. Lipson, Katherine C. Sharrock, Eliza Gardiner, and Laura G. Duncan. 2009. "Pooled Energy Budget and Human Life History." *American Journal of Human Biology* 21(4): 421–429.

Reimer, Paula J., William E. N. Austin, Edouard Bard, Alex Bayliss, Paul G. Blackwell, Christopher Bronk Ramsey, Martin Butzin, Hai Cheng, R. Lawrence Edwards, Michael Friedrich, Pieter M. Grootes, Thomas P. Guilderson, Irka Hajdas, Timothy J. Heaton, Alan G. Hogg, Konrad A. Hughen, Bernd Kromer, Sturt W. Manning, Raimund Muscheler, Jonathan G. Palmer, Charlotte Pearson, Johannes van der Plicht, Ron W. Reimer, David A. Richards, E. Marian Scott, John R. Southon, Christian S. M. Turney, Lukas Wacker, Florian Adolphi, Ulf Büntgen, Manuela Capano, Simon M. Fahrni, Alexandra Fogtmann-Schulz, Ronny Friedrich, Peter Köhler, Sabrina Kudsk, Fusa Miyake, Jesper Olsen, Frederick Reinig, Minoru Sakamoto, Adam Sookdeo, and Sahra Talamo. 2020. "The IntCal20 Northern Hemisphere Radiocarbon Age Calibration Curve (0–55 cal KBP)." *Radiocarbon* 1–33. DOI:10.1017/RD.C..2020.41.

Reuther, Joshua D. 2013. "Late Glacial and Early Holocene Geoarchaeology and Terrestrial Paleoecology in the Lowlands of the Middle Tanana Valley, Subarctic Alaska." Unpublished Ph.D. dissertation, University of Arizona.

Reuther, Joshua D., Ben A. Potter, Sam A. Coffman, Holly J. Smith, and Nancy Bigelow. 2019. "Revisiting the Timing of the Northern Lobe of the White River Ash Volcanic Event in Eastern Alaska and Western Yukon." *Radiocarbon.* DOI:10.1017/RD.C..2019.110.

Reuther, Joshua D., Ben A. Potter, Charles E. Holmes, James K. Feathers, François B Lanoë, and Jennifer Kielhofer. 2016. "The Rosa-Keystone Dunes Field: The Geoarchaeology and Paleoecology of a Late Quaternary Stabilized Dune Field in Eastern Beringia." *The Holocene* 26(12): 1939–1953.

Richardson, Don. 1974. *Peace Child.* Gospel Light, Ventura, California.

Richardson, Pamela. 2010. "Agricultural Ethics, Neurotic Natures, and Emotional Encounters: An Application of Actor-Network Theory." *Ethics, Place & Environment,* 7: 3, 195–201.

Richerson, Peter J., and Robert Boyd. 2008. "Not by Genes Alone: How Culture Transformed Human Evolution." *Journal of Bioeconomics* 10(2): 193–198.

Richter, Donald H., Cindi C. Pretter, Keith A. Labay, and Nora B. Shew. 2006. "Geologic Map of the Wrangell-Saint Elias National Park and Preserve, Alaska." Scientific Investigations Map 2877. U.S. Geological Survey, Alexandria, VA.

Riehle, James R. 1985. "A Reconnaissance of the Major Holocene Tephra Deposits in the Upper Cook Inlet Region, Alaska." *Journal of Volcanology and Geothermal Research* 26: 37–74.

Riehle, James R., Peter M. Bowers, and Thomas A. Ager. 1990. "The Hayes Tephra Deposits, and Upper Holocene Marker Horizon in South-Central Alaska." *Quaternary Research* 33(3): 276–290.

Riley, Wayne J. 2012. "Health Disparities: Gaps in Access, Quality, and Affordability of Medical Care." *Transactions of the American Clinical and Climatological Association* 123: 167–174.

Ritter, John, and Daniel Johnson. 1978. *Han Noun Dictionary*. Whitehorse: Yukon Native Language Center.

Rogers, Monty. 2015. "The Role of Quartz in the Lithic Technology of the Western Upper Cook Inlet Ancestral Dena'ina." Unpublished M.A. thesis, Department of Anthropology, University of Alaska Anchorage.

Rogers, Monty, and Daniel Stone. 2010. "Looking beyond Dena'ina House Pits and Cache Pits: There Is Something Else Out There." Paper Presented at the 2010 Alaska Anthropological Association Annual Meeting, Anchorage, Alaska.

Sanger, David, and M. A. P. Renouf, eds. 2006. *The Archaic of the Far Northeast*. Orono: The University of Maine Press.

Sapir, Edward. 1916. *Time Perspective in Aboriginal American Culture: A Study in Method*. Canada Department of Mines, Geological Survey, Memoir 90. Anthropological Series, No. 13.

Sarche, Michelle, and Paul Spicer. 2008. "Poverty and Health Disparities for American Indian and Alaska Native Children: Current Knowledge and Future Prospects." *Annals of the New York Academy of Sciences*. 1136: 126–136. DOI:10.1196/annals.1425.017.

Schiffer, Michael B. 1987. *Formation Processes of the Archaeological Record*. Albuquerque: University of New Mexico Press.

Schneider, William S. 2018. *The Tanana Chiefs: Native Rights and Western Law*. Fairbanks: University of Alaska Press.

Schwatka, Frederick. 1893. *A Summer in Alaska*. St. Louis: J. W. Henry.

Shaepe, David M. 1998. "Revisiting the Maurer Site: Household Archaeology in the Upper Fraser Valley." *The Midden* 30(4): 6–11.

Shahack-Gross, Ruth, Fiona Marshall, Kathleen Ryan, and Steve Wiener. 2004. "Reconstruction of Spatial Organization in Abandoned Maasi Settlements: Implications for Site Structure in the Pastoral Neolithic of East Africa." *Journal of Archaeological Science* 31: 1395–1411.

Shennan, Stephen. 2001. "Demography and Cultural Innovation: A Model and Its Implications for the Emergence of Modern Human Culture." *Cambridge Archaeological Journal* 11: 5–16.

Sherratt, Andrew, and Susan Sherratt. 1997. "The Archaeology of Indo-European: An Alternative View." *Antiquity* 62: 584–595.

Sheppard, William L. 2001. "Archaeological Testing and Survey in the Upper Tanana Region, Alaska, 2000." Report Submitted to the U.S. Fish and Wildlife Service, Sheppard Research, Portland.

Sheppard, William L., Amy F. Steffian, David P. Staley, and Nancy H. Bigelow. 1991. "Late Holocene Occupations at the Terrace Site, Tok, Alaska." Report Prepared for US Air Force, Electronic Systems Division. Arctic Environmental Information and Data Center, University of Alaska, Anchorage, Anchorage.

Shinkwin, Anne D. 1974. "Dakah De'nin's Village, an Early Historic Atna Site." *Arctic Anthropology* 9: 54–64.

Shinkwin, Anne D. 1979. "Dakah De'nin's Village and the Dixthada Site: A Contribution to Northern Athapaskan Prehistory." National Museum of Man. Mercury Series, Archaeological Survey of Canada Paper No. 91. Ottawa: National Museum of Canada.

Shinkwin, Anne, Jean Aigner, and Elizabeth Andrews. 1980. "Land Use Patterns in the Upper Tanana Valley, Alaska." *Anthropological Papers of the University of Alaska* 19(2): 43–53.

Sicard, Karri R., Travis J. Naibert, Trent D. Hubbard, Evan Twelker, Alicja Wypych, Melanie B. Werdon, Amanda L. Willingham, Robert J. Gillis, Lauren L. Lande, and Rainer J. Newberry. 2017. "Explanation of Map Units: Geologic Map of the Tok River Area, Tanacross A-5 and A-6 Quadrangles, Eastern Alaska Range, Alaska (1: 63,360 scale)." Preliminary Interpretive Report 2017-3. State of Alaska Department of Natural Resources, Division of Geological and Geophysical Surveys, Anchorage.

Simeone, William E. 1995. *Rifles, Blankets, and Beads: Identity, History, and the Northern Athapaskan Potlatch.* Norman: University of Oklahoma Press.

Simeone, William E. 1998. "The Northern Athabaskan Potlatch in East-Central Alaska, 1900–1930." *Arctic Anthropology* 35(2): 113–125.

Simeone, William E. 2007a. "The Arrival: Native and Missionary Relations on the Upper Tanana River, 1915." *Alaska Journal of Anthropology* 5(1): 83–94.

Simeone, William E. 2007b. "Niche Construction and the Behavioral Context of Plant and Animal Domestication." *Evolutionary Anthropology* 16: 188–199.

Simeone, William E. 2009. "Nataełde, "Roasted Salmon Place": A Summary History of Batzulnetas." In *Chasing the Dark: Perspectives on Place, History and Alaska Native Land Claims,* edited by Kenneth L. Pratt, 88–97. Anchorage: United States Department of the Interior, Bureau of Indian Affairs, Alaska Region, Division of Environmental and Cultural Resources Management, ANCSA Office.

Simeone, William E. 2011. "General Patterns of Niche Construction and the Management of 'Wild' Plant and Animal Resources by Small-Scale Pre-Industrial Societies." *Philosophical Transactions of the Royal Society B: Biological Sciences,* 366(1566): 836–848.

Simeone, William E. 2018. *Ahtna: The People and Their History.* Glennallen, AK: Ahtna, Inc.

Simeone, William E., Wilson Justin, Michelle Anderson, and Kathryn Martin. 2019. "The Ahtna Homeland." *Alaska Journal of Anthropology* 17(1&2): 102–119.

Skoog, Ronald O. 1968. "Ecology of the Caribou (Rangifer tarandus granti) in Alaska." Ph.D. dissertation, University of California.

Smith, Bruce D. 2007a. "The Ultimate Ecosystem Engineers." *Science* 315: 1797–1798.

Smith, Bruce D. 2007b. "Niche Construction and the Behavioral Context of Plant and Animal Domestication." *Evolutionary Anthropology* 16: 188–199.

Smith, Bruce D. 2011. "General patterns of niche construction and the management of 'wild' plant and animal resources by small-scale pre-industrial societies." *Philosophical Transactions of the Royal Society B: Biological Sciences,* 366(1566): 836–848.

Smith, Eric Alden. 1981. "The Application of Optimal Foraging Theory to the Analysis of Hunter-Gatherer Group Size." In *Hunter-Gatherer Foraging Strategies*, edited by Bruce Winterhalder and Eric Smith, 35–65. Chicago: University Press.

Smith, Gerad M. 2012. "Highland Hunters: Prehistoric Resource Use in the Yukon-Tanana Uplands." Unpublished M.A. thesis, Department of Anthropology, University of Alaska Fairbanks.

Smith, Gerad M. 2019. "Geoarchaeology of Glacial Lakes Susitna and Atna." *Alaska Journal of Anthropology* 17(1&2): 6–27. 2020a. "Ethnoarchaeology of the Middle Tanana Valley, Alaska." Ph.D. Dissertation, Department of Anthropology, University of Alaska Fairbanks.

Smith, Gerad M. 2020a. "Ethnoarchaeology of the Middle Tanana Valley, Alaska." Unpublished Ph.D. dissertation, Department of Anthropology, University of Alaska Fairbanks.

Smith, Gerad M., Eleanor M. Bishop, and Margan A. Grover. 2020. "Prehistoric Settlement Patterns and the Role of Caribou (Rangifer tarandus) in the Region of the Western Chugach Mountains, Elmendorf Moraine, and Anchorage Lowlands." *Alaska Journal of Anthropology* 18(2): 62–73.

Smith, Gerad M., and Evelynn Combs. 2020. "Experimental Approaches to Understanding Traditional Dene Copper Production." Paper presented at the 47th meeting of the Alaska Anthropological Association, Fairbanks, Alaska.

Smith, Gerad M., Ted Parsons, Ryan P. Harrod, Charles E. Holmes, Joshua D. Reuther, and Ben A. Potter. 2019. "A Track in the Tanana: Forensic Analysis of a Late Holocene Footprint from Central Alaska." *Journal of Archaeological Science: Reports.* 24: 900–912. DOI:10.1016/j.jasrep.2019.03.016.

Smith, Holly. 2020b. "Human and Ecological Responses to the Northern White River Ash Eruption." Unpublished M.A. thesis, Department of Anthropology, University of Alaska Fairbanks.

Smith, Michael E. 2009. "V. Gordon Childe and the Urban Revolution: A Historical Perspective on a Revolution in Urban Studies." *Town Planning Review* 80: 2–29.

Solka, Paul Jr. 1994. *The Lost Goldmine of the Upper Tanana.* Fairbanks: Commercial Printing Co.

Speakman, Robert J., Charles E. Holmes, and Michael D. Glascock. 2007. "Source Determination of Obsidian Artifacts from Swan Point (XBD-156), Alaska." *Current Research in the Pleistocene* 24: 143–145.

Spencer, Robert F. 1959. *The North Alaska Eskimo. A Study in Ecology and Society.* Bureau of American Ethnology Bulletin, 171. Washington, D.C.: Smithsonian Institution, US Government Printing Office.

Stanish, Charles H. 1989. "Household Archaeology: Testing Models of Zonal Complementarity in the South-Central Andes." *American Anthropologist* 91(1): 7–24.

Stebing, Holly Miowak. 2009. "Rewriting the History of Racial Segregation in Alaska." Undergraduate Honors Thesis. Stanford University.

Stephenson, Robert O., S. Craig Gerlach, R. Dale Guthrie, C. Richard Harington, Robin O. Mills, and Gregory Hare. 2001. "Wood Bison in Late Holocene Alaska and Adjacent Canada: Paleontological, Archaeological, and Historical Records." In *People and Wildlife in Northern North American: Essays in Honor of R. Dale*

Guthrie, edited by S. Craig Gerlach and Maribeth S. Murray, 125–159. Oxford: Archaeopress.

Sterelny, Kim. 2007. "Social Intelligence, Human Intelligence, and Niche Construction." *Philosophical Transactions of the Royal Society B*. 362: 719–730.

Steward, Julian. 1942. "The Direct Historical Approach to Archaeology." *American Antiquity* 7(4): 337–343.

Steward, Julian. 1977. "The Direct Historical Approach to Archaeology." In *Evolution and Ecology*, by Julian Steward, edited by Jane C. S. Steward and Robert F. Murphy, 201–207. Urbana: University of Illinois Press.

Stiner, Mary C., Steven L. Kuhn, Stephen Weiner, and Ofer Bar-Yosef. 1995. "Differential Burning, Recrystallization, and Fragmentation of Archaeological Bone." *Journal of Archaeological Science* 22: 223–237.

Street, Steven R. 1995. "Report of Investigation for Whitefish Lake Camp, Ahtna Inc., BLM AA-11127B." Report prepared by the Bureau of Indian Affairs, ANCSA Office, Anchorage, AK.

Strong, B. Stephen. 1976. "Historical Sequence of the Patterns of Production of the Ahtna Athabascan Indians of the Upper Copper Valley, Alaska: The Development of Capitalism in Alaska." Ph.D. dissertation in Anthropology, McGill University.

Stubben, Jerry D. 2000. "The Indigenous Influence Theory of American Democracy." *Social Science Quarterly*, 81(3): 716–731.

Sulas, Frederica, and Marco Madella. 2012. "Archaeology at the Micro-Scale: Micromorphology and Phytoliths at a Swahili Stonetown." *Journal of Archaeological and Anthropological Science*. DOI:10.1007/s12520-012-0090-7.

Surovell, Todd A. 2003. "The Behavioral Ecology of Folsom Lithic Technology." Unpublished Ph.D. dissertation, Dept. of Anthropology, University of Arizona.

Surovell, Todd A. 2009. *Toward a Behavioral Ecology of Lithic Technology: Cases from Paleoindian Archaeology*. Tucson: University of Arizona Press.

Suttles, Wayne, ed. 1990. *Handbook of North American Indians, Vol. 7: Northwest Coast*. Washington, D.C.: Smithsonian Institution.

Sydney, Angela. 1980. *Place Names of the Tagish Region, Southern Yukon*. Whitehorse: Yukon Native Language Center.

Tanana Chiefs Conference (TCC). 2017. *Legacy of Our Elders, Volume 2*. Fairbanks, Alaska: Tanana Chiefs Conference.

Tanana Chiefs Conference (TCC). 2018. *Legacy of Our Elders, Volume 5*. Fairbanks, Alaska: Tanana Chiefs Conference.

Tanana Chiefs Conference (TCC). n.d. "Our History." Retrieved from https://www.tananachiefs.org/about/our-history/. Accessed January 2021.

Tedor, Randolph M. and Charles E. Holmes. 2011. "The Hollembaek Hill Site (XBD-376): A First Loo,k at Another Stratified Site in the Tanana Valley, Alaska." Paper presented at Session: Late Pleistocene/Early Holocene Archaeology in Northwest North America, 38th annual Alaska Anthropology Association meeting, Fairbanks, Alaska.

Ten Brink, Norman W. 1983. "Glaciation of the Northern Alaska Range." In *Glaciation in Alaska, Extended Abstracts from a Workshop*. Alaska Quaternary Center Occasional Paper, 2, edited by Robert M. Thorson and Thomas D. Hamilton, 82–91. Fairbanks: Alaska Quaternary Center.

Thaler, Richard H. 2015. *Misbehaving: The Making of Behavioral Economics.* New York: W. W. Norton and Co..

Thomas, Christian Daniel, P. Gregory Hare, Joshua D. Reuther, Jason S. Rogers, H. Kory Cooper, and E. James Dixon. 2020. "Yukon First Nation use of Copper for End-Blades on Hunting Arrows." *Journal of Glacial Archaeology* 3.2: 109–131. DOI:10.1558/jga.40685.

Thomas, Kenny. 2005. *Crow Is My Boss: Taatsǫǫ' Shaa K'exalthet the Oral History of a Tanacross Athabascan Elder,* edited by Craig Mishler. Norman: University of Oklahoma Press.

Thomas, Tay. 1967. *Cry in the Wilderness: Hear Ye the Voice of the Lord.* Anchorage: Alaska Council of Churches, 1967.

Thompson, Chad. 1990. *K'etetaalkkaanee/The One Who Paddled among the People and Animals: An Analytical Companion Volume.* Fairbanks: Yukon Koyukuk School District and the Alaska Native Language Center.

Thompson, Lenore. 2016. "Copper Characterisation Analysis." Draft report prepared by Lenore Thompson, the Department of Archaeology, University of Sheffield.

Thornton, Thomas F. 2008. *Being and Place among the Tlingit.* Seattle: University of Washington Press.

Thornton, Thomas F., Douglas Duer, and Bert Adams. 2019. "Raven's Work in Tlingit Ethno-geography." In *Language and Toponymy in Alaska and Beyond: Papers in Honor of James Kari,* edited by Gary Holton and Thomas F. Thornton, 39–55. Language Documentation and Conservation Special Publication 17. Fairbanks: Alaskan Native Language Center press.

Tilley, Christopher. 1994. *A Phenomenology of Landscape.* Bridgend, United Kingdom: WBC Bookbinders.

Tirol, Jean. 2002. "Rational Iirrationality: Some Economics of Self-Management." *European Economic Review* 46(4–5): 633–655.

Tolton, Gordon E. 2014. *Healy's West: The Life and Times of John J. Healy.* Missoula: Mountain Press.

Tom, Gertie. 1987. *Èkeyi Gyò Cho Chú, My Country, Big Salmon River: Place Names of the Big Salmon River Region, Yukon Territory.* Whitehorse: Yukon Native Language Center.

Townsend, Joan B. 1981. "Tanaina." In *Handbook of North American Indians, Vol. 6: Subarctic,* edited by June Helm, 623–640. Washington, D.C.: Smithsonian Institution.

Townsend, Joan B. 1983. "Firearms against Native Arms: A Study in Comparative Efficiencies with an Alaskan Example." *Arctic Anthropology* 20(2): 1–33.

Tremayne, Andrew H. 2018. "A Survey of Human Migration in Alaska's National Parks through Time." *Series: Alaska Park Science* 17(1). https://www.nps.gov/articles/aps-17-1-2.htm. January 30, 2020.

Tremayne, Andrew H., and Bruce Winterhalder. 2017. "Large Mammal Biomass Predicts the Changing Distribution of Hunter-Gatherer Settlements in Mid-Late Holocene Alaska." *Journal of Anthropological Archaeology* 45: 81–97.

Trigger, Bruce G. 2009. *A History of Archaeological Thought, Second Edition.* Cambridge: Cambridge University Press.

Tringham, Ruth. 1990. "Conclusion: Selevac in the Wider Context of European Prehistory." In *Selevac: a Neolithic Village in Yugoslavia*, edited by Ruth Tringham and D. Krstic, pp. 567–616. Monumenta Archaeologica 15. Los Angeles: University of California Los Angeles Institute of Archaeology Press.

Tringham, Ruth. 2012. "Households through a Digital Lens." In *New Perspectives on Household Archaeology*, edited by Bradley J. Parker and Catherine P. Foster, 81–122. Winona Lake, Indiana: Eisenbrauns.

Tucker, Bram, and Lisa Rende Taylor. 2007. "The Human Behavioral Ecology of Contemporary World Issues: Applications to Public Policy and International Development." *Human Nature* 18(3): 181–189.

Tuhiwai Smith, Linda. 2012. *Decolonizing Methodologies: Research and Indigenous Peoples, Second Edition*. London: Zed Books.

Turck, Thomas J., and Diane L. Lehman Turck. 1992. "Trading Posts along the Yukon River: Noochuloghoyet Trading Post in Historical Context." *Arctic* 45(1): 51–61.

Turner, Billie L., and Jeremy A. Sabloff. 2012. "Classic Maya Collapse in the Central Lowlands." *Proceedings of the National Academy of Sciences* 109(35): 13908–13914.

Tweiten, Carl O. 1990. *Alaska, Goodpaster, and the Big Delta Region*. Puyallup, WA: Valley Press.

United States Army Corps of Engineers (USACE). 2004. "Chemical Data Report: Herbicide Residue Survey, Haines-Fairbanks Pipeline, Alaska." Materials Section, Engineering Services Branch. Alaska District, Elmendorf AFB.

United States Geological Survey (USGS). 2015. "Coordinated Effort between the United States Department of Agriculture-Natural Resources Conservation Service (USDA-NRCS), the United States Geological Survey (USGS), and the Environmental Protection Agency (EPA)." The Watershed Boundary Dataset (WBD) was created from a variety of sources from each state and aggregated into a standard national layer for use in strategic planning and accountability. Watershed Boundary Dataset for {county, state, or HUC#}, State [Online WWW]. Available URL: "http: //datagateway.nrcs.usda.gov" [Accessed April 28, 2015].

University of Alaska Museum of the North (UAMN). n.d. "Artifact of the Month: Moose Creek Bluff Pictographs." UA Museum of the Month Archaeology. https://uamnarchaeology.tumblr.com/post/154181493943/artifact-of-the-month-moose-creek-bluff/amp. Accessed July 1, 2020.

Urban, Thomas M., Jeffrey Rasic, Ian Buvit, Robert W. Jacob, Jillian Richie, Steven Hackenberger, Sydney Hanson, William Ritz, Eric Wakeland, and Sturt W. Manning. 2016. "Geophysical Investigation of a Middle Holocene Archaeological Site along the Yukon River, Alaska." *The Leading Edge*, 345–349.

Vajda, Edward. 2018. "Dene-Yeniseian, Progress, and Unanswered Questions." *Diachronica* 35: 2: 270–295.

Vajda, Edward. 2019. "Overview of the Dene-Yeniseian Linguistic Hypothesis." Supplementary Information, Section 13, *Nature* 570: 236–240.

VanderHoek, Richard, James E. Dixon, Nicholas L. Jarman, and Randolph M. Tedor. 2012. "Ice Patch Archaeology in Alaska: 2000–10." *Arctic* 65(Supplement 1): 153–164. DOI.10.14430/arctic4190.

Van Stone, James W. 1974. *Athapaskan Adaptations: Hunters and Fishermen of the Subarctic Forests*. Chicago: Adline Publishing Co.

Van Stone, James W. 1984. "Mainland Southwest Alaska Eskimo." In *Handbook of North American Indians, Vol. 5: Arctic*, edited by David Damas, 224–242. Washington, D.C.: Smithsonian Institution.

Vitt, Ramone B. 1971. "Hunting Practices of the Upper Tanana Athapaskans." Unpublished M.A. thesis, Department of Anthropology, University of Alaska Fairbanks.

Waldrop, M. Mitchell. 1992. *Complexity: The Emerging Science at the Edge of Order and Chaos*. New York: Simon and Schuster.

Wallace, Kristi L., Michelle L. Coombs, Leslie A. Hayden, and Christopher F. Waythomas. 2014. "Significance of a Near-Source Tephra-Stratigraphic Sequence to the Eruptive History of Hayes Volcano, Southcentral Alaska." US Geological Survey Scientific Investigations Report 2014-5133.

Wallis, Velma. 2004. *Two Old Women: An Alaska Legend of Betrayal, Courage and Survival*. Kenmore, Washington: Epicenter Press.

Weiner, Stephen. 2010. *Microarchaeology: Beyond the Visible Archaeological Record*. Cambridge: Cambridge University Press.

Weiss, Elizabeth, and James W. Springer. 2020. *Repatriation and Erasure of the Past*. Gainsville, Florida: University of Florida Press.

West, Charles E. 1978. "Archaeology of the Birches Site, Lake Minchumina, Alaska." Unpublished M.A. thesis, Department of Anthropology, University of Alaska Fairbanks.

West, Frederick H., Brian S. Robinson, and Mary Lou Curran. 1996a. "Phipps Site." In *American Beginnings: The Prehistory and Paleoecology of Beringia*, edited by Frederick H. West, 381–386. Chicago: University of Chicago Press.

West, Frederick H., Brian S. Robinson, and R. Greg Dixon. 1996b. "Sparks Point." In *American Beginnings: The Prehistory and Paleoecology of Beringia*, edited by Frederick H. West, 394–398. Chicago: University of Chicago Press.

West, Frederick H., Brian S. Robinson, and Constance F. West. 1996c. "Whitmore Ridge." In *American Beginnings: The Prehistory and Paleoecology of Beringia*, edited by Frederick H. West, 386–394. Chicago: University of Chicago Press.

West, K. D., and J. D. Donaldson. 2000. "Evidence for Winter Eruption of the White River Ash (Eastern Lobe), Yukon Territory, Canada." GeoCanada 200—The Millennium Geoscience Summit, Conference CD.

Whitehead, Hal, and Patricia L. Hope. 1991. "Sperm Whalers off the Galápagos Islands and in the Western North Pacific, 1830–1850: Ideal-Free Whalers?" *Ethology and Sociobiology* 12: 147–161.

Whittle, Alasdair. 1996. *Europe in the Neolithic: The Creation of New Worlds*. Cambridge: Cambridge University Press.

Wiessner, Polly. 1982. "Risk, Reciprocity and Social Influences on !Kung San Economics." In *Politics and History in Band Societies*, edited by E. Leacock and R. Lee, 61–84. Cambridge: Cambridge University.

Wiles, Gregory C., David J. Barclay, and Nicolás E. Young. 2010. "A Review of Lichenometric Dating of Glacial Moraines in Alaska." *Geographic Annals*. 92A(1): 101–109.

Wiles, Gregory C., Rosanne D. D'Arrigo, Ricardo Villalba, Parker E. Calkin, and David J. Barclay. 2004. "Century-Scale Solar Variability and Alaskan Temperature Change over the Past Millennium." *Geophysical Research Letters* 31(L15203): 1–4.

Wilk, Richard R., and William L. Rathje. 1982. "Household Archaeology." *American Behavioral Scientist* 25(6): 617–640.

Willems, Emilio. 1970. "Peasantry and City: Cultural Persistence and Change in Historical Perspective, a European Case." *American Anthropologist* 72(3): 528–544.

Willey, Gordon R., and Phillip Phillips. 1958. *Method and Theory in American Archaeology.* Chicago: University of Chicago Press.

Williams, Maria. 2009. "The Comity Agreement: Missionization of Alaska Native People." In *The Alaska Native Reader,* edited by Maria Shaa Tlaa Williams, 151–162. London: Duke University Press.

Wilson, Aaron K. 2007. "Mid-Holocene Occupation History and Activities at Agiak Lake: Two Northern Archaic Settlements in the Central Brooks Range, Alaska." Unpublished M.A. thesis, Department of Anthropology, University of Alaska Anchorage.

Wilson, Aaron K., and Jeffrey T. Rasic. 2008. "Northern Archaic Settlement and Subsistence Patterns at Agiak Lake, Brooks Range, Alaska." *Arctic Anthropology* 45(2): 128–145.

Wilson, Aaron K., and Natalia S. Slobodina. 2007. "Two Northern Archaic Tent Ring Settlements at Agiak Lake, Central Brooks Range, Alaska." *Alaska Journal of Anthropology* 5(1): 43–58.

Wilson, Frederic H., James H. Dover, Dwight C. Bradley, Florence R. Weber, Thomas K. Bundtzen, and Peter J. Haeussler. 1998. *Geologic Map of Central (Interior) Alaska Northeastern Region.* Open-File Report 98-133 Part A, Sheet 1 of 3. Produced in cooperation with the Alaska Divisions of Oil and Gas and Geological and Geophysical Surveys, Fairbanks.

Winterhalder, Bruce, and Eric Alden Smith, eds. 1981. *Hunter-Gatherer Foraging Strategies.* Chicago: University Press.

Woodman, Lyman L., ed. 1984. *Lieutenant Castner's Alaska Exploration, 1898: A Journey of Hardship and Suffering.* Anchorage: Cook Inlet Historical Society.

Wooller, Matthew J., Joshua Kurek, Benjamin V. Gaglioti, Les C. Cwynar, Nancy Bigelow, Joshua D. Reuther, Carol Gelvin-Reymiller, and John P. Smol. 2012. "An ~11,200 Year Paleolimnological Perspective for Emerging Archaeological Findings at Quartz Lake, Alaska." *Journal of Paleolimnology.* DOI 10.1007/ s10933-012-9610-9.

Workman, William B. 1974. "The Cultural Significance of a Volcanic Ash Which Fell in the Upper Yukon Basin About 1400 Years Ago." In *International Conference on the Prehistory and Paleoecology of Western North American Arctic and Subarctic,* edited by Scott Raymond and Peter Schledermann, pp. 239–261, Archaeological Association, Department of Archaeology, University of Calgary, Calgary.

Workman, William B. 1976. "Archaeological Investigations at GUL-077, A Prehistoric Site Near Gulkana, Alaska." Unpublished report, Alaska Methodist University, Anchorage.

Workman, William B. 1978. *Prehistory of the Aishihik-Kluane area, Southwest Yukon Territory.* National Museum of Man Mercury Series No. 74. Ottawa: Archaeological Survey of Canada.

Workman, William B. 1979. "The Significance of Volcanism in the Prehistory of Subarctic Northwest North America." In *Volcanic Activity and Human Ecology*, edited by P. D. Sheets and Donald K. Grayson, 339–371. New York: Academic Press.

Woster, Cassandra R. 2016. "Beacons of Civilization: The Roadhouses of the Richardson Highway." Unpublished M.A. thesis, Cornell University.

Wright, Arthur R. 1977. *First Medicine Man: The Tale of Yobaghu-Talyonunh.* Anchorage: O. W. Frost.

Wygal, Brian T. 2009. "Prehistoric Colonization of Southcentral Alaska: Human Adaptations in a Post Glacial World." Unpublished Ph.D. dissertation, Department of Anthropology, University of Nevada.

Wygal, Brian T. 2011. "The Microblade/Non-Microblade Dichotomy: Climatic Implications, Toolkit Variability, and the Role of Tiny Tools in Eastern Beringia." In *From the Yenisei to the Yukon: Interpreting Lithic Assemblage Variability in Late Pleistocene/Early Holocene Beringia*, edited by Ted Goebel and Ian Buvit, 234–254. College Station: Texas A&M Press.

Yamagishi, Toshio, Yutaka Horita, Haruto Takagishi, Mizuho Shinada, Shigehito Tanida, and Karen S. Cook. 2009. "The Private Rejection of Unfair Offers and Emotional Commitment." *Proceedings of the National Academy of Sciences* 106(28): 11520–11523.

Yarborough, Michael R. 2003. "Documentation for Determination of Eligibility for XBD-235, XBD-246, and XBD-247." Report prepared for the Pogo Gold Mine Project. On file at the State Historic Preservation Office, Anchorage.

Yesner, David R. 1980. "Caribou Exploitation in Interior Alaska: Paleoecology at Paxson Lake." *Anthropological Papers of the University of Alaska.* 19: 15–31.

Yesner, David R. 1981. "Archaeological Applications of Optimal Foraging Theory: Harvest Strategies of Aleut Hunter-Gatherers." In *Hunter-Gatherer Foraging Strategies* edited by Bruce Winterhalder and Eric Smith, 148–170. Chicago: University Press.

Yesner, David R. 1989. "Moose Hunters of the Boreal Forest? A Re-Examination of Subsistence Patterns in the Western Subarctic." *Arctic* 42: 97–108.

Yoffee, Norman, ed. 2007. *Negotiating the Past in the Past: Identity, Memory, and Landscape in Archaeological Research.* Tucson: The University of Arizona Press.

Younie, Angela. 2015. "Linda's Point and the Village Site: A New Look at the Chindadn Complex and Archaeological Record at Healy Lake, Alaska." Unpublished Ph.D. dissertation, Department of Anthropology, Texas A&M University.

Zazula, Grant D., Elizabeth Hall, P. Gregory Hare, Christian Thomas, Rolf Mathewes, Catherine La Farge, André L. Martel, Peter D. Heintzman, Beth Shapiro. 2017. "A Middle Holocene Steppe Bison and Paleoenvironments from the Versleuce Meadows, Whitehorse, Yukon, Canada." *Canadian Journal of Earth Sciences* 54(11): 1138–1152.

Zdanowicz, Christian M., Gregory. A. Zielinski, and Mark S. Germani. 1999. "Mount Mazama Eruption: Calendrical Age Verified and Atmospheric Impact Assessed." *Geology* 27(7): 621–624.

Zeanah, David W., James A. Carter, Daniel P. Dugas, Robert G. Elston, and Julia E. Hammett. 1995. "An Optimal Foraging Model of Hunter-Gatherer Land Use in the Carson Desert." Report prepared by Intermountain Research for the U.S. Fish and Wildlife Service and the U.S. Department of the Navy.

Zeder, Melinda A. 2016. "Domestication as a Model System for Niche Construction Theory." *Evolutionary Ecology* 30: 325–348.

Znamenski, Andrei A. 2003. *Through Orthodox Eyes: Russian Missionary Narratives of Travels to the Dena'ina and Ahtna, 1850s-1930s*. Historical Translation Series 13. Fairbanks: The University of Alaska Press.

Zurro, Debora, Marco Madella, Ivan Briz, and Assumpció Vila. 2009. "Variability of the Phytolith Record in Fisher-Hunter-Gatherer: An Example from the Yamana Society (Beagle Channel, Tierra del Fuego, Argentina)." *Quaternary International* 193(1–2): 184–191.

Index

Page references for figures are italicized.

Tanana Chiefs Conference 13–17, 20,
22, 65, 69, 187
Tanana:
River, 11, 20, 23, 25, 28, 30, 44, 46,
48, 52, 56, 58, 60, 65, 80, 107, 113,
127, 129, 144, 158, 159, 215, 221,
223, 235;
Valley, 12, 14–17, 20, 30–34, 43,
44, 46, *49*, 51, 54, 56, 62, 66, 69, 74,
107, 108, 110, 118, 123, 130–132,
142, 145, 150, 158, 160, 162, 164–
168, 171, 173–177, 185, 197, 207,
214, 215, 229, 239;
village, 15
taphonomy, 95, 103, 105, 147, 149, 174,
211
tattoo, 53
technological investment model, 89,
102, 180, 230, 231, 237
tephra, 154, 155, 158, 160–164, 167,
217
Tetlin, 15, 20
theory:
complexity, 98–100, 105, 106, 160;
building, 4, 6, 7, 103–105, 113;
Feminist, 4, 103, 104;
high range, 97, 105;
intersectionality, 4, 95, 104;
middle range, 97;
Neo-Marxist, 95, 103, 106;
Niche Construction, 100, 159;
Optimal Foraging, 96, 97, 102, 105,
106;
Proto-Dene Lex Loci, 108, 113, 119,
122, 133;
social complexity, 42, 43, 54, 56,
101, 102, 106, 200, 231, 240
Third Age, 41
Thomas, Kenny, 1, 51, 52, 57, 75, 76,
78, 182
Thornton, Thomas F., 81, 114, 115, 122,
123, 233
toponomy, 26, 66, 110, 113–127, 132,
133, 225

toolkit, 77–79, 89, 166, 173, 175, 213,
225, 236
Townsend, Joan B., 43, 77
Trade, 14, 20–22, 25, 26, 28–33, 36, 37,
42, 52, 54, 73, 77–79, 82, 86, 89, 91,
102, 107, 124, 125, 139, 161, 200,
237
Traditional Cultural Knowledge, 7
Traditional Ecological Knowledge, 7,
123
Transitional Period, 12, 166, 167, 172,
207, 208
trauma, 35, 87, 125, 136
Traveler, 34, 35, 40–42, 66, 81, 83, 121,
215
tree cultivation, *85*, 91
Tremayne, Andrew H., 142, 201
Tribal membership, 15
trickster, 40, 81
Tringham, Ruth, 95, 103
Tutchone, 8, 54, 56, 129, 130,
Tweiten, Carl O., 25, 58, 85, 224

University of Alaska Fairbanks, 45, 119,
145
Upper Kuskokwim, 8, 15, 132, 137
Upper Tanana:
language, *8*, 48, 127, 130, 133, 221;
people, *8*, 15, 20, 32, 33, 43, 46, 53,
54, 56, 65, 66, 69, 85, 130, 135, 162,
176, 197, 200, 238, 240;
region, 18, 20, 21, 29, 47, 50, 53, 56,
127, 130, 131, 133, 145, 161, 162,
168, 214, 229, 235, 239
US Army Signal Corps, 25, 26
US Military, *16*, 18, 20, 22, 24, 25, 30,
32, 126

Vajda, Edward, 110, 132
Valdez-Fairbanks Trail, 24, 25
Van Stone, James W., 42, 54
VanderHoek, Richard, 79, 144, 185
variable, 94, 97, 99, 160, 166, 168, 172
Village Site, 11, 39, 70

About the Author

Gerad M. Smith is an affiliate researcher in the Department of Anthropology at the University of Alaska Fairbanks (UAF). He received his Ph.D. in anthropology from the UAF, and has spent over a decade working as an archaeologist across Alaska, Hawaii, and Montana. In Alaska, he has extensively studied Northern Archaic and Athabascan tradition sites throughout the Tanana, Copper, Susitna, and Kuskokwim River basins.

www.ingramcontent.com/pod-product-compliance
Lightning Source LLC
Chambersburg PA
CBHW050629280326
41932CB00015B/2578